An Introduction to Communication

First Edition

Edited by Boatema Boateng, Zeinabu
Davis, and Brian Goldfarb

University of California, San Diego

Bassim Hamadeh, CEO and Publisher
Christopher Foster, General Vice President
Michael Simpson, Vice President of Acquisitions
Jessica Knott, Managing Editor
Kevin Fahey, Cognella Marketing Manager
Jess Busch, Senior Graphic Designer
Seidy Cruz, Acquisitions Editor
Sarah Wheeler, Project Editor
Stephanie Sandler, Licensing Associate

First published in the United States of America in 2013 by Cognella, Inc.

Printed in the United States of America

ISBN: 978-1-62131-389-2 (pbk)/ 978-1-62131-390-8 (br)

www.cognella.com 800.200.3908

Contents

Communication and Media

By Raymond Williams

These short discussions of two central concepts to our reader are excerpted from Williams'
Keywords. The book examines important words in cultural theory that are at once famil-
iar and challenging to define.

COMMUNICATION

Communication in its most general modern meaning has been in the language since
C15. Its fw is *communicacion,* oF, from *communicationem,* L, a noun of action from the
stem of the past participle of *communicare,* L, from rw *communis,* L—common: hence *communicate*—make common to many, impart. Communication was first this action, and then,
from lC15, the object thus made common: a communication. This has remained its main
range of use. But from lC17 there was an important extension to the *means* of communication,
specifically in such phrases as *lines of communication.* In the main period of development
of roads, canals and railways, communications was often the abstract general term for these
physical facilities. It was in C20, with the development of other means of passing information
and maintaining social contact, that communications came also and perhaps predominantly
to refer to such MEDIA (q.v.) as the press and broadcasting, though this use (which is earlier in
USA than in UK) is not settled before mC20. The communications industry, as it is now called,
is thus usually distinguished from the *transport industry*: communications for information
and ideas, in print and broadcasting; *transport* for the physical carriage of people and goods.

In controversy about communications systems and communication theory, it is often useful to recall the unresolved range of the original noun of action, represented at its extremes by *transmit*, a one-way process, and *share* (cf. communion and especially communicant), a common or mutual process. The intermediate senses—make common to many, and impart—can be read in either direction, and the choice of direction is often crucial. Hence the attempt to generalize the distinction in such contrasted phrases as *manipulative communication(s)* and *participatory communication(s)*.

MEDIA

Medium, from *medium,* L—middle, has been in regular use in English from lC16, and from at latest eC17 has had the sense of an intervening or intermediate agency or substance. Thus Burton (1621): 'To the Sight three things are required, the Object, the Organ, and the Medium'; Bacon (1605): 'expressed by the Medium of Wordes'. There was then a conventional C18 use in relation to newspapers: 'through the medium of your curious publication' (1795), and this was developed through C19 to such uses as 'considering your Journal one of the best possible mediums for such a scheme' (1880). Within this general use, the description of a newspaper as a medium for advertising became common in eC20. The mC20 development of media (which had been available as a general plural from mC19) was probably mainly in this context. Media became widely used when broadcasting as well as the press had become important in COMMUNICATIONS (q.v.); it was then the necessary general word. MASS (q.v.) media, media people, media agencies, media studies followed.

There has probably been a convergence of three senses: (i) the old general sense of an intervening or intermediate agency or substance; (ii) the conscious technical sense, as in the distinction between print and sound and vision as media; (iii) the specialized capitalist sense, in which a newspaper or broadcasting service—something that already exists or can be planned—is seen as a medium for something else, such as advertising. It is interesting that sense (i) depended on particular physical or philosophical ideas, where there had to be a substance intermediate between a sense or a thought and its operation or expression. In most modern science and philosophy, and especially in thinking about language, this idea of a medium has been dispensed with; thus language is not a medium but a primary practice, and writing (for print) and speaking or acting (for broadcasting) would also be practices. It is then controversial whether print and broadcasting, as in the technical sense (ii), are media or, more strictly, material *forms* and sign systems. It is probably here that specific social ideas, in which writing and broadcasting are seen as DETERMINED (q.v.) by other ends—from the relatively neutral 'information' to the highly specific 'advertising' and 'propaganda'—confirm the received sense but then confuse any modern sense of COMMUNICATION (q.v.). The technical sense of medium, as something with its own specific and *determining* properties (in one version taking absolute priority over anything actually said or written or shown), has in practice been compatible with a social sense of media in which the practices and institutions are seen as agencies for quite other than their primary purposes.

It might be added that in its rapid popularization since the 1950s media has come often to be used as a singular (cf. *phenomena*).

Living in the Number One Country

By Herbert Schiller

For more than sixty years my life's experiences have been shaped by the large-scale events of the twentieth century. From depression childhood to insecure student, from governmental employee to enlisted soldier, from military government worker to university professor, this introduction is a résumé of some of the encounters and episodes of a turbulent era as they impinged on one life.

I grew up in New York City in the depression years, having been born in 1919, two years after the Bolshevik Revolution and one year after the end of the bloody World War I. In my small family, hard times began in 1929. In the fall of that year, at the onset of the Great Depression, my father, a craftsman jeweler, lost his job. Except for local relief work, he remained unemployed until the war in Europe broke out. In 1940 he was hired by an aircraft factory, brought back into production by war-stimulated orders.

In the 1930s we escaped destitution and dispossession. We remained in our one-bedroom apartment—my parents slept on the living room couch and gave me the bedroom. Nourishing food was never absent. Occasionally clothing was purchased, mostly for me. My uncle helped pay the monthly rent. My mother found cleaning jobs in the public school system. She came home exhausted from her day's work and the long subway ride and prepared the evening meal.

Yet these economic difficulties did not interrupt my education, and I attended public school, high school, and the free City College of New York (CCNY), from which I graduated in 1940. Though I did not contribute to the family income, I did work and make enough to pay for transportation, lunch, and small entertainment expenditures, a few movies, subway rides, occasional sodas. All of this is to say that, compared with millions of others, our existence was far from desperate, though never free of anxiety.

There was always the money worry and the uncertainty of the near future. There were frequent quarrels, most of which had an economic origin. It was at this time that I could see how my father's continuing joblessness was viewed by my mother as weakness and inadequacy. In my separate life—I was out of the apartment most of the day—I knew this was unfair and wrong. Yet there seemed no way to contradict it. This atmosphere penetrated my being with sadness and resentment. I have never forgotten how the deprivation of work erodes human beings, those not working and those related to them. And from that time on, I loathed an economic system that could put a huge part of its workforce on the streets with no compunction.

As I see it now, there was one condition favorable to my general well-being and development that I could not appreciate at the time: the total absence of formal religious observance in our household. It was not the consequence of deliberate choice or a grounded atheistic ideal. It was, rather, the complete preoccupation of my parents with getting food on the table and securing for their son the best education they could not actually afford.

Not only was everything else secondary, it did not even come into question. In this somewhat austere secular environment, I may have missed some rich cultural history. But I have always felt fortunate to have escaped from the confines of orthodoxy and parochialism. I was starting out with one less pair of shackles. I am aware that today, this notion of liberation has been rejected by many in the postwar years.

It should not be concluded that this freedom from religious ritual and orthodoxy made for an enlightened adolescence. In my high school freshman class, for example, a straw poll was taken about student preferences in the approaching 1932 national elections. I was one of a handful of kids that chose Herbert Hoover. The overwhelming majority supported Franklin Delano Roosevelt.

My choice was influenced entirely by what I heard my parents say. No other political views at that time entered my consciousness. That an unemployed worker and his wife would, in the depth of the Great Depression, vote for the candidate of big business says much about early-twentieth-century mind control.

When my father finally got full-time, well-paying work in a war factory, I learned another enduring lesson. Ten years of human wastage through unemployment finally was overcome by a still vaster and more impersonal human wastage, the oncoming of world war. This was the not-so-secret stimulus to production and employment in the privately organized U.S. economy. Without it, there was no telling when the economic crisis would have ended. I, too, benefited from the newly created war economy. After worrying through four years of college about finding work when I would graduate, the problem dissolved in an explosion of war-connected employment.

After Pearl Harbor, the war became a total national involvement, which pulled me in the following year. But from 1941 until my induction, the expanding war agencies in Washington were hiring, and, like my father, I got a war-created job. Washington offered an escape from my family-monitored and financially restricted New York life. For a year, the freedom of a relatively well paid job; my own, though shared, apartment; new friends; and the inescapable feeling of living on borrowed time until military service, generated great energy.

I joined a union, the United Federal Workers. I tried to recruit, mostly unsuccessfully, other employees. This attracted the attention of the dollar-a-year industrial executives who staffed the upper echelons of my agency, the War Production Board, who had not left their antiunion sentiments and practices back at their home companies.

Washington, D.C., in 1941–42 was a still segregated metropolitan area. The dynamic center of the war effort to defeat the Nazis and the fascists was itself a profoundly antidemocratic place. To a twenty-one-year-old raised in New York City, Washington's overt racism was a shock.

Education and daily routines in New York at the time were scarcely less segregated. Getting to City College, which was located at 138th Street and Convent Avenue, daily on the trolley, I passed through an adjacent sector of Harlem, the major black community. City College itself, in my recollection, did not have one black student in my 1,000-strong class. Perhaps there were a few African-Americans on the campus, but I never met or saw them. So New York apartheid was very real, but not understandable, at least to me then, as a legally coercive system.

Washington was different. The evidence of apartness, buttressed with force, was everywhere. I remember my sense of disbelief on crossing the bridge from the District of Columbia into Virginia and seeing signs that warned that "Negroes" were not permitted in local parks. In government cafeterias in Washington, separate dining rooms and food lines rigidly divided the races. Washington offered a stark prelude to what I would soon encounter overseas in the former colonies of the imperialist European states.

Drafted in the fall of 1942, I spent a year in a dozen army camps up and down California, mostly in southern California around Los Angeles, and in and out of the desert. In that year before being shipped overseas, I marveled at how the war was experienced in this loony part of the country. It was a big party that even I, an anonymous corporal, could wander into from one weekend to the next. Stepping out onto the highway to hitch a ride to Los Angeles could lead to a two-day merry-go-round of invitations to house parties throughout the area. The war plants in southern California were working three shifts. Thousands of workers would come off their jobs at midnight, revved up and raring to join the nightlife that was organized on a round-the-clock schedule—restaurants, bars, bowling alleys, movies, dance halls, whatever. Consumption needed no encouragement, coming after a ten-year depression. It was supported by full paychecks.

These scenes contrasted wildly with my arrival in North Africa in September 1943, and my limited travels in Europe over the next two years. It was shockingly clear that, with few exceptions, Americans had no idea of the costs of the war. The impoverished countrysides, the bombed cities and villages, the haggard civilians, the acute shortages of the most elemental necessities, escaped the U.S. troops' notice. In the United States (not all but many) people were, if not partying, then leading satisfying lives, while the world was suffering unimaginable disasters.

In American army camps, the post exchanges—commissaries—stocked huge quantities of goods. Overseas life for noncombat soldiers—a relatively small percentage of the Armed Forces—was not a hardship existence. In many places, post exchange goods were blackmarketed by the GIs, contributing further to the enormous gulf separating the U.S. war experience from that of much of the world's population. Over the decades that followed, this gap in common experience partly explains the recklessness of U.S. leadership in many international encounters, and the widely differing attitudes to the risk of provoking a new war that separated American from world public opinion.

Almost two and a half years of my military service was spent in North Africa: Tunisia briefly, Algiers for six months, and Casablanca in Morocco for two years.

Before my overseas sojourn, my knowledge of mass poverty was pretty vague. I knew of bread lines in Depression-stricken America. I had seen slums in New York City. I heard about "Hoovervilles," shack towns on the outskirts of cities during the bad years of the 1930s. Yet none of these prepared me for what I found in North Africa.

In Casablanca, *bidonvilles,* tin can settlements, made up of discarded oil drums and cardboard cartons, surrounded the city, homes to thousands of people. These unfortunates shared one or two open water faucets and utterly lacked the most primitive sanitation facilities. Though the French were still the reigning colonial power across the rim of North Africa, it was clear, even in 1943, their rule was coming to a close. The French still made air raids on defenseless villages viewed as troublesome. Local newspapers were routinely censored, often leaving blank columns on the pages. These efforts were in vain, however.

The U.S. presence was the new pole of power. American heavy transport filled the roads. Large numbers of local people were employed at the many U.S. installations. At night, on the edge of a GI audience watching an outdoor screening of an American film, Moroccan kids and adults followed the images intently. The new power, with its material riches and dazzling images, was nonchalantly elbowing out the once-dominating authority. This pattern was to be repeated in one colonial site after another. Inevitable as it turned out to be, it also carried with it the expectation of improvement, material and social. What would the United States do with its enormous capability to influence developments worldwide? Despite initial widespread hope, as time passed, the United States became a modernized model of domination.

For me, the North African interlude was a powerful prod to consciousness. What later came to be called, always euphemistically and often deceitfully, the Third World, the developing world, and, most recently, "emerging markets," continues to be, as I then began to understand it, the part of the world where great numbers of people live and die under frightfully deprived conditions. In their midst are enclaves of lavish wealth and power. Over time, I realized that these tragic destinies continue to be ordered by foreign owners and investors, and local oligarchs, whose one public concern is undisturbed profit making. This was the burden that the "advanced" West, and the United States in particular, imposed, and continues to impose, on the poorest and weakest peoples worldwide for half a century.

My next significant learning experience came after the defeat of Nazi Germany and its subsequent occupation by victorious British, French, Soviet, and U.S. forces. I returned from North Africa demobilized in the late fall of 1945 and spent three months at home in New York City. I did not seem able to jump into the postwar boom that was swirling about me, and so I traveled to another damaged society: I accepted a civilian job with the U.S. Military Government in Germany. By March 1946, I was living in Berlin, and part of the presumably democratizing process in West Germany.

In Germany I received hard-to-come-by instruction on how a terribly battered industrialized, market economy is rehabilitated by a self-interested class ally. This was not everyday learning. Well before I went into the army in 1942, I had a good stretch of higher education. I graduated from college with a degree in social science and a major in economics. I also had a master's degree in economics from Columbia University.

I mention this only because one might have assumed that this much formal education would have produced an individual knowledgeable about the basic relationships that comprise the prevailing system of production and consumption. Wrong assumption! My university education had been a shallow and superficial enterprise. The central driving forces of the economy I lived in were either ignored or left vague, to the point of meaninglessness.

When I returned to the States in mid-1948, thoroughly disgusted with official U.S. policy in Germany, it was evident that a terribly wrong and falsified assessment of Russian aims had gained wide and growing acceptance. Anticommunism, which dated back at least to the Russian Revolution thirty years earlier, had grown to constitute a full-blown national environment.

But there was still some resistance to the anticommunist propaganda steamroller that had the enthusiastic support of the national information dispensers. Elections were coming in November, and in July, the Progressive Party, with former Vice President Henry Wallace and Senator Glen Taylor heading the ticket, was founded. It seemed to be successfully questioning the anti-Soviet foreign policy of the Truman Administration. I attended their founding convention rally in Shibe Park, Philadelphia, days after returning from Europe, and felt buoyed by the enthusiasm and spirit that infused the huge gathering.

Soon enough I received another lesson in applied political science. To meet the challenge of the Progressives, the Truman forces quickly adopted, in collaboration with the Republicans, two tactics. First, a frenzied hunt for Communist spies in the government, real or imagined, fueled the rising anticommunist sentiment in the country.

At the same time, Truman demagogically sent an emissary and offered to meet with the Russians. This was the proffer of good faith and moderation to balance the hysteria the basic policy was provoking. These initiatives served to persuade the electorate that Truman was pursuing a reasonable course and that the Progressive alternative, of active cooperation with the Soviets, could be safely ignored. Truman squeaked by, and the Progressive Party disintegrated.

This was the onset of an era of implacable anticommunism, what came to be known as McCarthyism, though it far outlasted the Senator. It continued as a lowgrade infection in the 1960s and 1970s and flared up aggressively in the Reagan 1980s. It is by no means extinguished in the 1990s.

Facing this atmosphere, saturated with fear and hatred for a good part of my life, has required constant examination of my own beliefs and of my ability to analyze the social scene. How could I be so distant from the general thinking of the population? Was it a personality matter, some strained sense of uniqueness? Not too much time was spent worrying about this, but it did remain a source of wonderment.

Later, my attention became focused on how the process of inculcation worked. Who organized it? How were the messages shaped and transmitted? Who controlled the dissemination networks? How far did the networks extend? But before being able to study these matters, by the early 1950s I had a family with two children, and I was the only wage earner. I taught full-time at the Pratt Institute in Brooklyn, an arts school, and part-time, at night, at the City College business school at Twenty-third Street and Lexington Avenue.

These were trying years. My beginning salary at Pratt was less than $2,000, the teaching load a punishing five-course schedule, with two additional courses at night at City College. Some days I would have seven classroom preparations. Most of the time I was exhausted. The pervasive political atmosphere was overhung by the reality of investigating commissions, firings, the blacklist, and the generalized repression and coercion. Most of this was marginal to my own life but I knew many for whom these developments were traumatic. Notwithstanding some popular nostalgic sentiments about that period in the 1990s, I couldn't wait to see the end of the political environment of the 1950s, and the miasma in which that decade was engulfed.

After Truman's election in November 1948, oppositional views to the course that Washington was pursuing were less and less visible, eventually approaching underground status. The world was being reshaped by American power, though anticommunism provided the daily news and entertainment menu. A curtain had come down in America, smothering free discussion.

And so it was in 1949–1950, when most middle-class professionals were scurrying as rapidly as they could away from anything that they feared might bring them to the attention of the new vigilantism, that I chose to become a part-time, unpaid, radical journalist. Starting out in an era of semi-hysteria, I began to write weekly or biweekly articles on American foreign economic policy for the Labor Research Association (LRA), a tiny research group that critically scrutinized the corporate features of the American economy. The director of LRA at the time was Bob Dunn, one of the most considerate and sweetest men I've ever met, then or since. Working with Dunn was the remarkable Grace Hutchins, who had spent a lifetime in the radical movement.

My connection to LRA was limited to delivering personally, whenever I had written it, a short article I hoped might challenge at least a small sector of the approved and distorted conventional press coverage that overwhelmed the nation. I did not use my own name; the byline was LRA. Willing as I was to contribute my analytical skills, such as they were, to express an alternative view, I had no desire to be subjected to the kind of ferocious state-directed intimidation that was all too evident and pervasive.

I couldn't help feeling more than a little anxiety. Each visit I made to the LRA office on East Eighteenth Street in New York City to deliver my fragment of oppositional journalism seemed fraught. Paranoia prevailed in the country at large, and I was entitled to exhibit mine by walking rapidly, or averting my face, and worrying incessantly that I was being photographed entering the building or the office. This continued for several years, though my productivity, and my paranoia tailed off after the mid-1950s.

My full-time job at the Pratt Institute began in 1950, and my starting salary, as I said, was around $2,000. It increased incrementally about a thousand dollars a year. The other job, teaching evenings at City College, was on an hourly basis, something like $4 an hour. Pitiful as these jobs were monetarily, they would have disappeared immediately if my extracurricular activity had become known.

What were the subjects I addressed in this forbidding time? One overall theme ran through my work. It continues to this day. It was, and remains, the use of American power—so dominant over the period—to extract privilege and prevent social change that might limit that privilege. The places and instances where this was occurring spanned the globe, but I gave my attention to those locales about which I had some, though limited, personal experience. One was the Western European social order, which was "threatened" not, as was asserted by our leadership, by Soviet aggression, but by its own indigenous radical movements.

At the end of World War II, largely as a result of their antifascist leadership during the war, the major parties and movements in Europe were led by Communists and socialists. In both France and Italy the Communist parties were the biggest political formations. In the early fall of 1945, on a trip to France while still in the army, I remember the very visible presence of the

French Communist Party—the billboards, placards, announcement of rallies, and the like—in Nice, hardly the industrial belt of the country.

The U.S. government, with the active assistance of the CIA, did everything it could to weaken and disrupt these movements. The records of these interventions remain secret, fifty years later, despite continued presidential assurances that the documentation will be released.[1]

Even so, we know plenty. Noam Chomsky, condensing a good bit of the history of the process in postwar Europe, wrote:

> Marshall Plan aid was strictly contingent on exclusion of Communists—including major elements of the antifascist resistance and labor—from the government; "democracy," in the usual sense.
>
> In France, the postwar destitution was exploited to undermine the French labor movement, along with direct violence. Desperately needed food supplies were withheld to coerce obedience, and gangsters were organized to provide goon squads and strike-breakers, a matter that is described with some pride in semi-official U.S. labor histories, which praise the AFL for its achievements in helping to save Europe by splitting and weakening the labor movement (thus frustrating alleged Soviet designs) and safeguarding the flow of arms to Indochina for the French war of reconquest, another prime goal of the U.S. labor bureaucracy. The CIA reconstituted the Mafia for these purposes, in one of its early operations. The quid pro quo was restoration of the heroin trade. The U.S. government connection to the drug boom continues until today.[2]

The other focus of my writing was the former colonial territories, many of them recently politically liberated but actually totally dependent economically, militarily, and culturally. The not-so-secret U.S. objective was to secure this vast area with its huge populations and untold resource wealth, for private corporate exploitation. As was the situation in Western Europe, the populations and most of the leadership in the ex-colonial world had a different vision, a socially planned perspective, generally with its own specific characteristics.

This, of course, created big problems for U.S. policy makers. But even in this early postcolonial period, U.S. power was applied relentlessly to recovering the region(s) for profit making. All of this proceeded under a terminology that manipulatively linked freedom and choice with private ownership while associating noncapitalist regimes of varying character with tyranny and despotism and, worst of all, communism.

Having seen the devastation in Europe and the unspeakable conditions in colonial North Africa, I found it astonishing that the efforts being made in many places to find new ways to approach social reconstruction were regarded by Washington as threats to peace and American well-being. It was this astonishment, and frustration at the refusal of the informational system to divulge what was occurring, that drove my journalistic impulses.

One of my first pieces, in August 1949, examined American business and governmental perspectives that sought to reverse the very mild postwar reforms of the British Labour Party. This was significant, I thought, because it demonstrated early on the willingness of U.S. capitalism to intervene outside the country against working people on behalf of capital. More important, it was an early display of American leadership's unwillingness to accept the most limited modifications in an ally's private profit-making economy that might ease the lives of England's majority.

At that time, and ever since, U.S. power, governmental and private, has come down on the side of capital against the living standards and well-being of the laboring classes. Unemployment and austerity have been the policies endorsed and applied to troubled economies by U.S. checkbook-holding leaders. These interventions constitute the history of the last half-century and are as much a part of the concluding years of the twentieth century as they were fifty years ago.

In 1998 U.S. Treasury Secretary Robert Rubin, on an inspection tour of the world market system the United States largely dominates, had this advice to offer the newly elected South African government, which was faced with the cumulative devastation of centuries of colonial rule. Before it took power in 1994, the African National Congress, it may be remembered, had a socialist outlook and favored nationalization and full employment. Rubin brushes this aside. His formula for the South Africans, hardly updated from the recommendations his predecessors gave to the British in 1949, emphasizes "austere budgets, open markets, vigorous competition and the sale of state-owned companies … and greater flexibility from labor unions."[3]

Unfortunately, this advice can be disregarded only at a terrible price. If the South Africans demur, their access to capital will be shut off and their currency and economy put under siege. Here, as in all the other instances of U.S. pressure and intervention around the world, social alternatives are foreclosed and nations and people locked into the dominant system, with all its inequalities and ferocious imbalances.

Efforts to improve working conditions and allow labor a stronger voice in decision making, wherever undertaken over the decades, have been bitterly, and generally successfully, resisted by Washington power. The disappearance of the non-market sector of the world—the disintegration of the Soviet Union—has further strengthened the worldwide offensive of property against labor.

A second vital interest of the new U.S. superpower in 1945 was, and continues to be, the economic overlordship of as much of the world as possible. This became my other journalistic sphere of attention. In achieving this end, the great economic wealth and power of the United States has been used as a lever either to bribe or to coerce the compliance of others. The weaker the targeted country, the stronger the exactions demanded. Consider, for example, the conditions extracted for Western "aid" from South Koreans, and other Southeast Asian states, in 1997–98.

The *New York Times* account is headlined "Asia's Surrender: Reeling from Blows to Their Economies, Countries Agree to Financial Concessions" (December 14, 1997). Elaborating, another report described the mechanism of control:

> On a general level, the [IMF's] growing role in overhauling the private sector is making it a more explicit advocate of the style of capitalism long championed by the United States, centered on free markets, reduced government involvement in business decisions, and more openness. … The fund has also become the closest thing the world has to a global financial regulator.[4]

The world has changed greatly over the last fifty years, but the technique of extorting advantage, through the use of heavily conditioned economic assistance, from weak or ailing economies has been a durable feature of the period. Actually, one of the earliest applications was while World War II was in its concluding stage. The instrumentality was the United Nations Relief and Rehabilitation Administration (UNRRA).

Established as an emergency relief organization to alleviate the hunger and distress that would accompany the liberation of the Nazi-occupied areas of eastern and central Europe, UNRRA provided an early model for later international bodies that would engage in the aid business. Its membership was international—as far as that was possible at that time—but its chief contributor, and therefore most influential member, was the United States.

The efforts of the United States to steer UNRRA away from helping Eastern Europe and the Soviet states, unless they complied with rules set down by the dominant grant-giving state, were a preview of what would become the standard pattern when the war was over and the United States took up its self-assumed role as the world's rule maker.[5]

One international organization after another came into existence at war's end. The United Nations, with a number of related, function-based organizations (World Health [WHO]; Food and Agriculture [FAO]; and Educational, Scientific, and Cultural [UNESCO]), formed the overarching structure. But of greater influence were the economic structures, also newly created, that operated outside the UN framework. These followed the organizational pattern of the UN, with one crucial difference. The national contributions to these economic-financial bodies were calculated on a rough scale of economic strength, as they were in the UN; but while in the UN each state had one vote, voting rights in these structures were distributed according to the member's economic contribution.

It followed that in the World Bank and in the International Monetary Fund (IMF), the two most important institutions, the United States had, by virtue of the size of its contribution, the dominant voice and the absolute prerogative to veto any decision that displeased it. This "principle" has disfigured international decision making since 1945 and has been the source of an untold number of grievous decisions and actions. Yet viewed from the perspective of the North American power complex, it has been of inestimable value in securing as much of the globe as possible for the U.S.-led market system.

I looked into the World Bank's structure and activities in a piece I wrote in 1950, titled "The World Bank: Agency for Wall Street's Cold War," which provides an account of how economic assistance was withheld from poor, socialist, or socialist-inclined states in the postwar years. Fifty years later, in dramatic contrast, capital is being lavishly funneled into many of those places—Russia, Indonesia, Mexico, Korea, and so on—as long as they adopt the private market economy and abandon their public sector. Then and now, withholding or disbursing capital is the United States' lever of control.

By the late 1950s my career as a radical journalist had taken a new direction. This was due in part to a gradual slackening of the national repressive atmosphere, though U.S. global interventions continued unabated. It also coincided with an opportunity to join the faculty of the University of Illinois in 1961. This afforded me space to research and write on a regular basis—a very welcome change from my heavy teaching schedules in New York, which had taken almost all my energy.

Though communication was a relatively new subject in academic studies, it became the core of my work for twenty-five years. Personal, local, and global factors combined to encourage my new area of interest. The University of Illinois had a strong record in the field from early on, housing several of the first communication scholars. Dallas Smythe, for example, who had single-handedly created the study of the political economy of communication, was still teaching there, and we became friends. When Dallas left the University to return to Canada, I inherited, so to speak, his graduate course. Additionally, the Bureau of Economics and Business Research, to which I was appointed, was led by an experienced and wonderfully open-minded director, V. Lewis Bassie. Bassie, without any questions asked, permitted me to do my research—a considerable extension of the bureau's customary projects.

Actually, Bassie's work was in economic forecasting. He was one of the few at that time who still remembered and understood the susceptibility of a market economy to damaging booms and busts. He predicted a downturn that didn't materialize, as the long postwar boom temporarily interrupted the business cycle. This put him outside the conventional thinking and had the effect of making him an exemplary overseer of my own against-the-mainstream work.

But larger forces were at work. U.S. interventions around the world were multiplying: Cuba, the Dominican Republic, and Vietnam, where U.S. troops were fighting a barbarous colonial war with the most advanced weaponry. How these bloody and cruel events were being presented to the American public offered a key to understanding how the far-reaching control of popular consciousness in the country was being managed. The war also offered a unique example of how the control system could be challenged, with the rapid growth of a real opposition.

The antiwar movement grew stronger as the war continued, but the propaganda for the war was no less intense, as the specter of one anticommunist domino after another falling to the Reds became an unrelieved Washington refrain. And the media were fully complicit in supporting the war in the early years of the conflict. What turned the tide was the strength of the Vietnamese resistance, as the costs of waging the war reduced the national budget to a shambles. The decisive cost at home, however, was in the lost blood and lives of American youth. When domestic anger and shock reached a level dangerous to social stability, parts of the establishment and the media broke the prowar consensus and the unraveling was underway.

Even in such a relatively remote place as central Illinois, long the site of a "jock" university with row upon row of fraternity and sorority houses, the war jolted the campus out of its play routines. Student demonstrations led twice to university administrators summoning the National Guard. Mirroring the temporary loss of conventional governing control, some of the players on the football team showed up at antiwar parties and events. This was one of those all-too-infrequent times in the last half century when the experiences of (enough) people propelled them to reject the policies and explanations of the governing class. As also could be expected, after the event, the media claimed that they had prompted the antiwar effort with their reporting. Washington and the military knew better. The staggering losses of American youth changed the informational climate, and eventually government policy.

Vietnam is now more than a quarter of a century behind us, and the changes in the domestic informational system since the war have been far-reaching. What was at that time a powerful and concentrated structure has become a globally integrated multimedia machine, owned by a few dozen, at most, giant private communication enterprises. Yet before this pyramid of global information power became the new standard, I was engaged in the short-lived efforts of the ex-colonial world to restructure the global economy into a more equitable and life-enhancing living space. For a few brief years, numbers of poor nations, some still led by their liberation heroes—Nehru in India, Sukarno in Indonesia, Tito in Yugoslavia, Castro in Cuba, Nasser in

Egypt, Ben Bella in Algeria, Nkrumah in Ghana, and others in Kenya, Angola, Mozambique, and elsewhere—sought to change economic and informational structures worldwide.

Here again, as in Europe, in 1945–50, an opportunity appeared to move away from the disastrous policies of domination and privilege. Once more, on a global grid, the United States and a few allies resisted substantive changes that would have reconfigured the global distribution of resources.

In the end, the Third World's demands came to nothing. With the exception of the oil-producing states' attempt to gain greater control of their vital natural resource, the ambitious objectives of the ninety-plus poor countries possessed no leverage to apply to the Western dominators, especially the United States. There were no indispensable resources they could withhold. Their military capability was practically nonexistent. They were compelled, for lack of alternatives, to issue their challenge in the international bodies created after World War II; essentially the United Nations and its subsidiary organization, UNESCO (the United Nations Educational, Scientific, and Cultural Organization).

The have-nots' claims to a new international economic order, and subsequently a new international information order, were expressed in the meetings of these bodies. Invariably, after a comprehensive exposition of the inequities and injustices of the prevailing structures, the issues would be voted on, and recommendations for changes would be passed by overwhelming majorities. And that was the end of it; there was no mechanism for implementation. More to the point, the powerful nations in control of the system had no intention of accepting even the most modest limitations on their privileged arrangements. The demands put forth to improve these crucial areas of human existence, however valid and just their bases, had no chance of overturning the realities of economic, military, and technological power. Actually, the situation corresponded closely to my previous historical experiences in Germany. All the same, I spent a good deal of my time in the late 1960s and throughout the 1970s involved in the global informational debate.

Mass Communications and American Empire (1969) and *Communication and Cultural Domination* (1976) were my contributions to the global discussion.[6] Attacks on these works evidenced the semihysterical opposition in the West to any structural modifications of the privileged corporate networks of information control. For example, the executive director of Freedom House overstated my importance to the opposition in grotesque and even comical terms, casting me in the role of ventriloquist to a distinguished Chilean diplomat, Juan Somavia, at that time director of the Latin American Institute for Transnational Studies (ILET), and currently the Chilean ambassador to the United Nations.

Analyzing a speech given by Somavia at that time, Freedom House found that "at the outset, Somavia describes, exactly as Schiller does, the origins of the Third World media challenge: the continuation of colonial domination from the 'center' to the 'periphery,' from the transnational power structure to the dominated Third World; from the controller of information to its recipient." It concluded: "Woven into [Somavia's conclusions] were Herbert Schiller's concepts": for instance, the use of "center" to refer to dominating countries and "periphery" for the dominated nations.[7] Much as I might want to, I cannot take credit for these terms, which were first formulated by distinguished Latin American dependency theorists, one of whom is, at this writing, the president of Brazil.

Yet still larger social forces were at work, and well before the "Third World Media Challenge" to the West subsided, new transformations were making the have-nots' goals of economic and informational equality recede further. These developments coincided with changes in my personal living and working arrangements.

In the fall of 1970 I left Illinois and moved to southern California, where I became a professor of communication in a newly created college at the University of California, San Diego. Once again, my education received an unexpected and unconventional widening. The new college had been established as a result of student demonstrations—in fact, by the seizure of buildings. The aim of the students was to secure an educational enterprise that would seriously concern itself with the needs of the nation's "minorities," African-Americans, Chicanos (Mexican-Americans), and Native Americans.

That the demands of the students were partly met, temporarily, was itself remarkable. But it reflected the turbulence of the times and the volatile condition on the nation's campuses during the Vietnam War. In this instance, the students, and some faculty sympathetic to their goals, were authorized to organize a curriculum for the new college. Four main areas were chosen for study: Third World studies; science and technology; urban and rural studies; and communication. Each was to focus on the special needs of the minority students. This domestic objective was of a piece with the Third World movement for a new international economic and information order, with local specifications.

I was hired, after intense student interviews—a rarity in itself—to head the communication program. Departmental status was promised quickly. The importance of this is hard to exaggerate; a program has no autonomy and cannot make its own appointments. These are the prerogatives of a department.

I set forth as the "coordinator" of the program, with three nontenured faculty borrowed from the literature and sociology departments—hardly a secure base for a project seeking to develop major changes in the educational enterprise. My obligation to the new college and the students, as I understood it, was to create a meaningful set of courses in the communication field that would enable those enrolled to develop their understanding and consciousness and overcome the mental servitude instilled in oppressed classes and groups.

I interpreted my task as trying to explain how the powerful communication system in all its spheres (film, television, publishing, the press, recording, and education) was structured, and how it created, or at least justified, inequality. This perspective, as might be expected, did not secure the confidence and administrative support that was accorded conventional modes of study. Our tiny unit was treated by administrative power as an annoying infection that it hoped to quickly cauterize.

One circumstance alone protected and enabled us to survive in the initial period: The students found our relatively few courses stimulating and meaningful. The daily news—what it reported, how it reported it, and what was left out or distorted—supplied my major texts. Much of this material appeared in *The Mind Managers* in 1973. (Years later, in 1981, I used television to disseminate similar critiques in a series of half-hour shows titled *Herb Schiller Reads* The New York Times.[8])

Our popularity with the students continued to grow. Our enrollment numbers exceeded those of most of the traditional departments. This guaranteed our survival, since the university has become no less a retailer in need of "customers" than any department store, yet general campus support for our efforts continued to be meager. Across the university, communication was regarded as a subject lacking substance and taught by ideologues. Compounding the problem, no established discipline would admit to the slightest possibility that its field might have an ideological slant.

The suspicion of communication on the campus was reinforced by extra-university pressure. One example was an article by two nationally syndicated columnists, Roland Evans and Robert Novak, describing me as a white radical brought in to mold the minds of minority students. These minds were regarded by the writers, and probably by many others, as malleable clay, waiting to be shaped by manipulative fingers.

Our courses critically examined the actual world; and another development worked steadily on behalf of our program. Silently, and almost invisibly, the underlying structure of the national economy was changing. These transformations included the growth of the service sector and the relative decline of the industrial sector, the ever-enlarging role of the transnational corporation in production and distribution, and the rapid development of new communication technologies, the propellants of an increasingly information-using economy.

In the mid-1970s these developments were still in formation, but their presence could not be ignored. Their implications and impact on the national scene soon became overwhelming, and we were affected locally as well. Communication and "information society" became daily popular references. How then could the university disregard a sphere of knowledge that was becoming ever more prominent in the popular mind and press? It couldn't, and we owed our survival in part to the emergence of an alleged information society.

While the structural shifts noted above were making themselves felt throughout the economy, equally significant changes were underway in the national information condition. It was to these that my attention turned in the 1980s and '90s. Let me give the context.

My wife, Anita Schiller, had been a librarian since the 1950s. When we moved to Illinois, she joined the University of Illinois Library Research Center, the first such unit in the country devoted to library research issues. Her assignment was to select and study questions of concern to libraries. One of her first efforts was to design and carry out a survey of college and university librarians. Her main finding, at the time revelatory, was that though women comprised the largest part of the library workforce, they were the "disadvantaged majority" in terms of salary and job level.

Beyond this study, which received national attention, the Library Research Center offered a unique opportunity to gain an overview of what was happening in the library field. And this was no parochial landscape. Libraries were caught up, almost unwittingly, in the most fundamental changes occurring in American society. The momentous shifts in the information world, were first turning up as library problems affecting the daily work and experiences of the nation's leading libraries and librarians.

For example, computerization, privatization, and commoditization of information first appeared as library developments. As such, their implications for the economy at large were practically disregarded. Libraries historically had been treated as marginal institutions—respected and given rhetorical support, but far outside the areas of decision-making power. It was not surprising, therefore, that fundamental trends appearing first in the library sphere, passed almost unnoticed in the general perception of what were considered important national developments. My own recognition and partial understanding of what was occurring I attribute completely to Anita's experiences, commentary, and early writings on these trends. A first indication of what was happening with remarkable speed was the privatization of information as commercial online database services were introduced, and libraries that historically had been centers of information freely available to all users found themselves engaged in policy making about whether charges should be levied on the new computer services—the fee versus free debate.

This was and is no trivial issue. It goes to the heart of a profound change spreading across the economy—the steady expansion of commercial transactions at the expense of public and community activity. And it was only one of many issues that emerged in the library field but were connected to the transformation of the whole economy by spreading computerization under corporate auspices. The libraries served also as early experiment and testing centers for familiarizing the workforce and general population with the new instrumentation. In the process libraries, starting with the big research facilities, became early users and enthusiasts of the new information technologies. This contributed greatly to the success of the changes underway.

As these developments became more clear, it was also apparent that the entire social order was being reshaped in a most undemocratic way, while the beneficiaries publicized these changes as freedom-enhancing developments. Much as the "democratization" of Germany was heralded, as was "development" in the Third World, the shaping of a corporate global electronic environment has most recently been presented as promising universal benefit. These contradictory conditions set the central themes of my writing and work in the 1980s and '90s. My task, as I interpreted it, was to analyse and explore the contradictions and deceptions of the proponents of the new information age. I tried to demonstrate how the industrial and technological transformations then sweeping across the country benefited the already most powerful force in the system—the big global corporations. Additionally, I claimed that despite all the changes observable in daily life, the main characteristics and dynamics of the centuries-old private profit-making system remained in place, if not intact.

In 1998 the International Monetary Fund (IMF) largely replaced the World Bank as the source of capital to beleaguered states. Its structure of decision making is basically the same as that of the World Bank. The determining criteria for obtaining capital from the IMF are no different, though perhaps more onerous, than they were fifty years ago. There is today, hard as it is to imagine, even less balance in the world community than there was in 1945. Investor and creditor interests are paramount; social need and an equitable society hardly come into consideration. When President Clinton visited Moscow in September 1998, he told the bankrupt Russians that U.S. aid would be resumed only if the international investors were satisfied with the terms. The Russian people, on the edge of total impoverishment, didn't come into the discussion.[9]

In the early postwar years, two other closely related goals motivated Washington's international policies. The central objective was to secure as large a part as possible of the ex-colonial world for the world market system. The dangers of slippage at that time seemed very high. Nationalist leaders with social vision were in the command positions of many new nations; how to forestall such developments occupied the attention of U.S. military and intelligence services and the financial establishment.

Yet while doing everything it could to thwart alternative courses of social development in these new states, American power also sought to reassure their leaderships, and the U.S. public, that its intentions were honorable and that, unlike the old imperialists, the United States sought no special advantages.

In the half century since the end of the war, U.S. companies have been transformed into global enterprises, extending their interests from raw materials acquisition to production plants and financial subsidiaries in scores of countries. In 1949 the British and the French and others were told that they had to restrict their consumption and discourage their workers from demanding decent wages because of the competition of the powerful, postwar American economy. In 1999 countries are given the same advice, with the justification that the competitive pressure of the "global economy" demands it.

Basically, the issue is who benefits in a privately structured society. Capital is in a position to see that its interests are taken care of, but it doesn't quite come out that way as public information. How could it when the worldwide presence and activity of U.S. corporate business are now handled by massive public relations firms, phalanxes of lobbyists, and information massaging services that make the earlier "Point Four" claims sound primitive?

Shuttling back and forth over a half century's developments can be confusing. Yet these historical observations of a time long past serve to highlight the extraordinary feature of the entire age—the pervasive application of one power's authority to the world scene. Washington's policies and actions today are the direct descendants of those prevailing over a span of five decades. Modifications in some cases have been made, and new practices introduced, but the fundamentals are unchanged. The United States remains the center of a globally expansive system, one that still strives to eliminate critical opposition. The system administrators, governmental and business, have had to take into account global power shifts—the disappearance of the rival Soviet sphere, the emergence of China as a potentially great world force, and the efforts of Europe to become a unified entity and a likely economic challenger to the United States. Withal, the impulse of Washington and the power complex it represents remains one of command and domination.

Many of the deformations in American society of the twentieth century have their roots in a vast enterprise of deception that has reached into almost every crevice of the social order. A mixture of concocted threats of aggression, external and internal, has been central to a masterfully arranged scenario whose creation and staging have been effected by thorough collaboration of the leaders of the country's main institutions. Little of this social transformation has been planned or coordinated; it developed out of the drives and assumptions of a newly emerged corporate order that found itself in an unprecedented position of global power.

Military force, espionage, and disinformation campaigns figured into and contributed to the U.S. effort to keep as much of the world as possible in its bailiwick. The record over the period is one of incessant military interventions, military buildups, spy scares, witch hunts, classifications of information, universities sanitized by academic purges or the threat of them, and Cold War curricula. Paraded before us in popular culture, on TV and in films, has been an army of invaders and secret operatives who perform, in full special effects regalia, dramas that numb the intellect and channel the passions. The total absorption in commercial translations that permeates the tightest echelons of the social order filters down to all levels.

What then can be concluded from this bare-bones review of more than half a century's social developments seen from the point of view of their personal impact on one individual? Perhaps it has been the need to express my concern, often my outrage, over a course of events that could have had different outcomes. I could not imagine either accommodation or passivity in the face of what sometimes seemed lunatic, at other times calculated, aggressions against ordinary people's lives and well-being. In 1998, for example, a government report estimated that the

United States had spent over *five trillion dollars* since World War II on nuclear weaponry.[10] We would be living in a different world had those staggering expenditures been invested in a socially productive manner.

Yet far more costly has been the unwillingness of U.S. leadership to allow other nations and peoples the freedom to pursue different directions in their economic and social life. American policy and actions have for half a century repeatedly frustrated initiatives for a better and more diverse world. It is an awesome indictment.

REFERENCES

1. Tim Weiner, "CIA, Breaking Promises, Puts off Release of Cold War Files," *The New York Times,* July 15, 1998, A-13.
2. Noam Chomsky, *Deterring Democracy* (New York: Verso, 1991), 343.
3. Donald G. McNeil, Jr., "Visiting South Africa, Rubin Sides with the Free Marketers," *The New York Times,* July 15, 1998, C-5.
4. Richard W. Stevenson and Jeff Gerth, "IMF's New Book: A Far Deeper Role in Lands in Crisis," *The New York Times,* December 8, 1997, 1.
5. Herbert I. Schiller, "The U.S. and UNRRA," Ph.D. diss., New York University, 1960.
6. Herbert I. Schiller, *Mass Communications and American Empire* (New York: A. Kelley, 1969); Schiller, *Communication and Cultural Domination* (White Plains, N.Y.: International Arts and Sciences Press, 1976).
7. Leonard R. Sussman, "Mass News Media and the Third World Challenge," *The Washington Papers,* Vol. 5 (46) (Beverly Hills, Calif.: Sage, 1977).
8. Herbert I. Schiller, *The Mind Managers* (Boston: Beacon Press, 1973); *Herb Schiller Reads* The New York Times, Paper Tiger Television, 1981.
9. "Clinton and Yeltsin Press Conference," *The New York Times,* September 3, 1998, A-10.
10. *Atomic Audit* (Washington, D.C.: Brookings Press, 1998), quoted in Peter Passell, *The New York Times,* July 9, 1998, C-2.

The Self, the I, and the Me

By George Herbert Mead

We can distinguish very definitely between the self and the body. The body can be there and can operate in a very intelligent fashion without there being a self involved in the experience. The self has the characteristic that it is an object to itself, and that characteristic distinguishes it from other objects and from the body. It is perfectly true that the eye can see the foot, but it does not see the body as a whole. We cannot see our backs; we can feel certain portions of them, if we are agile, but we cannot get an experience of our whole body. There are, of course, experiences which are somewhat vague and difficult of location, but the bodily experiences are for us organized about a self. The foot and hand belong to the self. We can see our feet, especially if we look at them from the wrong end of an opera glass, as strange things which we have difficulty in recognizing as our own. The parts of the body are quite distinguishable from the self. We can lose parts of the body without any serious invasion of the self. The mere ability to experience different parts of the body is not different from the experience of a table. The table presents a different feel from what the hand does when one hand feels another, but it is an experience of something with which we come definitely into contact. The body does not experience itself as a whole, in the sense in which the self in some way enters into the experience of the self.

It is the characteristic of the self as an object to itself that I want to bring out. This characteristic is represented in the word "self," which is a reflexive, and indicates that which can be both subject and object. This type of object is essentially different from other objects, and in the past it has been distinguished as conscious, a term which indicates an experience with, an experience of, one's self. It was assumed that consciousness in some way carried this capacity of being an object to itself. In giving a behavioristic statement of consciousness we have to look for some sort of experience in which the physical organism can become an object to itself.

When one is running to get away from someone who is chasing him, he is entirely occupied in this action, and his experience may be swallowed up in the objects about him, so that he has, at the time being, no consciousness of self at all. We must be, of course, very completely occupied to have that take place, but we can, I think, recognize that sort of a possible experience in which the self does not enter. We can, perhaps, get some light on that situation through those experiences in which in very intense action there appear in the experience of the individual, back of this intense action, memories and anticipations. Tolstoi as an officer in the war gives an account of having pictures of his past experience in the midst of his most intense action. There are also the pictures that flash into a person's mind when he is drowning. In such instances there is a contrast between an experience that is absolutely wound up in outside activity in which the self as an object does not enter, and an activity of memory and imagination in which the self is the principal object. The self is then entirely distinguishable from an organism that is surrounded by things and acts with reference to things, including parts of its own body. These latter may be objects like other objects, but they are just objects out there in the field, and they do not involve a self that is an object to the organism. This is, I think, frequently overlooked. It is that fact which makes our anthropomorphic reconstructions of animal life so fallacious. How can an individual get outside himself (experientially) in such a way as to become an object to himself? This is the essential psychological problem of selfhood or of self-consciousness; and its solution is to be found by referring to the process of social conduct or activity in which the given person or individual is implicated. The apparatus of reason would not be complete unless it swept itself into its own analysis of the field of experience; or unless the individual brought himself into the same experiential field as that of the other individual selves in relation to whom he acts in any given social situation. Reason cannot become impersonal unless it takes an objective, non-affective attitude toward itself; otherwise we have just consciousness, not *self*-consciousness. And it is necessary to rational conduct that the individual should thus take an objective, impersonal attitude toward himself, that he should become an object to himself. For the individual organism is obviously an essential and important fact or constituent element of the empirical situation in which it acts; and without taking objective account of itself as such, it cannot act intelligently, or rationally.

The individual experiences himself as such, not directly, but only indirectly, from the particular standpoints of other individual members of the same social group, or from the generalized standpoint of the social group as a whole to which he belongs. For he enters his own experience as a self or individual, not directly or immediately, not by becoming a subject to himself, but only in so far as he first becomes an object to himself just as other individuals are objects to him or in his experience; and he becomes an object to himself only by taking the attitudes of other individuals toward himself within a social environment or context of experience and behavior in which both he and they are involved.

The importance of what we term "communication" lies in the fact that it provides a form of behavior in which the organism or the individual may become an object to himself. It is that sort of communication which we have been discussing—not communication in the sense of the cluck of the hen to the chickens, or the bark of a wolf to the pack, or the lowing of a cow, but communication in the sense of significant symbols, communication which is directed not only to others but also to the individual himself. So far as that type of communication is a part of behavior it at least introduces a self. Of course, one may hear without listening; one may see things that he does not realize; do things that he is not really aware of. But it is where one does respond to that which he addresses to another and where that response of his own becomes a part of his conduct, where he not only hears himself but responds to himself, talks and replies to himself as truly as the other person replies to him, that we have behavior in which the individuals become objects to themselves.

Such a self is not, I would say, primarily the physiological organism. The physiological organism is essential to it, but we are at least able to think of a self without it. Persons who believe in immortality, or believe in ghosts, or in the possibility of the self leaving the body, assume a self which is quite distinguishable from the body. How successfully they can hold these conceptions is an open question, but we do, as a fact, separate the self and the organism. It is fair to say that the beginning of the self as an object, so far as we can see, is to be found in the experiences of people that lead to the conception of a "double." Primitive people assume that there is a double, located presumably in the diaphragm, that leaves the body temporarily in sleep and completely in death. It can be enticed out of the body of one's enemy and perhaps killed. It is represented in infancy by the imaginary playmates which children set up, and through which they come to control their experiences in their play.

The self, as that which can be an object to itself, is essentially a social structure, and it arises in social experience. After a self has arisen, it in a certain sense provides for itself its social experiences, and so we can conceive of an absolutely solitary self. But it is impossible to conceive of a self arising outside of social experience. When it has arisen we can think of a person in solitary confinement for the rest of his life, but who still has himself as a companion, and is able to think and to converse with himself as he had communicated with others. That process to which I have just referred, of responding to one's self as another responds to it, taking part in one's own conversation with others, being aware of what one is saying and using that awareness of what one is saying to determine what one is going to say thereafter—that is a process with which we are all familiar. We are continually following up our own address to other persons by an understanding of what we are saying, and using that understanding in the direction of our continued speech. We are finding out what we are going to say, what we are going to do, by saying and doing, and in the process we are continually controlling the process itself. In the conversation of gestures what we say calls out a certain response in another and that in turn changes our own action, so that we shift from what we started to do because of the reply the other makes. The conversation of gestures is the beginning of communication. The individual comes to carry on a conversation of gestures with himself. He says something, and that calls out a certain reply in himself which makes him change what he was going to say. One starts to say something, we will presume an unpleasant something, but when he starts to say it he realizes it is cruel. The effect on himself of what he is saying checks him; there is here a conversation of gestures between the individual and himself. We mean by significant speech that the action is one that affects the individual himself, and that the effect upon the individual himself is part of the intelligent carrying-out of the conversation with others. Now we, so to speak, amputate that social phase and dispense with it for the time being, so that one is talking to one's self as one would talk to another person.

This process of abstraction cannot be carried on indefinitely. One inevitably seeks an audience, has to pour himself out to somebody. In reflective intelligence one thinks to act, and to act solely so that this action remains a part of a social process. Thinking becomes preparatory to social action. The very process of thinking is, of course, simply an inner conversation that goes on, but it is a conversation of gestures which in its completion implies the expression of that which one thinks to an audience. One separates the significance of what he is saying to others from the actual speech and gets it ready before saying it. He thinks it out, and perhaps writes it in the form of a book; but it is still a part of social intercourse in which one is addressing other persons and at the same time addressing one's self, and in which one controls the address to other persons by the response made to one's own gesture. That the person should be responding to himself is necessary to the self, and it is this sort of social conduct which provides behavior within which that self appears. I know of no other form of behavior than the linguistic in which the individual is an object to himself, and, so far as I can see, the individual is not a self in the reflexive sense unless he is an object to himself. It is this fact that gives a critical importance to communication, since this is a type of behavior in which the individual does so respond to himself.

We realize in everyday conduct and experience that an individual does not mean a great deal of what he is doing and saying. We frequently say that such an individual is not himself. We come away from an interview with a realization that we have left out important things, that there are parts of the self that did not get into what was said. What determines the amount of the self that gets into communication is the social experience itself. Of course, a good deal of the self does not need to get expression. We carry on a whole series of different relationships to different people. We are one thing to one man and another thing to another. There are parts of the self which exist only for the self in relationship to itself. We divide ourselves up in all sorts of different selves with reference to our acquaintances. We discuss politics with one and religion with another. There are all sorts of different selves answering to all sorts of different social reactions. It is the social process itself that is responsible for the appearance of the self; it is not there as a self apart from this type of experience.

A multiple personality is in a certain sense normal, as I have just pointed put. There is usually an organization of the whole self with reference to the community to which we belong, and the situation in which we find ourselves. What the society is, whether we are living with people of the present, people of our own imaginations, people of the past, varies, of course, with different individuals. Normally, within the sort of community as a whole to which we belong, there is a unified self, but that may be broken up. To a person who is somewhat unstable nervously and in whom there is a line of cleavage, certain activities become impossible, and that set of activities may separate and evolve another self. Two separate "me's" and "I's," two different selves, result, and that is the condition under which there is a tendency to break up the personality. There is an account of a professor of education who disappeared, was lost to the community, and later turned up in a logging camp in the West. He freed himself of his occupation and turned to the woods where he felt, if you like, more at home. The pathological side of it was the forgetting, the leaving out of the rest of the self. This result involved getting rid of certain bodily memories which would identify the individual to himself. We often recognize the lines of cleavage that run through us. We would be glad to forget certain things, get rid of things the self is bound up with in past experiences. What we have here is a situation in which there can be different selves, and it is dependent upon the set of social reactions that is involved as to which self we are going to be. If we can forget everything involved in one set of activities, obviously we relinquish that part of the self. Take a person who is unstable, get him occupied by speech, and at the same time get his eye on something you are writing so that he is carrying on two separate lines of communication, and if you go about it in the right way you can get those two currents going so that they do not run into each other. You can get two entirely different sets of activities going on. You can bring about in that way the dissociation of a person's self. It is a process of setting up two sorts of communication which separate the behavior of the individual. For one individual it is this thing said and heard, and for the other individual there exists only that which he sees written. You must, of course, keep one experience out of the field of the other. Dissociations are apt to take place when an event leads to emotional upheavals. That which is separated goes on in its own way.

The unity and structure of the complete self reflects the unity and structure of the social process as a whole; and each of the elementary selves of which it is composed reflects the unity and structure of one of the various aspects of that process in which the individual is implicated. In other words, the various elementary selves which constitute, or are organized into, a complete self are the various aspects of the structure of that complete self answering to the various aspects of the structure of the social process as a whole; the structure of the complete self is thus a reflection of the complete social process. The organization and unification of a social group is identical with the organization and unification of any one of the selves arising within the social process in which that group is engaged, or which it is carrying on.

The phenomenon of dissociation of personality is caused by a breaking up of the complete, unitary self into the component selves of which it is composed, and which respectively correspond to different aspects of the social process in which the person is involved, and within which his complete or unitary self has arisen; these aspects being the different social groups to which he belongs within that process. …

Rational society, of course, is not limited to any specific set of individuals. Any person who is rational can become a part of it. The attitude of the community toward our own response is imported into ourselves in terms of the meaning of what we are doing. This occurs in its widest extent in universal discourse, in the reply which the rational world makes to our remark. The meaning is as universal as the community, it is necessarily involved in the rational character of that community; it is the response that the world made up out of rational beings inevitably makes to our own statement. We both get the object and ourselves into experience in terms of such a process; the other appears in our own experience in so far as we do take such an organized and generalized attitude.

If one meets a person on the street whom he fails to recognize, one's reaction toward him is that toward any other who is a member of the same community. He is the other, the organized, generalized other, if you like. One takes his attitude over against one's self. If he turns in one direction one is to go in another direction. One has his response as an attitude within himself. It is having that attitude within himself that makes it possible for one to be a self. That involves something beyond the mere turning to the right, as we say, instinctively, without self-consciousness. To have self-consciousness one must have the attitude of the other in one's own organism as controlling the thing that he is going to do. What appears in the immediate experience of one's self in taking that attitude is what we term the "me." It is that self which is able to maintain itself in the community, that is recognized in the community in so far as it recognizes the others. Such is the phase of the self which I have referred to as that of the "me."

Over against the "me" is the "I." The individual not only has rights, but he has duties; he is not only a citizen, a member of the community, but he is one who reacts to this community and in his reaction to it, as we have seen in the conversation of gestures, changes it. The "I" is the response of the individual to the attitude of the community as this appears in his own experience. His response to that organized attitude in turn changes it. As we have pointed out, this is a change which is not present in his own experience until after it takes place. The "I" appears in our experience in memory. It is only after we have acted that we know what we have done; it is only after we have spoken that we know what we have said. The adjustment to that organized world which is present in our own nature is one that represents the "me" and is constantly there. But if the response to it is a response which is of the nature of the conversation of gestures, if it creates a situation which is in some sense novel, if one puts up his side of the case, asserts himself over against others and insists that they take a different attitude toward himself, then there is something important occurring that is not previously present in experience.

The Less Space We Take the More Powerful We'll Be

How Advertising Uses Gender to Invert Signs of Empowerment and Social Equality

By Vickie Rutledge Shields

How do advertisements show us and tell us how to "gender" ourselves through the images and messages in their content? Within the field of media studies, questions of content, gender, and advertising have a long and fruitful albeit internally tense history. Researchers in the fields of communication, marketing, sociology and philosophy, to name a few, have been actively addressing this question for about 30 years (see Shields, 1996). Scholars began to approach the issue through empirical analyses. Early research implying mimetic effects evolved to more sophisticated quantitative and qualitative research. By the turn of the century, scholars, activists, and industry all draw from this long tradition to come out with research, strategies, and ads that both exploit the findings and attempt to create more gender sensitive ads. However, given that ads are a crucial component of the circulation of goods in a capitalist system, all of this research, activism, and ad production occur in a setting where commodification parameters themselves are seldom challenged.

The 1970s US was infused with second-wave feminist politics, increasing support for an Equal Rights Amendment, and the increase of female researchers in higher education. In this climate feminist scholars raced to produce empirical analyses of sex-role stereotyping found in print and television. This type of research originating then and, to a lesser extent continuing on today, is commonly referred to as *sex-roles* research. Through the use of content analysis these studies investigated questions pertaining to gender difference and inequality within the *content* of ads. Specifically, early sex-roles research revealed that women in advertising were portrayed by restrictive categories, such as housewife or sex-object, and that advertising reflected a false picture of women's real lives (see Courtney & Whipple, 1974). This type of research fit in nicely with the research methods already established in communication studies while serving a political imperative, the improvement of the representation of women in the media (Rakow, 1986).

Early researchers in the area of sex-role stereotyping in the mass media examined large numbers of ads at a time in order to classify and count particular types of representations. For example, a typical content analysis might examine 500–1,000 ads in popular fashion magazines. These ads would be examined for categories such as: how many times males appeared in business roles, how many times females appeared in bathrooms, how many times females were posed as sex-objects, and so on. The aim of this research was to demonstrate how prevalent sex-role stereotypes were in advertising.

By shining a light on the gender inequities in advertising through empirical analysis, these researchers hoped to show where the most harmful and most frequent stereotyping occurs. The expectations were that the results of this type of research would have two types of effects. First, the research would reveal to the producers of ads where and how they could improve their campaigns to more adequately reflect "real" gender relations in society. Second, the research was intended to reveal to all audiences of advertising how the images viewed each day, and generally taken for granted, were really showing us a warped, sexually inequitable vision of our society.

The rush to research the image of gender portrayal across the mass media in the 1970s could be attributed to at least two major factors. The first was the re-emergence of feminist writing in the academy spurred on by Betty Friedan's (1963) *The Feminine Mystique*. Second, advertising and print journalism received special attention because women were dominating, more than ever, many of the consumer groups targeted by advertisers and common sense dictated that the ways in which women viewed themselves in ads might greatly impact the effectiveness of commercial marketing campaigns (Lundstrom & Sciglimpaglia, 1977; Morrison & Sherman, 1972; Wise, King, & Merenski, 1974; Wortzel & Frisbie, 1974). This research was concerned with advertising "effectiveness," examining whether, and under what conditions, more progressive, less stereotyped portrayals may be preferred to traditional ones. Of foremost concern was the measurement of causal relationships between women's heightened attitudes about "Women's Liberation," role portrayal, and product desirability. Several studies, for instance, hypothesized that women would view products more positively if the role portrayal were that of women in jobs or careers (Wortzel & Frisbie, 1974).

Alice Courtney and Sarah Lockeretz's (1971) content analysis of the portrayal of men and women in print advertising was one of the first and also one of the most widely cited and replicated research studies on the subject. These authors concluded that four general stereotypes of women existed across advertisements in eight major general-interest magazines in the years 1958, 1968, and 1978: 1) a woman's place is in the home; 2) women do not make important decisions or do important things; 3) women are dependent and need men's protection; and 4) men regard women primarily as sex objects (Courtney, 1983, p. 7).

Issues and findings from content analyses of television advertisements showed very similar results. Television studies showed that: 1) prevalent female roles were—maternal, housekeeping", and aesthetic; 2) women and girls were seen less frequently than men; 3) women were shown to have different characteristics than males (less authoritative, decisive, powerful, rational); 4) women were housewives or in subservient, low-status occupations; and 5) women were depicted as less intelligent than men (Ferrante, Haynes, & Kingsley, 1988; Kimball, 1986; Lazier & Kendrick, 1993). It is important to note that the findings in the print advertising research and the television advertising research revealed similar results. Because we as audience members do not generally experience only one mass medium in any given day or week, but are instead positioned within a web of media viewing, the greater the consistency of messages, such as gender stereotypes, across the media the more powerful their potential effect is on how audiences transfer that knowledge to their social relationships.

Studies charting progress in these images in the next few years also charted new problems. Louis Wagner and Janis Banos (1973) found that the percentage of women in working roles had increased, but in non-working roles women were being seen less in family settings and more in decorative capacities. Further, women were seldom depicted interacting with one another or making major purchases without a male also in the picture. These authors concluded that stereotypes pre-dating the women's movement remained and advertising was not keeping up with the times in failing to portray realistically the diversity of women's roles (see also Belkaoui & Belkaoui, 1976).

Little attention was paid to male sex-role portrayal in print ads at this time, with the exception of one major study replicating Courtney and Lockeretz's sample from a male standpoint (Wohleter & Lammers, 1980) and one minor study (Skelly & Lundstrom, 1981). These studies found that men were more likely to be shown working outside the home and to be involved in the major purchases of expensive goods. All of these studies concluded that roles of men and women in print advertisements had changed little over twenty years (Busby, 1975; Dominick & Rauch, 1972; Fejes, 1992). Men were depicted in mainstream advertising as autonomous; pictured outdoors or in business settings; and are less likely to be at home than women and they are more likely to advertise alcohol, vehicles, and business products (Downs, 1981; Fejes, 1992; Fowles, 1996).

In the 1980s and early 1990s there has been a decrease in the number of sex-roles studies conducted than was the case in the 1970s. Furthermore, recent empirical studies investigate highly specialized areas such as "women's adoption of the business uniform" (Saunders & Stearn, 1986), sex-role stereotyping of children on TV (Furnham, Abramsky, & Gunter, 1997; Peirce, 1989), women in advertisements in medical journals (Hawkins & Aber, 1993), perception studies (Rossi & Rossi, 1985), achievement studies (Geis et al., 1984), and self-consciousness variables studies (Gould, 1987). Additional recent studies have examined cross-cultural or international perspectives on gender representation in advertising (Furnham, 1989; Gilly, 1988; Griffin, Viswanath, & Schwartz 1992; Mazzella et al., 1992; Neto & Pinto, 1998).

Most recent sex-roles research, however, have used the vast data collected over the last 20 to 30 years to: 1) either advance theory on sex-role representation and possible debilitating "effects" stereotypical images can have for society or 2) revisit this early research, replicating studies to see whether advertising images have progressed in the past 20 years (Whipple & Courtney, 1985). According to Linda Lazier and Alice Kendrick (1993), stereotyping of portrayals of women was still important to study because the portrayals were not only debilitating and demeaning, but they continue to be "inaccurate." Advertisements "do not reflect the significant strides (both socially and statistically) made by women in the past two decades into the work force" (p. 201). Further, women were still not seen as decision makers for major purchases (although women actually make more family financial decisions than do men) and finally, "by using outdated stereotypes, ads are simplistically ignoring the complexities of modern women's lives" (p. 201).

Lynn Lovdal (1989), in a study of 354 TV commercials, found that men's voices were still dominant in voice-overs and that men were portrayed in three times the variety of occupational roles as were women. Other recent research has found that men were more likely to be portrayed in independent roles in relation to women who were portrayed in a variety of stereotyped roles such as wife, mother, bride, waitress, actress, dancer (Bred & Cantor, 1988; Gilly, 1988; Lazier & Kendrick, 1993). Even the feminist publication, Ms., whose editorial policy states that it will not run advertising harmful to women, did not fare well under the scrutiny of content analysis. A 1990 study by Jill Ferguson, Peggy Kreshel, and Spencer Tinkham found that a substantial proportion of advertising promoted products considered harmful, such as cigarettes and alcohol. Further, although images of women in subordinate and decorative capacities had decreased overall in the ads in *Ms.*, the amount of ads depicting women as alluring sex-objects increased. The editors of Ms. found that pleasing advertisers and offering serious feminist-oriented articles were often in conflict. In 1990 *Ms.* adopted a no-ads policy much as a result of Gloria Steinem's own critical proclamation in the pages of *Ms.* as its founding editor that "what became more and more clear is how few media are able to give consumers facts that may displease their advertisers" (p. 17). Although *Ms.* magazine is now more expensive to purchase, the no-ads policy has allowed *Ms.* to "present a renewed vision of feminism" (McKinnon, 1995).

In 1989 Linda Lazier-Smith conducted research replicating the three major studies of Suzanne Pingree, Robert Hawkins, Matilda Butler and William Paisley (1976), Erving Goffman (1976), and Jeane Kilbourne (1987). In her research the author replicated the method, categories and procedures of Pingree and Hawkins' "Consciousness Scale of Sexism" and reapplied it along with Goffman's and Kilbourne's sexism in representation categories to one full year of advertisements in *Ms.*, *Playboy*, *Time* and *Newsweek*. Lazier-Smith found no significant change between the 1970s analyses and the 1988 representations. The authors reported that preliminary results showed a decrease in (sex object/decoration/bimbo) portrayals, however, the categories applying to women's subordination to men were still as prevalent.

Sex-roles research, in particular, has played an important part in diffusing the concept of the "sexual stereotype" throughout the language of this culture. A review of Alice Courtney and Thomas Whipple's (1974) four categories of sexual stereotyping in advertising are instructive here: (1) a woman's place is in the home; (2) women do not make important decisions or do important things; (3) women are dependent and need men's protection; and (4) men regard women primarily as sex objects. Although the variety of roles of women represented in ads has increased, current feminist literature on gender and advertising argues that these content categories have changed very little. These roles are masked by the appearance of variety. Stereotypical representations seem less harmful when served up smorgasbord style.

ADVERTISING CONTENT: A DIFFERENT VIEW

When exploring how people discuss the content of ads, we are really asking how advertising images that we see over and over again affect our thoughts, emotions and behaviors. Cultural studies scholar and Media Education Foundation video entrepreneur, Sut Jhally, levels an important critique at sex-roles research in *Codes of Advertisements* (1987). According to Jhally, content analysis research of gender stereotyping in advertising places its emphasis on the truth or falsity of representation, when in fact "advertisement images are neither false nor true reflections of social reality because they are in fact *part* of social reality" (p. 135). As such, advertising needs to be studied as a constituent part of our social reality, not as a distorted reflection of it. Therefore, emphasis must shift from questions of trueness or falseness to processes of "signification," or the ability of advertisements to "communicate" to social actors. This change marks a theoretical and methodological shift in advertising research focused on gender from analyses of manifest content to analyses of the "symbolic potential" of that content.

The work of Erving Goffman provides one of the first significant examples in this shift in emphasis from the examination of manifest content to the symbolic potential of ads. In the midst of the flurry of content analysis research, Goffman (1976) published his own empirical manifesto on the nature of advertising portrayals in *Gender Advertisements*. However, Goffman asked very different questions of his data than sex-roles researchers and also employed a very different method for analyzing his results. Guided by the tenets of symbolic interactionism and sociology, Goffman suggested that the most relevant questions we can ask of advertising are: of what aspects of real life do advertisements provide us a fair picture, and what social effects do the advertisements have upon the lives purportedly pictured in them?

Goffman's *Gender Advertisements* was one of the first and is to this day one of the most influential textual analyses of the symbolic potential of advertising images. Central to his view of how gender operates in advertising is his notion of "gender display": "[I]f gender be defined as the culturally established correlates of sex (whether in consequence of biology or learning), then gender display refers to conventionalized portrayals of these correlates" (p. 1). The key, then, to understanding how gender is communicated through advertisements is to understand the notion that advertisements present to us familiar ritual-like displays. However, gender displays in advertising are *polysemic* (containing myriad possible meanings). More than one piece of cultural information may be encoded into them. Further, once a display becomes well-established and stylized the stylization itself becomes the object of attention. Standardization, exaggeration and simplification are found to an extended degree in advertising. Gender displays in advertising are familiar because they show us ritual—that is, bits of behaviors in which we engage in real life.

Goffman's research was unique at the time for employing a method now being labeled "semiotic content analysis." His analysis focused on message structures across the entire discourse of print advertisements containing gender components. Goffman revealed patterns in messages about gender that when repeated constantly and consistently provide a picture of reality that seems natural and real, but is in fact over stylized and conventionalized, or what Goffman called *hyper-ritualized*. Five prominent hyper-ritualizations, or for coding purposes, categories emerged from Goffman's empirical analysis: (1) Relative Size—women in ads are shown as smaller or lower relative to men. (2) Feminine Touch—women are constantly touching themselves, others or objects in ads. (3) Function Ranking—male occupations rank higher in ads than female occupations, consistently. (4) Ritualization of Subordination—women and children are often lower in the frame of the ad, lying on floors or beds or canting the body in ways that convey submission. (5) Licensed Withdrawal—women are never quite part of the scene in a meaningful way.

Goffman's analysis forced the reader to reconsider the relationship between advertising and reality. "He also uncovers the assumptions underlying the interpretive codes buried in advertisements and the way advertising acts as an accomplice in perpetuating regressive forms of social relations" (Leiss, Kline, & Jhally, 1986, p. 169). In all its familiarity, advertising does not merely reflect reality. Although it draws its materials from everyday life, from real gender displays for instance, the bits of everyday life used are selected carefully and much is habitually omitted. By selecting some things to integrate continuously into the message system of advertising (a good example is the ideal female body image), and continuously omitting others (say, the "fleshy" female body), ads create new meanings that are not found elsewhere necessarily. Cultural critics of communication have attempted to build upon, as well as push beyond, Goffman's ideas of gender display. Taken in historical context, these new directions in theorizing are beginning to address more adequately how gender relations can be reproduced when viewed across time and symbolic conventions (Coward, 1982; Hay, 1989; Kilbourne, 1999, 1987; Masse & Rosenblum, 1988; Millium, 1975; Myers, 1982, 1986; Williamson, 1986; Winship, 1981, 1985). Prominent themes have emerged in this body of work that are of particular relevance here.

The first of these themes involves the "photographic cropping" (Millium, 1975) of female body parts to substitute for the entire body in advertising representations. Women in advertising are very often signified in a fragmented way, by their lips, legs, hair, eyes or hands. The "bit" (lips, legs, breasts, etc.) represents the whole: the sexualized woman (Winship, 1981, p. 25). Men, on the other hand, are less likely to be "dismembered" in this way in advertisements. Jeane Kilbourne (1999, 1987), in particular, describes the cropping of photographs of women in advertising as one of the major elements that present the female as dehumanized and as an object, which is the first step toward the legitimation of committing violence toward that person. This, she argues, contributes to a general climate of violence against women. Kilbourne identifies at least two other hyper-ritualizations in gender advertisements: (1) Innocence is Sexy—ads tend to sexualize female youth and (2) Food and Sex—in recent advertisements food and eating are portrayed as modern woman's sin, replacing sex.

In her analysis of the relationship between the positioning of hands and sexuality in advertising, Janice Winship (1981) brings together the theme of photographic cropping with a second theme, "the public male and the domestic female." Male and female hands are a part of an entire message system of social representation signifying appropriate gender behavior. In her analysis, Winship juxtaposes an ad of a man's hand holding an open pack of Rothman's cigarettes, the "World Leader," and a woman's hand pouring a pitcher of Bird's custard over a dessert, the caption reading, "home-made goodness." A switching of the hands would disrupt the meanings with which each gender imbues the ad:

> A woman's hand does not signify "world leader"; a man's hand does not signify "home-made." But as it is, the appropriately gendered hand allows us to key into familiar ideologies of masculinity and femininity. Those ideologies see "naturally" masculine or feminine, and the represented hand is "naturally" a man's or a woman's. (p. 30)

In 1997 Mee-Eun Kang published a "conceptual replication" of Goffman's *Gender Advertisements*. He sampled over 500 advertisements in all picturing human subjects. One half of the sample was drawn from 1979 magazines and the other half was drawn from the 1991 counterparts to those magazines. Kang added the categories of (1) Body Display—females in ads are often scantily clad or nude and (2) Independence and Self-Assertiveness—how self reliant and independent does the woman appear in the ad?, to Goffman's original five categories. Kang found that few changes had occurred in the representation of women in magazine ads since 1979 (three years after Goffman's findings were published). Although "Function Ranking" and "Relative Size" featured less prominently in 1991 than in 1979, in the two categories of "Licensed Withdrawal" and "Body Display" the 1991 ads showed more stereotyping of women than in 1979.

RACE AND GENDER DISPLAY

In media theory, the serious under-representation of a particular group has been coined "symbolic annihilation" (Gerbner & Gross, 1976; Tuchman, Daniels & Benet, 1978). Symbolic annihilation refers to the most profound inequities in "the spectrum of mediated representations of social groups" (see Kielwasser & Wolf, 1992, p. 351). Those consistently annihilated from visual representation in mainstream ads include: Native Americans, Latinos, Asians, gays, lesbians, fat people and little people, to name a few. Blacks, on the other hand, have appeared in advertising almost from its beginning. However, the nature of those representations until very recently has been dubious at best. In her study of the "raceing" of advertising featuring women between 1876 and 1900, Marilyn Maness Mehaffy (1997) charts how negative depictions of Black women were instrumental to the construction of the ideal White female consumer. In image after image the "visual narrative of ideal (White) consuming domesticity takes shape through her juxtaposition with a mirroring Black female figure, typically associated, in contrast, with pre-industrial technologies and economies of home production" (p. 135). The Black woman was the "domestic" to ideal domesticity occupied by the White woman (consumer).

> In today's putatively race- and gender-blind era, the raced-gender allocations of late nineteenth-century advertising cards haunt the rhetorics of contemporary media, and, in the perennial, dually raced invocations of "welfare queens" and sanctified white motherhood, they haunt contemporary politics and government as well. (p. 172)

Since World War II until very recently, women of color were required to be light-skinned fine-featured, resembling the European ideal of beauty, in order to be represented as anything other than a Mammy-figure in print or television advertising. Feminist scholars such as Roach and Felix (1989) suggest that we live in a culture where the dominant gaze is not only male, but white. Up until the last decade or so, representations of African Americans were mostly excluded, but when included highly stereotyped and ghettoized, placed outside "natural" and "beautiful" representation in advertising and positioned as "other." However, unlike the "exotic other" of the Hawaiian or Philippino "girls" in suntan advertisements (see Williamson, 1986), African Americans are society's mundane other, (Cui, 2000; Fredrickson, 1988; McLaughlin & Goulet, 1999; Miles, 1989; Omi & Winant, 1986).

Scott Coltrane and Melinda Messineo (2000) content analyzed 1,699 television commercials that aired on programs with high ratings from 1992 to 1994 in order to study the interrelationship between race and gender in advertising. The authors suggest that

> television commercials do more than offer people images of selves defined through the consumption of products. In addition, they shape images of others and sustain group boundaries that come to be taken for granted. Feelings of entitlement, subtle forms of prejudice, and institutional racism are thus reproduced in and through commercial television imagery. (p. 385)

Coltrane and Messineo found that although African-American images were more plentiful than in previous decades, the ways they are represented still reinforce established prejudices. Characters in television commercials still "enjoy more prominence and exercise more authority" if they are White or men. Women and Whites occupy most family-oriented commercial imagery. "In general, 1990s television commercials tend to portray White men as powerful, White women as sex objects, African-American men as aggressive, and African-American women as inconsequential" (p. 363).

THE SEMIOTICS OF GENDER IN ADVERTISING

Many of the most illuminating studies of advertising images have employed some variation of semiology (see Barthes, 1977, 1988; Leiss, Kline, & Jhally, 1986; Nichols, 1981; Williamson, 1978, 1986). By treating the advertising image as a "text," semiotic analyses concentrate on the relationships between the ads' internal meaning structures as they relate to the larger cultural codes shared by viewers. Semiology's relationship to advertising is explained succinctly by Sut Jhally (1987):

> Semiology is the study of signs, or more specifically the *system of signs*. A sign is something that has significance within a system of meaning and is constituted of two key elements: the signifier (the material vehicle) and the signified (the mental construct, the idea). The two elements are equally necessary and can be separated only analytically … This is the difference between the signifier and the sign. A diamond as signifier is *empty* of meaning. The diamond as sign is *full* of meaning. … production produces commodities as signifiers while advertising produces them as signs, (p. 130)

Advertising operates in the realm of symbols, drawing from those already familiar, and inventing new signs where none existed before. The symbol is a sign that has been arbitrarily imbued with meaning, either through culture, habit, or through the intentional strategy of marketing. For example, the signifier of a rose is literally the plant (its petals, stem, leaves, thorns, pigment). However, in this culture the most prevalent signifieds of rose are "love," "affection," and "beauty." These meanings are arbitrary in that there is nothing in the plant itself that either resembles or points to these things. However, culture has "naturalized" these connotations for us. Marketing campaigns achieve this. For example when the early 1990s marketing campaign for Guess? jeans repeatedly used the photographic image of super model Claudia Schiffer in their ads, the image of Claudia Schiffer became a symbol of Guess? jeans, or, more accurately, a symbol of the Guess? style and "look." This pairing of Schiffer and Guess? jeans was arbitrary.

The meaning of any given sign is culturally defined and culturally specific. When advertising and marketing campaigns attempt to sell commodities (signifiers) to the public, they either work with the cultural connotations with which the commodity is already imbued, or, in the case of a new product (a generic commodity), the significance of the commodity is invented entirely in the process of advertising. For example, the long-running "Diamonds are Forever" ad campaign draws on cultural meanings of a diamond familiar to consumers, but then imbues particular types of diamond rings (signifiers) with very particular signifieds. The eternity diamond ring, for example, through the magic of this advertising campaign now signifies to us, "marriage anniversary," or "milestones within marriage" such as the birth of a child. The ad campaign draws heavily on the persuasive appeal of "guilt" to convey especially to the male consumer that if he lets these milestones go by without rewarding "her" with an eternity diamond ring, he is some kind of clod. So, in this regard, the "Diamonds are Forever" campaign signifies as much about what it means if one has reached these marital milestones and does *not* own an eternity ring, as it signifies about what it means *to* own and wear a diamond eternity ring. The campaign presents us with the diamond eternity ring as a full sign, both in its presence and in its absence (Shields, 2002).

Pioneering scholars in the area of semiotics and advertising such as Judith Williamson (1978), Bill Nichols (1981) and Sut Jhally (1987) were concerned with how individual advertisements are interdependent on one another for meaning—as a *code*. "Signs do not occur singly; they occur in groups … placing signs into appropriate groupings stresses that meaning arises not solely, not even primarily, from the relationship of signifier to signified but relations between signs" (Leeds-Hurwitz, 1993, p. 51). A code is not a mere grouping of signs, however. A code is a system of associations governed by rules agreed upon (explicitly or implicitly) between members of a culture. The code unifies the different elements of the process of meaning construction. In advertising, a code is the store of experience upon which both the advertiser and audience draw in their participation in the construction of "commodity meaning" (Jhally, 1987, p. 140).

As cultural codes shift within dominant ideologies some signs acquire different signifieds, sometimes in direct opposition to the previous signifieds—such is the case with the sign of the cigarette. In the 1950s celebrities with squeaky clean images, like Donna Reed, advertised for Chesterfields, while major league baseball players endorsed Camels, and Lucky Strikes used images of teenage cheerleaders. In the 1950s the cigarette was a somewhat empty signifier and the challenge for advertisers was differentiating between brands of a fairly generic product. Today the cigarette itself is a "full sign" of negative connotations before advertisers try to invest it with a particular image. The challenge for advertisers today is to deal with the fullness of the sign in the first place, and then attach some kind of positive signification to it (Shields, 2002). Camel has done it with a cartoon character; Malboro is still using the image of the rugged outdoorsman; and Virginia Slims has attempted to incorporate advances from the women's movement into their campaigns. Many cigarette ads marketed to women still implicitly push them as an appetite suppressant and aid in weight-loss.

Advertising insists that we differentiate what kind of person we "are" in relation to a specific product. Differentiation cannot be interpreted as a wholly overt and cognitively conscious process, however. Differentiation is often emotional and sensual. Many fashion advertisements, for example, operate at a level of social significance that is once-removed from the utility of the product being advertised (Shields, 1990). The sensuality of the image does not define the commodity, so much as it differentiates the sensuousness of one commodity from the sensuousness of another.

The transfer of codes of sexuality to commodities in this culture is widely accessible to both males and females because the transfer has become "naturalized" in our popular iconography. More specifically, the transfer of codes of ideal female beauty or attractiveness to commodities has become common sense, even though the relationship between, say, a woman in a swimsuit and a can of beer is in itself arbitrary. However, the sign of the ideal female body, in this culturally naturalized state takes on an exchange-value all its own. It is an ambiguous discourse that can be visually attached to virtually any commodity in order to lend the commodity value. Therefore, when the woman in the swimsuit appears in an advertisement for beer, the relationship between the sexuality of the female body and the commodity (beer) does not appear to be arbitrary. The sexuality of the female body has a general exchange-value lent in this case to the value of beer, but could just as easily be lent to the value of an automobile or cigarettes (Shields, 1996).

IDEOLOGIES OF THE BODY IN ADS

The "general exchange-value" of the ideal female body reaches far beyond advertising in this culture. This exchange-value is what John Berger (1972) coined, a cultural way of seeing. Ways of seeing the female body are culturally imbued codes which are consistent across not only advertising images but other visual images as well such as film, television programs, music videos, soft-porn and even portraiture. This consistency in representation helps define what is "natural" to be seen and enjoyed—what is ideal. A photograph or an advertising image is a selective view of reality. In this culture, advertising images of females frequently contain an invisible yet implicit man who approves of and defines the feminine ideal. Thus, the "point-of-view" in advertisements featuring the perfect female body is most always that of an implied male spectator. This implied approval by an often invisible male spectator is referred to by feminist scholars as the "male gaze." Seen through the lens of the "male gaze" females are the objects of the gaze as opposed to the subjects of the gaze.

The male gaze connotes significantly more than mere voyeurism. It is a controlling gaze. "To possess the image of a woman's sexuality is, however mass-produced the image, also in some way to possess, to maintain a degree of control over the woman in general (Kuhn, 1985, p. 11)." Laura Mulvey (1975) further explains the concept of the gendered gaze:

> In a world ordered by sexual imbalance, pleasure in looking has been split between active/male and passive/female. The determining male gaze projects its fantasy onto the female figure, which is styled accordingly. In their traditional exhibitionist role women are simultaneously looked at and displayed, with their appearance coded for strong visual and erotic impact so that they can be said to connote *to-be-looked-at-ness*. (p. 366)

For Rosalind Coward (1985), the male gaze encoded in photographic images is an extension of how men view women in the streets. The naturalness of this way of seeing the female body follows from its pervasiveness in all arenas of female representation as well as experience. In this schema, the female looking at an image is always a "split-subject." Women in patriarchal cultures are placed in a position of always being the embodiment of the object of the sight for someone else's pleasure and simultaneously being aware that she is this object of the sight. It also allows for a way of seeing that seems natural in appeal to both male and female spectators. If aesthetic appeal of the female body is naturalized for both males and females, it also seems natural that the female body is represented as sexualized more often than the male body.

Patricia Mellencamp (1995) explains the phenomena in this way:

> It is precisely this misrecognition [the split between a woman's self-image and her mirror image], a real alienation effect—woman divided against her inadequate self, body versus mind, mother versus daughter or son, woman versus woman—that must be overcome. After all, the body is an image and a sack of flesh; it is a historical, personal fiction or style as much as a reality. Certainly, the body is neither self nor identity nor value; we are much more, much

greater, than our bodies. Sex and the body don't grant identity, as Michel Foucault said over a decade ago, yet we keep looking there for answers. (p. 3)

WEIGHT AND DISCIPLINE

Just as the female body is the site of idealization and spectacle for the male gaze, it is also the site of anxiety and insecurity for women, who, constrained by the gaze, feel less embodied than objectified and reach out for ways to transform the body into the ideal, or as close as possible. The symbolic annihilation of body fat within the realm of the media means that we rarely ever see role models of heavy women looking attractive, receiving love or attention, particularly from handsome men. Moreover, when images of heavier women are shown, they tend to be negative images—jealous, angry villains like Ursula of Disney's *The Little Mermaid*, Sally Struthers in *South Park*, Mimi of *The Drew Carey Show*, or child-like pathetic creatures (the suicidal girl of *Heathers*, the mother of *What's Eating Gilbert Grape*).

As a culture, then we conceive of fat as being something outside the norm or linked to socially unacceptable behavior. When the vast percentage of media stars, actresses, and models we see are extraordinarily thin, many women and girls in particular begin to lose perspective on what really is the average weight of most women, and get a sense of the "norm" as being accurately represented in print, on TV and in film. In fact the "normal" weight of actresses and models is far below what is actually the average weight of everyday women, generally by up to 23 percent less (Women's Action Coalition, 1993).

In *Unbearable Weight* (1993), Susan Bordo convincingly shows how narcissism, the self-directed gaze, is a logical extension of a long tradition of Western thought: the epistemological and philosophical obsession with dualism. Dualism is the splitting of the head (the self, the "me," the part that thinks and reasons, the spiritual self) from the body. Bordo observes that the "self" in dualist thought is identified as that which has control, while the body has historically been conceived of as the enemy. The body is subject to disease and distracts the mind from thinking or spiritual activity because of its need for food, warmth, rest and other bodily functions. Importantly, women, as "irrational" and representative of nature, have been depicted as being closer to the body, while men, who have been depicted as the rational architects of society, are seen to be closer to "the mind" (Shields, 2002).

Bordo shows how contemporary views on the virtues of slenderness simply reiterate the way that the "self" is expected to control and discipline the body. Just as today we make assumptions about an individual's worth, self-liking, or laziness based on their weight, in the past the ascetic values of fasting monks and saints were represented by their wasted flesh. The saints' ability to fast, to deny the needs of their body, was a way of demonstrating their control, and thus the superiority of their mind and spirit, over the unholy body. The spirit was seen as separated from the body. In other words, one measure of our mental and spiritual control, indeed, our morality, is through how well we control our bodies. Slenderness thus becomes not only a sign of our mental health, but represents our status as a good person.

As Bordo reveals, this theme reappears today as thin people are likewise popularly represented as having mental control (will power and self-discipline). In contrast, fat is associated with the lack of will—the inability to control the needs and processes of one's body and hunger. Fat is seen as a demonstration of the person's lack of control over their demanding body. So, in addition to being symbolically annihilated, when they do appear in the media or in literature, heavy people are characterized as out of control, greedy, childish, or even mentally unwell. Carole Spitzack (1990) has likewise observed that fat people are often portrayed as disliking themselves.

As Susie Orbach (1978) has noted, fat is a particularly sensitive issue for women not only because of the historical association between women and the body, but because of women's position in the cultural pecking order and access to resources. Cultural and feminist scholars like Orbach, Bordo, Spitzack, and Naomi Wolf (1991) have all examined the ways that female consumption—of food and other resources—for both nourishment and pleasure has been suppressed throughout history. Consequently, female hunger for food, like female desire for sex or knowledge, has been derided and suppressed.

Following Michel Foucault (1977), Rowe, like Bordo (1993) and Spitzack (1990), describes how social groups maintain control over their members by setting standards of "normalcy." In a famous example, Foucault describes the idea of the panopticon in which prisoners are so used to being observed by the prison guards that they begin to police their own behavior to conform to the set standards of the prison (or society). The body that refuses to follow the aesthetic standards of its culture whether in bodily beauty or behavior can thus "communicate resistance to social discipline" (Rowe, 1995, p. 65). Therefore, women whose bodies show their willingness to eat, to have sex, or who break the rules of femininity in other ways are perceived as transgressing against the social bounds of propriety. At some level they are refusing to limit themselves, refusing to pretend that their hunger and desires do not exist—and thereby posing an unspoken threat to patriarchy. Thus, Rowe argues that female fat is hated in part because "it signifies a disturbing unresponsiveness to social control" (Rowe, 1995, p. 61). In today's culture, body fat may be read, albeit unconsciously, as a sign of women rebelling against the male gaze by refusing to conform to standards of beauty. Female fat also signifies a woman's ability and desire to consume for herself as subject—rather than to merely exist as object and for the pleasures of others.

In *Confessing Excess* (1990), Carole Spitzack suggests that this arrangement is aided by an ideology of women's health that condones policing the body in order to reap the reward of "freedom" or "release" from the unhealthy fat body. In order to maintain the healthy liberated body, one must continuously discipline it, police its cravings and excesses, and reprimand the self when discipline falters. Advertisements for diet products, fitness gyms, clothing and cosmetics tap into this ideology of the female body. These advertisements offer "solutions" to the disjuncture between the image of fashion models' bodies and real women's bodies by disciplining the body in the name of fitness—the triumph of culture over nature. The 1980s ushered in a new female physique complementary to aerobic exercise and activity. This curvaceous, muscular look, which is now most closely associated in its ideal form with supermodel Heidi Klum, is the combination of cultural antitheses: thin and muscular, hard and curvaceous, it suggests power and yet a slender boyishness; furthermore those very muscles which empower are also the material of feminine curves (Shields, 2002).

Achieving this combination of attributes is difficult, involving an investment of large amounts of time, money and effort on "body work." As Susan Bordo (1993) has observed, the ultra-thin look of the 1960s and 1970s could be achieved through starvation diets alone, but today, thinness without muscle tone falls short of the ideal feminine physique. The ideal must be achieved through a regimen of diet plus exercise.

As Spitzack argues, "Women are socialized to view the ongoing surveillance of their bodies as a form of empowerment that arises from self-love. The newly slender woman purchases a new wardrobe, presumably, because she likes herself now that she is thin: when fat, she did not like herself and consequently did not give adequate attention to appearance" (p. 35). These competing discourses surrounding body reduction help to position the discourse of thinness with "health," thereby placing weightiness or fatness in binary opposition with "health," as "disease." These discourses work with numerous other institutions and practices to encourage self-correction and, therefore, "liberation" from the disease of fat, especially for women. Thus, women, whose bodies are made to put on weight, find their natural bodies represented as diseased and abnormal. The possession of fat itself—of femaleness itself—is a sign of disease.

SELLING WOMEN THEIR "NEW FREEDOM"

In the past 10 years or so marketers have made a concerted effort to develop ad campaigns that seem to speak directly to female experience. Advertisers have tried also to capitalize on the fact that women are more conscious than ever before; that blindly striving toward the

idealized body in ads, film and on MTV shouldn't be their raison d'être; and that the rewards are hollow and the time and effort lost could be put to more meaningful and sustaining use (Shields, 2002). Advertisers have also picked up on the fact that women are tired of the size four body being presented as "everywoman." However, most of these ad campaigns offer "a wink" toward women and not a viable alternative to traditional sex-sells campaigns. Advertising scholar Daniel Nicholson (1997) describes the wink—or self-referentiality within an ad: when advertisers want the reader to recognize that "we know you know what we're trying to do, but because we're letting you know we know, it makes it okay—because we're so hip to your hipness. Get it?" (182–3). Just as Sprite was marketed to teens as the only soft drink that respects its consumer's media savvy, brands such as Special K, Levi's, Chic and Virginia Slims have tried to "anti-market" to women.

Take recent advertisements for Special K cereal. A television ad campaign for Special K in the mid-1990s suggested that women shouldn't be taken in by the prescriptions they see in the media, they should accept themselves. This particular campaign doesn't linger visually on any female body, but features a woman, probably in her forties, moving to light music as if in a yoga class. She is shot in soft-focus and no full body shots are revealed and no body fetishes are lingered over. This campaign showed that Special K could provide an intervention if they really tried; however can we as consumers above the age of 35 really forget that it was Special K commercials that got the whole nation obsessing in the 1970s about whether we could "pinch an inch"? Yet, this quickly became another measure of whether one was too fat in the 1970s. Pinching an inch of flesh was shameful and meant one needed to get right to work on the body. Their campaign tapped completely and directly into a culture of thin-obsessed girls and women who were willing to take advice from almost anywhere, even a cereal commercial, to achieve that "goal" of ultra-thinness (Shields, 2002).

The marketers of Special K seemed to suffer from a type of schizophrenia in the 1990s. Around the same time they were suggesting that women just relax and accept their bodies and themselves, a print ad in women's magazines featured a small floral bikini simply lying against a white background. The caption reads "it's not doing any good in your drawer." Again, Special

K couldn't resist tapping into one of women's phobias—being seen in a bathing suit. A recent ad for Special K seems to be one of the biggest winks toward women yet. The television ad features supermodel Cindy Crawford first making fun of her/our participation in fashion trends and then suggesting it is just as silly to participate in eating fads, finally suggesting that Special K always has been and remains a sensible diet food; positioned somehow outside of diet trends. A very natural looking and un-glamorous Crawford is metaphorically winking at us saying, "I know that you know I've probably done as much as anybody to make you feel paranoid about your body, but when we are all in our jeans and t-shirts we are just the same—responsible grown-ups who can live both in and outside of diet trends and fads—Right?"

MORE THAN A WINK: INTERVENING IN THE IMAGERY LANDSCAPE

Stuart Hall and Sut Jhally in their writings, but more explicitly in their respective Media Education Foundation videos, "Media and Representation" (1996) and "Dreamworlds II" (1995), theorize that the changes in media representation that will radically improve the image landscape for those currently or traditionally symbolically annihilated needs to come from within the oppressive media forms themselves. Alternative media has its important place in activism and disruption to traditional media systems in the form of exposing viewers to alternatives. However, the leftist agenda of concentrating its creative energies primarily on alternative interventions has left the stifling codes and conventions of white, male, heterosexist media to flourish in the twentieth century and into the new millennium.

There are current media images of women that are attempting to implode cultural expectations for women's beauty, bodies and lives from *within* the aesthetics and conventions of well-established and popular media forms such as the women's magazine and the 60-second commercial radio and TV ad. Several magazines now exist which are geared towards larger women—both in content and in ads. Of these magazines, *Mode* (in circulation from 1977 to 2001) has perhaps received the most publicity for its stated intent to provide attractive images of women that reflect the diversity of women, both size-wise and racially. In fact, unlike *Big, Bold and Beautiful*, a magazine that caters to larger women, *Mode's* stated goal is to promote positive self-image of women of all sizes. It presents itself as not only anti-fat oppression, but anti-sizeism.

For example, in the February 2000 issue under the regular feature "Mode Matters" a story titled, "Can't Lick It!" addresses how sizeism affects all women, thick or thin:

> Size discrimination in Hollywood has taken a new turn. Lara Flynn Boyle, Jennifer Aniston, Calista Flockhart, and others are being referred to as "The Lollipop Girls" (big heads, stick bodies). After our initial snicker, we realized that it's still size discrimination. We believe no one should look to anyone for validation. Give your body what it needs to live a happy life. Oh, and of course, read *Mode* for real inspiration. (Day, 2000, p. 32)

Reflecting the unwillingness to label by size, until January, 2000 the cover of *Mode* used to read *"Mode: 12, 14, 16 …"* Now it simply reads *"Mode: The new shape in fashion."*

The slightly knowing, "in with the joke" tone in the last sentence of "Lollipop Girls" cues us into another quality of *Mode*. It presumes and plays upon a high level of media literacy and the fact that its readers are cognizant of the pressures found in mainstream advertising. In other words, its readers are already presumed to be negotiating or resistant readers. This is clearly evidenced in the letters to the editor section, which offer much more interesting and often critical responses to the content of *Mode* than are found in other magazines. For example, in the February, 2000 edition, MH writes:

> Regarding your recent query about *Mode* men, please don't go there!!! Virtually every other women's magazine on the market has scores of articles on men, sex, dating, etc. The very thing that keeps me hooked on *Mode* is that it helps me (at size 14–16) look the best I can. I don't need any more advice on relationships or men or anything else. Please keep your wonderful magazine in its original, fresh, relevant, and helpful state. (21)

Unlike *Ms.*, *Mode* does not take a "feminist" perspective per se and is not presented as an "alternative" magazine. *Mode's* glossy paper is like that of any mainstream fashion magazine. The advertisements reflect both "traditional" advertising aesthetics, but also offer more images of "normal" sized women. Indeed, the content, format and style of *Mode* is much like any other fashion magazine. The articles deal with dating tips, new seasonal styles, a health and fitness section, and make-up tips and bridal pages. The products offered inside its covers are primarily clothing and make-up, with an occasional car ad or other product featured. *Mode* stresses the feet that all women want to be and can be stylish. The similarity of *Mode* to other fashion magazines means that women can read *Mode* as a familiar genre without feeling ostracized from other women. The magazine is not positioned as alternative or "other," but as addressing the same concerns other women's magazines have, except for allowing greater diversity of size.

However, while the rhetoric of anti-sizeism is clear and there is a repeated editorial insistence on the dangers of labeling, *Mode* actually does quite a bit of size labeling. Many letters to the editor feature profiles on notable women, and blurbs on the magazine models feature some kind of reference to their size, framed usually within a clothing size (14–16 or 22). While on one hand this reinforces the idea of size as a label, it also projects and speaks what is usually unspoken for women of normal and heavier weights and/or sizes. By speaking and naming the size as 22 or 18, those sizes seem more acceptable. Yet this also reinforces the idea of women fitting into pre-categorized shapes.

Just My Size Pantyhose has created a series of ads that are quite successful in this tactic, titled "Just My Opinion," that consistently run in *Mode* magazine. In one ad the left-hand bottom shows a color picture of an African-American woman partially reclining against some pillows with one leg stretched in the air and her hand caressing her leg. She wears a black bra, white pearls, a wedding band on her finger, and a pair of pantyhose. She is smiling and looking out at the spectator. While part of her stomach is hidden by her arm and leg, we can see the fleshy creases around her lower belly, and her legs and partially-exposed bottom appear thick. Her skin has rich brown sheen. Her eyes sparkle. She looks like she is glowing. Partially printed across this image are the words "I am the product of a lifetime of learning." The image works against the grain of the anti-age aesthetic by stressing the "lifetime of learning"; weight is somehow being associated with knowledge and experience. That experience, as suggested by the wedding ring, includes a man. Her pearls signify economic stability.

The woman in this ad is clearly posed in a way that is sexual. Half dressed, she reclines on what appears to be a couch, but there is a blanket that is half pulled off. The fact that it is clearly daytime, the couch, her state of undress, and her provocative pose suggests that she has recently had or is about to have a noontime sexual rendezvous. Obviously the sight of a large-sized woman being shown in dishabille and posed sexually is new, even for the pages of *Mode*. The idea of "looseness" that the ad urges goes against most traditional ideas of advertising. Most ads urge for control over "loose" bodies that threaten to go out of control. This *Just My Size* ad clearly equates a large, lived-in body with sexuality, a romantic life and comfort.

The power of this image, particularly for those who have not seen their images represented as attractive or sexual, cannot be overlooked. The psycho-sexual rejection of many fat women, the exclusion from "normalcy," is powerful in its negativity. Exclusion means that not only is one different—but in an odd way one is almost inhuman. A fat woman loses her right to sexuality—the very thing that defines her as a woman (supposedly). If she cannot appeal sexually she loses the right to not only representation, but to things like sex, men, a home and family. The image of a thicker woman in this ad is revolutionary in that not only does it (partly) reveal a heavy body, but suggests the sexuality of that body. Moreover, unlike most ads, it does not associate fat bodies with negativity or low self-esteem, but high self-esteem.

There appears to be a contradiction here. Feminist scholars generally argue against the objectification of woman. Why then might it be desirable to objectify large women anymore than thin women? The difference is in the right to be seen as a sexual object. Ads gain their meaning from context—from their relationship to other ads as well as their relationship to the larger world. As Sut Jhally (1990) has observed, there is nothing inherently bad about visual objectification. It is part of human nature to objectify and to want to be objectified at times. The evaluation of that objectification as positive or negative comes from the image's relationship to other images in a system. In a sign system in which female sexuality and objectification is a sign of female success, the absence of objectified heavy women as sexual means that they are symbolically annihilated from being seen as sexual beings. And, in not being shown as sexual objects, fat women lose the right to be seen as laying claim to the privileges of that objectification—love, marriage, children and other aspects of "feminine" success.

The *Just My Size* campaign offers its audience images of women that directly confront ideas of women as lacking subjectivity. They feature an attitude that heavily promotes ideas of individualism, physical freedom and choice. This is not itself an unusual tactic; most ads do this. However, in contrast to many ads discussed earlier, the *Just My Size* campaign places notions of individuality in a slightly different context, suggesting that the women are already there. These ads feature images of happy women who are happy because they already possess the right attitude. Her subjectivity will not be created by the use of a new product. Her subjectivity will occur when she recognizes she already has it. Obviously in a culture and an advertising standard that continually urges women to take up less space and control their desires, these *Just My Size* ads are radical in that they present an idea of the woman as being already refined.

RESISTANT ENCODING: NARAL ADS

At least one series of ads work, not by distancing themselves from the concepts of individuality utilized by most advertisers, but, curiously, by co-opting them; reframing messages of individuality, placing them in a new context in a way that does work for feminist goals. These advertising campaigns may be read as interventions in that they consciously deal with the female body as a contested terrain over which political and ideological battles are fought.

In the mainstream media, we often see the female body being depicted as a sexualized object. As an object, of course, female bodies lose subjectivity and individuality. The attitude that fosters this dehumanization of the female body is accompanied by and linked to attitudes in which the female becomes separated from her body. Depicting women as dehumanized objects removes their subjectivity, their capacity to be seen as individuals and to make individual choices. If the female body is an object to be enjoyed and controlled by others, then the female herself has no right to her body. No right to control her body against the advances of others, no right to sexual pleasure in her own body, and particularly lacking in the ability to control her reproductive choices.

The NARAL (National Abortion and Reproductive Rights Action League) "Choice for America" advertising campaign co-opts the rhetoric and discourses of right-wing politics and pro-life factions. These ads frame reproductive rights as being intrinsically linked to "American" values of individuality and freedom—the foundation of subjectivity. They also co-opt the language of faith and responsibility frequently used in pro-life rhetoric. By using these tactics, NARAL promotes female subjectivity at the same time the body is presented for examination, asking us to reconsider meanings of that bodily representation.

NARAL ads play with themes of individuality and concepts of individual freedom as an essential "American" quality. They also explicitly reference the battles that Americans have fought, equating the pro-choice position with protection against the "invasion" of foreign forces. This is a typical right-wing rhetoric used against the perceived threat of forces that would "invade" and take over the "American" way of life—such as Islamic extremists. The ad appeals to the history of the American military by evoking images of battle and bravery and America as a nation of fighters.

The use of the word "blessed" is telling. It presents freedom as a "natural" gift and also suggests that NARAL is articulating a religious view. In contrast to those who would argue that abortion is a godless act, the ad suggests that not only does God exist, but that God sanctions a woman's right to choose. The appeal to the pro-life ideal of protecting life is twisted as the ad references social responsibility as including concern for the well-being of woman and child.

In NARAL ads, a woman's body becomes linked to a sense of eternity, infinity and the always-existing value of "freedom." By doing so, the body becomes imbued with an over-determination of meaning connected to individuality. In this way the NARAL campaign has moved from the body as object, to one in which the body becomes a sign of individuality, of movement and identity bursting beyond restraint. This visual technique echoes other new media forms which are representing the female body in new and different ways, such as the female action hero in such television shows as *Buffy the Vampire Slayer*, *La Femme Nikita* and *Xena: Warrior Princess* (Heinecken, 1999).

CONCLUSION

The analysis of the content of gender advertisements has been studied from a variety of methodological, theoretical and epistemological perspectives since the rash of sex-roles research and Goffman's semiotic content analysis in the 1970s. Scholars replicating the early content analyses of pioneers such as Courtney and Whipple and those testing the longevity of Goffman's categories reported little difference in the representation of women from the 1970s to the 1990s.

Feminist scholars, in particular, have been instrumental in focusing their analyses of gender and advertising in the larger theoretical and epistemological debates bubbling up in feminist scholarship, the social sciences and humanities in order to better understand the consistent ideology of the body portrayed in ads. For example, scholars such as Judith Williamson and Ros Coward employed advances in film theory, psychoanalysis and structuralism to analyze how our gender subjectivities are positioned through advertising. The psychoanalytic perspective can be credited with giving scholars of gender advertising the theoretical tools to analyze the concept of the "male gaze" encoded in most mass media in this society. Further, feminist scholars of gender advertising have relied heavily on the construct of the "split-consciousness" of the female subject to theorize how advertising works to encourage women to continuously view themselves as objects to be improved upon for the male other, rather than to view themselves as subjects of their own femaleness.

Obviously advertising is not produced or consumed in a vacuum; to a great extent, the liberatory potential of any image is reliant upon the social structures that surround it. To that extent, changing imagery is not enough. The culture itself must change, from being one in which girls and women are devalued to one in which they are cherished. Yet positive imagery must also play a role. Pipher (1994) argues that "Adolescent girls need a more public place in our culture, not as sex objects, but as interesting and complicated human beings" (p. 289). Similarly, more positive images of women may be central in influencing females' self-perception. More positive reporting on female public figures like politicians, athletes and women in entertainment are necessary. Women's magazines and their advertisements play a central role.

In recent years, advertisers seem to have recognized that women are tired of being presented with uniform, unrealistic visions of the "ideal" woman. As a result, they have created campaigns that on one hand seem to address women's concerns, while on the other hand offer only "a wink" toward women. The wink is a way of addressing the audience, suggesting that social equality for women has already been achieved. However, closer examination reveals that the wink is one way that traditionally conservative ideals are recycled into a more palatable "feminist" or progressive framework, while in fact achieving no real significant change in how women are represented.

Nonetheless, there are an increasing number of media forms that seem to be seriously trying to present more positive images of women. *Mode* magazine presents itself as an "anti-sizeist" fashion magazine. While *Mode* often fails to present truly progressive images, it has been somewhat successful in normalizing some images, like those of large-size women, that have previously been outside the dominant frame. The success of such ads can at least partly be measured by letters to *Mode's* editor that consistently express the joy readers feel at finally recognizing themselves in ads. However, one possible reason for the success of *Mode's* ads is that there is really very little difference between them and mainstream ads. The different sizes and shapes of *Mode's* models, no matter how revolutionary, remain contextualized within a traditional discourse of individuality and consumer choice.

Such rhetoric has also been co-opted by at least one ad campaign that is truly revolutionary and progressive, consciously dealing with the female body as a site where political and ideological battles are fought. NARAL's recent campaign reinforces notions of individuality. Recalling the way that men's bodies have been glorified in western and action films, the women of the NARAL ads always seem to be *more* than their bodies, imbued with an over-determination of meaning connected to individuality. In this way NARAL ads move from presenting the female body as object, to one in which the body becomes a sign of subjectivity. Unlike Special K's mythology of the individual women's new-found body acceptance as a means to sell cereal, NARAL ads tie their imagery to a truly feminist goal.

REFERENCES

Barthes, R. (1977). *Image Music Text*. New York: The Noonday Press.

Barthes, R. (1988). *The Semiotic Challenge* (trans. R. Howard). New York: Hill and Wang.

Belkaoui, A. and Belkaoui, J. M. (1976). A comparative study of the roles portrayed by women in print advertisements: 1958, 1969, 1972. *Journal of Marketing Research*, 13, 168–72.

Berger, J. (1972). *Ways of Seeing*. London: British Film Institute.

Bordo, S. (1993). *Unbearable Weight*. Los Angeles: University of California Press.

Bretl, D.J. and Cantor, J. (1988). The portrayal of men and women in U.S. television commercials: A recent content analysis and trends over 15 years. *Sex Roles*, 18(9/10), 595–609.

Busby, L.J. (1975). Sex-role research on the mass media. *Journal of Communication*, 25(4), 107–31.

Coltrane, S. and Messineo, M. (2000). The perpetuation of subtle prejudice: Race and gender imagery in 1990s television advertising. *Sex Roles*, 42(5–6), 363–89.

Courtney, A. E. (1983). *Sex Stereotyping in Advertising*. Lexington, MA: Lexington Books.

Courtney, A. E. and Lockeretz, S. W. (1971). A woman's place: An analysis of the roles portrayed by women in magazine advertisements. *Journal of Marketing Research*, 8(1), 92–5.

Courtney, A. E. and Whipple, T. W. (1974). Women in TV commercials. *Journal of Communication*, 24(2), 110–18.

Coward, R. (1982). Sexual violence and sexuality. *Feminist Review*, 1(11), 9–22.

Coward, R. (1985). *Female Desires: How they are sought, bought and packaged*. New York: Grove Press.

Cui, G. (2000). Advertising of alcoholic beverages in African-American and women's magazines: Implications for health communication. *Howard Journal of Communication*, 11, 279–93.

Day, H. (2000). Can't lick it. *Mode Magazine,* February, 32.

Dominick, J. R. and Ranch, G. E. (1972). The image of women in network TV commercials. *Journal of Broadcasting*, 16(3), 259–65.

Downs, A. C. (1981). Sex-role stereotyping on prime-time television. *The Journal of Genetic Psychology*, 138, 253–8.

Fejes, F. (1992). Masculinity as fact: A review of empirical mass communication research on masculinity. In S. Craig (ed.), *Men, Masculinity, and the Media*. Newbury Park, CA: Sage, pp. 219–22.

Ferguson, J. H., Kreshel, P. J., and Tinkham, S. F. (1990). In the pages of *Ms.*: Sex role portrayals of women in advertising. *Journal of Advertising*, 19(1), 40–51.

Fcrrante, C. L., Haynes, A. M., and Kingsley, S. M. (1988). Image of women in television advertising. *Journal of Broadcasting and Electronic Media*, 32(2), 231–7.

Foucault, M. (1977). *Discipline and Punish: The birth of the prison* (trans. A. Sheridan). London: Penguin Press.

Fowles, J. (1996). *Advertising and Popular Culture*. Thousand Oaks, CA: Sage.

Fredrickson, G. M. (1988). *The Arrogance of Race: Historical perspectives on slavery, racism, and social inequality*. Middleton, CT: Wesleyan University Press.

Friedan, B. (1963). *The Feminine Mystique*. New York: Dell.

Furnham, A. (1989). Gender stereotypes in Italian television advertisements. *Journal of Broadcasting and Electronic Media*, 33(2), 175–85.

Furnham, A., Abramsky, S., and Gunter, B. (1997). A cross-cultural content analysis of children's television advertisements. *Sex Roles*, 37(1–2), 91–9.

Geis, F. L., Brown, V., Jennings, J., and Porter, N. (1984). TV commercials as achievement scripts for women. *Sex Roles*, 10(7/8), 513–25.

Gerbner, G. and Gross, L. (1976). Living with television: The violence profile. *Journal of Communication*, 26(2), 172–99.

Gilly, M. C. (1988). Sex roles in advertising: A comparison of television advertisements in Australia, Mexico, and the United States. *Journal of Marketing*, 52, 75–85.

Goffman, E. (1976). *Gender Advertisements*. New York: Harper and Row.

Gould, S. J. (1987). Gender differences in advertising response and self-consciousness variables. *Sex Roles*, 16(5/6), 215–25.

Griffin, M., Viswanath, K., and Schwartz, D. (1992). *Gender Advertising in the U.S. and India: Exporting cultural stereotypes*. Minneapolis: University of Minnesota School of Journalism and Mass Communication.

Hall, S. (1996). *Representation and the Media*. Video. Amherst, MA: Media Education Foundation.

Hawkins, J. W. and Aber, C. S. (1993). Women in advertisements in medical journals. *Sex Roles*, 28(3/4), 233–42.

Hay, J. (1989). Advertising as a cultural text (rethinking message analysis in a recombinant culture). In B. Dervin, L. Grossberg, B. J. O'Keefe and E. Wartella (eds.), *Rethinking Communication*. Newbury Park, CA: Sage, pp. 129–51.

Heinecken, D. (1999). The Warrior Women of TV: A feminist cultural analysis of the new female body in popular culture. Doctoral dissertation. Bowling Green State University, Bowling Green, OH.

Jhally, S. (1987). *Codes of Advertising*. London: Frances Pinter.

Jhally, S. (1990). *Dreamworlds*. Video. Amherst, MA: Media Education Foundation.

Jhally, S. (1995). *Dreamworlds II: Desire, sex and power in music videos*. Video. Amherst, MA: Media Education Foundation.

Kang, M. (1997). The portrayal of w omen's images in magazine advertisements: Goffman's gender analysis revisited. *Sex Roles*, 37(11–12), 979–97.

Kiehvasser, A. P. and Wolf, M. A. (1992). Mainstream television, adolescent homosexuality, and significant silence. *Critical Studies in Mass Communication*, 9(4), 350–73.

Kilbourne, J. (1987). *Still Killing Us Softly: Advertising images of women*. Film. Cambridge.

Kilbourne, J. (1999). *Deadly Persuasion: Why women and girls must fight the addictive power of advertising*. New York: The Free Press.

Kimball, M. M. (1986). Television and sex-role attitudes. In T. M. Williams (ed.), *The Impact of Television: A natural experiment in three communities*. New York: Academic Press, pp. 265–84.

Kuhn, A. (1985). *The Power of the Image*. Boston: Routledge & Kegan Paul.

Lazier, L. and Kendrick, A. G. (1993). Women in advertisements: Sizing up the images, roles, and functions. In P. J. Creedon (ed.), *Women in Mass Communication* (2nd edn.). Newbury Park, CA: Sage, pp. 199–219.

Lazier-Smith, L. (1989). A new "generation" of images to women. In P. J. Creedon (ed.), *Women in Mass Communication: Challenging gender values*. Newbury Park, CA: Sage.

Leeds-Hurwitz (1993). *Semiotics and Communication: Signs, codes, cultures*. Hillsdale, NJ: Lawrence Erlbaum.

Leiss, W., Kline, S., and Jhally, S. (1986). *Social Communication in Advertising: Persons, products, and images of well being*. London: Methuen.

Lovdal, L. T. (1989). Sex role messages in television commercials: An update. *Sex Roles*, 21(11/ 12), 715–24.

Lundstrom, W. J. and Sciglimpaglia, D. (1977). Sex role portrayals in advertising. *Journal of Marketing*, 72–9.

Masse, M. A. and Rosenblum, K. (1988). Male and female created they them: The depiction of gender in the advertising of traditional women's and men's magazines. *Women's Studies International Forum*, 11(2), 127–44.

Mazzella, C., Durkin, K., Cerini, E., and Buralli, P. (1992). Sex role stereotyping in Australian television advertisements. *Sex Roles*, 26(7/8), 243–59.

McKinnon, L. M. (1995). *Ms.*ing the free press: The advertising and editorial content of *Ms.* magazine, 1972–1992. In D. Abrahamson (ed.), *The American Magazine: Research perspectives and prospects*. Aimes, IA: Iowa State University Press, pp. 98–107.

McLaughlin, T. L. and Goulet, N. (1999). Gender advertisements in magazines aimed at African Americans: A comparison to their occurrence in magazines aimed at Caucasians. *Sex Roles*, 40(1–2), 61–71.

Mehaffy, M. M. (1997). Advertising race/raceing advertising: The feminine consumer(-nation), 1876–1900. *Signs*, 23(1), 131–74.

Mellencamp, P. (1995). *A Fine Romance: Five ages of film feminism*. Philadelphia: Temple University Press.

Miles, R. (1989). *Racism*. London: Routledge.

Millium, T. (1975). *Images of Women: Advertising in women's magazines*. London: Chatto and Windus.

Mode Magazine (2000). February.

Morrison, B. J. and Sherman. (1972). Who responds to sex in advertising? *Journal of Advertising Research*, 12(2), 15–19.

Mulvey, L. (1975). Visual pleasure and narrative cinema. *Screen*, 16(3), 6–18.

Myers, K. (1982). Fashion 'n' passion. *Screen*, 23(2–3), 89–97.

Myers, K. (1986). *Understains: The sense and seduction of advertising*. London: Comedia.

Neto, F. and Pinto, I. (1998). Gender stereotypes in Portuguese television advertisements. *Sex Roles*, 39(1–2), 153–64.

Nichols, B. (1981). *Ideology and the Image*. Bloomington: University of Indiana Press.

Nicholson, D. (1997). The Diesal jeans and workwear advertising campaign and the commodification of resistance. In K. Frith (ed.), *Undressing the Ad: Reading culture in advertising*. New York: Peter Lang, pp. 175–96.

Omi, M. and Winant, H. (1986). *Racial Formation in the United States from the 1960s to the 1980s*. London: Routledge.

Orbach, S. (1978). *Fat is a Feminist Issue*. London: Hamlyn.

Peirce, K. (1989). Sex-role stereotyping of children on television: A content analysis of the roles and attributes of child characters. *Sociological Spectrum*, 9, 321–8.

Pingree, S., Hawkins, R. P., Butler, M., and Paisley, W. (1976). Equality in advertising/A scale for sexism. *Journal of Communication*, 26(2), 193–200.

Pipher, M. (1994). *Reviving Ophelia: Saving the selves of adolescent girls*. New York: Baliantine.

Press, A. (1996). Toward a qualitative methodology of audience study: Using ethnography to study. In J. Hay, L. Grossberg, and E. Wartella (eds.), *The Audience and its Landscape*. Boulder, CO: Westview, pp. 113–30.

Rakow, L. (1986). Rethinking gender in communication. *Journal of Communication*, 36(4), 11–26.

Roach, J. and Felix, P. (1989). Black looks. In L. Gamman and M. Marshment (eds.), *The Female Gaze: Women as viewers of popular culture*. Seattle: The Real Comet Press, pp. 130—12.

Rossi, S. R. and Rossi, J. S. (1985). Gender differences in the perception of women in magazine advertising. *Sex Roles*, 12(9/10), 1033–9.

Rowe, K. (1995). *The Unruly Woman*. Austin: The University of Texas Press.

Saunders, C. S. and Stearn, B. A. (1986). Women's adoption of a business uniform: A content analysis of magazine advertisements. *Sex Roles*, 15(3/4), 197–205.

Shields, V. R. (1990). Advertising visual images: Gendered ways of seeing and looking. *Journal of Communication Inquiry*, 14(2), 25–39.

Shields, V. R. (1996). Selling the sex that sells: Mapping the evolution of gender advertising research across three decades. In B. Burleson (ed.), *Communication Yearbook 20*. Thousand Oaks, CA: Sage, pp. 71–109.

Shields, V. R. (2002). *Measuring Up: How advertising affects self image*. Philadelphia: University of Pennsylvania Press.

Skelly, G. U. and Lundstrom, W. J. (1981). Male sex roles in magazine advertising, 1959–1979. *Journal of Communication*, Autumn, 52–7.

Spitzack, C. (1990). *Confessing Excess: Women and the politics of body reduction*. Albany: State University of New York Press.

Steinem, G. (1990). Sex, lies, and advertising. *Ms.*, 1(1), 1–20.

Tuchman, G., Daniels, A. K., and Benet, J. (eds.) (1978). *Hearth and Home: Images of women in the mass media*. New York: Oxford University Press.

Wagner, L. C. and Banos, J. B. (1973). A woman's place: A follow-up analysis of the roles portrayed by women in magazine advertisements. *Journal of Marketing Research*, 10, 213–14.

Whipple, T. W. and Courtney, A. E. (1985). Female role portrayals in advertising and communication effectiveness: A review. *Journal of Advertising*, 14(3), 4–8.

Williamson, J. (1978). *Decoding Advertisements*. London: Methuen.

Williamson, J. (1986). Woman is an island: Femininity and colonization. In T. Modleski (ed.), *Studies in Entertainment: Critical approaches to mass culture*. Bloomington and Indianapolis: Indiana University Press, pp. 99–118.

Winship, J. (1981). Handling sex. *Media, Culture and Society*, 3(3), 25–41.

Wiriship, J. (1985). "A girl needs to get street-wise": Magazines of the 1980s. *Feminist Review*, 21, 25–46.

Wise, G. L., King, A. L., and Merenski, J. P. (1974). Reactions to sexy ads vary with age. *Journal of Advertising Research*, 14(4), 11–16.

Wohleter, M. and Lammers, B. H. (1980). An analysis of male roles in print advertisements over a 20-year span: 1958–1978. In J. C. Olson (ed.), Advances in Consumer Research, vol. 7. Ann Arbor: Association for Consumer Research, pp. 138–50.

Wolf, N. (1991). *The Beauty Myth: How images of beauty are used against women*. New York: Anchor Books.

Women's Action Coalition (1993). *The Facts about Women*. New York: The New Press.

Wortzel, L. and Frisbie, J. M. (1974). Women's role portrayal preferences in advertisements. *Journal of Marketing*, 38, 41–6.

Soft-Soaping Empire

Commodity Racism and Imperial Advertising

By Anne McClintock

Soap is Civilization

—Unilever Company Slogan

Doc: My, it's so clean.
Grumpy: There's dirty work afoot.

—Snow White and the Seven Dwarfs

SOAP AND CIVILIZATION

At the beginning of the nineteenth century, soap was a scarce and humdrum item and washing a cursory activity at best. A few decades later, the manufacture of soap had burgeoned into an imperial commerce; Victorian cleaning rituals were peddled globally as the God-given sign of Britain's evolutionary superiority, and soap was invested with magical, fetish powers. The soap saga captured the hidden affinity between domesticity and empire and embodied a triangulated crisis in value: the *undervaluation* of women's work in the domestic realm, the *overvaluation* of the commodity in the industrial market and the *disavowal* of colonized economies in the arena of empire. Soap entered the realm of Victorian fetishism with spectacular effect, notwithstanding the fact that male Victorians promoted soap as the icon of nonfetishistic rationality.

Both the cult of domesticity and the new imperialism found in soap an exemplary mediating form. The emergent middle class values—monogamy ("clean" sex, which has value), industrial capital ("clean" money, which has value), Christianity ("being washed in the blood of the lamb"), class control ("cleansing the great unwashed") and the imperial civilizing mission ("washing and clothing the savage")—could all be marvelously embodied in a single household commodity. Soap advertising, in particular the Pears' soap campaign, took its place at the vanguard of Britain's new commodity culture and its civilizing mission.

In the eighteenth century, the commodity was little more than a mundane object to be bought and used—in Marx's words, "a trivial thing."[1] By the late nineteenth century, however, the commodity had taken its privileged place not only as the fundamental form of a new industrial economy but also as the fundamental form of a new cultural system for representing social value.[2] Banks and stock exchanges rose up to manage the bonanzas of imperial capital. Professions emerged to administer the goods tumbling hectically from the manufactories. Middle-class domestic space became crammed as never before with furniture, clocks, mirrors, paintings, stuffed animals, ornaments, guns and myriad gewgaws and knicknacks. Victorian novelists bore witness to the strange spawning of commodities that seemed to have lives of their own, and huge ships lumbered with trifles and trinkets plied their trade among the colonial markets of Africa, the East and the Americas.[3]

The new economy created an uproar not only of things but of signs. As Thomas Richards has argued, if all these new commodities were to be managed, a unified system of cultural representation had to be found. Richards shows how the Great Exhibition at the Crystal Palace served as a monument to a new form of consumption: "What the first Exhibition heralded so intimately was the complete transformation of collective and private life into a space for the spectacular exhibition of commodities."[4] As a "semiotic laboratory for the labor theory of value," the World Exhibition showed once and for all that the capitalist system had not only created a dominant form of exchange but was also in the process of creating a dominant form of representation to go with it: the voyeuristic panorama of surplus as spectacle. By exhibiting commodities not only as goods but as an organized system of images, the World Exhibition helped fashion "a new kind of being, the consumer and a new kind of ideology, consumerism."[5] The mass consumption of the commodity spectacle was born.

Victorian advertising reveals a paradox, however, for, as the cultural form that was entrusted with upholding and marketing abroad those founding middle-class distinctions—between private and public, paid work and unpaid work—advertising also from the outset began to confound those distinctions. Advertising took the intimate signs of domesticity (children bathing, men shaving, women laced into corsets, maids delivering nightcaps) into the public realm, plastering scenes of domesticity on walls, buses, shopfronts and billboards. At the same time, advertising took scenes of empire into every corner of the home, stamping images of colonial conquest on soap boxes, matchboxes, biscuit tins, whiskey bottles, tea tins and chocolate bars. By trafficking promiscuously across the threshold of private and public, advertising began to subvert one of the fundamental distinctions of commodity capital, even as it was coming into being.

From the outset, moreover, Victorian advertising took explicit shape around the reinvention of racial difference. Commodity kitsch made possible, as never before, the mass marketing of empire as an organized system of images and attitudes. Soap flourished not only because it created and filled a spectacular gap in the domestic market but also because, as a cheap and portable domestic commodity, it could persuasively mediate the Victorian poetics of racial hygiene and imperial progress.

Commodity racism became distinct from scientific racism in its capacity to expand beyond the literate propertied elite through the marketing of commodity spectacle. If, after the 1850s, scientific racism saturated anthropological, scientific and medical journals, travel writing and novels, these cultural forms were still relatively class-bound and inaccessible to most Victorians, who had neither the means nor the education to read such material. Imperial kitsch as consumer spectacle, by contrast, could package, market and distribute evolutionary racism on a hitherto unimagined scale. No preexisting form of organized racism had ever before been able to reach so large and so differentiated a mass of the populace. Thus, as domestic commodities were mass marketed through their appeal to imperial jingoism, commodity jingoism itself helped reinvent and maintain British national unity in the face of deepening imperial competition and colonial resistance. The cult of domesticity became indispensable to the consolidation of British national identity, and at the center of the domestic cult stood the simple bar of soap.[6]

Yet soap has no social history. Since it purportedly belongs in the female realm of domesticity, soap is figured as beyond history and beyond politics proper.[7] To begin a social history of soap, then, is to refuse, in part, to accept the erasure of women's domestic value under imperial capitalism. It cannot be forgotten, moreover, that the history of European attempts to impose a commodity economy on African cultures was also the history of diverse African attempts either to refuse or to transform European commodity fetishism to suit their own needs. The story of soap reveals that fetishism, far from being a quintessentially African propensity, as nineteenth-century anthropology maintained, was central to industrial modernity, inhabiting and mediating the uncertain threshold zones between domesticity and industry, metropolis and empire.

SOAP AND COMMODITY SPECTACLE

Before the late nineteenth century, clothes and bedding washing was done in most households only once or twice a year in great, communal binges, usually in public at streams or rivers.[8] As for body washing, not much had changed since the days when Queen Elizabeth I was distinguished by the frequency with which she washed: "regularly every month whether she needed it or not."[9] By the 1890s, however, soap sales had soared, Victorians were consuming 260,000 tons of soap a year, and advertising had emerged as the central cultural form of commodity capitalism.[10]

Before 1851, advertising scarcely existed. As a commercial form, it was generally regarded as a confession of weakness, a rather shabby last resort. Most advertising was limited to small newspaper advertisements, cheap handbills and posters. After midcentury, however, soap manufacturers began to pioneer the use of pictorial advertising as a central part of business policy.

The initial impetus for soap advertising came from the realm of empire. With the burgeoning of imperial cotton on the slave plantations came the surplus of cheap cotton goods, alongside the growing buying power of a middle class that could afford for the first time to consume such goods in large quantities. Similarly, the sources for cheap palm oil, coconut oil and cottonseed oil flourished in the imperial plantations of West Africa, Malay, Ceylon, Fiji and New Guinea. As rapid changes in the technology of soapmaking took place in Britain after midcentury, the prospect dawned of a large domestic market for soft body soaps, which had previously been a luxury that only the upper class could afford.

Economic competition with the United States and Germany created the need for a more aggressive promotion of British products and led to the first real innovations in advertising. In 1884, the year of the Berlin Conference, the first wrapped soap was sold under a brand name. This small event signified a major transformation in capitalism, as imperial competition gave rise to the creation of monopolies. Henceforth, items formerly indistinguishable from each other (soap sold simply as soap) would be marketed by their corporate signature (Pears, Monkey Brand, etc). Soap became one of the first commodities to register the historic shift from myriad small businesses to the great imperial monopolies. In the 1870s, hundreds of small soap companies plied the new trade in hygiene, but by the end of the century, the trade was monopolized by ten large companies.

In order to manage the great soap show, an aggressively entrepreneurial breed of advertisers emerged, dedicated to gracing each homely product with a radiant halo of imperial glamour and racial potency. The advertising agent, like the bureaucrat, played a vital role in the imperial expansion of foreign trade. Advertisers billed themselves as "empire builders" and flattered themselves with "the responsibility of the historic imperial mission." Said one: "Commerce even more than sentiment binds the ocean sundered portions of empire together. Anyone who increases these commercial interests strengthens the whole fabric of the empire."[11] Soap was credited not only with bringing moral and economic salvation to Britain's "great unwashed" but also with magically embodying the spiritual ingredient of the imperial mission itself.

In an ad for Pears, for example, a black and implicitly racialized coalsweeper holds in his hands a glowing, occult object. Luminous with its own inner radiance, the simple soap bar glows like a fetish, pulsating magically with spiritual enlightenment and imperial grandeur, promising to warm the hands and hearts of working people across the globe.[12] Pears, in particular, became intimately associated with a purified nature magically cleansed of polluting industry (tumbling kittens, faithful dogs, children festooned with flowers) and a purified working class magically cleansed of polluting labor (smiling servants in crisp white aprons, rosy-cheeked match girls and scrubbed scullions).[13]

Nonetheless, the Victorian obsession with cotton and cleanliness was not simply a mechanical reflex of economic surplus. If imperialism garnered a bounty of cheap cotton and soap oils from coerced colonial labor, the middle class Victorian fascination with clean, white bodies and clean, white clothing stemmed not only from the rampant profiteering of the imperial economy but also from the realms of ritual and fetish.

Soap did not flourish when imperial ebullience was at its peak. It emerged commercially during an era of impending crisis and social calamity, serving to preserve, through fetish ritual, the uncertain boundaries of class, gender and race identity in a social order felt to be threatened by the fetid effluvia of the slums, the belching smoke of industry, social agitation, economic upheaval, imperial competition and anticolonial resistance. Soap offered the promise of spiritual salvation and regeneration through commodity consumption, a regime of domestic hygiene that could restore the threatened potency of the imperial body politic and the race.

THE PEARS' CAMPAIGN

In 1789 Andrew Pears, a farmer's son, left his Cornish village of Mevagissey to open a barbershop in London, following the trend of widespread demographic migration from country to city and the economic turn from land to commerce. In his shop, Pears made and sold the powders, creams and dentifrices used by the rich to ensure the fashionable alabaster purity of their complexions. For the elite, a sun-darkened skin stained by outdoor manual work was the visible stigma not only of a class obliged to work under the elements for a living but also of far-off, benighted races marked by God's disfavor. From the outset, soap took shape as a technology of social purification, inextricably entwined with the semiotics of imperial racism and class denigration.

In 1838 Andrew Pears retired and left his firm in the hands of his grandson, Francis. In due course, Francis' daughter, Mary, married Thomas J. Barratt, who became Francis' partner and took the gamble of fashioning a middle-class market for the transparent soap. Barratt revolutionized Pears by masterminding a series of dazzling advertising campaigns. Inaugurating a new era of advertising, he won himself lasting fame, in the familiar iconography of male birthing, as the "father of advertising." Soap thus found its industrial destiny through the mediation of domestic kinship and that peculiarly Victorian preoccupation with patrimony.

Through a series of gimmicks and innovations that placed Pears at the center of Britain's emerging commodity culture, Barratt showed a perfect understanding of the fetishism that structures all advertising. Importing a quarter of a million French centime pieces into Britain, Barratt had the name Pears stamped on them and put the coins into circulation—a gesture that marvelously linked exchange value with the corporate brand name. The ploy worked famously, arousing much publicity for Pears and such a public fuss that an Act of Parliament was rushed through to declare all foreign coins illegal tender. The boundaries of the national currency closed around the domestic bar of soap.

Georg Lukacs points out that the commodity lies on the threshold of culture and commerce, confusing the supposedly sacrosanct boundaries between aesthetics and economy, money and art. In the mid-1880s, Barratt devised a piece of breathtaking cultural transgression that exemplified Lukacs' insight and clinched Pears' fame. Barratt bought Sir John Everett Millais' painting "Bubbles" (originally entitled "A Child's World") and inserted into the painting a bar of soap stamped with the totemic word *Pears*. At a stroke, he transformed the artwork of the best-known painter in Britain into a mass produced commodity associated in the public mind with Pears.[14] At the same time, by mass reproducing the painting as a poster ad, Barratt took art from the elite realm of private property to the mass realm of commodity spectacle.[15]

In advertising, the axis of possession is shifted to the axis of spectacle. Advertising's chief contribution to the culture of modernity was the discovery that manipulating the semiotic space around the commodity, the unconscious as a public space could also be manipulated. Barratt's great innovation was to invest huge Sums of money in the creation of a visible aesthetic space around the commodity. The development of poster and print technology made possible the mass reproduction of such a space around the image of a commodity.[16]

In advertising, that which is disavowed by industrial rationality (ambivalence, sensuality, chance, unpredictable causality, multiple time) is projected onto image space as a repository of the forbidden. Advertising draws on subterranean flows of desire and taboo, manipulating the investment of surplus money. Pears' distinction, swiftly emulated by scores of soap companies including Monkey Brand and Sunlight, as well as countless other advertisers, was to invest the aesthetic space around the domestic commodity with the commercial cult of empire.

EMPIRE OF THE HOME: RACIALIZING DOMESTICITY

The Soap

Four fetishes recur ritualistically in soap advertising: soap itself, white clothing (especially aprons), mirrors and monkeys. A typical Pears' advertisement figures a black child and a white child together in a bathroom. The Victorian bathroom is the innermost sanctuary of domestic hygiene and by extension the private temple of public regeneration. The sacrament of soap offers a reformation allegory whereby the purification of the domestic body becomes a metaphor for the regeneration of the body politic. In this particular ad, a black boy sits in the bath, gazing wide-eyed into the water as if into a foreign element. A white boy, clothed in a white apron—the familiar fetish of domestic purity—bends benevolently over his "lesser" brother, bestowing upon him the precious talisman of racial progress. The magical fetish of soap promises that the commodity can regenerate the Family of Man by washing from the skin the very stigma of racial and class degeneration.

Soap advertising offers an allegory of imperial progress as spectacle. In this ad, the imperial topos that I call panoptical time (progress consumed as a spectacle from a point of privileged invisibility) enters the domain of the commodity. In the second frame of the ad, the black child is out of the bath and the white boy shows him his startled visage in the mirror. The black boy's body has become magically white, but his face—for Victorians the seat of rational individuality and self-consciousness—remains stubbornly black. The white child is thereby figured as the agent of history and the male heir to progress, reflecting his lesser brother in the European mirror of self-consciousness. In the Victorian mirror, the black child witnesses his predetermined destiny of imperial metamorphosis but remains a passive racial hybrid, part black, part white, brought to the brink of civilization by the twin commodity fetishes of soap and mirror. The advertisement discloses a crucial element of late Victorian commodity culture: the metaphoric transformation of imperial *time* into consumer *space-imperial* progress consumed at a glance as domestic spectacle.

The Monkey

The metamorphosis of imperial time into domestic space is captured most vividly by the advertising campaign for Monkey Brand Soap. During the 1880s, the urban landscape of Victorian Britain teemed with the fetish monkeys of this soap. The monkey with its frying pan and bar of soap perched everywhere, on grimy hoardings and buses, on walls and shop fronts, promoting the soap that promised magically to do away with domestic labor: "No dust, no dirt, no labor." Monkey Brand Soap promised not only to regenerate the race but also to magically erase the unseemly spectacle of women's manual labor.

In an exemplary ad, the fetish soap-monkey sits cross-legged on a doorstep, the threshold boundary between private domesticity and public commerce—the embodiment of anachronistic space. Dressed like an organ grinder's minion in a gentleman's ragged suit, white shirt and tie, but with improbably human hands and feet, the monkey extends a frying pan to catch the surplus cash of passersby. On the doormat before him, a great bar of soap is displayed, accompanied by a placard that reads: "My Own Work." In every respect the soap-monkey is a hybrid: not entirely ape, not entirely human; part street beggar, part gentleman; part artist, part advertiser. The creature inhabits the ambivalent border of jungle and city, private and public, the domestic and the commercial, and offers as its handiwork a fetish that is both art and commodity.

Monkeys inhabit Western discourse on the borders of social limit, marking the place of a contradiction in social value. As Donna Haraway has argued: "the primate body, as part of the body of nature, may be read as a map of power."[17] Primatology, Haraway insists, "is a Western discourse … a political order that works by the negotiation of boundaries achieved through ordering differences."[18] In Victorian iconography, the ritual recurrence of the monkey figure is eloquent of a crisis in value and hence anxiety at possible boundary breakdown. The primate body became a symbolic space for reordering and policing boundaries between humans and nature, women and men, family and politics, empire and metropolis.

Simian imperialism is also centrally concerned with the problem of representing *social change*. By projecting history (rather than fate, or God's will) onto the theater of nature, primatology made nature the alibi of political violence and placed in the hands of "rational science" the authority to sanction and legitimize social change. Here, "the scene of origins," Haraway argues, "is not the cradle of civilization, but the cradle of culture … the origin of sociality itself, especially in the densely meaning-laden icon of the family."[19] Primatology emerges as a theater for negotiating the perilous boundaries between the family (as natural and female) and power (as political and male).

The appearance of monkeys in soap advertising signals a dilemma: *how to represent domesticity without representing women at work*. The Victorian middle-class house was structured around the fundamental contradiction between women's paid and unpaid domestic work. As women were driven from paid work in mines, factories, shops and trades to private, unpaid work in the home, domestic work became economically undervalued and the middle-class definition of femininity figured the "proper" woman as one who did not work for profit. At the same time, a *cordon sanitaire* of racial degeneration was thrown around those women who did work publicly and visibly for money. What could not be incorporated into the industrial formation (women's domestic economic value) was displaced onto the invented domain of the primitive, and thereby disciplined and contained.

Monkeys, in particular, were deployed to legitimize social boundaries as edicts of nature. Fetishes straddling nature and culture, monkeys were seen as allied with the dangerous classes: the "apelike" wandering poor, the hungry Irish, Jews, prostitutes, impoverished black people, the ragged working class, criminals, the insane and female miners and servants, who were collectively seen to inhabit the threshold of racial degeneration. When Charles Kingsley visited Ireland, for example, he lamented: "I am haunted by the human chimpanzees I saw along that hundred miles of horrible country … But to see white chimpanzees is dreadful; if they were black, one would not feel it so much, but their skins, except where tanned by exposure, are as white as ours."[20]

In the Monkey Brand advertisement, the monkey's signature of labor ("My Own Work") signals a double disavowal. Soap is masculinized, figured as a male product, while the (mostly female) labor of the workers in the huge, unhealthy soap factories is disavowed. At the same time, the labor of social transformation in the daily scrubbing and scouring of the sinks, pans and dishes, labyrinthine floors and corridors of Victorian domestic space vanishes—refigured as anachronistic space, primitive and bestial. Female servants disappear and in their place crouches a phantasmic male hybrid. Thus, domesticity—seen as the sphere most separate from the marketplace and the masculine hurly-burly of empire—takes shape around the invented ideas of the primitive and the commodity fetish.

In Victorian culture, the monkey was an icon of metamorphosis, perfectly serving soap's liminal role in mediating the transformations of nature (dirt, waste and disorder) into culture (cleanliness, rationality and industry). Like all fetishes, the monkey is a contradictory image, embodying the hope of imperial progress through commerce while at the same time rendering visible deepening Victorian fears of urban militancy and colonial misrule. The soap-monkey became the emblem of industrial progress and imperial evolution, embodying the double promise that nature could be redeemed by consumer capital and that consumer capital could be guaranteed by natural law. At the same time, however, the soap-monkey was eloquent of the degree to which fetishism structures industrial rationality.

The Mirror

In most Monkey Brand advertisements, the monkey holds a frying pan, which is also a mirror.. In a similar Brooke's Soap ad, a classical female beauty with bare white arms stands draped in white, her skin and clothes epitomizing the exhibition value of sexual purity and domestic leisure, while from the cornucopia she holds flows a grotesque effluvium of hobgoblin angels. Each hybrid fetish embodies the doubled Victorian image of woman as "angel in the drawing room, monkey in the bedroom," as well as the racial iconography of evolutionary progress from ape to angel. Historical time, again, is captured as domestic spectacle, eerily reflected in the frying pan/mirror fetish.

In this ad, the Brooke's Soap offers an alchemy of economic progress, promising to make "copper like gold." At the same time, the Enlightenment idea of linear, rational time leading to angelic perfection finds its antithesis in the other time of housework, ruled by the hobgoblins of dirt, disorder and fetishistic, nonprogressive time. Erupting on the margins of the rational frame, the ad displays the irrational consequences of the idea of progress. The mirror/frying pan, like all fetishes, visibly expresses a crisis in value but cannot resolve it. It can only embody the contradiction, frozen as commodity spectacle, luring the spectator deeper and deeper into consumerism.

Mirrors glint and gleam in soap advertising, as they do in the culture of imperial kitsch at large. In Victorian middle-class households, servants scoured and polished every metal and wooden surface until it shone like a mirror. Doorknobs, lamp stands and banisters, tables and chairs, mirrors and clocks, knives and forks, kettles and pans, shoes and boots were polished until they shimmered, reflecting in their gleaming surfaces other object-mirrors, an infinity of crystalline mirrors within mirrors, until the interior of the house was all shining surfaces, a labyrinth of reflection. The mirror became the epitome of commodity fetishism: erasing both the signs of domestic labor and the industrial origins of domestic commodities. In the domestic world of mirrors, objects multiply without apparent human intervention in a promiscuous economy of self-generation.

Why the attention to surface and reflection? The polishing was dedicated, in part, to policing the boundaries between private and public, removing every trace of labor, replacing the disorderly evidence of working women with the exhibition of domesticity as veneer, the commodity spectacle as surface, the house arranged as a theater of clean surfaces for commodity display. The mirror/commodity renders the value of the object as an exhibit, a spectacle to be consumed, admired and displayed for its capacity to embody a twofold value: the man's market worth and the wife's exhibition status. The house existed to display femininity as bearing exhibition value only, beyond the marketplace and therefore, by natural decree, beyond political power.

An ad for Stephenson's Furniture Cream figures a spotless maid on all fours, smiling up from a floor so clean that it mirrors her reflection. The cream is "warranted not to fingermark." A superior soap should leave no telltale smear, no fingerprint of female labor. As Victorian servants lost individuality in the generic names their employers imposed on them, so soaps erased the imprint of women's work on middle-class history.

DOMESTICATING EMPIRE

By the end of the century, a stream of imperial bric-a-brac had invaded Victorian homes. Colonial heroes and colonial scenes were emblazoned on a host of domestic commodities, from milk cartons to sauce bottles, tobacco tins to whiskey bottles, assorted biscuits to toothpaste, toffee boxes to baking powder.[21] Traditional national fetishes such as the Union Jack, Britannia, John Bull and the rampant lion were marshaled into a revamped celebration of imperial spectacle. Empire was seen to be patriotically defended by Ironclad Porpoise Bootlaces and Sons of the Empire soap, while Henry Morton Stanley came to the rescue of the Emin of Pasha laden with outsize boxes of Huntley and Palmers Biscuits.

Late Victorian advertising presented a vista of Africa conquered by domestic commodities.[22] In the flickering magic lantern of imperial desire, teas, biscuits, tobaccos, Bovril, tins of cocoa and, above all, soaps beach themselves on far-flung shores, tramp through jungles, quell uprisings, restore order and write the inevitable legend of commercial progress across the colonial landscape. In a Huntley and Palmers' Biscuits ad, a group of male colonials sit in the middle of a jungle on biscuit crates, sipping tea. Moving toward them is a stately and seemingly endless procession of elephants, loaded with more biscuits and colonials, bringing tea time to the heart of the jungle. The serving attendant in this ad, as in most others, is male. Two things happen in such images: women vanish from the affair of empire, and colonized men are feminized by their association with domestic servitude.

Liminal images of oceans, beaches and shorelines recur in cleaning ads of the time. An exemplary ad for Chlorinol Soda Bleach shows three boys in a soda box sailing in a phantasmic ocean bathed by the radiance of the imperial dawn. In a scene washed in the red, white and blue of the Union Jack, two black boys proudly hold aloft their boxes of Chlorinol. A third boy, the familiar racial hybrid of cleaning ads, has presumably already applied his bleach, for his skin is blanched an eery white. On red sails that repeat the red of the bleach box, the legend of black people's purported commercial redemption in the arena of empire reads: "We are going to use 'Chlorinol' and be like de white nigger."

The ad vividly exemplifies Marx's lesson that the mystique of the commodity fetish lies not in its use value but in its exchange value and its potency as a sign: "So far as [the commodity] is a value in use, there is nothing mysterious about it." For three naked children, clothing bleach is less than useful. Instead, the whitening agent of bleach promises an alchemy of racial upliftment through historical contact with commodity culture. The transforming power of the civilizing mission is stamped on the boat-box's sails as the objective character of the commodity itself.

More than merely a *symbol* of imperial progress, the domestic commodity becomes the *agent* of history itself. The commodity, abstracted from social context and human labor, does the civilizing work of empire, while radical change is figured as magical, without process or social agency. Hence the proliferation of ads featuring magic. In similar fashion, cleaning ads such as Chlorinol's foreshadow the "before and after" beauty ads of the twentieth century, a crucial genre directed largely at women, in which the conjuring power of the product to alchemize change is all that lies between the temporal "before and after" of women's bodily transformation.

The Chlorinol ad displays a racial and gendered division of labor. Imperial progress from black child to "white nigger" is consumed as commodity spectacle—as panoptical time. The self-satisfied, hybrid "white nigger" literally holds the rudder of history and directs social change, while the dawning of civilization bathes his enlightened brow with radiance. The black children simply have exhibition value as potential consumers of the commodity, there only to uphold the promise of capitalist commerce and to represent how far the white child has evolved—in the iconography of Victorian racism, the condition of "savagery" is identical to the condition of infancy. Like white women, Africans (both women and men) are figured not as historic agents but as frames for the commodity, valued for *exhibition* alone. The working women, both black and white, who spent vast amounts of energy bleaching the white sheets, shirts, frills, aprons, cuffs and collars of imperial clothes are nowhere to be seen. It is important to note that in Victorian advertising, black women are very seldom rendered as consumers of commodities, for, in imperial lore, they lag too far behind men to be agents of history. Imperial domesticity is therefore a domesticity without women.

In the Chlorinol ad, women's creation of social value through housework is displaced onto the commodity as its own power, fetishistically inscribed on the children's bodies as a magical metamorphosis of the flesh. At the same time, military subjugation, cultural coercion and economic thuggery are refigured as benign domestic processes as natural and healthy as washing. The stains of Africa's disobligingly complex and tenacious past and the inconvenience of alternative economic and cultural values are washed away like grime.

Incapable of themselves actually engendering change, African men are figured only as "mimic men," to borrow V. S. Naipaul's dyspeptic phrase, destined simply to ope the epic white march of progress to self-knowledge. Bereft of the white raimants of imperial godliness, the Chlorinol children appear to take the fetish literally, content to bleach their skins to white. Yet these ads reveal that, far from being a quintessentially African propensity, the faith in fetishism was a faith fundamental to imperial capitalism itself.

THE MYTH OF FIRST CONTACT

By the turn of the century, soap ads vividly embodied the hope that the commodity alone, independent of its use value, could convert other cultures to "civilization." Soap ads also embody what can be called *the myth of first contact*: the hope of capturing, as spectacle, the pristine moment of imaginary contact fixed forever in the timeless surface of the image. In another Pears ad, a black man stands alone on a beach, examining a bar of soap he has picked from a crate washed ashore from a shipwreck. The ad announces nothing less than the "The Birth

Of Civilization." Civilization is born, the image implies, at the moment of first contact with the western commodity. Simply by touching the magical object, African man is inspired into history. An epic metamorphosis takes place, as Alan the Hunter-gatherer (anachronistic man) evolves instantly into Alan the Consumer. At the same time, the magical object effects a gender transformation, for the consumption of the domestic soap is racialized as a male birthing ritual, with the egg-shaped commodity as the fertile talisman of change. Since women cannot be recognized as agents of history, it is necessary that a man, not a woman, be the historic beneficiary of the magical cargo and that the *male* birthing occur on the beach, not in the home.[23]

In keeping with the racist iconography of the gender degeneration of African men, the man is subtly feminized by his role as historic exhibit. His jaunty feather represents what Victorians liked to believe was African men's fetishistic, feminine and lower-class predilection for decorating their bodies. Thomas Carlyle, in his prolonged cogitation on clothes, *Sartor Resdrtus*, notes, for example: "The first spiritual want of a barbarous man is Decoration, as indeed we still see amongst the barbarous classes in civilized nations."[24] Feminists have explored how, in the iconography of modernity, women's bodies are exhibited for visual consumption, but very little has been said about how, in imperial iconography, black men were figured as 'spectacle'; for commodity exhibition. If, in scenes set in the Victorian home, female servants are *racialized* and portrayed as frames for the exhibition of the commodity, in advertising scenes set in the colonies, African men are *colonized* and portrayed as exhibition frames for commodity display. Black women, by contrast, are rendered virtually invisible. Essentialist assumptions about a universal "male gaze" elide a great many important historical complexities.

Marx noted how under capitalism "the exchange value of a commodity assumes an independent existence."[25] Toward the end of the nineteenth century, the commodity itself disappears from many ads, and the corporate signature, as the embodiment of pure exchange value in monopoly capital, finds an independent existence. Another ad for Pears features a group of disheveled Sudanese "dervishes" awestruck by a white legend carved on the mountain face: PEARS SOAP IS THE BEST. The significance of the ad, as Richards notes, is its representation of the commodity as a magical medium capable of enforcing and enlarging British power in the colonial world, even without the rational understanding of the mesmerized Sudanese.[26] What the ad more properly reveals is the colonials' own fetishistic faith in the magic of brand names to work the causal power of empire. In a similar ad, the letters BOVRIL march boldly over a colonial map of South Africa—imperial progress consumed as spectacle, as panoptical time. In an inspired promotional idea, the world had been recognized as tracing the military advance of Lord Roberts across country, yoking together, as if writ by nature, the simultaneous lessons of colonial domination and commodity progress. In this ad, the colonial map explicitly enters the realm of commodity spectacle.

The poetics of cleanliness is a poetics of social discipline. Purification rituals prepare the body as a terrain of meaning, organizing flows of value across the self and the community and demarcating boundaries between one community and another. Purification rituals, however, can also be regimes of violence and constraint. The people who have the power to invalidate the boundary rituals of another people thereby demonstrate their capacity to violently impose their culture on other's. Colonial travel writers, traders, missionaries and bureaucrats carped constantly at the supposed absence in African culture of "proper domestic life," in particular Africans' purported lack of hygiene.[27] But the inscription of Africans as dirty and undomesticated, far from being an accurate depiction of African cultures, served to legitimize the imperialists' violent enforcement of their cultural and economic values, with the intent of purifying and thereby subjugating the unclean African body imposing market and cultural values more useful to the mercantile and imperial economy. The myth of imperial commodities beaching on native shores, there to be welcomed by awestruck natives, wipes from memory the long and intricate history of European commercial trade with Africans and the long and intricate history of African resistance to Europe and colonization. Domestic ritual became a technology of discipline and dispossession.

The crucial point is not simply the formal contradictions that structure fetishes, but also the more demanding historical question of how certain groups succeed, through coercion or hegemony, in foreclosing the ambivalence that fetishism embodies by successfully imposing their economic and cultural system on others.[28] Culturally, imperialism does not mean that the contradictions are permanently resolved nor that they cannot be used against the colonials themselves. Nonetheless, it is crucial to recognize that what has been vaunted by some as the permanent unavoidability of cultural signs can also be violently and decisively foreclosed by superior military power or hegemonic dominion.

FETISHISM IN THE CONTEST ZONE

Enlightenment and Victorian writers frequently figured the colonial encounter as the journey of the rational European (male) mind across a liminal space (ocean, jungle or desert) populated by hybrids (mermaids and monsters) to a prehistoric zone of dervishes, cannibals and fetish-worshippers. Robinson Crusoe, in one of the first novelistic expressions of the idea, sets Christian lands apart from those whose people "prostrate themselves to Stocks and Stones, worshipping Monsters, Elephants, horrible shaped animals and Statues, or Images of Monsters."[29] The Enlightenment mind was felt to have transcended fetish worship and could look indulgently upon those still enchanted by the magical powers of "stocks and stones." But as Mitchell notes, "the deepest magic of the commodity fetish is its denial that there is anything magical about it."[30] Colonial protestations notwithstanding, a decidedly fetishistic faith in the magical powers of the commodity underpinned much of the colonial civilizing mission.

Contrary to the myth of first contact embodied in Victorian ads, Africans had been trading with Europeans for centuries by the time the British Victorians arrived. Intricate trading networks were spread over west and north Africa, with complex intercultural settlements and long histories of trade negotiations and exchanges, sporadically interrupted by violent conflicts and conquests. As John Barbot, the seventeenth-century trader and writer, remarked of the Gold Coast trade: "The Blacks of the Gold Coast, having traded with Europeans since the 14th century, are very well skilled in the nature and proper qualities of all European wares and merchandise vended there."[31] Eighteenth-century voyage accounts reveal, moreover, that European ships plying their trade with Africa were often loaded not with "useful" commodities but with baubles, trinkets, beads, mirrors and "medicinal" potions.[32] Appearing in seventeenth-century trade lists, among the salt, brandy, cloth and iron, are items such as brass rings, false pearls, bugles (small glass beads), looking glasses, little bells, false crystals, shells, bright rags, glass buttons, small brass trumpets, amulets and arm rings.[33] Colonials indulged heavily in the notion that, by ferrying these cargoes of geegaws and knick-knacks across the seas, they were merely pandering to naive and primitive African tastes. Merchant trade lists reveal, however, that when the European ships returned from West Africa, they were laden not only with gold dust and palm oil but also with elephant tusks, "teeth of sea-horses" (hippopotami), ostrich feathers, beeswax, animal hides and "cads of tusk."[34] The absolute commodification of humanity and the colonial genuflection to the fetish of profit was most grotesquely revealed in the indiscriminate listing of slaves amongst the trifles and knick-knacks.

By defining the economic exchanges and ritual beliefs of other cultures as "irrational" and "fetishistic," the colonials tried to disavow them as legitimate systems. The huge labor that went into transporting cargoes of trifles to the colonies had less to do with the appropriateness of such fripperies to African cultural systems than with the systematic undervaluation of those systems with respect to merchant capitalism and market values in the European metropolis.

A good deal of evidence also suggests that the European traders, while vigorously denying their own fetishism and projecting such "primitive" proclivities onto white women, Africans and children, took their own "rational" fetishes with the utmost seriousness.[35] By many accounts, the empire seems to have been especially fortified by the marvelous fetish of Eno's Fruit Salt. If Pears could be entrusted with cleaning the outer body, Eno's was entrusted with "cleaning" the inner body. Most importantly, the internal purity guaranteed by Eno's could be relied upon to ensure male potency in the arena of war. As one colonial vouched: "During the Afghan war, I verily believe Kandahar was won by us all taking up large supplies of ENO'S FRUIT SALT and so arrived fit to overthrow half-a-dozen Ayub Khans."[36] He was not alone in strongly recommending Eno's power to restore white supremacy. Commander A. J. Loftus, hydrographer to His Siamese Majesty, swore that he never ventured into the jungle without his tin of Eno's. There was only one instance, he vouched, during four years of imperial expeditions that any member of his party fell prey to fever: "and that happened after our supply of FRUIT SALT ran out."[37] Fetishism became an intercultural space in that both sides of the encounter appear occasionally to have tried to manipulate the other by mimicking what they took to be the other's specific fetish. In Kenya, Joseph Thomson posed grandly as a white medicine man by conjuring an elaborate ruse with a tin of Eno's for the supposed edification of the Masai: "Taking out my sextant," he records with some glee:

> and putting on a pair of kid gloves—that accidentally I happened to have and that impressed the natives enormously, I intently examined the contents … getting ready some ENO'S FRUIT SALT, I sang an incantation—in general something about "Three Blue Bottles"—over it. My voice … did capitally for a wizard's. My preparations complete and Brahim [*sic*] being ready with a gun, I dropped the Salt into the mixture; simultaneously the gun was fired and, lot up fizzed and sparkled the carbonic acid … the chiefs with fear and trembling taste as it fizzes away.[38]

While amusing himself grandly at the imagined expense of the Masai, Thomson reveals his own faith in the power of his fetishes (gloves as a fetish of class leisure, sextant and gun as a fetish of scientific technology and Eno's as a fetish of domestic purity) to hoodwink the Masai. "More amusing," however, as Hindley notes, is Thomson's own naivete, for the point of the story is that "to persuade the Masai to take his unfamiliar remedies, Thomson laid on a show in which the famous fruit salt provided only the 'magic' effects."[39] Eno's power as domestic fetish was eloquently summed up by a General Officer, who wrote and thanked Mr. Eno for his god-sent powder: "Blessings on your Fruit Salt," he wrote, "I trust it is not profane to say so, but I swear by it. There stands the cherished bottle on the Chimney piece of my sanctum, my little idol—at home my household god, abroad my vade mecum."[40] The manufacturers of Eno's were so delighted by this fulsome dedication to their little fetish that they adopted it as regular promotional copy. Henceforth, Eno's was advertised by the slogan: "At home my household god, abroad my vade mecum."

In the colonial encounter, Africans adopted a variety of strategies for countering colonial attempts to undervalue their economies. Amongst these strategies, mimicry, appropriation, revaluation and violence figure the most frequently. Colonials carped rancorously at the African habit of making off with property that did not belong to them, a habit that was seen not as a form of protest, nor as a refusal of European notions of property ownership and exchange value, but as a primitive incapacity to understand the value of the "rational" market economy. Barbot, for example, describes the Eket as "the most trying of any of the Peoples we had to deal with … Poor Sawyer had a terrible time; the people had an idea they could do as they liked with the factory keeper and would often walk off with the goods without paying for them, that Mr Sawyer naturally objected to, usually ending in a free fight, sometimes my people coming off second best."[41] Richards notes how Henry Morton Stanley, likewise, could not make Africans (whom he saw primarily as carriers of western commodities) understand that he endowed the goods they carried with an abstract exchange value apart from their use value. Since these goods "lack any concrete social role for them in the customs, directives and taboos of their tribal lives, the carriers are forever dropping, discarding, misplacing, or walking away with them. Incensed, Stanley calls this theft."[42]

From the outset, the fetishism involved an intercultural contestation that was fraught with ambiguity, miscommunication and violence. Colonials were prone to fits of murderous temper when Africans refused to show due respect to their flags, crowns, maps, clocks, guns and soaps. Stanley, for one, records executing three African carriers for removing rifles, even though he admits that the condemned did not understand the value of the rifles or the principle for which they were being put to death.[43] Other carriers were executed for infringements such as dropping goods flyers.

Anecdotes also reveal how quickly colonial tempers flared when Africans failed to be awestruck by the outlandish baubles the colonials offered them, for it wasn't long before the non-Europeans' curiosity and tolerance turned to derision and contempt. In Australia, Cook carped at the local inhabitants' ungrateful refusal to recognize the value of the baubles he brought them: "Some of the natives would not part with a hog unless they received an axe in exchange; but nails and beads and other trinkets, that, during our former voyages, had so great a run at this island, were now so much despised, that few would deign so much to look at them."[44]

De Bougainville similarly recalls how a native from the Moluccas, when given "a handkerchief, a looking-glass and some other trifles … laughed when he received these presents and did not admire them. He seemed to know the Europeans."[45] As Simpson points out: "The handkerchief is an attribute of 'civilization,' the tool for making away with the unseemly sweat of the brow, the nasal discharge of cold climates and perhaps the tears of excessive emotion." The white handkerchief was also (like white gloves) the Victorian icon of domestic purity and the erasure of signs of labor. The Moluccan's refusal of handkerchiefs and mirror expressed a frank refusal of two of the central icons of Victorian middle-class consumerism.[46]

In some instances, elaborate forms of mimicry were created by Africans to maintain control of the mercantile trade. As the Comaroffs point out, the Tlhaping, the southernmost Tswana, having obtained beads for themselves, tried to deter Europeans from venturing further into the interior by mimicking European stereotypes of black savagery and portraying their neighbors as "men of ferocious habits" too barbaric to meddle with.[47]

In the imperial contest zone, fetishes embodied conflicts in the realm of value and were eloquent of a sustained African refusal to accept Europe's commodities and boundary rituals on the colonials' terms. The soap saga and the cult of domesticity vividly demonstrates that fetishism was original neither to industrial capitalism nor to precolonial economies, but was from the outset the embodiment and record of an incongruous and violent encounter.

NOTES

1. Karl Marx, "Commodity Fetishism," *Capital*, vol. 1 (New York: Vintage Books, 1977), p. 163.

2. See Thomas Richards's excellent analysis, *The Commodity Culture of Victorian Britain: Advertising and Spectacle, 1881–1914* (London: Verso, 1990), especially the introduction and chapter 1.

3. See David Simpson's analysis of novelistic fetishism in *Fetishism and Imagination: Dickens, Melville, Conrad* (Baltimore: Johns Hopkins University Press, 1982).

4. Richards, *The Commodity Culture*, p. 72.

5. Richards, *The Commodity Culture*, p. 5.

6. In 1889, an ad for Sunlight Soap featured the feminized figure of British nationalism, Britannia, standing on a hill and showing P. T. Barnum, the famous circus manager and impresario of the commodity spectacle, a huge Sunlight Soap factory stretched out below them. Britannia proudly proclaims the manufacture of Sunlight Soap to be: "The Greatest Show On Earth." See Jennifer Wicke's excellent analysis of P. T. Barnum in *Advertising Fiction: Literature, Advertisement and Social Reading* (New York: Columbia University Press, 1988).

7. See Timothy Burke, " 'Nyamarira That I Loved': Commoditization, Consumption and the Social History of Soap in Zimbabwe," *The Societies of Southern Africa in the 19th and 20th Centuries: Collected Seminar Papers*, vol. 17, no. 42 (London: University of London, Institute of Commonwealth Studies, 1992), pp. 195–216.

8. Leonore Davidoff and Catherine Hall, *Family Fortunes: Men and Women of the English Middle Class* (Routledge: London, 1992).

9. David T. A. Lindsey and Geoffrey C. Bamber, *Soap-Making: Past and Present, 1876–1976* (Nottingham: Gerard Brothers Ltd, 1965), p. 34.

10. Lindsey and Bamber, *Soap-Making*, p. 38. Just how deeply the relation between soap and advertising became embedded in popular memory is expressed in words such as "soft-soap" and "soap opera." For histories of advertising, see also Blanche B. Elliott, *A History of English Advertising* (London: Business Publications Ltd., 1962); and T. R. Nevett, *Advertising in Britain: A History* (London: Heinemann, 1982).

11. Quoted in Diana and Geoffrey Hindley, *Advertising in Victorian England, 1837–1901* (London: Wayland, 1972), p. 117.

12. Mike Dempsey, ed., *Bubbles: Early Advertising Art from A. & F. Pears Ltd.* (London: Fontana, 1978).

13. Laurel Bradley, "From Eden to Empire: John Everett Millais' Cherry Ripe," *Victorian Studies*, vol. 34, no. 2 (Winter 1991): 179–203. See also, Michael Dempsey, *Bubbles*.

14. Barratt spent £2200 on Millais' painting and £30,000 on the mass production of millions of individual reproductions of the painting. In the 1880s, Pears was spending between £300,000 and £400,000 on advertising alone.

15. Furious at the pollution of the sacrosanct realm of art with economics, the art world lambasted Millais for trafficking (publicly instead of privately) in the sordid world of trade.

16. See Jennifer Wicke, *Advertising Fiction*, p. 70

17. Donna Haraway, *Primate Visions: Gender; Race, and Nature in the World of Modern Science* (London: Routledge, 1989), p. 10.

18. Haraway, *Primate Visions*, p. 10.

19. Haraway, *Primate Visions*, pp. 10–11.

20. Charles Kingsley, Letter to his wife, 4 July 1860, in *Charles Kingsley: His Letters and Memories of His Life*, Francis E. Kingsley, ed. (London; Henry S. King and Co, 1877), p. 107. See also Richard Kearney, ed., *The Irish Mind* (Dublin: Wolfhound Press, 1985); L. P. Curtis Jr., *Anglo-Saxons and Celts: A Study of Anti-Irish Prejudice in Victorian England* (Bridgeport; Conference on British Studies of University of Bridgeport, 1988); and Seamus Deane, "Civilians and Barbarians," *Ireland's Field Day* (London: Hutchinson, 1985), pp. 33–42.

21. During the Anglo-Boer War, Britain's fighting forces were seen as valiantly fortified by Johnston's Corn Flour, Pattisons' Whiskey and Frye's Milk Chocolate. See Robert Opie, *Trading on the British Image* (Middlesex; Penguin, 1985), for an excellent collection of advertising images.

22. In a brilliant chapter, Richards explores how the imperial conviction of the explorer and writer Henry Morton Stanley that he had a mission to civilize Africans by teaching them the value of commodities "reveals the major role that imperialists ascribed to the commodity in propelling and justifying the scramble for Africa." Richards, *The Commodity Culture*, p. 123.

23. As Richards notes; "A hundred years earlier the ship offshore would have been preparing to enslave the African bodily as an object of exchange; here the object is rather to incorporate him into the orbit of exchange. In either case, this liminal moment posits that capitalism is dependent on a noncapitalist world, for only by sending commodities into liminal areas where, presumably, their value will not be appreciated at first can the endemic overproduction of the capitalist system continue." Richards, *The Commodity Culture*, p. 90.

24. Thomas Carlyle, *Sartor Resartus*, in *The Works of Thomas Carlyle*, vol. 1 (London: Chapman and Hall, 1896–1899), p. 30.

25. Karl Marx, "Theories of Surplus Value," quoted in G. A. Cohen, *Karl Marx's Theory of History: A Difference* (Princeton: Princeton University Press, 1978), pp. 124–25.

26. Richards, *The Commodity Culture*, pp. 122–23.

27. But palm-oil soaps had been made and used for centuries in west and equatorial Africa. In *Travels in West Africa* Mary Kingsley records the custom of digging deep baths in the earth, filling them with boiling water and fragrant herbs, and luxuriating under soothing packs of wet clay. In southern Africa, soap from oils was not much used, but clays, saps and barks were processed as cosmetics, and shrubs known as "soap bushes" were used for cleansing. Mary H. Kingsley, *Travels in West Africa* (London: Macmillan, 1899). Male Tswana activities like hunting and war were elaborately prepared for and governed by taboo. "In each case," as Jean and John Comaroff write, "the participants met beyond the boundaries of the village, dressed and armed for the fray, and were subjected to careful ritual washing (go foka marumo)." Jean and John Comaroff, *Of Revelation and Revolution: Christianity, Colonialism and Consciousness in South Africa*, vol. 1 (Chicago: University of Chicago Press, 1991), p. 164. In general, people creamed,

glossed and sheened their bodies with a variety of oils, ruddy orchres, animal fats and fine colored clays.

28. For an excellent exploration of colonial hegemony in Southern Africa see Jean and and John L. Comaroff, *Of Revelation and Revolution*, … long, it seems, for Africans to invent their own subterfuges to hoodwink the Europeans and win the exchange. By Barbot's account, they would half-fill their oil casks with wood, add water to their oil, or herbs to the oil to make it ferment and thus fill up casks with half the oil. Kingsley, *Travels in West Africa*, p. 582.

29. Jean and John L. Comaroff, *Of Revelation and Revolution*, p. 166.

What Does It Mean?

How Humans Represent the World

By Marcel Danesi

The whole visible universe is but a storehouse of images and signs to which the imagination will give a relative place and value; it is a sort of pasture which the imagination must digest and transform.

—Charles Baudelaire (1821–67)

Martha's videotape of the restaurant scene contains many more interesting episodes for the semiotician to digest and ponder. In one segment, Ted's attention is caught by a pin that Cheryl has on her dress. Noticing its unconventional shape, he inquires: "What an interesting design. What does it *mean?*" Cheryl answers as follows: "It *represents* a water spirit in Chinese culture. The water spirit symbolizes the vitality of life."

Such questions and answers are common in human affairs, even though we rarely give them much consideration, beyond the fact that they allow us to satisfy our curiosity. But human curiosity is a remarkable thing. The crux of semiotic analysis is, in effect, to unravel what something *means,* or more accurately, *represents.* It is the *science of representation,* and its primary objective is to develop notions and ideas that can be applied to deciphering the meanings of even seemingly trivial things like cigarettes and high heels. … Notions such as *sign, code,* and *text* allow us to understand with much more accuracy how we extract meaning from the things and actions that we come across routinely in our society.

These also made it quite evident that even something as ordinary as flirting can hardly be considered random behavior. Rather, it unfolds as a recognizable form of behavior inherited through the channel of cultural history. Semiotically, culture can be defined as a *container* of the *meaning-making strategies* and *forms of behavior* that people employ to carry out their daily routines. Culture is the phenomenon that sets the human species apart from all other species. Humans transmit what they have learned, not through the genetic code, but through the *cultural codes* that undergird the customs, traditions, languages, art works, and scientific practices that fill the world's *cultural containers*. These may differ substantively in contents, and may show considerable variation from one historical epoch to another, but at their core they are all reflexes of a universal need for meaning.

The ability to create and make use of a vast repertoire of signs can be traced to the development within the human species of an extremely large brain, averaging 1400 cc/85.4 cu. in., more than two million years ago. The brain's great size, complexity, and slow rate of maturation, with connections among its nerve cells being added through the pre-pubescent years of life, has made it possible for humanity, in effect, to step outside the slow forces of biological evolution and to meet new material demands by means of conscious rapid adjustments rather than by force of genetic adaptation. This is why humans have the ability to survive in a wide range of habitats and in extreme environmental conditions without further mutations. However, on balance, the prolonged juvenile stage of brain and skull development in relation to the time required to reach sexual maturity has exposed newly born human beings to an unparalleled risk among animals. Each new infant is born with relatively few innate traits yet with a vast number of potential behaviors and, therefore, must be reared in a cultural setting to achieve its biological potential. Without such rearing, survival is unlikely. So, while culture may have taken over from biology in charting humanity's future course, it has done so at a considerable risk. No one really knows why this has come about in our species, although there certainly are no lack of theories attempting to explain it.

The world's *sign* systems provide key pieces of evidence for solving the riddle of culture and for probing the mystery behind the human *meaning quest*. But, what is *meaning*? As it turns out, the word has many *meanings* itself. In 1923 two scholars, C. K. Ogden and I. A. Richards, found 16 common meanings for this word in English:[1] In a sentence like "Does life have a meaning?" for instance, the term is equivalent to "purpose." This is a universal concept which reveals that the human animal, aware of its mortality, is distinguished by its need to know if its life has a purpose. The human meaning search is a real phenomenon. It is what art, philosophy, and religion have always sought to understand. However, in sentences such as "What does love mean to you?" or "A green light means go," the term *meaning* is equivalent to "conveyance" or "indication." This is what we called *referential* or *representational* meaning in the previous chapter. In general, when we ask "What does it mean?" we are really asking, "What does it *stand for* or *represent?*" *Representation* is literally "presenting again" (re-presenting) some aspect of the world through signs, codes, or texts.

Representation implies *classification,* that is, the organization of the meanings captured and conveyed by signs, codes, and texts into *categories*. This makes the world much more understandable in human terms. But classification does not tell the whole truth, and is in fact highly variable across cultures. To get a firmer grasp of what this means, consider the world of plants and animals. In theory, human beings are capable of classifying this physically perceivable world by simple trial and error into *edible* (non-perilous) and *non-edible* (perilous)—that is, people living anywhere on earth are capable of classifying any species of plant or animal that they find by experimentation to cause disease or death as non-edible, and any species that does not as edible. But, in practice, the inclusion of a particular non-perilous species in one or the other category is a culture-specific decision. Rabbits, many kinds of flowers, and silkworms, for instance, would be classified by and large as non-edible by North American society, even though they cause no harm to health. On the other hand, many Europeans regularly consume rabbit meat and various types of flowers and Mexicans eat cooked silkworms with no adverse physical reactions whatsoever. But if any of these were to be presented to North Americans in a cooked form, chances are that they would react adversely if told what they were about to eat. Thus the *meaning* of "rabbit" or "silkworm" is clearly different from culture to culture. World-views are built up from the acquisition of such meanings, or categories, in specific cultural contexts.

The fact that a particular culture predisposes its users to attend to certain meanings does not imply that members of other cultures are incapable of perceiving the world in similar ways. Indeed, although people from a different culture might construe a cigarette differently from how we defined it in the previous chapter, they can easily understand what it means in our culture if we simply explain to them its meaning as a sexual prop. They might react with surprise or consternation, but they will nevertheless be able to grasp its meaning. Practical *knowledge* of the world is culture-specific, built on the categories used to classify the world that an individual acquires in social context; but the capacity for knowing is limitless, and can easily transcend the very culture-specific categories that commonly guide it.

The act of *representation* entails a corresponding act of *interpretation*. Simply defined, this is the ability to extract an appropriate meaning from some sign or text. Although interpretation is subject to much individual variation, it is not an open-ended process; it involves familiarity with the meanings of signs in specific contexts, with the type of code to which they belong, and with the nature of their referents—concrete referents are less subject to variation than are abstract ones. Without such familiarity, communication would be virtually impossible in common social settings. In essence, interpretation is a purposeful selection of specific meanings among the boundless meanings of which the human mind is capable. In art and performance, one talks of interpretation as if it were less than the original creation of the work of art. But this is not correct. The interpreter is a creator of meanings as well. The late Canadian pianist Glen Gould was no less an artist for not having composed *The Well-Tempered Clavier,* which he so masterfully played. He effaced himself the better to serve Bach's model. The more successful was he at his task, the more deeply involved did he become in Bach's art form. Every touch, every turn of phrase, became a mirror of his own creative imagination.

TYPES OF MEANING

Now, let's take a closer look at the process of *representation*, the way a semiotician would. First, there are two levels of representation—the *denotative* and the *connotative*. You already have a sense of what this involves when you use everyday words. Think of the word *red*. What does it mean? At one level, it refers to a color at the lower end of the visible spectrum, but at another level, it refers to such things as an emotional state ("I'm red with anger"), a financial predicament ("I'm in the red"), or a political ideology ("He's been a red communist all his life"). Virtually all words have such levels of meaning. So, the discussion that follows will not be totally foreign to you. It is intended simply to formalize what you already know intuitively.

A sign represents something observed, perceived, felt, or thought. This is what it *denotes,* or calls attention to. The word *red* denotes a color on the spectrum. The word *house* denotes a "structure for human habitation." The kind of "habitation structure" that it refers to is not specific, but rather, prototypical (a perfect example of a particular type). The word *house* can thus be used to denote many different types—large, small, cubical, spherical. In our society, this word will normally evoke the image of a cubical, rather than a spherical habitation structure, because that is the typical shape of our houses. But, in others, such as the Dogon society of the Sudan or the settlements of Zambian herders, the equivalent words will denote a spherical or conical structure.

A sign can also have a different level of meanings, known as *connotative*. The uses of the word *red* to refer to an "emotional state," a "financial predicament," or a "political ideology" are examples of connotative meanings. These allow people to use a manageable set of signs to represent a large array of potential meanings. There are three basic kinds of connotative processes: *extensional, emotive,* and *symbolic*.

The additional set of meanings that a sign acquires through usage are its *connotative extensions*. The word *house* connotes a "legislative quorum," an "audience," and a "dormitory" by *extension*, as can be seen in such sentences as "The house is in session," "The house roared with laughter," and "They sleep in one of the houses at Harvard University." These new meanings are *extensional* because they presuppose "structures" of certain kinds that are "inhabited" in some specific way by "humans."

The emotional nuances that can be conveyed through a sign are called its *emotive connotations*. The word *yes* in English denotes "affirmation," but one can communicate doubt or incredulity through this same word by simply raising one's voice as in a question: *Yes?* Similarly, one can convey conviction by stressing it: *Yessss!* The same kinds of emotive connotations can be imparted through the word *house*: "Are you sure that's a house? It looks more like a garage." (= incredulity); "Yes, it's a *house*, not a garage!" (= conviction).

The additional meanings that a sign acquires in specific social contexts at particular moments of its history are its *symbolic connotations*. In the expressions "the house of God" and the "house of ill repute," *house* connotes a church and a prostitution establishment respectively. These differ from the extensional connotations of *house*, discussed above, because they cannot be figured out solely in terms of the word's prototypical meaning, but must be learned from their use in social context. The meanings of cigarettes, high heels, perfumes, brand names of cars and of clothes, and other such things, are all similarly symbolic.

In 1957, the psychologists C. E. Osgood, G. J. Suci, and P. H. Tannenbaum developed an interesting technique for fleshing out the connotations of words, known as the *semantic differential*.[2] By posing a series of questions to subjects about a specific concept—Is it good or bad? Weak or strong?—as seven-point scales, with the opposing adjectives at each end, they were able to sift out any general pattern from them using statistical techniques. As an example, suppose you ask a group of people to evaluate the concept *U.S. President* in terms of categories such as young–old, practical–idealistic, modern–traditional, attractive–bland, friendly–stern, each on a scale of 1 to 7, as shown in Figure 6-1.

Figure 6-1. *Connotations of "President"*

modern								traditional
	1	2	3	4	5	6	7	

young								old
	1	2	3	4	5	6	7	

attractive								bland
	1	2	3	4	5	6	7	

practical								idealistic
	1	2	3	4	5	6	7	

friendly								stern
	1	2	3	4	5	6	7	

Those who feel that the President should be modern, would place a mark towards the corresponding end of that scale. Those who believe that the President should not be too young or too old would place a mark near the middle of the young–old scale. People who think that the President should be bland-looking, would place a mark towards the corresponding end of the attractive–bland scale, and so on. If you were to ask larger and larger groups of people to rate the President in terms of such scales, you would then be able to draw a profile of the presidency in terms of what it connotes to people. Remarkably, research utilizing the semantic differential has shown that, while the connotations of concepts are subject to personal interpretation and subjective feelings, the range of variation is rarely a matter of randomness. In other words, the experiments using the semantic differential have shown that connotation is constrained by culture, and thus prototypical. For example, the word *noise* turns out to be a highly emotional concept for the Japanese, who rate it consistently at the emotional ends of the scales presented to them; whereas it is a fairly neutral concept for Americans who place it in the mid-range of the same scales.

In a fundamental sense, the semiotician is a "scientist of connotations," as the French semiotician Roland Barthes (1915–80) claimed throughout his career. The aim of our analysis of Cheryl and Ted's smoking performance in the previous chapter was, in fact, to sift out the sexual connotations that cigarettes and high-heel shoes have in specific situations. Recall that it would not have been possible to decipher those connotations without taking into account the physical and social *context* of the scene. If you came across a crumpled up and discarded cigarette package on a sidewalk on a city street, you would interpret it as a piece of rubbish. But if you saw the very same package encased in a picture frame, hanging on a wall in an art gallery, autographed by some artist, and given the title *Waste*, then you would hardly perceive it as garbage. You would interpret it in a markedly different way—as a symbol of a "throw-away society," as a metaphor of a "materialistic culture," or as some other symbol. Clearly, the package's *context* of occurrence—its location on a sidewalk versus its insertion in a picture frame displayed in an art gallery—determines the kind of meaning you will extract from it. But note that the *meaning* of the context, too, is determined by culture. Only those living in cultures with art galleries in it will know enough to interpret the cigarette displayed on the gallery's walls as a "work of art."

The art gallery is a perfect example of a *code,* because it entails recognizing what a painting is, how paintings differ from each other, and how they can be arranged (on walls, in sections of the gallery). A code is an organizing grid of signs; it is what allows individuals to extract meanings from signs. There are many codes in a culture. These regulate how the members of the culture make messages and meanings together. Indeed, semiotically speaking culture itself is one huge code, or *macrocode,* constituting a *signifying network* that unites individual signs into a cohesive circuitry of intertwined meanings. Signs are linked to each other in this network as circuits are linked in an electrical system.

A face-to-face conversation, for instance, is a code-based event, involving not only the deployment of a language code, but also gestural, facial, and other nonverbal codes. When people talk to each other, they not only use words, but unconsciously use hand gestures, facial expressions, and other kinds of body language. The verbal message is "woven together" with the resources of different codes into a *text.* Not only routine conversations, but musical compositions, stage plays, dance styles, and ceremonies, are also the products of our *text-making* capacity. The terms *message* and *text* are not synonymous. A message refers to *what one* wishes to communicate; a text refers to *how* the message is constructed.

TYPES OF SIGNS

Much work within semiotics has been devoted to identifying and understanding the main types of signs of which the human brain is capable. The American semiotician Thomas A. Sebeok has identified six types—*symptom, signal, index, icon, symbol,* and *name.*[3] Although some semioticians would exclude symptom and signal from their purview of investigation, Sebeok correctly insists that their inclusion would force semiotics to consider the relation of biological factors to cultural ones more seriously in its investigation of *semiosis*—the ability to produce and comprehend signs.

Let's consider this idea a little further. Symptoms are bodily signs that are indicative of physical states or conditions. But their identification as such is filtered culturally. Facial acne, for example, is recognized as a chronic disease of the skin afflicting adolescents and young adults, linked in large part to lifestyle factors (diet, stress, etc.) in Western cultures. The symptoms associated with this condition are pimples (furuncles) on the face, back, and chest. But the appearance of pimples on the face is not seen as indicative of disease in other cultures, as attested by the lack of words equivalent to *acne* in many of the world's languages. The Inuit tribes in northern Manitoba do not recognize the physical conditions associated with *rickets*—a softening and, often, bending of the bones usually caused by a lack of vitamin D and insufficient exposure to sunlight—as symptomatic. As their lack of a word for this condition testifies, the people living in those cultures do not perceive this pattern of bone formation as indicative of an abnormality of the skeletal system. This is akin to our lack of recognition of the syndrome that Malaysian, Japanese, Indonesian, and Thai peoples call *latah,* which results from sudden fright. Lacking an equivalent term for this state, we simply do not recognize it as a condition, although it clearly exists (as people living in these other cultures would avow). As such examples show, the whole process of diagnosing a disease is a semiotic one, since it involves deciphering and establishing what constitutes a symptom in cultural terms.

A *signal* is a bodily emission (sound, odor, etc.) or movement (head tilt, eye wink, etc.). In most species, signals have the primary function of identifying the sex and species of an animal's potential mate. For example, a fish called the stickleback uses a system of interlocking releasers to orchestrate its mating. When its breeding season arrives, the underside of each male turns bright red. This color attracts females, but also provokes attacks by other males. Red objects of almost any description will trigger male stickleback aggression. A female responds to the male's red signal with a curious approach posture that displays her swollen belly full of eggs. This incites the male to perform a zigzag dance that leads the female to the tunnel-like nest he has built for her. The female snuggles into the nest, whereupon the male touches her tail with his nose and quivers. The ensuing vibration causes the female to release her eggs for the male to fertilize. If the male fails to perform the last part of the dance, the female will not lay her eggs. Vibrating the female with a pencil will also work perfectly well, but the male in this case, not having gone through the last stage of the ritual, will refuse to fertilize the eggs and eats them instead.

Signaling can, of course, have other functions. Worker honey bees, for instance, are endowed with a sophisticated system for signaling the location of a cache of food to their hive members. Upon returning to the hive from foraging trips, these bees have the extraordinary capacity to inform the other bees in the hive, through movement sequences, about the direction, distance, and quality of the food with amazing accuracy. This signaling system is known as a dance because its movements resemble the actions of human dancing. The remarkable thing about bee dancing is that it is representational, thus sharing with human signs the feature of conveying information about something in the absence of the thing to which it refers. Several kinds of dance patterns have been documented by zoologists. In the "round" dance, the bee moves in circles, alternating to the left and to the right. This dance is apparently used by the bees to signal that the cache of food is nearby. When the food source is farther away, the bee dances in a "wagging" fashion, moving in a straight line while wagging its abdomen from side to side and then returning to its starting point. The straight line in this dance points in the direction of the food source, the energy level of the dance indicates how rich the food source is, and the tempo provides information about its distance from the hive.

Despite their noteworthiness, such examples of signaling are hardly ever deliberate in the human sense. They are instinctual, even though they sometimes do not appear to us to be so. A classic example of how easily we are duped by our own perceptions of animal signaling is the well-documented case of Clever Hans. Clever Hans was a world-famous German "talking horse" who lived at the turn of the twentieth century. He appeared to understand human language and communicate human answers to questions by tapping the alphabet with his front hoof—one tap for *A*, two taps for *B*, and so on. A panel of scientists ruled out deception by the horse's owner. The horse, it was claimed, could talk! Clever Hans was awarded honors and proclaimed an important scientific discovery. Eventually, however, an astute member of the committee of scientists who had examined the horse, the Dutch psychologist Oskar Pfungst, discovered that Clever Hans could not talk without *observing* his questioners. The horse decoded signals that humans transmit and over which they have no conscious control. Clever Hans sensed when to tap his hoof and when not to tap it in response to inadvertent cues from his human handler, who would visibly relax when the horse had tapped the proper number of times. To show this, Pfungst simply blindfolded Clever Hans who, as a consequence, ceased to be so clever. The "Clever Hans phenomenon," as it has come to be known in the annals of psychology, has been demonstrated with other animals—for instance, a dog will bark in response to inadvertent human signals.

Many human signals are also instinctual. Psychological studies have shown, for instance, that men are sexually attracted to women with large pupils, which signal strong sexual interest and make a female look younger. This might explain the vogue in central Europe during the 1920s and 1930s of women using a pupil-dilating crystalline alkaloid eye-drop liquid derived from the drug known popularly as *belladonna* ("beautiful woman" in Italian) as a cosmetic to enhance facial appearance. But human beings also have the ability to send out signals consciously and intentionally. A look or tilt of the head can be used to indicate to someone the presence in the room of a certain person; a wink of the eye can be used to communicate the need to maintain secrecy or sexual interest; and so on.

INDEXES, ICONS, AND SYMBOLS

The power of human *semiosis* (sign-making) lies in the fact that it is not limited to instinctual signaling. The signs that humans make allow them to carry the world "around in their heads," because they permit the recall of the things, beings, events, feelings, to which they refer, even if these are *displaced* in space and time, that is, not physically present for the person to observe and perceive. This *displacement* property of signs has endowed the human species with the remarkable capacity to think about the world beyond the realm of responses to stimuli to which most other species are constrained, and thus to reflect upon it at any time or in any context whatsoever.

Consider, for instance, the action of pointing a finger at an object, say, a ball. This action will invariably direct someone's eye to its location. The pointing index finger is an example of a remarkable type of sign known, logically enough, as an *index*. But there is more to *indexicality* (the capacity for indexical representation), than just finger-pointing. Words such as *here, there, up, down,* are also indexical signs. When someone says "I am here, you are there," he or she is referring to the relative position of persons to each other. Personal pronouns such as *I, you, he, she* are also indexes because they refer to different people in relation to where they are located in the line of sight—*I* is the origin, *you* is closer to the origin than is *he,* and so on.

In addition to such forms, there are many examples of abstract forms of indexicality in languages across the world. Take, for instance, the English expressions *think up, think over,* and *think out:* "When did you think up that preposterous idea?" "You should think over carefully what you just said"; "You should think out the entire problem." Even though these refer to abstract ideas, they nonetheless refer to them in ways that presuppose location and movement: *think up* elicits a mental image of upward movement, portraying the activity of thinking as if it were an object being extracted physically from a kind of imaginary mental terrain; *think over* evokes the image of an internal eye scanning the mind; *think out* suggests the action of taking a deeply buried thought out of the mind so that it can be held up, presumably, for the mind's eye to see and examine.

The presence of such expressions in languages across the world suggests something rather intriguing about the possible origins of language. Representing abstract concepts in accordance with the laws of physical perception suggests an evolutionary link between language, cognition, and the senses. Languages across the world show the same feature of representing ideas as if they were objects in time and space, with physical properties: in Sanskrit the word *maya* (perceiving form in thought) contains the particle *ma* (to measure or lay out); in Italian, the verb *pensarci* (to think about something, to think over), is constructed with the indexical particle *ci* (here, there); in English, *perceive* derives from Latin *cipio* (to seize) and *per* (through), *examine* from *agmen* (to pull out from a row) and *ex* (from), and *prospect* from Latin *spectus* (looking) and *pro* (forward, ahead).

Now, consider the ball again. If location is not a requirement of the situation, one could alternatively refer to the same object by *showing* what a ball looks like. To do this, one could use gesture, cupping one's hands and moving them as if one were "drawing" the ball in space: that is, moving the left hand in a counterclockwise circular motion and the right one in a clockwise motion at the same time. One could do virtually the same thing on a piece of paper with a pencil in each hand. In both cases, the sign that results is a circular figure resembling the outline of a ball. This type of sign is known as an *icon*.

An icon is a sign that simulates, replicates, reproduces, imitates, or resembles properties of its referent. A portrait, for instance, is contrived as a reproduction of the actual face of a person from the perspective of the artist; a perfume scent is made chemically to simulate a natural aroma or fragrance; words such as *drip, bang, screech* were obviously coined as attempts to imitate certain sounds. *Iconicity* (the capacity for iconic representation) is clearly based on sensory knowledge. Its presence in the system of everyday life is so pervasive that people are hardly aware of it. If you have a Macintosh computer or a Windows program for your IBM, you will see icons displayed on a screen, representing available functions or resources in a visual way. On the doors of public toilets, you will see figures representing males and females also in a visual way. If you listen carefully to Beethoven's *Pastoral* symphony or Rossini's *William Tell Overture*, for instance, you will hear musical icons that are evocative of the sounds found in nature (bird calls, thunder, wind). Icons are everywhere.

One of the key figures of semiotics, Charles Peirce, … saw iconicity as the primary, or default, way of representing the world, precisely because it is tied to sensory knowledge. This is why its handiwork shows up even in prehistoric etchings, small sculptures, and relief carvings of animals and female figures found in caves throughout Europe that go back some 30,000 to 40,000 years. The appearance of such art is probably the end-result of something that is not much different from the kind of hand gesture made to represent the ball described above. With some cutting, sculpting, or drawing instrument in one's hands, it would be a fairly straightforward task to transfer the imaginary picture of the ball made through gesture onto some surface, using the same kinds of movements. Indeed, this is probably what happened in human prehistory. It was only at a later point in time that the hand movements used to make those works of art became more abbreviated. At that point, figures became more condensed and abstract, leading to the invention of picture writing. Archeological research suggests, in fact, that the origins of alphabetic writing lie in symbols previously made out of elemental shapes that were used as image-making objects—much like the molds that figurine and coin-makers use today. Only later did they take on more abstract qualities.[4]

The persistence of gesture in human communication is also a testament to the ancient origins of iconicity. Although vocal language is our primary mode of communication, the evolutionary link between speech and gesture is still clearly noticeable. The linguist David McNeill has shown that when people speak they gesture unconsciously, literally "drawing" the concepts they are conveying orally.[5] Over a ten-year period, he painstakingly examined how individuals—of different cultures, children as well as adults, some even neurologically impaired—invariably represent mental images in terms of gesture. For instance, when people talk of "large" things, they typically cup their hands moving them outward in imitation of a swelling motion. When they talk of "small" things, they typically cup their hands moving them inward, mimicking a shrinking motion. McNeill's research suggests that, although vocal language has become the dominant form of communication in humans, the use of the hands has not vanished, but remains a functional subsystem. The story of gesture as a servant of vocal communication is, however, incomplete. Indeed, gesture persists today as the default form of communication when an interaction is otherwise impossible. This happens typically when two people speak different languages. Of course, in individuals with impaired vocal organs, gesture constitutes the primary mode of communication.

This innate "drawing" capacity is also evident in the development of children. The ability to draw the outlines of rudimentary figures emerges at approximately the same time as the first verbal utterances. If a drawing instrument is put in a child's hand at this point in life, he or she will instinctively make random scribbles on a surface. As time passes, the scribbling becomes more and more controlled; shapes become suggestive of geometric figures which, with adult prompting, are soon labeled as "suns" or "faces." At first, children do not appear to draw anything in particular but instead spontaneously produce forms, which become refined through practice into precise, repeatable shapes. They draw for the pleasure of it, without larger or more explicit associations of meaning. Drawing in early childhood is, in effect, an example of "art for art's sake."

In a generic sense, indexes and icons are types *of symbols,* because they can be used to represent something *displaced,* that is, not physically present for the person to observe and perceive. In semiotic parlance, a sign becomes increasingly *symbolic* the more it has this property of *displacement.* In such cases, its meaning can be gleaned only in terms of convention. Consider the ball again. The easiest and most efficient way to refer to the object in question is to use the word *ball.* But this can be done only if one knows the English language. The word ball is, in fact, a symbol, a sign that stands for a referent in an arbitrary or conventional way and which, therefore, must be learned in social context. Words, in general, are symbolic signs. But any sig-nifier—an object, a sound, a figure—can be used symbolically. A cross can symbolize the concept "Christianity," a "V" configuration made with the index and middle fingers can symbolize the concept "peace," and so on.

The interconnection between symbols and other kinds of signs is not always evident. Take, for instance, a word such as *flow.* It probably was coined as an icon, because the sounds that comprise it suggest an attempt to represent the sound made by moving water. Indeed, a word made with other kinds of sounds would seem, intuitively, to be inappropriate for referring to a stream—*klop, twing, yoot,* for example, do not seem suitable; but *flow* does. The reason why the word flow sounds more "natural" is because it is more *representative* of the sound made by water. Over time, the word has become

Figure 6-2. *A Railroad Crossing Sign*

detached from its sonority and is now understood mainly *symbolically.* Time dims the sounds that many words attempt to capture when they are first coined—a story that repeats itself with virtually every kind of human sign. Practically everything in human representation tends towards the symbolic. This is why the twentieth-century philosopher Ernst Cassirer (1874–1945) characterized the human animal as a *symbolic animal.*

As Charles Peirce also argued, signs are often amalgams of iconic, indexical, and purely arbitrary modes of representation, because they tend to enfold more than one way of referring to something. Take, as an example, the common traffic sign for a crossroads, as seen in Figure 6-2.

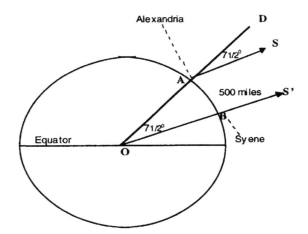

Figure 6-3. *Eratosthenes' Representation*

The "cross" on this sign is both an icon and a symbol. It is iconic because its form visually represents the outline of a crossing. However, since the cross figure could be used to represent a church in other contexts (with minor changes to its shape), it is also conventional insofar as we need to know that it has been chosen to refer specifically to a crossing. Finally, the sign is an index because when it is placed near a railway crossing it indicates that we are about to reach it. In parallel ways, most signs are amalgams, and will be interpreted as more or less iconic, indexical, or conventional depending on their uses, their forms, and their purposes.

Nowhere has the use of symbols borne more remarkable fruits than in mathematics and science. Mathematical symbols have given us a unique opportunity to represent the physical world in abstract (displaced) ways, and then experiment with it in a purely intellectual and imaginary fashion. The results of this mental experimentation can then be redirected to the real world to see what they yield. Often, this leads to real discoveries about that world. Symbolic reasoning in such areas of human thought carries the burden over intuition.

One of the early impressive examples of what this type of reasoning can achieve is the calculation of the earth's circumference by the Greek astronomer, geometer, and geographer, Eratosthenes (275–194 B.C.). Standing, during the summer solstice, at Alexandria, and knowing that it was due north of the city of Syene, with the distance between the two cities being 500 miles, Eratosthenes used an ingenious method for measuring the earth's circumference—without having to physically measure it. At the summer solstice he knew, as an astronomer, that the noon sun was directly overhead at Syene, shining directly down upon it. Thus, he drew a diagram, showing the earth as a circle, labeling the center of the equator with the letter O and the cities of Alexandria and Syene with A and B, respectively, as shown in Figure 6-3.

He then represented the *direction of the sun* (S′) over Syene as BS′ and he reasoned that joining this line to the earth's center O would form the straight line OBS′, since at that instant the sun was shining straight overhead: that is, at Syene the *overhead direction* and the *direction of the sun* were coincident. At the same moment in Alexandria, he argued, the *direction of the sun* (S) could thus be represented with AS, a line parallel to BS′ because, as he knew, sun rays are parallel to each other. Then, on the diagram he extended the line OA—the line joining the center of the earth to Alexandria—to an arbitrary point D. The line OAD thus represented the *overhead direction* at Alexandria. Now, Eratosthenes reasoned, since AS was parallel to BS′, the angles DAS and AOB, formed by the line OAD cutting the two parallel lines AS and OBS′, were equal by a theorem of Euclidean geometry. On the basis of this knowledge, Eratosthenes had only to measure DAS, which he was able to do easily, being in Alexandria, by measuring the angle of the shadow made by a well near which he was standing. This was the difference between the *overhead direction* and the *direction of the sun* at Syene. He found it to be 7½°. This, then, was also the size of angle AOB on the diagram. Moreover, Eratosthenes reasoned, this angle is 7½° of 360° since the earth is virtually a sphere and therefore forms almost a 360° angle. Thus, he proved the angle AOB as being ¼⁸ of the entire angle at O (7½° of 360°), the circumference of the earth. From another fact of geometry, Eratosthenes knew that the arc AB, the distance between Alexandria and Syene, was also ¼⁸ of the circumference. Therefore, Eratosthenes concluded, the circumference was 48 times the length of that arc: 48 x 500 = 24,000 miles. His calculation of 24,000 miles was, in fact, in close agreement with the modern value of 24,844 miles.

This classic episode in the history of science shows how powerful symbolic representation is. Symbols can replace physical intervention, allowing humans to model the world in abstract ways and then discover real properties of that world. But it must not be forgotten that the reason why representations such as the one by Eratosthenes produce the results that they do is because they are extrapolations of experiences and observations. The derivation of the term *geometry* is "measuring the earth," and this is, in fact, an accurate description of what the early geometers did: they measured the size of fields and laid out accurate right angles for the corners of buildings. This type of empirical geometry, which flourished in ancient Egypt, Sumer, and Babylon, was refined and systematized by the Greeks. It was in the sixth century B.C. that the Greek mathematician Pythagoras (580?–500? B.C.) laid the cornerstone of scientific reasoning by showing that the various measurements made by geometers held a hidden pattern in them. When he tied three pieces of string or rope together to form a right-angled triangle, the square on the hypotenuse of the triangle was always equal to the sum of the squares on the other two sides. Pythagoras' great achievement was essentially to develop a convenient shorthand for this pattern and demonstrate its generalizability.

NAMES

There is one kind of symbol that merits separate consideration—the *name*. The name is a word-symbol that identifies a person, place, or by connotative extension, a brand, an animal, a tropical storm, etc. At first thought, names would seem to be like other symbols, having no particular emotional significance. But that is not the case. It is, in fact, impossible to think of a human being without a name—if an individual is not given a name by his or her family, then society steps in to do so. Names define the human person. This is why children tend to become rather upset when someone calls them by a name other than their birth name, or else makes fun of that name.

The personal name, known technically as an *anthroponym,* constitutes a truly significant chapter in the history of the human species. Throughout the world a newly born child is not considered a full-fledged member of this species until he or she is given a name. In Inuit cultures an individual is perceived as having a body, a soul, and a name; a person is not seen to be complete without all three. This is true, to varying degrees, in all cultures. A few decades ago, a British television program, *The Prisoner,* played on this theme. It portrayed a totalitarian world in which people were assigned numbers instead of traditional names—Number 1, Number 2, etc. The idea was that a person could be made to conform more submissively and to become more controllable if he or she did not have a name. The use of numbers to identify prisoners and slaves throughout history has constituted an act designed to negate the humanity or the existence of certain people. *The Prisoner* was, in essence, a portrayal of the struggle that humans feel to discover the meaning of self.

Naming is an intrinsic feature of a society's *signifying network,* mentioned above, that unites all forms of representation into a congruous system of intertwined meanings. In our culture, for instance, given names are commonly derived from the names of the months (April, June), precious stones (Ruby, Pearl), popular personalities (Franklin, Liza), flowers (Rose, Violet), places (Georgia), legendary figures (Diana, Jason). Although name-giving is very much influenced by vogue and fashion in Western cultures, rather than exclusively by tradition, modern societies vary widely in this respect. Britain and the United States permit all kinds of names, but in some countries there are approved lists of names that must be given to a child if he or she is to be legally recognized. In Brazil, for example, a child must be given an appropriate Christian name before he or she will be issued a birth certificate.

Sometimes one name is not sufficient to identify individuals. Historically, *surnames*—literally "names on top of names"—became necessary when name duplications in growing societies made it difficult to differentiate between people. Surnaming accomplished this typically by representing an individual with reference to his or her place of origin, occupation, or descendancy. In England, for example, a person living near or at a place where apple trees grew was called *John* "where-the-apples-grow," hence, *John Appleby.* Regional or habitation names, such as *Wood, Moore, Church,* or *Hill* are products of the same kind of surnaming process. Surnames denoting an occupation are *Chapman* (merchant or trader), *Miller,* and *Baker.* Parentage surnames in Scotland or Ireland are often indicated by prefixes such as *Mac, Mc—McTavish, McManus,* etc.—or in England by suffixes such as *son—Johnson, Harrison,* and *Maryson* (son of John, son of Harry, son of Mary). Compound surnames are also used in some countries where retaining both family names is the custom. Thus, in Spain, Juan the son of Manuel Chávez and Juanita Fernandez would be named *Juan Chavez (y) Fernández.* The surname is also an index of ethnicity, since it reveals to which family, society, or culture the individual probably belongs—the surname *Smith* indicates that the person is of Anglo-American heritage, *Bellini* (Italian), *Lamontaigne* (French), and so on.

The story of naming does not stop at surnames. People create *nicknames,* for instance, to emphasize a physical characteristic (*Lefty*) or a personality trait (*Cranky*), and *pseudonyms* (false names) to conceal sex (*George Sand,* pseudonym of Amandine Aurore Lucie Dupin), the past (*O. Henry,* pseudonym of William Sydney Porter), or simply as a personal whim (*Mark Twain,* a Mississippi River phrase meaning "two fathoms deep," pseudonym of Samuel Clemens). Some pseudonyms have become better known than the real name, as in the case of *Mark Twain* or *Lewis Carroll,* whose real name was Charles Dodgson.

People also name things other than human beings. Throughout the world, people give names to deities, vehicles (ships, boats), and to geographical spaces and formations—countries, states, islands, rivers, streets, houses, fields, mountains, valleys—known technically as *toponyms.* Toponyms may have historical significance (*Washington,* a city named after the first president of the United States), religious significance (*Santa Cruz* means "holy cross"), or some other kind of culture-specific connotation. Some are simply descriptive: *Honolulu,* "safe harbor," *Dover,* "water," *Doncaster,* "camp on the Don." A rough estimate is that 3.5 million place names exist in the United States alone, one for each square mile. Many of these reflect Native American influence (*Niagara, Potomac, Tennessee*). Others are of various origins: Spanish (*Florida, Santa Fe*), French (*Lake Champlain, Baton Rouge*), Dutch (*Brooklyn, Harlem*), Russian (*Kotzebue, Tolstoi Point*), and so on. Nations typically have regulatory agencies that supervise and recommend geographical names. In the United States, the agency is the Board on Geographic Names of the Department of the Interior.

In modern cultures, naming has been extended in a variety of ways—to identify products (*brand names*), to recognize teams (*New York Yankees, Dallas Cowboys*), to name tropical storms (*Hazel, Harry*), and so on. Aware that a product with a name has a more personal quality to it, marketing and advertising people pay close attention to the choice of a brand name. The intentional creation of a name for a product engenders a personality for that product that is meant to appeal to specific consumers. Sometimes the brand name becomes so well-known that it is used to represent the whole category of products: *Scotch tape* for adhesive tape, *Skidoo* for snowmobile, *Kleenex* for facial tissue, and so on. The names given to cosmetics and beauty products are created to elicit desirable connotations such as natural beauty (*Moondrops, Natural Wonder, Rainflower, Sunsilk, Skin Dew*), scientific authority (*Eterna 27, Clinique, Endocil, Equalia*), or masculinity (*Brut, Cossak, Denim, Aramis, Devin*).

STRUCTURE

Recall Ted's question at the beginning of this chapter regarding the meaning of the design of the pin Cheryl was wearing (a Chinese water spirit). In terms of semiotics, Ted asked that question because he did not recognize the design as meaning anything in the framework of any of the codes he knew. For any sign to bear meaning, it must have some *differential* physical feature that individuals recognize as code-based. What does this imply? Consider words such as *pin, bin, fun, run, duck, luck.* As a speaker of English, you will instantly recognize these as separate, meaning-bearing words because you perceive the initial sounds of successive pairs (*p* versus *b* in *pin-bin, f* versus *r* in *fun-run, d* Versus *l* in *duck-luck*) as *differential.* In technical terms, this *differentiation* feature in the make-up of signs is known as *paradigmatic structure.* For any sign to bear meaning, it must have some physical feature in its make-up that individuals recognize as keeping it distinct within some specific code. People are intuitively aware of this feature of signs, even though they may never have consciously reflected upon it. It is the reason why, for example, people can easily recognize (a, b, …) and (1, 2, 3, …) as pertaining to separate codes (the *Roman alphabet code,* the *positive integer code*) and as distinct elements of each code.

Words such as *pin* and *bin* are not only recognizable as distinct signs through their differing initial sounds, but also by the way in which their constituent sounds have been put together. In technical terms, this *combination* feature in the make-up of signs is called *syntagmatic structure.* For any sign to bear meaning, it must not only have some physical feature in its make-up that keeps it distinct, but also be constructed according to some recognizable pattern. The word *pin* is recognizable as a legitimate English word because of the way in which its constituent sounds, $p + i + n$, have been linked. On the other hand, the form *pfin* is not recognizable as an English word because the sequence $p + f + i + n$ violates English combinatory (*syntagmatic*) structure. So, too, the integers (1, 2, 3, 4, 5, …) can be combined to form numerals larger than nine according to specified rules of *horizontal* combination—12, 345, 9870, etc.; but they cannot be put one under the other *vertically,* because we do not form numerals in that way. In sum, paradigmatic structure involves *differentiation,* syntagmatic structure involves *combination.*

The notion of *structure* is a crucial one. So, it is worth mulling over with an analogy to solitaire. Solitaire is the term applied to a variety of card games that can be played by one person. In all versions, the cards are dealt to the table according to a plan or pattern, known as a *tableau.* The game develops out of the undealt portion of the deck, known as the *hand,* which is turned up one card or more at a time. The object of most solitaire games is to build columns of cards in ascending or descending order. The rules of play may require that these be built-up in one color, in alternating colors, in some number-value arrangement, or in one suit alone. Playing solitaire, therefore, entails both the ability to recognize the distinctive features of cards (suit and number value) and knowledge of how to put the individual cards together in vertical columns. In other words, solitaire is a *code* in which the various cards (signs) are distinguishable *paradigmatically* from each other by suit, color, and number, and placeable *syntagmatically* into columns in certain specified ways.

To summarize, forms are recognized as legitimate meaning-bearing signs when they fit *structurally* into their respective *codes*—language, number systems, card games, etc. Signs are like pieces of a jigsaw puzzle, which have visible features on their faces that keep them distinct from each other, as well as differently shaped edges that allow the puzzle-solver to join them together in specific ways to complete the overall picture. The words *pin, bin, fun, run, duck, luck* are acceptable words in English not only because they are kept *distinct* by different initial sounds (paradigmatic structure), but also because the sound *combinations* that were used to construct them are consistent with English syllable structure. Codes can be thought of as formatted computer disks. The *speech code,* or more precisely the *sound system,* of a language, has a format that permits only certain types of sounds along with a finite set of sound-combination patterns in the formation of syllables; a specific type of *dress code* has a format that allows the wearing of only certain clothing items that can be worn in specific combinations.

Codes are both restrictive and liberating. They are restrictive in that they impose upon individuals born and reared in a specific culture an already-fixed system of meaning; this system will largely determine how they will come to understand the world around them—that is, through the *structure* of the language, music, myths, rituals, technological systems, and the other codes to which they are exposed in social context. Code-based *structure* influences beliefs, attitudes, world-view, and even sensory perception. To grasp how a particular type of *visual code* to which you have become accustomed can influence your own visual perception, look at Figure 6-4.

People reared in Western cultures are typically fooled by these lines. Lines AB and CD are actually *equal* in length, but the *orientation* of the arrowheads fools the Western eye into seeing

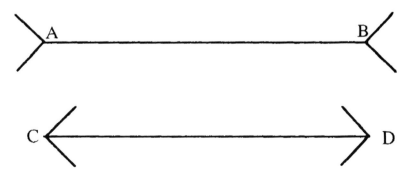

Figure 6-4. *A Visual Illusion*

AB as longer than CD. As psychologists have found, many people living in non-Western cultures do not experience the same illusion. The reason why people from Western cultures see one line as longer than the other is because they have become conditioned by their upbringing to view drawings in a certain *perspective.* Perspective refers to the ability to create an illusion of depth or length. Visual artists in our culture, from painters to graphic designers, learn how to manipulate and guide perspective by means of line, shape, color, value, and texture so as to induce a specific range of interpretations to their visual texts. Their craft dates back to the Renaissance (from the fourteenth to the sixteenth centuries) when the Italian artist Filippo Brunelleschi (1377–1446) discovered and popularized the technique of perspective. Since then, the Western eye has become accustomed to reading pictures in terms of Brunelleschi's technique. Pictures are thus perceived as having depth, figures within them as being far or near, and so on. This way of seeing is a consequence of Brunelleschi's *visual code,* which now structures our experience of viewing visual texts.

The story of culture does not end on the rather worrisome note that we are all caught in a predetermined cultural system of perception. Paradoxically, the very same *perception-structuring* system of signification in which we are reared is also liberating because it provides the means by which we can seek new meanings. The great artistic, religious, scientific, and philosophical texts to which we are exposed in cultural contexts open up the mind, stimulate creativity, and engender freedom of thought. As a result, human beings tend to become restless for new meanings, new messages. For this reason, codes are constantly being modified by new generations of artists, scientists, philosophers, thinkers, and others to meet new demands, new ideas, new challenges. Therein lies the paradox of culture.

REFERENCES

1. C. K. Ogden and I. A. Richards, *The Meaning of Meaning* (London: Routledge and Kegan Paul, 1923).
2. C. E. Osgood, G. J. Suci, and P. H. Tannenbaum, *The Measurement of Meaning* (Urbana: University of Illinois Press, 1957).
3. Thomas A. Sebeok, *Signs* (Toronto: University of Toronto Press, 1994).
4. See D. Schmandt-Besserat, "The Earliest Precursor of Writing," *Scientific American* 238 (1978), pp. 50–9.
5. David McNeill, *Hand and Mind: What Gestures Reveal about Thought* (Chicago: University of Chicago Press, 1992).

Representation

Cultural Representations and Signifying Practices

By Stuart Hall

INTRODUCTION

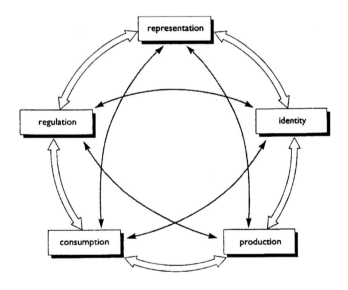

Figure 7-1. *The Circuit of Culture*

The chapters in [Hall's] volume all deal, in different ways, with the question of representation. This is one of the central practices which produce culture and a key 'moment' in what has been called the 'circuit of culture' (see **du Gay, Hall et al.,** 1997)[1]. But what does representation have to do with 'culture': what is the connection between them? To put it simply, culture is about 'shared meanings'. Now, language is the privileged medium in which we 'make sense' of things, in which meaning is produced and exchanged. Meanings can only be shared through our common access to language. So language is central to meaning and culture and has always been regarded as the key repository of cultural values and meanings.

But how does language construct meanings? How does it sustain the dialogue between participants which enables them to build up a culture of shared understandings and so interpret the world in roughly the same ways? Language is able to do this because it operates as a *representational system*. In language, we use signs and symbols—whether they are sounds, written words, electronically produced images, musical notes, even objects—to stand for or represent to other people our concepts, ideas and feelings. Language is one of the 'media' through which thoughts, ideas and feelings are represented in a culture. Representation through language is therefore central to the processes by which meaning is produced. This is the basic, underlying idea which underpins all six chapters in [Hall's] book. Each chapter examines 'the production and circulation of meaning through language' in different ways, in relation to different examples, different areas of social practice. Together, these chapters push forward and develop our understanding of how representation actually *works*.

'Culture' is one of the most difficult concepts in the human and social sciences and there are many different ways of defining it. In more traditional definitions of the term, culture is said to embody the 'best that has been thought and said' in a society. It is the sum of the great ideas, as represented in the classic works of literature, painting, music and philosophy—the 'high culture' of an age. Belonging to the same frame of reference, but more 'modern' in its associations, is the use of 'culture' to refer to the widely distributed forms of popular music, publishing, art, design and literature, or the activities of leisure-time and entertainment, which make up the everyday lives of the majority of 'ordinary people'—what is called the 'mass culture' or the 'popular culture' of an age. High culture versus popular culture was, for many years, the classic way of framing the debate about culture—the terms carrying a powerfully evaluative charge (roughly, high = good; popular = debased). In recent years, and in a more 'social science' context, the word 'culture' is used to refer to whatever is distinctive about the 'way of life' of a people, community, nation or social group. This has come to be known as the 'anthropological' definition. Alternatively, the word can be used to describe the 'shared values' of a group or of society—which is like the anthropological definition, only with a more sociological emphasis. You will find traces of all these meanings somewhere in [Hall's] book. However, as its title suggests, 'culture' is usually being used … in a somewhat different, more specialized way.

What has come to be called the 'cultural turn' in the social and human sciences, especially in cultural studies and the sociology of culture, has tended to emphasize the importance of *meaning* to the definition of culture. Culture, it is argued, is not so much a set of *things*—novels and paintings or TV programmes and comics—as a process, a set of *practices*. Primarily, culture is concerned with the production and the exchange of meanings—the 'giving and taking of meaning'—between the members of a society or group. To say that two people belong to the

---

1   A reference in bold indicates another book, or another chapter in another book, in the series.

same culture is to say that they interpret the world in roughly the same ways and can express themselves, their thoughts and feelings about the world, in ways which will be understood by each other. Thus culture depends on its participants interpreting meaningfully what is happening around them, and 'making sense' of the world, in broadly similar ways.

This focus on 'shared meanings' may sometimes make culture sound too unitary and too cognitive. In any culture, there is always a great diversity of meanings about any topic, and more than one way of interpreting or representing it. Also, culture is about feelings, attachments and emotions as well as concepts and ideas. The expression on my face 'says something' about who I am (identity) and what I am feeling (emotions) and what group I feel I belong to (attachment), which can be 'read' and understood by other people, even if I didn't intend deliberately to communicate anything as formal as 'a message', and even if the other person couldn't give a very logical account of how s/he came to understand what I was 'saying'. Above all, cultural meanings are not only 'in the head'. They organize and regulate social practices, influence our conduct and consequently have real, practical effects.

The emphasis on cultural practices is important. It is participants in a culture who give meaning to people, objects and events. Things 'in themselves' rarely if ever have any one, single, fixed and unchanging meaning. Even something as obvious as a stone can be a stone, a boundary marker or a piece of sculpture, depending on *what it means*—that is, within a certain context of use, within what the philosophers call different 'language games' (i.e. the language of boundaries, the language of sculpture, and so on). It is by our use of things, and what we say, think and feel about them—how we represent them—that we *give them a meaning*. In part, we give objects, people and events meaning by the frameworks of interpretation which we bring to them. In part, we give things meaning by how we use them, or integrate them into our everyday practices. It is our use of a pile of bricks and mortar which makes it a 'house'; and what we feel, think or say about it that makes a 'house' a 'home'. In part, we give things meaning by how we *represent* them—the words we use about them, the stories we tell about them, the images of them we produce, the emotions we associate with them, the ways we classify and conceptualize them, the values we place on them. Culture, we may say, is involved in all those practices which are not simply genetically programmed into us—like the jerk of the knee when tapped—but which carry meaning and value for us, which need to be *meaningfully interpreted* by others, or which *depend on meaning* for their effective operation. Culture, in this sense, permeates all of society. It is what distinguishes the 'human' element in social life from what is simply biologically driven. Its study underlines the crucial role of the *symbolic* domain at the very heart of social life.

Where is meaning produced? Our 'circuit of culture' suggests that, in fact, meanings are produced at several different sites and circulated through several different processes or practices (the cultural circuit). Meaning is what gives us a sense of our own identity, of who we are and with whom we 'belong'—so it is tied up with questions of how culture is used to mark out and maintain identity within and difference between groups (which is the main focus of **Woodward**, ed., 1997). Meaning is constantly being produced and exchanged in every personal and social interaction in which we take part. In a sense, this is the most privileged, though often the most neglected, site of culture and meaning. It is also produced in a variety of different *media*; especially, these days, in the modern mass media, the means of global communication, by complex technologies, which circulate meanings between different cultures on a scale and with a speed hitherto unknown in history. (This is the focus of **du Gay**, ed., 1997.) Meaning is also produced whenever we express ourselves in, make use of, consume or appropriate cultural 'things'; that is, when we incorporate them in different ways into the everyday rituals and practices of daily life and in this way give them value or significance. Or when we weave narratives, stories—and fantasies—around them. (This is the focus of **Mackay**, ed., 1997.) Meanings also regulate and organize our conduct and practices—they help to set the rules, norms and conventions by which social life is ordered and governed. They are also, therefore, what those who wish to govern and regulate the conduct and ideas of others seek to structure and shape. (This is the focus of **Thompson**, ed., 1997.) In other words, the question of meaning arises in relation to *all* the different moments or practices in our 'cultural circuit'—in the construction of identity and the marking of difference, in production and consumption, as well as in the regulation of social conduct. However, in all these instances, and at all these different institutional sites, one of the privileged 'media' through which meaning is produced and circulated is *language*.

So, in [Hall's] book, where we take up in depth the first element in our 'circuit of culture', we start with this question of meaning, language and representation. Members of the same culture must share sets of concepts, images and ideas which enable them to think and feel about the world, and thus to interpret the world, in roughly similar ways. They must share, broadly speaking, the same 'cultural codes'. In this sense, thinking and feeling are themselves 'systems of representation', in which our concepts, images and emotions 'stand for' or represent, in our mental life, things which are or may be 'out there' in the world. Similarly, in order to *communicate* these meanings to other people, the participants to any meaningful exchange must also be able to use the same linguistic codes—they must, in a very broad sense, 'speak the same language'. This does not mean that they must all, literally, speak German or French or Chinese. Nor does it mean that they understand perfectly what anyone who speaks the same language is saying. We mean 'language' here in a much wider sense. Our partners must speak enough of the same language to be able to 'translate' what 'you' say into what 'I' understand, and vice versa. They must also be able to read visual images in roughly similar ways. They must be familiar with broadly the same ways of producing sounds to make what they would both recognize as 'music'. They must all interpret body language and facial expressions in broadly similar ways. And they must know how to translate their feelings and ideas into these various languages. Meaning is a dialogue—always only partially understood, always an unequal exchange.

Why do we refer to all these different ways of producing and communicating meaning as 'languages' or as 'working like languages'? How do languages work? The simple answer is that languages work through *representation*. They are 'systems of representation'. Essentially, we can say that all these practices 'work like languages', *not* because they are all written or spoken (they are not), but because they all use some element to stand for or represent what we want to say, to express or communicate a thought, concept, idea or feeling. Spoken language uses sounds, written language uses words, musical language uses notes on a scale, the 'language of the body' uses physical gesture, the fashion industry uses items of clothing, the language of facial expression uses ways of arranging one's features, television uses digitally or electronically produced dots on a screen, traffic lights use red, green and amber—to 'say something'. These elements—sounds, words, notes, gestures, expressions, clothes—are part of our natural and material world; but their importance for language is not what they *are* but what they *do*, their function. They construct meaning and transmit it. They signify. They don't have any clear meaning *in themselves*. Rather, they are the vehicles or media which *carry meaning* because they operate as *symbols*, which stand for or represent (i.e. symbolize) the meanings we wish to communicate. To use another metaphor, they function as *signs*. Signs stand for or *represent* our concepts, ideas and feelings in such a way as to enable others to 'read', decode or interpret their meaning in roughly the same way that we do.

Language, in this sense, is a signifying practice. Any representational system which functions in this way can be thought of as working, broadly speaking, according to the principles of representation through language. Thus photography is a representational system, using images on light-sensitive paper to communicate photographic meaning about a particular person, event or scene. Exhibition or display in a museum or gallery can also be thought of as 'like a language', since it uses objects on display to produce certain meanings about the subject-matter of the exhibition. Music is 'like a language' in so far as it uses musical notes to communicate feelings and ideas, even if these are very abstract, and do not refer in any obvious way to the 'real world'. (Music has been called 'the most noise conveying the least information'.) But turning up at football matches with banners and slogans, with faces and bodies painted in certain colours or inscribed with certain symbols, can also be thought of as 'like a language'—in so far as it is a symbolic practice which gives meaning or expression to the idea of belonging to a national culture, or identification with one's local community. It is part of the language of national identity, a discourse of national belongingness. Representation, here, is closely tied up with both identity and knowledge. Indeed, it is difficult to know what 'being English', or indeed French, German, South African or Japanese, *means* outside of all the ways in which our ideas and images of national identity or national cultures have been represented. Without these 'signifying' systems, we could not take on such identities (or indeed reject them) and consequently could not build up or sustain that common 'life-world' which we call a culture.

So it is through culture and language *in this sense* that the production and circulation of meaning takes place. The conventional view used to be that 'things' exist in the material and natural world; that their material or natural characteristics are what determines or constitutes them; and that they have a perfectly clear meaning, *outside* of how they are represented. Representation, in this view, is a process of secondary importance, which enters into the field only after things have been fully formed and their meaning constituted. But since the 'cultural turn' in the human and social sciences, meaning is thought to be *produced*—constructed—rather than simply 'found'. Consequently, in what has come to be called a 'social constructionist approach', representation is conceived as entering into the very constitution of things; and thus culture is conceptualized as a primary or 'constitutive' process, as important as the economic or material 'base' in shaping social subjects and historical events—not merely a reflection of the world after the event.

'Language' therefore provides one general model of how culture and representation work, especially in what has come to be known as the *semiotic* approach—*semiotics* being the study or 'science of signs' and their general role as vehicles of meaning in culture. In more recent years, this preoccupation with meaning has taken a different turn, being more concerned, not with the detail of how 'language' works, but with the broader role of *discourse* in culture. Discourses are ways of referring to or constructing knowledge about a particular topic of practice: a cluster (or *formation*) of ideas, images and practices, which provide ways of talking about, forms of knowledge and conduct associated with, a particular topic, social activity or institutional site in society. These *discursive formations*, as they are known, define what is and is not appropriate in our formulation of, and our practices in relation to, a particular subject or site of social activity; what knowledge is considered useful, relevant and 'true' in that context; and what sorts of persons or 'subjects' embody its characteristics. 'Discursive' has become the general term used to refer to any approach in which meaning, representation and culture are considered to be constitutive.

There are some similarities, but also some major differences, between the *semiotic* and the *discursive* approaches ... One important difference is that the *semiotic* approach is concerned with the *how* of representation, with how language produces meaning—what has been called its 'poetics'; whereas the *discursive* approach is more concerned with the *effects and consequences* of representation—its 'politics'. It examines not only how language and representation produce meaning, but how the knowledge which a particular discourse produces connects with power, regulates conduct, makes up or constructs identities and subjectivities, and defines the way certain things are represented, thought about, practised and studied. The emphasis in the *discursive* approach is always on the historical specificity of a particular form or 'regime' of representation: not on 'language' as a general concern, but on specific *languages* or meanings, and how they are deployed at particular times, in particular places. It points us towards greater historical specificity—the way representational practices operate in concrete historical situations, in actual practice.

The general use of language and discourse as models of how culture, meaning and representation work, and the 'discursive turn' in the social and cultural sciences which has followed, is one of the most significant shifts of direction in our knowledge of society which has occurred in recent years. The discussion around these two versions of 'constructionism'—the semiotic and discursive approaches—is threaded through and developed in the six chapters which follow. The 'discursive turn' has not, of course, gone uncontested. You will find questions raised about this approach and critiques offered, as well as different variants of the position explored, by the different authors in [Hall's] volume. Elsewhere in [the]series (in **Mackay**, ed., 1997, for example) alternative approaches are explored, which adopt a more 'creative', expressive or performative approach to meaning, questioning, for example, whether it makes sense to think of music as 'working like a language'. However, by and large, with some variations, the chapters ... adopt a broadly 'constructionist' approach to representation and meaning.

1. REPRESENTATION, MEANING AND LANGUAGE

In this chapter we will be concentrating on one of the key processes in the 'cultural circuit' (see **du Gay, Hall et al.**, 1997 ...)—the practices of *representation*. The aim of this chapter is to introduce you to this topic, and to explain what it is about and why we give it such importance in cultural studies.

The concept of representation has come to occupy a new and important place in the study of culture. Representation connects meaning and language to culture. But what exactly do people mean by it? What does representation have to do with culture and meaning? One common-sense usage of the term is as follows: 'Representation means using language to say something meaningful about, or to represent, the world meaningfully, to other people.' You may well ask, 'Is that all?' Well, yes and no. Representation *is* an essential part of the process by which meaning is produced and exchanged between members of a culture. It *does* involve the use of language, of signs and images which stand for or represent things. But this is a far from simple or straightforward process, as you will soon discover.

How does the concept of representation connect meaning and language to culture? In order to explore this connection further, we will look at a number of different theories about how language is used to represent the world. Here we will be drawing a distinction between three different accounts or theories: the *reflective*, the *intentional* and the *constructionist* approaches to representation. Does language simply reflect a meaning which already exists out there in the world of objects, people and events (*reflective*)? Does language express only what the speaker or writer or painter wants to say, his or her personally intended meaning (*intentional*)? Or is meaning constructed in and through language (*constructionist*)? You will learn more in a moment about these three approaches.

Most of the chapter will be spent exploring the *constructionist* approach, because it is this perspective which has had the most significant impact on cultural studies in recent years. This chapter chooses to examine two major variants or models of the constructionist approach—the *semiotic* approach, greatly influenced by the great Swiss linguist, Ferdinand de Saussure, and the *discursive* approach, associated with the French philosopher and historian, Michel Foucault. Later chapters in [Hall's] book will take up these two theories again, among others, so you will have an opportunity to consolidate your understanding of them, and to apply them to different areas of analysis. Other chapters will introduce theoretical paradigms which apply constructionist approaches in different ways to that of semiotics and Foucault. All, however, put in question the very nature of representation. We turn to this question first.

1.1 Making Meaning, Representing Things

What does the word **representation** really mean, in this context? What does the process of representation involve? How does representation work?

To put it briefly, representation is the production of meaning through language. The *Shorter Oxford English Dictionary* suggests two relevant meanings for the word:

1. To represent something is to describe or depict it, to call it up in the mind by description or portrayal or imagination; to place a likeness of it before us in our mind or in the senses; as, for example, in the sentence, 'This picture represents the murder of Abel by Cain.'
2. To represent also means to symbolize, stand for, to be a specimen of, or to substitute for; as in the sentence, 'In Christianity, the cross represents the suffering and crucifixion of Christ.'

The figures in the painting *stand in the place of*, and at the same time, *stand for* the story of Cain and Abel. Likewise, the cross simply consists of two wooden planks nailed together; but in the context of Christian belief and teaching, it takes on, symbolizes or comes to stand for a wider set of meanings about the crucifixion of the Son of God, and this is a concept we can put into words and pictures.

Activity 1

Here is a simple exercise about representation. Look at any familiar object in the room. You will immediately recognize what it is. But how do you *know* what the object is? What does 'recognize' mean?

Now try to make yourself conscious of what you are doing—observe what is going on as you do it. You recognize what it is because your thought-processes decode your visual perception of the object in terms of a concept of it which you have in your head. This must be so because, if you look away from the object, you can still *think* about it by conjuring it up, as we say, 'in your mind's eye'. Go on—try to follow the process as it happens: There is the object … and there is the concept in your head which tells you what it is, what your visual image of it *means*.

Now, tell me what it is. Say it aloud: 'It's a lamp'—or a table or a book or the phone or whatever. The concept of the object has passed through your mental representation of it to me *via* the word for it which you have just used. The word stands for or represents the concept, and can be used to reference or designate either a 'real' object in the world or indeed even some imaginary object, like angels dancing on the head of a pin, which no one has ever actually seen.

This is how you give meaning to things through language. This is how you make sense of the world of people, objects and events, and how you are able to express a complex thought about those things to other people, or communicate about them through language in ways which other people are able to understand.

Why do we have to go through this complex process to represent our thoughts? If you put down a glass you are holding and walk out of the room, you can still *think* about the glass, even though it is no longer physically there. Actually, you can't think with a glass. You can only think with *the concept* of the glass. As the linguists are fond of saying, 'Dogs bark. But the concept of "dog" cannot bark or bite.' You can't speak with the actual glass, either. You can only speak with the *word* for glass—GLASS—which is the linguistic sign which we use in English to refer to objects which you drink water out of. This is where *representation* comes in. Representation is the production of the meaning of the concepts in our minds through language. It is the link between concepts and language which enables us to *refer* to either the 'real' world of objects, people or events, or indeed to imaginary worlds of fictional objects, people and events.

So there are *two* processes, two **systems of representation**, involved. First, there is the 'system' by which all sorts of objects, people and events are correlated with a set of concepts or *mental representations* which we carry around in our heads. Without them, we could not interpret the world meaningfully at all. In the first place, then, meaning depends on the system of concepts and images formed in our thoughts which can stand for or 'represent' the world, enabling us to refer to things both inside and outside our heads.

Before we move on to look at the second 'system of representation', we should observe that what we have just said is a very simple version of a rather complex process. It is simple enough to see how we might form concepts for things we can perceive—people or material objects, like chairs, tables and desks. But we also form concepts of rather obscure and abstract things, which we can't in any simple way see, feel or touch. Think, for example, of our concepts of war, or death, or friendship or love. And, as we have remarked, we also form concepts about things we never have seen, and possibly can't or won't ever see, and about people and places we have plainly made up. We may have a clear concept of, say, angels, mermaids, God, the Devil, or of Heaven and Hell, or of Middlemarch (the fictional provincial town in George Eliot's novel), or Elizabeth (the heroine of Jane Austen's *Pride and Prejudice*).

We have called this a *'system* of representation'. That is because it consists, not of individual concepts, but of different ways of organizing, clustering, arranging and classifying concepts, and of establishing complex relations between them. For example, we use the principles of similarity and difference to establish relationships between concepts or to distinguish them from one another. Thus I have an idea that in some respects birds are like planes in the sky, based on the fact that they are similar because they both fly—but I also have an idea that in other respects they are different, because one is part of nature whilst the other is man-made. This mixing and matching of relations between concepts to form complex ideas and thoughts is possible because our concepts are arranged into different classifying systems. In this example, the first is based on a distinction between flying/not flying and the second is based on the distinction between natural/man-made. There are other principles of organization like this at work in all conceptual systems: for example, classifying according to sequence—which concept follows which—or causality—what causes what—and so on. The point here is that we are talking about, not just a random collection of concepts, but concepts organized, arranged and classified into complex relations with one another. That is what our conceptual system actually is like. However, this does not undermine the basic point. Meaning depends on the relationship between things in the world—people, objects and events, real or fictional—and the conceptual system, which can operate as *mental representations* of them.

Now it could be the case that the conceptual map which I carry around in my head is totally different from yours, in which case you and I would interpret or make sense of the world in totally different ways. We would be incapable of sharing our thoughts or expressing ideas about the world to each other. In fact, each of us probably does understand and interpret the world in a unique and individual way. However, we are able to communicate because we share broadly the same conceptual maps and thus make sense of or interpret the world in roughly similar ways. That is indeed what it means when we say we 'belong to the same culture'. Because we interpret the world in roughly similar ways, we are able to build up a shared culture of meanings and thus construct a social world which we inhabit together. That is why 'culture' is sometimes defined in terms of 'shared meanings or shared conceptual maps' (see **du Gay, Hall et al.**, 1997).

However, a shared conceptual map is not enough. We must also be able to represent or exchange meanings and concepts, and we can only do that when we also have access to a shared language. Language is therefore the second system of representation involved in the overall process of constructing meaning. Our shared conceptual map must be translated into a common language, so that we can correlate our concepts and ideas with certain written words, spoken sounds or visual images. The general term we use for words, sounds or images which carry meaning is *signs*. These signs stand for or represent the concepts and the conceptual relations between them which we carry around in our heads and together they make up the meaning-systems of our culture.

Signs are organized into languages and it is the existence of common languages which enable us to translate our thoughts (concepts) into words, sounds or images, and then to use these, operating as a language, to express meanings and communicate thoughts to other people. Remember that the term 'language' is being used here in a very broad and inclusive way. The writing system or the spoken system of a particular language are both obviously 'languages'. But so are visual images, whether produced by hand, mechanical, electronic, digital or some other means, when they are used to express meaning. And so are other things which aren't 'linguistic' in any ordinary sense: the 'language' of facial expressions or of gesture, for example, or the 'language' of fashion, of clothes, or of traffic lights. Even music is a 'language', with complex relations between different sounds and chords, though it is a very special case since it can't easily be used to reference actual things or objects in the world (a point further elaborated in **du Gay**, ed., 1997, and **Mackay**, ed., 1997). Any sound, word, image or object which functions as a sign, and is organized with other signs into a system which is capable of carrying and expressing meaning is, from this point of view, 'a language'. It is in this sense that the model of meaning which I have been analysing here is often described as a 'linguistic' one; and that all the theories of meaning which follow this basic model are described as belonging to 'the linguistic turn' in the social sciences and cultural studies.

At the heart of the meaning process in culture, then, are two related 'systems of representation'. The first enables us to give meaning to the world by constructing a set of correspondences or a chain of equivalences between things—people, objects, events, abstract ideas, etc.—and our system of concepts, our conceptual maps. The second depends on constructing a set of correspondences between our conceptual map and a set of signs, arranged or organized into various languages which stand for or represent those concepts. The relation between 'things', concepts and signs lies at the heart of the production of meaning in language. The process which links these three elements together is what we call 'representation'.

1.2 Language and Representation

Just as people who belong to the same culture must share a broadly similar conceptual map, so they must also share the same way of interpreting the signs of a language, for only in this way can meanings be effectively exchanged between people. But how do we know which concept stands for which thing? Or which word effectively represents which concept? How do I know which sounds or images will carry, through language, the meaning of my concepts and what I want to say with them to you? This may seem relatively simple in the case of visual signs, because the drawing, painting, camera or TV image of a sheep bears a resemblance to the animal with a woolly coat grazing in a field to which I want to refer. Even so, we need to remind ourselves that a drawn or painted or digital version of a sheep is not exactly like a 'real' sheep. For one thing, most images are in two dimensions whereas the 'real' sheep exists in three dimensions.

Visual signs and images, even when they bear a close resemblance to the things to which they refer, are still signs: they carry meaning and thus have to be interpreted. In order to interpret them, we must have access to the two systems of representation discussed earlier: to a conceptual map which correlates the sheep in the field with the concept of a 'sheep'; and a language system which in visual language, bears some resemblance to the real thing or 'looks like it' in some way. This argument is clearest if we think of a cartoon drawing or an abstract painting of a 'sheep', where we need a very sophisticated conceptual and shared linguistic system to be certain that we are all 'reading' the sign in the same way. Even then we may find ourselves wondering whether it really is a picture of a sheep at all. As the relationship between the sign and its referent becomes less clear-cut, the meaning begins to slip and slide away from us into uncertainty. Meaning is no longer transparently passing from one person to another …

So, even in the case of visual language, where the relationship between the concept and the sign seems fairly straightforward, the matter is far from simple. It is even more difficult with written or spoken language, where words don't look or sound anything like the things to which

Figure 7-2. *William Holman Hunt, Our English Coasts,* Strayed Sheep, *1852.*

they refer. In part, this is because there are different kinds of signs. Visual signs are what are called *iconic* signs. That is, they bear, in their form, a certain resemblance to the object, person or event to which they refer. A photograph of a tree reproduces some of the actual conditions of our visual perception in the visual sign. Written or spoken signs, on the other hand, are what is called *indexical*.

They bear no obvious relationship at all to the things to which they refer. The letters T, R, E, E, do not look anything like trees in nature, nor does the word 'tree' in English sound like 'real' trees (if indeed they make any sound at all!). The relationship in these systems of representation between the sign, the concept and the object to which they might be used to refer is entirely *arbitrary*. By 'arbitrary' we mean that in principle any collection of letters or any sound in any order would do the trick equally well. Trees would not mind if we used the word SEERT—'trees' written backwards—to represent the concept of them. This is clear from the fact that, in French, quite different letters and a quite different sound is used to refer to what, to all appearances, is the same thing—a 'real' tree—and, as far as we can tell, to the same concept a large plant that grows in nature. The French and English seem to be using the same concept. But the concept which in English is represented by the word, TREE, is represented in French by the word, ARBRE.

1.3 Sharing the Codes

The question, then, is: how do people who belong to the same culture, who share the same conceptual map and who speak or write the same language (English) know that the arbitrary combination of letters and sounds that makes up the word, TREE, will stand for or represent the concept 'a large plant that grows in nature'? One possibility would be that the objects in the world themselves embody and fix in some way their 'true' meaning. But it is not at all clear that real trees *know* that they are trees, and even less clear that they know that the word in English which represents the concept of themselves is written TREE whereas in French it is written ARBRE! As far as they are concerned, it could just as well be written COW or VACHE or indeed XYZ. The meaning is *not* in the object or person or thing, nor is it *in* the word. It is we who fix the meaning so firmly that, after a while, it comes to seem natural and inevitable. The meaning is *constructed by the system of representation*. It is constructed and fixed by the *code*, which sets up the correlation between our conceptual system and our language system in such a way that, every time we think of a tree, the code tells us to use the English word TREE, or the French word ARBRE. The code tells us that, in our culture—that is, in our conceptual and language codes—the concept 'tree' is represented by the letters T, R, E, E, arranged in a certain sequence, just as in Morse code, the sign for V (which in World War II Churchill made 'stand for' or represent 'Victory') is Dot, Dot, Dot, Dash, and in the 'language of traffic lights', Green = Go! and Red = Stop!

One way of thinking about 'culture', then, is in terms of these shared conceptual maps, shared language systems and the *codes which govern the relationships of translation between them*. Codes fix the relationships between concepts and signs. They stabilize meaning within different languages and cultures. They tell us which language to use to convey which idea. The reverse is also true. Codes tell us which concepts are being referred to when we hear or read which signs. By arbitrarily fixing the relationships between our conceptual system and our linguistic systems (remember, 'linguistic' in a broad sense), codes make it possible for us to speak and to hear intelligibly, and establish the translatability between our concepts and our languages which enables meaning to pass from speaker to hearer and be effectively communicated within a culture. This translatability is not given by nature or fixed by the gods. It is the result of a set of social conventions. It is fixed socially, fixed in culture. English or French or Hindi speakers have, over time, and without conscious decision or choice, come to an unwritten agreement, a sort of unwritten cultural covenant that, in their various languages, certain signs will stand for or represent certain concepts. This is what children learn, and how they become, not simply biological individuals but cultural subjects. They learn the system and conventions of representation, the codes of their language and culture, which equip them with cultural 'know-how' enabling them to function as culturally competent subjects. Not because such knowledge is imprinted in their genes, but because they learn its conventions and so gradually *become* 'cultured persons'—i.e. members of their culture. They unconsciously internalize the codes which allow them to express certain concepts and ideas through their systems of representation—writing, speech, gesture, visualization, and so on—and to interpret ideas which are communicated to them using the same systems.

You may find it easier to understand, now, why meaning, language and representation are such critical elements in the study of culture. To belong to a culture is to belong to roughly the same conceptual and linguistic universe, to know how concepts and ideas translate into different languages, and how language can be interpreted to refer to or *reference* the world.

To share these things is to see the world from within the same conceptual map and to make sense of it through the same language systems. Early anthropologists of language, like Sapir and Whorf, took this insight to its logical extreme when they argued that we are all, as it were, locked into our cultural perspectives or 'mind-sets', and that language is the best clue we have to that conceptual universe. This observation, when applied to all human cultures, lies at the root of what, today, we may think of as cultural or linguistic *relativism*.

Activity 2

You might like to think further about this question of how different cultures conceptually classify the world and what implications this has for meaning and representation.

The English make a rather simple distinction between sleet and snow. The Inuit (Eskimos) who have to survive in a very different, more extreme and hostile climate, apparently have many more words for snow and snowy weather. Consider the list of Inuit terms for snow from the Scott Polar Research Institute in Table 7-1. There are many more than in English, making much finer and more complex distinctions. The Inuit have a complex classificatory conceptual system for the weather compared with the English. The novelist Peter Hoeg, for example, writing about Greenland in his novel, *Miss Smilla's Feeling For Snow* (1994, pp. 5–6), graphically describes 'frazzil ice' which is 'kneaded together into a soapy mash called porridge ice, which gradually forms free-floating plates, pancake ice, which one, cold, noonday hour, on a Sunday, freezes into a single solid sheet'. Such distinctions are too fine and elaborate even for the English who are always talking about the weather! The question, however, is—do the Inuit actually experience snow differently from the English? Their language system suggests they conceptualize the weather differently. But how far is our experience actually bounded by our linguistic and conceptual universe?

One implication of this argument about cultural codes is that, if meaning is the result, not of something fixed out there, in nature, but of our social, cultural and linguistic conventions, then meaning can never be *finally* fixed. We can all 'agree' to allow words to carry somewhat different meanings—as we have for example, with the word 'gay', or the use, by young people, of the word 'wicked!' as a term of approval. Of course, there must be *some* fixing of meaning in language, or we would never be able to understand one another. We can't get up one morning and suddenly decide to represent the concept of a 'tree' with the letters or the word VYXZ, and expect people to follow what we are saying. On the other hand, there is no absolute or final fixing of meaning. Social and linguistic conventions do change over time. In the language of modern managerialism, what we used to call 'students', 'clients', 'patients' and 'passengers' have all become 'customers'. Linguistic codes vary significantly between one language and another. Many cultures do not have words for concepts which are normal and widely acceptable to us. Words constantly go out of common usage, and new phrases are coined: think, for example, of the use of 'down-sizing' to represent the process of firms laying people off work. Even when the actual words remain stable, their connotations shift or they acquire a different nuance. The problem is especially acute in translation. For example, does the difference in English between

Snow		ice	siku
blowing—	piqtuluk	—pan, broken—	siqumniq
is snowstorming	piqtuluktuq	—ice water	immiugaq
falling—	qanik	melts—to make water	immiuqtuaq
—is falling;—is snowing	qaniktuq	candle—	illauyiniq
light falling—	qaniaraq	flat—	qairniq
light—is falling	qaniaraqtuq	glare—	quasaq
first layer of—in fall	apilraun	piled—	ivunrit
deep soft—	mauya	rough—	ivvuit
packed—to make water	aniu	shore—	tugiu
light soft—	aquluraq	shorefast—	tuvaq
sugar—	pukak	slush—	quna
waterlogged, mushy—	masak	young—	sikuliaq
—is turning into *masak*	masaguqtuaq		
watery—	maqayak		
wet—	misak		
wet falling—	qanikkuk		
wet—is falling	qanikkuktuq		
—drifting along a surface	natiruvik		
—is drifting along a surface	natiruviktuaq		
—lying on a surface	apun		
snowflake	qanik		
is being drifted over with—	apiyuaq		

Table 7-1. *Inuit terms for snow and ice*

know and *understand* correspond exactly to and capture exactly the same conceptual distinction as the French make between *savoir* and *connaitre*? Perhaps; but can we be sure?

The main point is that meaning does not inhere *in* things, in the world. It is constructed, produced. It is the result of a signifying practice—a practice that *produces* meaning, that *makes things mean*.

1.4 Theories of Representation

There are broadly speaking three approaches to explaining how representation of meaning through language works. We may call these the reflective, the intentional and the constructionist or constructivist approaches. You might think of each as an attempt to answer the questions, 'where do meanings come from?' and 'how can we tell the "true" meaning of a word or image?'

In the **reflective approach**, meaning is thought to lie in the object, person, idea or event in the real world, and language functions like a mirror, to *reflect* the true meaning as it already exists in the world. As the poet Gertrude Stein once said, 'A rose is a rose is a rose'. In the fourth century BC, the Greeks used the notion of *mimesis* to explain how language, even drawing and painting, mirrored or imitated Nature; they thought of Homer's great poem, *The Iliad,* as 'imitating' a heroic series of events. So the theory which says that language works by simply reflecting or imitating the truth that is already there and fixed in the world, is sometimes called 'mimetic'.

Of course there is a certain obvious truth to mimetic theories of representation and language. As we've pointed out, visual signs do bear some relationship to the shape and texture of the objects which they represent. But ... , a two-dimensional visual image of a *rose* is a sign—it should not be confused with the real plant with thorns and blooms growing in the garden. Remember also that there are many words, sounds and images which we fully well understand but which are entirely fictional or fantasy and refer to worlds which are wholly imaginary—including, many people now think, most of *The Iliad*! Of course, I can use the word 'rose' to *refer* to real, actual plants growing in a garden, as we have said before. But this is because I know the code which links the concept with a particular word or image. I cannot *think* or *speak* or *draw* with an actual rose. And if someone says to me that there is no such word as 'rose' for a plant in her culture, the actual plant in the garden cannot resolve the failure of communication between us. Within the conventions of the different language codes we are using, we are both right—and for us to understand each other, one of us must learn the code linking the flower with the word for it in the other's culture.

The second approach to meaning in representation argues the opposite case. It holds that it is the speaker, the author, who imposes his or her unique meaning on the world through language. Words mean what the author intends they should mean. This is the **intentional approach**. Again, there is some point to this argument since we all, as individuals, do use language to convey or communicate things which are special or unique to us, to our way of seeing the world. However, as a general theory of representation through language, the intentional approach is also flawed. We cannot be the sole or unique source of meanings in language, since that would mean that we could express ourselves in entirely private languages. But the essence of language is communication and that, in turn, depends on shared linguistic conventions and shared codes. Language can never be wholly a private game. Our private intended meanings, however personal to us, have to *enter into the rules, codes and conventions of language* to be shared and understood. Language is a social system through and through. This means that our private thoughts have to negotiate with all the other meanings for words or images which have been stored in language which our use of the language system will inevitably trigger into action.

The third approach recognizes this public, social character of language. It acknowledges that neither things in themselves nor the individual users of language can fix meaning in language. Things don't *mean:* we *construct* meaning, using representational systems—concepts and signs. Hence it is called the constructivist or **constructionist approach** to meaning in language. According to this approach, we must not confuse the *material* world, where things and people exist, and the *symbolic* practices and processes through which representation, meaning and language operate. Constructivists do not deny the existence of the material world. However, it is not the material world which conveys meaning: it is the language system or whatever system we are using to represent our concepts. It is social actors who use the conceptual systems of their culture and the linguistic and other representational systems to construct meaning, to make the world meaningful and to communicate about that world meaningfully to others.

Of course, signs may also have a material dimension. Representational systems consist of the actual *sounds* we make with our vocal chords, the *images* we make on light-sensitive paper with cameras, the *marks* we make with paint on canvas, the digital *impulses* we transmit electronically. Representation is a practice, a kind of 'work', which uses material objects and effects. But the *meaning* depends, not on the material quality of the sign, but on its *symbolic function*. It is because a particular sound or word *stands for, symbolizes or represents* a concept that it can function, in language, as a sign and convey meaning—or, as the constructionists say, signify (sign-i-fy).

1.5 The Language of Traffic Lights

The simplest example of this point, which is critical for an understanding of how languages function as representational systems, is the famous traffic lights example. A traffic light is a machine which produces different coloured lights in sequence. The effect of light of different wavelengths on the eye—which is a natural and material phenomenon—produces the sensation of different colours. Now these things certainly do exist in the material world. But it is our culture which breaks the spectrum of light into different colours, distinguishes them from one another and attaches names—Red, Green, Yellow, Blue—to them. We use a way of *classifying* the colour spectrum to create colours which are different from one another. We *represent* or symbolize the different colours and classify them according to different colour-concepts. This is the conceptual colour system of our culture. We say 'our culture' because, of course, other cultures may divide the colour spectrum differently. What's more, they certainly use different actual *words* or *letters* to identify different colours: what we call 'red', the French call 'rouge' and so on. This is the linguistic code—the one which correlates certain words (signs) with certain colours (concepts), and thus enables us to communicate about colours to other people, using 'the language of colours'.

But how do we use this representational or symbolic system to regulate the traffic? Colours do not have any 'true' or fixed meaning in that sense. Red does not mean 'Stop' in nature, any more than Green means 'Go'. In other settings, Red may stand for, symbolize or represent 'Blood' or 'Danger' or 'Communism'; and Green may represent 'Ireland' or 'The Countryside' or 'Environmentalism'. Even these meanings can change. In the 'language of electric plugs', Red used to mean 'the connection with the positive charge' but this was arbitrarily and without explanation changed to Brown! But then for many years the producers of plugs had to attach a slip of paper telling people that the code or convention had changed, otherwise how would they know? Red and Green work in the language of traffic lights because 'Stop' and 'Go' are the meanings which have been assigned to them in our culture by the code or conventions governing this language, and this code is widely known and almost universally obeyed in our culture and cultures like ours—though we can well imagine other cultures which did not possess the code, in which this language would be a complete mystery.

Let us stay with the example for a moment, to explore a little further how, according to the constructionist approach to representation, colours and the 'language of traffic lights' work as a signifying or representational system. Recall the *two* representational systems we spoke of earlier. First, there is the conceptual map of colours in our culture—the way colours are distinguished from one another, classified and arranged in our mental universe. Secondly, there are the ways words or images are correlated with colours in our language—our linguistic colour-codes. Actually, of course, a *language* of colours consists of more than just the individual words for different points on the colour spectrum. It also depends on how they function in relation to one another—the sorts of things which are governed by grammar and syntax in written or spoken languages, which allow us to express rather complex ideas. In the language of traffic lights, it is the sequence and position of the colours, as well as the colours themselves, which enable them to carry meaning and thus function as signs.

Does it matter which colours we use? No, the constructionists argue. This is because what signifies is not the colours themselves but (a) the fact that they are different and can be distinguished from one another; and (b) the fact that they are organized into a particular sequence—Red followed by Green, with sometimes a warning Amber in between which says, in effect, 'Get ready! Lights about to change'. Constructionists put this point in the following way. What signifies, what carries meaning—they argue—is not each colour in itself nor even the concept or word for it. It is *the difference between Red and Green* which signifies. This is a very important principle, in general, about representation and meaning … Think about it in these terms. If you couldn't differentiate between Red and Green, you couldn't use one to mean 'Stop' and the other to mean 'Go'. In the same way, it is only the difference between the letters P and T which enable the word SHEEP to be linked, in the English language code, to the concept of 'the animal with four legs and a woolly coat', and the word SHEET to 'the material we use to cover ourselves in bed at night'.

In principle, any combination of colours—like any collection of letters in written language or of sounds in spoken language—would do, provided they are sufficiently different not to be confused. Constructionists express this idea by saying that all signs are 'arbitrary'. 'Arbitrary' means that there is no natural relationship between the sign and its meaning or concept. Since Red only means 'Stop' because that is how the code works, in principle any colour would do, including Green. It is the code that fixes the meaning, not the colour itself. This also has wider implications for the theory of representation and meaning in language. It means that signs themselves cannot fix meaning. Instead, meaning depends on *the relation between* a sign and a concept which is fixed by a code. Meaning, the constructionists would say, is 'relational'.

Activity 3

Why not test this point about the arbitrary nature of the sign and the importance of the code for yourself? Construct a code to govern the movement of traffic using two different colours—Yellow and Blue—as in the following:

When the yellow light is showing, …

Now add an instruction allowing pedestrians and cyclists only to cross, using Pink.

Provided the code tells us clearly how to read or interpret each colour, and everyone agrees to interpret them in this way, any colour will do. These are just colours, just as the word SHEEP is just a jumble of letters. In French the same animal is referred to using the very different linguistic sign MOUTON. Signs are arbitrary. Their meanings are fixed by codes.

As we said earlier, traffic lights are machines, and colours are the material effect of light-waves on the retina of the eye. But objects—things—can also function as signs, provided they have been assigned a concept and meaning within our cultural and linguistic codes. As signs, they work symbolically—they represent concepts, and signify. Their effects, however, are felt in the material and social world. Red and Green function in the language of traffic lights as signs, but they have real material and social effects. They regulate the social behaviour of drivers and, without them, there would be many more traffic accidents at road intersections.

1.6 Summary

We have come a long way in exploring the nature of representation. It is time to summarize what we have learned about the constructionist approach to representation through language.

Representation is the production of meaning through language. In representation, constructionists argue, we use signs, organized into languages of different kinds, to communicate meaningfully with others. Languages can use signs to symbolize, stand for or reference objects, people and events in the so-called 'real' world. But they can also reference imaginary things and fantasy worlds or abstract ideas which are not in any obvious sense part of our material world. There is no simple relationship of reflection, imitation or one-to-one correspondence between language and the real world. The world is not accurately or otherwise reflected in the mirror of language. Language does not work like a mirror. Meaning is produced within language, in and through various representational systems which, for convenience, we call 'languages'. Meaning is produced by the practice, the 'work', of representation. It is constructed through signifying—i.e. meaning-producing—practices.

How does this take place? In fact, it depends on two different but related systems of representation. First, the concepts which are formed in the mind function as a system of mental representation which classifies and organizes the world into meaningful categories. If we have a concept for something, we can say we know its 'meaning'. But we cannot communicate this meaning without a second system of representation, a language. Language consists of signs organized into various relationships. But signs can only convey meaning if we possess codes which allow us to translate our concepts into language—and vice versa. These codes are crucial for meaning and representation. They do not exist in nature but are the result of social conventions. They are a crucial part of our culture—our shared 'maps of meaning'—which we learn and unconsciously internalize as we become members of our culture. This constructionist approach to language thus introduces the symbolic domain of life, where words and things function as signs, into the very heart of social life itself.

All this may seem rather abstract. But we can quickly demonstrate its relevance by an example from painting.

Look at the painting of a still life by the Spanish painter, Juan Sanchez Cotán (1521–1627), entitled *Quince, Cabbage, Melon and Cucumber* (Figure 7-3). It seems as if the painter has made every effort to use the 'language of painting' accurately to reflect these four objects, to capture or 'imitate nature'. Is this, then, an example of a reflective or mimetic form of representation—a painting reflecting the 'true meaning' of what already exists in Cotán's kitchen? Or can we find the operation of certain codes?

Figure 7-3. *Juan Cotán,* Quince, Cabbage, Melon and Cucumber, *c. 1602.*

Language, Politics, and Power

By Robin Lakoff

The trial lawyers are selecting a jury for a capital case. The defense attorney is trying to discover whether a prospective juror is capable of voting either for death or for life imprisonment without parole in this case. The juror knows only the bare outlines of the case; what she might do *now* is less germane than what she might eventually be able to decide at the end of the trial. At the same time, the judge has cautioned against "speculative" questions, which are apt to elicit meaningless responses.

The defense tries: "Can you envision any mitigation outweighing the fact of two women having been killed?" The prosecutor objects to "envision" as encouraging "fantasy," meaning speculation: it's in his interests to constrain the form of this question as much as possible. The two go back and forth rancorously; the judge threatens contempt; finally, the prosecutor remarks that he doesn't see why the defense is insisting on this form of the question: "It's just semantics."

In other words, give me the decision, since it really doesn't matter, it's only words. But he and his adversary have just spent most of fifteen minutes wrangling over that very choice of words, wasting valuable time and trying the judge's temper (always inadvisable). Either he believes that language counts enough to justify the time and the risk, or he's behaving totally irrationally. Since he is a professional and since trial lawyers with any competence (and even his opponents acknowledge out of his hearing that he's pretty good) calculate their every move, we have to assume he has a good idea of what he's doing and has concluded that depriving the defense of this choice of phraseology is worth risking the judge's displeasure. But his remark does cause both the judge and the defense attorney to cool down and step back; and the latter agrees that, well, the words don't really matter so much after all, and tries something else.

Lawyers are particularly dependent on language; their success is a measure of their linguistic proficiency, their recognition of the ability of language to create, highlight, and distort reality, their power to force language to do their will. At the same time, they know that actual evidence—the blood-stained garment, the eyewitness identification—has potency where mere words fail. Their ambivalence, then, is not surprising. But they are not alone in taking a dual position on the relation between language and power.

Politics and power is a smoother juncture than *language and power*. The words belong to the same semantic realm. *Politics* is the game of *power;* politics allocates power and utilizes it. The promise of power makes politics worth the effort. Power in particular is vibrant, the very word conjuring up images of strength, force, action. Whether positive or negative, those images are strong. Power is physical: it changes reality, it gets things done or undoes what exists. It creates effects that can be seen, felt, and measured. Power is the engine of the 747 that lifts the behemoth off the runway; it is the "plow that broke the plains"; the firing squad; the nuclear bomb under discussion at the conference table; the parent who can give or withhold the keys to the car; the boss who can hire or fire at whim. All of these operate to change reality for better or worse. We may admire power or resent it, but we can see its operations and feel its physical effects on us. Politics distributes that power, determines who has it and how it can be used; it is the handmaiden of power—or better, its parliamentarian.

Politics, we might say, is the physicality of power made psychological, power as sentient humans experience it and use it. It is applicable to every form of human interaction. International politics concerns large and abstract entities: countries forming alliances; competing for trade or influence, determining war and peace. National politics allocates the perquisites of power (wealth, influence, comfort) among competing groups and convinces those who control that allocation that one choice rather than another represents their best interests.

Politics also works at an individual level, as we have come to realize recently. Families have political structures, like businesses and friendships.[1] As in the larger contexts, there are winners and losers: winners get the power, the means to do as they choose and to define their own actions and those of others. Losers get destroyed or devalued or otherwise reduced in status. In one form or another, power informs all human relationships and politics is the instrument by which power creates and defines those relations. Both are real; both have physical forms and effects.

But how does language, the third member of the triad, fit in alongside the other two? Not very well, it might seem. Language is as abstract as power is concrete; it is impalpable, an artifact of the mind rather than the body. Only metaphorically does language *strike* us or *move* us, and it changes us only in indirect ways. But as politics brings the brute physical reality of power into the sphere of the human mind and heart, language is the means of that transformation. Language drives politics and determines the success of political machinations. Language is the initiator and interpreter of power relations. Politics is language.

At the same time, language is politics. How well language is used translates directly into how well one's needs are met, into success or failure, climbing to the top of the hierarchy or settling around the bottom, into good or bad relationships, intimate and distant. Language allocates power through politics, defines and determines it, decides its efficacy.

When societies of humans confront ideas and realities that are profoundly moving and disturbing, they do something uniquely and essentially human: they create culture around them—myth, religion, art, and eventually science. By such means what feels chaotic and beyond control is reduced to the lawful and understood, the predictable. And around language all of these explainers have flourished, as culture after culture has sought ways to make sense of the intrinsic duality: language as rooted, one foot in the real and tangible, the other in the airy world of imagination; language as powerful and as powerless, and in fact, improbably, both at once.

One way we come to terms with unsatisfactory dichotomies like these (that is, dichotomies that are psychologically comforting but not accurate representations of observed fact) is to construct systems, mythological, legal, or artistic. Society after society offers two distinct views of language, its role, its power, and its tangibility, coexisting necessarily if uneasily. As advanced as we believe our culture is, as far as we have transcended, as we think, the rationalizations of myth and superstition, we enshrine those dualities as surely as anyone else.

THE TWO FACES OF LANGUAGE

Language is powerful; language is power. Language is a change-creating force and therefore to be feared and used, if at all, with great care, not unlike fire. Change itself is frightening, as is that which creates it (especially in abstract and undetectable ways).

Particularly evident in less scientifically advanced cultures (but by no means absent even from the most sophisticated) is the use of language in ceremonials, *as* ceremony: language as the maker of a mood, and thereby a force for efficacy. In fairy tales we encounter magic words: say "abracadabra" or "shazam!" and *something happens,* by the utterance of the words alone. But they must be just those words: slip on a syllable, misplace a word, and nothing happens, or worse. In old Roman law, for a contract to be valid the contracting parties had to pronounce a set of words (some so archaic they were no longer understood) precisely right, or it was null and void. Today contracts must be written according to specific and rigorous legal rules that do not necessarily contribute to clarity of meaning; if not, they can be broken.

Many fairy tales and legends center around the power of language for good or evil, the dangers of an ill-considered word, the value of silence. The Fisherman's Wife intemperately uses the last of her wishes to grow a sausage to her husband's nose. The young queen is warned that her brothers will be released from enchantment as geese only if she can spend seven years without saying a single word. Misunderstanding of language brings disaster. Odysseus tells the Cyclops, "My name is No-man." When he puts out the monster's eye, the latter's friends ask him who did it, against whom shall they seek revenge? "No-man injured me," says the creature; and his fellows reply that, if no man injured him, there's nothing to be done, it was his own fault. By learning Rumpelstiltskin's name, the princess achieves power over him.

Finally, like other societies we have proverbs and other guiding expressions that warn us to be careful what we say, that language is potent:

> Silence is golden.
> The pen is mightier than the sword.
> The tongue is the hangman of the mouth.

And, like other societies, we identify and reward those persons whose use of language is especially skillful. "From his tongue fell words sweeter than honey," says the *Iliad* of Nestor, who would otherwise, as an old man in warfare, which values youth, be a man without a role. Today we speak bemusedly of the "Great Communicator," wondering how Ronald Reagan's use of language seemingly rendered him impervious to criticism.

Along with testimony to the very real powers of language, we also find a collection of reverse folklore: tales, customs, and proverbs that use magical thinking to deny the potency of language by stressing its differences from the reality of deeds. Language, in this view, is weak, empty air:

by itself, without the force of reality behind it, it counts for nothing, accomplishes nothing. So, for instance, when it is important that language be forceful, we attempt to buttress it in some tangible ways. Thus, since treaties are no more than words on paper, cultures have from ancient times required backups: hostages exchanged between the negotiating parties to guarantee that they meant what they said. Often, too, under these and other solemn conditions (in courtrooms to the present day), oaths are exacted of those whose words must be truthful for the procedure to "work." Nowadays we often think of these oaths as mere words themselves, *pro forma* declarations. But they originated as dire threats: to swear by a deity, take the name of a god in vain, was to invite vengeance. Not only was lying ruinous to the perjurer, but the ruin, and its cause, were obvious to all. The very words *testify, testimony* recall one ancient link between words and reality. They are derived from the Latin *testes,* its meaning the same as in current English. In swearing, the Roman male (women were not allowed to participate in these procedures in the earliest times) placed his right hand upon his genitals; the implication was that, if he swore falsely, they would be rendered sterile—a potent threat. The need for such desperate measures suggests a fear (or hope) that words alone are not enough. We have proverbs and sayings to the same effect, from "No woman was ever seduced by a book" (in Federal Judge John M. Woolsey's 1933 opinion overturning the obscenity laws to allow the importation of James Joyce's *Ulysses* into the United States) to the more traditional:

> Talk is cheap.
> Words are feminine, deeds masculine.
> Sticks and stones may break my bones, but words can never harm me.

And when we wish to undermine another person's political use of language, we call it "mere words," "empty rhetoric," "just semantics."

So we are continually faced with the paradox that those words, pure air, that have no physical reality and that we are encouraged to disparage, have potent consequences in the real world every day: in the decisions of courtrooms, the actions of governments, the pronouncements of institutions, and the relationships with our nearest and dearest.

> "The question is," said Alice, "whether you *can* make words mean so many different things."
> "The question is," said Humpty Dumpty, "which is to be master—that's all."[2]

The paradox is not unsolvable. Words can be powerful or not. They can affect reality or not. Words become powerful because they can be used as tools: like a hammer or a gun, they don't make changes by themselves, but through a human being's use of them, skillful or clumsy. Guns don't kill people, the National Rifle Association likes to say: people kill people. By the same token, words don't change reality, people change reality. But like guns, words make it possible for people to achieve the effects they seek.

Language is a symbol, not a reality; the map, not the territory, as Alfred Korzybski, the general semanticist, put it many years ago. But symbols have tremendous potency, often more than the reality they stand for, because so much volatile emotion attaches to them. We all agree, for instance, that the American flag is a "symbol" of this country and its ideals: freedom, democracy, justice, and so forth. But as recent history demonstrates, the same people who are ready to rise up, in arms if necessary, in defense of "the flag" are quite willing to stand by uncaringly as blatant nonsymbolic injustices are perpetrated.

THE LANGUAGE OF PUBLIC PERSUASION

If we agree that language can be a source of power, we tend to see that as true for those people with special access to both language and power. If "they" choose, they can use language so skillfully and deceptively that we—the rest of us—will be helpless against them and their stratagems. They know something we don't; they have training we don't. We are the helpless and passive recipients of manipulative communication; they are the users of it and, through it, of us.

We put those special people into two or three major categories: economic persuaders, on the one hand, advertisers and salesmen; and political persuaders, on the other. Sometimes we divide the second into two groups: those who use language especially effectively but legitimately, "politicians" (or "statesmen" if we want to be respectful or they are dead); and those who use it in some illegitimate way, or for some illegitimate purpose, or both—"propagandists." We try from time to time to draw clear lines between the legitimate and the illegitimate persuaders, but too often these lines distinguish those with whose message we are in basic agreement from those whose appeal threatens us. Such a definition, based on the personal preferences of the definer, is not valid. Moreover, advertisers and politicians are not the only skilled users of powerful language: we all have some persuasive skills.

It is true that there are special, learnable skills that give those who have mastered them an advantage over amateurs. But the difference is quantitative, not qualitative. It is not that they know things of which we are totally innocent, but that they are better at the tricks we all know. After all, those smooth persuaders don't require that their audiences be specially trained and prepared, so the strategies they use must be ones we already know how to appreciate, even if we can't use them as effectively. There are some clever new strategies, but they are not ironclad or guaranteed: in fact, one thing both advertisers and politicians know too well is that the public becomes wise to their tactics remarkably fast; they have to keep replacing techniques to keep them working at all.

It is equally true that the twentieth century has provided a host of techniques, tactics, and strategies that render language more potently persuasive than it used to be. The development of modern psychology and the explicit discovery of the unconscious and its mechanisms, on the one hand, provide one route of access; and the development of new media provides another. The two go hand in hand. Freudian concepts, defenses, repression, sexual symbolism, and the rest can be used to get at us where we are not accustomed to being consciously manipulated; television provides a way to bring those messages home to us, where we feel safest and most protected. One of the century's pretty ironies is that public relations, perpetrator of some of the cleverest manipulative techniques, was pioneered by Edward L. Bernays, a nephew of Freud's on both sides of his family (his mother, Freud's sister, married Freud's wife's brother). But the human mind is if nothing else ingenious: no sooner does the therapist, or the propagandist, find a way to undermine the barrier of the defenses, than the mind finds a new and stronger defense. We can fight back, even if this version of who uses language and how is correct.

We construct worst-case scenarios, like Newspeak in Orwell's *Nineteen Eighty-Four*: a manipulation of language that not only empowers its creators but renders them unassailable.

But that scenario is only an exaggeration of our fears about the way it really is now. There is an amorphous *them* out there who know all the tricks and use them to play us like violins. Without our realizing it, we are moved to do as they say. Some years back Vance Packard's *The Hidden Persuaders* gave substance to those fears with the concept of subliminal advertising. Later research showed the fear to be exaggerated: subliminal advertising had only the most limited range of usefulness, if any, and claims for its effectiveness were greatly overrated. But we were left with the vague sense that *they* were using language in ways that *we* could neither fathom nor defend ourselves against; they had all the good words and the bad words; we were marionettes on their strings.

This kind of thinking has its comforting and its frightening aspects. It comforts us to divide the world in two, *them* versus *us*. It is comforting to think of ourselves as virtuous and innocent; and when we make stupid or dangerous decisions, to attribute that to *them* and their illicit persuasive techniques. But at the same time, that division makes us feel helpless and reinforces any tendencies we already have toward passivity. We don't try to be intelligent consumers: why bother? It's beyond us, utterly foreign, totally mysterious. We can't stop those sneaky communicators by heading them off at the pass with equal and opposite analytic strategies. Rather, we demand that the lawmakers protect us with legislation that covers each imaginable case. Since each case is different, such legislation is a patent impossibility, but we continue to hope and be outraged when we keep getting taken in and nobody steps in to prevent it.

EVERYBODY IS A POLITICIAN

This scenario, attractive though it may be, is inaccurate. We are not mere passive recipients of manipulative communicative strategies. Orwell and other worriers ignore the truth, whether unpleasant or happy: we all manipulate language, and we do it all the time. Our every interaction is political, whether we intend it to be or not; everything we do in the course of a day communicates our relative power, our desire for a particular sort of connection, our identification of the other as one who needs something from us, or vice versa. Often, perhaps usually, we are unaware of these choices; we don't realize that we are playing for high stakes even in the smallest of small talk. We may enter the transaction knowingly or not, we may function mainly as manipulator or manipulatee—but we are always involved in persuasion, in trying to get another person to see the world or some piece of it our way, and therefore to act as we would like them to act. If we succeed, we have power. Mostly we are without formal training, we work by intuition, and some of us have better instincts in language use than others. But we are all trying to do it, all the time.

Even the most innocent and well-intentioned conversational gambits entail power strategies. Most of us have participated, in one role or another, in dialogues similar to the following ones. On their face, most look guileless; no one is using finely honed Orwellian methods. But what is really going on in each?

He: Wanna go to the movies?
She: Oh, I don't know. … Do you?

This is one traditional form of the male-female game (although others can play as well). He has made a suggestion, and it's up to her to take it or propose another. Either course would entail self-assertion. She would be stating and taking responsibility for a personal preference. Particularly if she makes a counterproposal, she has to worry if it doesn't work out well. She will feel guilty. If she is deficient in self-esteem, she is likely to be fearful of that outcome—better, then, to avoid any sort of assertion and leave the decision making up to him. But then, she never does get to do what she wants; and if the decision is good, it proves to both of them that he's smart and she's not. It's a form of linguistic politics, to be sure: she is trying to retain what power she has by never being proved incompetent; by leaving the decision up to him, she gets him to make the commitment and run all risks. Women are often castigated for this sort of behavior, but it arises out of deep fears of incompetence that societies too often foist upon female children.

> She: Tell me how to fix this Xerox machine.
> He: Oh, don't you worry about that, honey. Leave it to me.

Now the shoe is on the other foot. This vignette illustrates one way that men maintain control over women, by reducing their self-confidence (and thereby leading to scenes like the first example). What is happening on the surface is different from the meaning at a deeper level. On the surface, he is being polite and considerate: he's saving her time and energy by doing the job himself. The "honey" offers intimacy and caring. But look again. The hidden message he is conveying is that she would not benefit from being told how to do it herself (which would give her power in the future: she wouldn't need to keep asking him for help). She probably couldn't do it anyway; fixing machinery is a man's job. Her only hope is to be able to cajole him into helping her each time she encounters a snag: she has to rely on him; her functioning is dependent on his goodwill. His words convey to her that she *should* lack self-confidence; she isn't really competent. And if she knows what's good for her, she'll remember to be deferential to him, now and in the future. He has set up their future relationship with himself in charge. The "honey" only helps in this: he assumes an intimacy that is not reciprocal (she probably can't call him "sweetie-pie" back), and this puts them in a relation analogous to adult-child (an adult can call a child "honey," but not vice versa). It does not matter whether the woman in the first case, and the man in the second, openly acknowledge that these were their intentions, or passionately deny it; this is the function of such language uses. They are strongly political; power is the topic under discussion.

Gender is not the only battlefield where struggles for power are waged:

> A: Have some of this chocolate mousse.
> B: I *told* you I was on a diet!

This colloquy can be perfectly innocent conversation on both sides, but it can also be treacherous. The interpretation depends on just how the sentences are said (as is generally true, bare words on the printed page tell us little). Much depends, too, upon what has preceded them: If A has been "complaining" about his or her inability to gain weight, then we might read into the offer some invidious intent. On the other hand, if A is the well-meaning hostess, it would be unreasonable to draw any negative inference. Now consider B's rejoinder: If it is accompanied by the marks of resentment and outrage—tears, a raised voice, a reproachful expression—it might signify, "You don't really care about me," or even, "I bet you want me to be fat." Since neither is said aloud in so many words, A is effectively helpless. A's possible hostility is not asserted by B, but presupposed, meaning that A cannot fend off the attack by saying, for instance, in response to B's outburst, "Of course, you are important to me," or "I like you just the way you are." The use of implications such as B's is an old and effective way of playing conversational politics: B wins the point because A cannot counterattack or defend. Nothing has been *said* that requires a defense, so that anything A says runs the risk of seeming to protest too much, getting the unfortunate A into still hotter water.

The games are not necessarily face to face. Imagine this telephone conversation:

A: So, I was wondering if you were free on Saturday, because I was thinking—
B: Oh, excuse me, there goes my other line. [*Hangs up.*]

With each innovation in communicative technology, the political possibilities are multiplied, and the more savvy and well-equipped the communicator, the more numerous the opportunities. The telephone has always allowed us to invent excuses for getting out of a conversation that, in person, would be impossible ("Oops, there's the doorbell!"). The phone is also good for making demands and accusations, since it's hard for most of us to behave badly to someone else while making eye contact. (It's probably also easier to lie on the telephone, and harder for the hearer to spot.) The initiator of the phone call is in a position of power: the caller chooses the time, has the facts ready, and normally terminates the call. (Clever people learn to play "telephone tag" to their advantage: when you're up to something, never allow the other person to call you back.) The recent advent of call-waiting has only added fuel to the fire. Advice columns not infrequently print letters from people outraged by being put on hold and hung up on by others, especially when the latter initiated the call. "Well," says B, when confronted in the preceding example, "what was I to do? The phone beeped! I had to answer!" True enough, but alongside the perfectly practical reasons for B's behavior and call-waiting in general, the innovation allows the user ingenious political manipulations and, at worst, convinces the victim on the other end that some political game is being played. The covert message that B may or may not intend, but A is likely to receive, is: "Let me see if it's someone more interesting on the other line." And if B "has to hang up" on A, the latter will be sure that someone more interesting is, in fact, waiting.

It is equally possible to play power games in person, in relatively public settings:

A: I have an appointment with Dr. Snarf at eleven forty-five.
B: Oh, Doctor's running late. Please have a seat.

Like call-waiting, being kept waiting by professionals engenders furious reactions, from private grumbling to letters to advice columnists. Tales are prevalent of people billing their doctors for time wasted sitting in offices, or even suing them in small claims court for compensation. It is not so much the actual time spent sitting there, nor the dog-eared copy of *Today's Health* that galls; it is the attitude and, specifically, the subliminal message: "Doctor is more important than you. You'd better be subservient, because you need us more than we need you." Salt is rubbed in the wounds (dubious medical procedure) by the receptionist's use of the honorific title "Doctor." Under few circumstances in this culture are people referred to (not addressed) by title alone; my secretary, for instance, does not tell callers, "Professor's fighting her computer. Call back later." In fact, professors are addressed as "Professor" only by non-academics—a mark of outsidership. The practice is most common in the rigid stratifications of the courtroom: a lawyer may be referred to (as well as addressed) as "Counsel," a judge as "His Honor" (though this is relatively uncommon). But in the egalitarian world of every day, most of us aspire to a general, at least superficial, *pro forma* equality. In fact, the only ordinary-world analogue to the receptionist's "Doctor" is "Mommy" and "Daddy" with children. ("Hi there, dear. Is Mommy home?") Even this may seem patronizing to some children if used by those outside the nuclear family. "Doctor," like "Mommy," presupposes a strongly unequal relationship and thus both justifies the enforced wait and makes objection to it more difficult, just as you'd better not talk back to Mommy. The polite imperative ("Please") that follows may make matters even worse: "What choice do I have?" the patient wonders. The politeness may be as fake as the aspidistra in the corner.

In each of the preceding imaginary dialogues, at least one of the participants uses linguistic form to achieve political ends, to create or reinforce a power imbalance that would, in turn, lead to further advantages. The linguistic politician may have worked the other into a position of responsibility for a past or future course of action; of inadequacy on any of various societally agreed-upon grounds; or of inferiority, requiring one to take what is offered however unsatisfactory it is. And, in most of the cases examined, the game is won by hidden means. No receptionist says, "I want you to know that Dr. Snarf considers you vermin, and you should be glad he lets you wait in his office at all." No, that is actionable. "Doctor is running late" has much the same subliminal effect, but if you are miffed, any attorney you consult will tell you it's in your mind, not in anything that was said. You bear the responsibility for the invidious interpretation. Politics is piled on politics.

MICRO AND MACRO

Whether speaking as a professional or in everyday life, one still plays the linguistic game according to hidden agendas, the unsaid being far more potent than the said. Furthermore, power drives power: those who already have it (advertisers and politicos) parlay it into authority, and their superior status enhances the credibility of their message, which in turn enhances their power over us. It is the use of our deepest and least-acknowledged fear, shame, desires, by speakers whose authority emanates from their apparent transcendence over those base needs, that allows linguistic power games to work between intimates and colleagues, in dealing with professionals, from higher-ups to lower-downs, and from powerful individuals to groups.

We can call one kind of power-oriented discourse *micropolitics;* the other, *macropolitics.* The first involves the development and use of strategies that create and enhance power differences among individuals; the second, strategies of group management. Micropolitical tactics tend to be personal, hinging on the establishment of a relationship and determining its rules: how close will the participants be? Who will make the decisions? Who will be dominant in which areas? How direct or indirect will communication be? Usually these negotiations are unconscious and implicit: participants are not aware that they have taken place; the relationship just seems to fall into a pattern. To bring these issues into the open, to articulate them, is to *metacommunicate,* to communicate about communication. This metacommunication is fraught with perils and, therefore, generally avoided. But the achievement of honesty in intimate relations, and the getting of satisfaction in more distant ones, is often contingent upon running those risks; otherwise, the games will continue.

Macropolitical discourse determines power relationships within and between groups, individuals functioning in cohesive units: nations, religions, races, and institutions, for instance. It may concern a struggle for power between two or more such groups, or the assertion by an individual of authority over a group. Linguistic power tactics are most apparent in struggles over a nation's choice of an "official" language as in Quebec. The frequency with which such issues develop into armed conflict demonstrates that they are more than a matter of administrative efficiency; the decision, by implicitly calling into question the individual identity of speakers of the nonchosen languages, thereby suggests that some identities are more valuable and valid than others. Macropolitics also covers the special languages of institutions: If your doctor tells you what your illness is in language you don't understand, or if laws and trial procedures are so cumbersome that only a lawyer can negotiate them, as an outsider you are rendered powerless over your fate; the institutions, by their development of and insistence upon special languages, both justify and underscore their authority and legitimacy and shield their members from scrutiny by the larger community. In this way they perpetuate the status quo, as official languages do, and are intended to do. Language can be a force for change; but, if controlled by those entrenched in power, it is a force for conservatism.

There are mixtures of micro and macro. For instance, women in most cultures use language differently from men, who, typically, hold political, social, and economic power. Therefore, women's ways of using language are disparaged as illogical (since men define logic according to their own practices). Therefore, it makes sense to deny women power, since they would not use it well. Therefore, too, women tend to get short shrift at all levels: in ordinary conversation, they are interrupted and the topics they broach ignored; in groups, they are not called on to speak, and if they are, their contributions are unrecognized or incorrectly attributed to others (men); women who seek power at the highest levels are seen as "shrill," "strident," "bitches," or slaves to raging hormones—often all the above. To change this and other situations where the linguistically proficient dominate those who are not, we must understand how we and others use linguistic politics.

ANALYZING THE LANGUAGE GAME

Whether in power or out of it, one plays the language game. Even one who has the upper hand and is an abuser of others will in turn be abused by someone still higher or more skilled, or by someone who possesses particular expertise. Only by learning how power is assigned and determined through linguistic structure, and what power is equitable, what not, can we work to develop fairer ways of communicating. Then, at last, we can stop being mystified and victimized by those who wield the power inherent in language. Then we can decide, in Humpty Dumpty's words, "which is to be master."

NOTES

The concept of the family as politically structured has been given much attention in recent years in several fields. A couple of the seminal works in this area are:

1. J. Haley 1963 and R. D. Laing 1967.
2. Lewis Carroll, *Through the Looking-Glass* (n.d.), p. 214.

Dude

By Scott Kiesling

INTRODUCTION

Older adults, baffled by the new forms of language that regularly appear in youth cultures, frequently characterize young people's language as "inarticulate," and then provide examples that illustrate the specific forms of linguistic mayhem performed by "young people nowadays." For American teenagers, these examples usually include the discourse marker *like*, rising final intonation on declaratives, and the address term *dude*, which is cited as an example of the inarticulateness of young men in particular. ... [T]his stereotype views the use of *dude* as unconstrained—a sign of inexpressiveness in which one word is used for any and all utterances. These kinds of stereotypes, of course, are based on a fundamental misunderstanding of the functions and meanings of these linguistic forms. As analyses of *like* and rising intonation have shown (e.g., Guy et al. 1986, McLemore 1991; Andersen 2001; Siegel 2002), these forms are constrained in use and elegantly expressive in meaning. *Dude* is no exception. In this article I outline the patterns of use for *dude*, and its functions and meanings in interaction. I provide some explanations for its rise in use, particularly among young men, in the early 1980s, and for its continued popularity since then.

Indeed, the data presented here confirm that *dude* is an address term that is used mostly by young men to address other young men; however, its use has expanded so that it is now used as a general address term for a group (same or mixed gender), and by and to women. *Dude* is developing into a discourse marker that need not identify an addressee, but more generally encodes the speaker's stance to his or her current addressee(s). The term is used mainly in situations in which a speaker takes a stance of solidarity or camaraderie, but crucially in a nonchalant, not-too-enthusiastic manner. *Dude* indexes a stance of effortlessness (or laziness, depending on the perspective of the hearer), largely because of its origins in the "surfer" and "druggie" subcultures in which such stances are valued. The reason young men use this term is precisely that *dude* indexes this stance of cool solidarity. Such a stance is especially valuable for young men as they navigate cultural Discourses of young masculinity,[1] which simultaneously demand masculine solidarity, strict heterosexuality, and non-conformity.

This indexicality also explains where *dude* appears in discourse structure, and why it tends to be used in a restricted set of speech events. The discussion that follows illuminates not only the meanings and use of this address term, but also the broader linguistic issue of how language-in-use creates and displays social relationships and identities, i.e., how language is socially meaningful. An understanding of the ways in which *dude* works thus leads to a better understanding of how everyday language-in-interaction is related to widespread, enduring cultural Discourses (i.e., the relationship between first- and second-order indexical meanings, in Silverstein's 1996 terms). I focus on gender meanings in this article, and how cultural Discourses of gender are recreated in interaction with the help of *dude*.

The crucial connection between these cultural Discourses and the everyday use of *dude* is the stance of cool solidarity which *dude* indexes. This stance allows men to balance two dominant, but potentially contradictory, cultural Discourses of modern American masculinity: *Masculine solidarity* and *heterosexism*. Connell (1995) argues that different types of masculinities are ordered in Western cultures, and that the most desired and honored in a particular culture is its *hegemonic masculinity*. Along with Carrigan et al. (1987), he shows that heterosexuality is one aspect of hegemonic masculinities in Western cultures, especially the United States. Kimmel (2002:282) argues more forcefully that "homophobia, men's fear of other men, is the animating condition of the dominant definition of masculinity in America, [and] that the reigning definition of masculinity is a defensive effort to prevent being emasculated," where "emasculated" is equivalent to being perceived as gay by other men. At the same time, there is a cultural Discourse of masculine solidarity—close social bonds between men. In this cultural Discourse, a bond with, and loyalty to, other men is a central measure of masculinity. This Discourse is epitomized in the ideal of loyalty within a military unit, as outlined for American war films by Donald (2002), and illustrated vividly in Swofford's (2002) *Jarhead*, a first-person account of the author's experiences as a U.S. Marine in the 1991 Persian Gulf War. Although this ideal of masculine solidarity could be understood to be consonant with the Discourse of heterosexism (i.e., by having a set of loyal close friends, a man need not be afraid that they will think he is gay), on another level masculine solidarity, in emphasizing closeness between men, is opposed to heterosexism, which emphasizes distance between men. Masculine solidarity and heterosexism thus delimit a narrow range of ratified, dominant, and hegemonic relationships between American men, since masculine solidarity implies closeness with other men, while heterosexism entails non-intimacy with other men. *Dude* allows men to create a stance within this narrow range, one of closeness with other men (satisfying masculine solidarity) that also maintains a casual stance that keeps some distance (thus satisfying heterosexism).

What follows provides data for these claims about *dude*, and fleshes out the details. My data are drawn from a number of complementary sources. Survey data come from three surveys of two types performed by classes at the University of Pittsburgh. Ethnographic and interaction data are drawn from my observations in 1993 of an American college fraternity.[2] I also draw from various media sources and from my own experience as a bona fide '*dude*-user' in the 1980s. These multiple sources of data come together to present a consistent picture of the uses, meanings, and recent history of the address term. I will first investigate the wider use of the term, and then excerpt several uses in the fraternity to illustrate its discourse functions and to show how it is used in interaction. I will also discuss the personalities of the men who use *dude* the most in the fraternity, then describe the most salient phonological aspect of the term—a fronted /u/—and possible connections between this aspect of *dude* and the ongoing fronting of this vowel across North America. Finally, I explain the rise and use of *dude* by exploring cultural Discourses of masculinity and American identity more generally in the 1980s.

HISTORY AND ORIGINS

The recent history of *dude* provides insight into its indexicalities as well as its rise in use in the United States. The discussion that follows is based on Hill's (1994) history of the term to the recent past (until approximately the 1980s). *Dudes* were originally old rags, and a *dudesman* a scarecrow. In the latter half of the nineteenth century, "*dude* became synonymous with *dandy* a term used to designate a sharp dresser in the western territories [of the United States]" (321). There was for a time a female version of the word, but it fell out of use. According to Hill, the use of *dude* as an address term developed in the 1930s and 1940s from groups of men, "Urban Mexican-American *pachuchos* and African-American *zoot-suiters*" (323), known for their clothes consciousness. These groups began to use it as an in-group term, and it soon was used as a general form of address among men. It seems that *dude* followed a well-worn linguistic path from stigmatized groups such as urban African Americans and Mexicans to whites through African-American music culture (much as *cool* and *groovy* did). Finally, in the 1980s, "[y]oung people began to use *dude* as an exclamation of delight and/or affection." (Hill 1994:325) Hill predicts that *dude* may follow *fuck* and its derivatives as being able to function in any grammatical slot (or as a single-word utterance that can mean anything in the right context). The history of the term, however, shows that from the time it began to be used as an address term, it was an in-group term that indicated solidarity.

It is this cool solidarity and in-group semantic that has remained with *dude* until the present, and it is the kind of stance indexed when the men in the fraternity use it. However, I show below that, while it is true that *dude* is used as more than simply an address term, it is restricted in where and how it is used grammatically, in discourse structure, and with what intonation.

THE DUDE CORPUS

As an assignment for two introductory undergraduate sociolinguistics classes (in 2001 and 2002), students were required to listen for and record the first 20 tokens of *dude* that they heard throughout a three-day period. They recorded the entire utterance as best as they could remember it, the gender and ethnicity of the speaker and addressee(s), the relationship between speaker and hearer, and the situation. I have compiled the results from both classes into a 519-token Dude Corpus (DC).[3] The impression that *dude* is used by young men (under 30) is confirmed by the survey, but young women also used the term a significant amount, particularly when speaking to other women, as shown in Figure 8-1.[4]

In addition to the overwhelming predominance of male-male uses of *dude* in these data,[5] it is important to note that the second most common speaker-addressee gender type is female-female, while in mixed-gender interactions there were relatively fewer uses of *dude*.

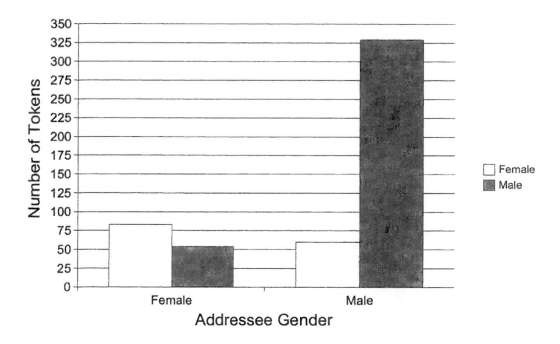

Figure 8-1. *Use of "dude" by gender of speaker and addressee. All interactions are between people under 38 years old.*

This correlational result suggests that *dude* indexes a solidary stance separate from its probable indexing of masculinity, unless for some reason women are apt to be more masculine (and men, less masculine) when speaking to women.

More clues to the solidarity aspect of *dude*'s indexicality can be found in the actual tokens used by women speakers to women addressees. The all-women tokens were not used in simple greetings, but mostly in situations where camaraderie was salient: Only one of the 82 woman-woman tokens (1.2%) were simple greetings (*Hey dude* or *What's up, dude*), as opposed to 7.6% (25/329) greetings in the men's tokens. The women tended to use *dude* 1) when they were commiserating about something bad or being in an unfortunate position; 2) when they were in confrontational situations; or 3) when they were issuing a directive to their addressee. In these last two uses by women, *dude* seems to function to ameliorate the confrontational and/or hierarchical stance of the rest of the utterance.

For example, one token of commiserating was said in a whisper during a class: "Dude, this class is soooo boring." An even clearer example of commiseration (and not masculinity) was recorded after the addressee had been describing a situation in which a man had been trying to 'hit on' her. Following the story, the woman who heard the story replied simply "dude," with "a tone of disbelief and disgust." An instance of a confrontational situation in which *dude* is used was recorded after the addressee had been teasing the speaker, who then said, "Dude, that's just not cool." Finally, a token used with a direct order while in a car: "Dude, turn signal!" There were also several instances of constructed dialogue[6] with men as addressees in the woman-woman tokens, which inflates the woman-woman tokens. However, these tokens also reveal information about the indexicality of *dude*, because all of these constructed dialogue tokens are used to express a stance of distance—or at least non-intimacy—from a man. For example, one token was recorded in the midst of telling a story about talking to a man. In the course of the narrative, the narrator says to the man "I'm like, dude don't touch me!" Such tokens are clearly being used to create stances of *distance* between the speaker and the addressee (*don't touch me*), and these tokens thus reveal the *non-intimate* indexicality of the term.

Dude thus carries indexicalities of both solidarity (camaraderie) and distance (non-intimacy), and can be deployed to create both of these kinds of stance, separately or together. This combined stance is what I call cool solidarity. The expansion of the use *dude* to women is thus based on its usefulness in indexing this stance, separate from its associations with masculinity. *Dude* is clearly used most by young, European-American men, and thus also likely indexes membership in this identity category, but by closely investigating women's use of the term, the separation between the first-order stance index (cool solidarity) and the second-order group-identity index (man) becomes evident. These data also suggest, as would be intuitively predicted by anyone living in North American Anglo culture, that there is an indexical connection between the stance of cool solidarity and that of young Anglo masculinity, and thus an indirect indexical connection, of the kind outlined by Ochs (1992), between *dude* and masculinity.

SELF-REPORT STUDY

The connection between the category 'men' and *dude* was further investigated by a project performed by a language and gender class at the University of Pittsburgh in Fall 2003. This class administered a self-report survey to their friends on the terms *dude*, *babe*, and *yinz* (a Pittsburgh dialect term for second-person plural). Respondents were asked how often they used the term, and then whether they would use the term with particular addressees (boyfriend/girlfriend, close friend, acquaintance, stranger, sibling, parent, boss, and professor) using a Likert scale

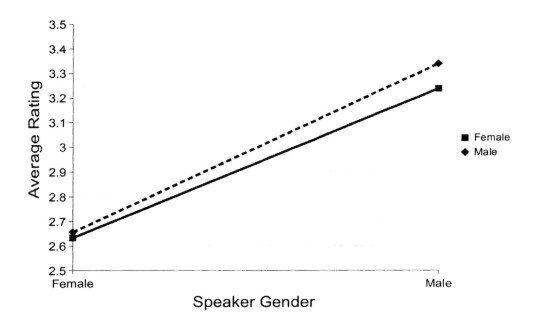

Figure 8-2. *Reported frequency of use of dude by gender of speaker and addressee.*

of 1 to 5. They were also asked why they used the term and what kind of people they typically think use the term.[7]

These self-report data corroborate the findings of the survey above: that *dude* is used primarily by men speaking to other men, but not exclusively so. The highest average frequency rating was for man-man interactions (3.34), but men reported using *dude* with women as well (the average man-woman frequency rating was 3.24). As shown in Figure 8-2, the gender of the survey respondent was more important than the gender of the addressee, since the difference between male and female speakers is greater than the difference between male and female addressees (i.e., the difference between the endpoints of the lines is greater than the difference between the two lines). However, there are again clues that *dude* is restricted to non-intimate solidarity stances. Consider Figure 8-3.[8] The first noticeable pattern in this figure is that the gender of the addressee makes more of a difference to the men than the women: For women respondents (represented by the two solid lines), there is almost no difference between male and female addressees in any category, while for men respondents (the dashed lines), the gender of the addressee makes a striking difference, especially in the close friend category. In fact, the female lines are almost always within the male lines in Figure 8-3. These data thus show that *dude* is associated with a male friendship for the men, and a non-hierarchic relationship for all respondents, indicated by the low values for parent and boss.

In addition, intimacy is *not* indexed by *dude*, especially for the men, as shown by the low ratings in the "heterosexual relationship" (*Hetero*) category. More importantly, the difference between the "different-gender, close-friend" and "heterosexual relationship" category is greater for men than for women (a difference of 0.63 for men and 0.55 for women). The disparity is even greater between "same-gender, close-friend" and "heterosexual relationship" (the difference for men is 1.85, while for women it is 0.33). Thus, intimate relationships with women are

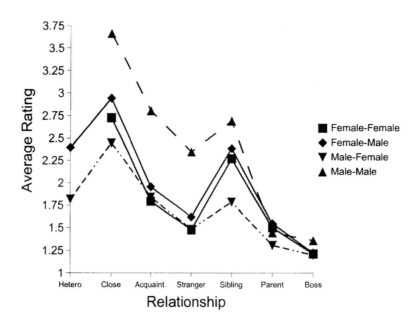

Figure 8-3. *Dude reported use by gender of speaker, addressee (speaker-addressee in the legend), and relationship.*

among the least likely addressee situations in which men will use *dude*, while a close female friend is the most likely woman to be addressed with *dude* by a man. In most simple terms, men report that they use *dude* with women with whom they are close friends, but not with women with whom they are intimate.

This survey, combined with the DC, thus supports the claim that *dude* indexes a complex and somewhat indeterminate combination of distance, casualness, camaraderie, and equality. The survey also suggests that speakers are aware of the association between *dude* use and masculinity: In the open-ended question asking who uses *dude*, all responses suggested men, specifically young, drug-using, men, often with descriptions such as *slacker*, *skater* (one who skateboards), or *druggie*. This second-order indexicality, or metapragmatic awareness (Silverstein 1996, Morford 1997) is one which connects the term to counter-culture, non-serious, masculinity.

These indexicalities are clearly represented in films such as *Fast Times at Ridgemont High* (1982), *Bill and Ted's Excellent Adventure* (1989), *Clerks* (1994), and *Dude, Where's My Car?* (2000), and in other popular representations of the term. In these films, some or all of the young male characters frequently use the term *dude*. The character Jeff Spicoli in *Fast Times at Ridgemont High*, played by Sean Penn, is one of the earliest, perhaps the best known, and most typical, of these characters. This film is a comedy about a year in a southern Californian high school, with Spicoli as the do-nothing, class-cutting, stoned, surfer. While he is clueless and often falls on hard times, Spicoli is consistently laid back, even in exasperation, and especially in encounters with authority. The male characters who use *dude* in the other films mentioned here have similar personalities. Although they manifest in slightly different ways, all take a laid back stance to the world, even if the world proves to be quite remarkable, as in *Bill and Ted's Excellent Adventure* (in which the protagonists travel through time). I was a teenager at the time *Fast Times* was released. The characters in this film resonated with me and my peers, because they represented a distillation of the dominant identity types found in my high school (mostly middle-class Euro-American). As such, these characters, especially Spicoli, became media 'linguistic icons' in Eckert's (2000) terminology. Many young men glorified Spicoli, especially his nonchalant blindness to authority and hierarchical division; in the early eighties we often spoke with Spicoli's voice. At first these quotes were only in stylized situations where we quoted from the movie, but eventually many of the features of Spicoli's speech, especially *dude*, became commonplace as we endeavored to emulate the stance Spicoli takes toward the world. I will return to this film when discussing the rise of *dude*, but for now I present it as more evidence of the stances associated with *dude* as represented in popular media.

Dude has also been featured in comic strips, … [for example] "Zits," which has as its main characters American teenagers. *Dude* is implicated in stereotypes of male communication as inexpressive and monosyllabic (see also Sattel 1983), but here again the speakers are performing an act of solidarity (offering and accepting chewing gum), but with limited enthusiasm. *Dude* is perfect for such an interaction, and again bolsters the understanding of *dude* as indexing cool solidarity, especially among men. … [In] a Doonesbury comic of a dialogue between two male college roommates[, o]ne of the roommates is distressed that the other has stopped calling him *dude*, and then interprets it as a symptom of being a more serious student overall. Here *dude* is clearly indexed with not being serious, since not using *dude* is seen as a symptom of becoming serious. All of these representations suggest that *dude*'s first order indexicality is one of cool solidarity, with a related second order indexicality of men who shun authority and the establishment. Gary Trudeau uses this indexicality for humorous effect when one of the characters in [his comic strip] joins the CIA; the humor is created by the clash of the "slacker" working for the agency that arguably represents the height of establishment power. The indexicalities of *dude* thus encompass not just stances but also specific kinds of masculinity, and the two are intimately bound with one another in an indexical web.

DUDE IN INTERACTION

Next we turn to investigate how this term is used in contextualized interactions among college-aged men in 1993, and to view some examples of its use in interaction, to understand how these indexicalities are put to use, I'll first outline where *dude* appears, and then the various functions it fulfills in interaction.

In reviewing the tokens of *dude* in the tapes from my year's ethnographic work in an American all-male fraternity (see Kiesling 1997, 1998, 2001a, 2001b), and in reviewing the tokens in the DC, I have found that *dude* appears overwhelmingly in utterance-initial or utterance-final position. The frequencies with which *dude* appears in these positions are presented in Table 8-1. It is also used regularly in certain sequential locations in interaction, such as greetings, leave-takings, the prefacing of important information, and exclamations.

Position	N	Frequency
Initial	309	59.5%
Final	140	27.0%
Medial	19	3.7%
Greeting	36	6.9%
Single (*dude* is entire utterance)	7	1.4%
Exclamation with *whoa*	8	1.5%
Total	519	100.0%

Table 8-1. *Frequency of positions of dude. Dude is final in all greetings and exclamations.*

I have also identified at least five specific interactional functions for *dude*. Almost all of its functions overlap and derive from its indexicalities of cool solidarity and laid-back masculinity, although these indexicalities are employed in different ways depending on the function. These functions also show how *dude* encapsulates the men's homosociality, i.e., the small zone of "safe" solidarity between camaraderie and intimacy. These functions include 1) marking discourse structure; 2) exclamation; 3) confrontational stance mitigation; 4) marking affiliation and connection; and 5) signaling agreement:

- **Discourse structure marking.** An individual use of *dude* may indicate some discourse structure, as described below, although a cool solidary stance is simultaneously indexed when *dude* is used in this way.
- **Exclamation.** *Dude* may be used on its own as an exclamation, to express both positive and negative reactions (commonly with another exclamative, especially *whoa*).

- **Confrontational stance attenuator.** *Dude* is often used when the speaker is taking a confrontational or "one-up" stance to the addressee. Through its indexing of solidarity, *dude* can attenuate or ameliorate the confrontation, signaling that the competitive or hierarchical aspect of the utterance is not serious. In the DC, there were many instances of this kind of use, especially in woman-woman situations. This use is as a positive politeness strategy in situations of negative face threat, in the terms of Brown and Levinson's (1987) politeness theory.
- **Affiliation and connection.** When *dude* is used as a true address term (i.e., it identifies the addressee), it is used to indicate a stance of affiliation or connection, but with cool solidarity as well.
- **Agreement.** *Dude* is commonly used when a stance of agreement is taken (either sympathizing with something [the] addressee said, or agreeing with the content of the utterance). As with the affiliation and connection function, when sympathy or agreement is expressed and *dude* is used, this sympathetic stance retains a measure of cool.

These functions are not all mutually exclusive; *dude* can perform more than one function in a single utterance, or left ambiguous. Some examples of each of the functions in use will help us to understand how speakers use this term in particular situations, and how its indexicalities work in these situations.

The first example, in which *dude* is used in its discourse-structure-marking function, is from a narrative told by Pete at the end of a meeting of fraternity members (during 'gavel;' see Kiesling 2001a). In this excerpt, Pete is telling about a road trip that he and Hotdog had taken during the previous weekend, in which they got lost. (This excerpt is not the entire narrative, which is very long and has numerous points which might be counted as evaluation and/or climax.)

Excerpt 1[9]

6	Pete:	I was like fuck it just take this road we'll be there.
7		end up,
8		at one o'clock in the morning,
9		in south Philly.
10		I don't know if any y'all been at south Philly,
11		but it ain't where you wanna be at one o'clock in the morning
12	Hotdog:	it's it's the northeast of Washington DC
13	Pete:	it is it's the southeast of Philadelphia
14		that's what it is.
15		I mean it's southeast
16		**dude**.
17		we're driving a 94 Geo Prism (.) with no tags, (1.1)
18		two White boys,
19		and we're like stuck behind this bu-
20		at one point,
21		we were stuck in an alley,
22		in an alley like cars parked on both sides, (.)
23		behind a bus,
24		and there's like two bars
25		like on both sides.

26	like (1.0) all these black people everywhere.
27	wasted.
28	fucked up.
29	lookin at us.
30	*just like* (1.8)
31	I was scared shitless,
32	I 'as like Hotdog go.
33	he was like there's a bus.
34	I don't care go go (0.7)
35	most nerve-racking time of my life—

Pete's use of *dude* in line 16 marks off an important segment of the narrative, a part in which he tells about the 'danger' he and Hotdog were in. In lines 6–9 he is setting up their arrival in South Philadelphia. In lines 10–15, he describes in general that South Philly is dangerous, with help from Hotdog in line 12, who explains the status of South Philadelphia by relating it to a similar neighborhood in Washington, D.C., with which his audience is familiar. He has some disfluency getting exactly the form he is looking for, and then in line 16 utters *dude*, with a complete intonation contour that has a falling intonation. *Dude* thus serves to break off the string of disfluencies from the following utterances, which Pete "resets" by giving it more volume and beginning with a higher pitch. The utterances following *dude* then resume his evocation of danger more specifically, and the climax of this part of the story comes in lines 26–29, in which he describes the 'dangerous' people around them, and then an evaluation in line 31 (*I was scared shitless*).

In this example, *dude* is not picking out a single addressee: Pete is addressing the entire meeting. Rather, *dude* has two functions related to the narrative structure and purpose. First, it delays the climax and resets the narrative, calling attention to the climax and evaluation to come. In this sense it is a discourse marker rather than an address term. So why does Pete use *dude* here, and not something more "discourse-focused" like *so* or *anyway*, which are sometimes used to return to the main thread of a conversation or narrative once it has been left? The answer is that *dude* also retains its indexicality of cool solidarity, and allows Pete to bring the audience into his story as if he were telling it to one person rather than many. Moreover, it invites the hearers to take Pete's perspective, thus further creating a separation between himself and the dangerous denizens of South Philly. Pete uses *dude* to build involvement, to use Tannen's (1989) term.

Later in the story, before Hotdog begins to co-narrate, Pete again uses *dude*:

Excerpt 2

40	Pete:	[**dude** it was like boys in the hood man ain't no: lie:
41	Hotdog:	[And they're all they're fucked up on crack, wasted
42		they're all lookin' at us they start comin' to the car,
43		so Pete's like FLOOR IT.
44		so I take off (.) and (.)

In this instance, Pete is using *dude* with an exclamatory function. But notice that the statement that follows is also a summary and evaluation of the situation he and Hotdog found themselves in, and continues the same involved, affiliative stance he used in the previous excerpt. We can make this conclusion based on his concurrent use of Southern vernacular language forms in *ain't no lie*, and the address term *man*, which is similar to *dude* but less pervasive in this group.

An instance in which Pete uses *dude* to both attenuate a competitive stance and create connection is shown in the following excerpt from the monopoly game:

Excerpt 3

44	Pete:	Fuckin' ay man.
45		Gimme the red Dave. **Dude**. (1.0)
46	Dave:	No.
47	Pete:	Dave **dude**, **dude** Dave hm hm hm hm
48	Dave:	I'll give you the purple one
49	Pete:	Oh *that's* a good trade

Pete is of course playing with the alliteration between Dave's name and *dude* in line 47 (Dave's real name also has an initial /d/). But Pete's use of *dude* in line 45 is coupled with a bald imperative (*gimme the red*), and *dude* is in fact added almost as an afterthought, with a falling intonation on Dave, before *dude* (although there is no pause between the two words). Dave responds with his own bald refusal (no), which continues the confrontational stance initiated by Pete. The next line serves a purely interactional purpose, as it contains only Dave's name and *dude* repeated once in chiasmus. This 'content-less' use of *dude* then, can only be performing an interactional function (it is not performing a necessary address term function, since Pete also uses Dave's first name). We can understand by Pete's chuckles after his use of the term that he is not taking a truly confrontational stance, so he is probably changing his strategy to get the red property by emphasizing his and Dave's friendship. Dave follows suit in this 'toning down' of the competition; he makes a conciliatory move by offering Pete another property after Pete's initial plea. In this excerpt, then, we see *dude* used in a purely affiliative way, and in its mitigating function, especially useful because Pete is in an inherently competitive but friendly activity (the monopoly game). These uses show how *dude* can be strategically placed so that the confrontation and the competition stays on a playful level. In this sense, it is a framing device as well as a stance indicator, indexing a "play" frame for the men (see Bateson 1972, Tannen 1979).

In the next example, Pete uses *dude* to create a stance of affiliation, but also 'cool.' Pete is in a bar with Dan, an out-of-town friend visiting another fraternity member. In this conversation, Pete agrees with many of the comments Dan enthusiastically makes, but plays down his enthusiasm (see Kiesling 2001b). Particularly important here is that Pete is not just agreeing, but doing so while keeping a cool, nonchalant stance that contrasts with Dan's enthusiasm about playing caps (a drinking game).

Excerpt 4

Dan:	I love playin' caps.
	That's what did me in last-| |last week.

Pete: |that's-|
        Everybody plays that damn game, **dude**.

Pete's use of *dude* in this excerpt matches the nonchalant stance of Pete's statement, thus helping to create that stance.

The next excerpt indexes a similar cool stance, but this time in a meeting. This example is Speed's first comment about which candidate should be elected chapter correspondent in an election meeting (see Kiesling 1997).

Excerpt 5

Speed: Ritchie. I like Ritchie 'cause he's smart
              and he probably (writes really good) too:.
              so let him do it **dude**.

Dude helps Speed create a "stand-offish" stance in this excerpt, as it is used with the phrase *let him do it*. Speed could have used something more active, such as "elect Ritchie," or "we need to put Ritchie in this position," but he frames his comments as a matter of simply stepping aside and letting Ritchie do the job. His relatively short comments are also consistent with this stance. Note also that Speed is speaking not to a single person, but to a roomful of members who are collectively his addressee, as Pete did in Excerpt 1. *Dude* in this case, then, is used purely to help create this stance of non-intervention, letting things take their course.

In the next excerpt, taken from a rush event (a social function held to attract potential members to the fraternity), Saul agrees with a potential member's (or *rush's*) assessment of the University of Virginia men's basketball team.

Excerpt 6

Rush: Junior Burroughs is tough he's gonna be (tough to beat)
Saul: Oh HELL yeah **dude**

This use of *dude* is especially interesting because it appears with an intensifier. The main part of Saul's utterance is his agreement with the rush, as expressed simply by *yeah*. But he intensifies this agreement with the use of *oh hell* before it, with the primary sentence stress on *hell*. This indexes a stance not just of agreement, but of enthusiastic agreement, in contrast to Pete's nonchalant agreement with Dan. This difference is characteristic of Saul and Pete's personal styles: the former more often takes an enthusiastic interpersonal stance while the latter more often takes a cool stance, as we have seen in several instances throughout the book. So it is not surprising that Saul should employ *dude* in a less cool, affiliative stance than Pete. Nevertheless, *dude* still serves to index both affiliation and distance, "toning down" the enthusiasm.

Finally, let us consider an instance of *dude* used in an interview. Mack uses it here in an answer to a question I had asked about who gets elected to offices, and whether the person who works hard or has the most ability actually gets elected to the office. In his answer, Mack takes me into his confidence about "the way things really work."

60	Mack:	You've been getting **dude**, what-
61		and this is, again what I'm coming down to
62	SK:	??
63	Mack:	It really—the guys have been telling you what is supposed to happen
64		they don't know.

Mack here takes a stance of the knowledgeable insider, one he takes habitually (see Kiesling 1997, 1998). In lines 63–64, he creates a dichotomy between what is supposed to happen, and what really happens, which only he and a few others know about. In line 60, he begins this course of argument *you've been getting* refers to the answers I had received from other members about how people are elected to office), and he uses *dude* to signal that he is taking me into his confidence; into the inner circle of members. So here *dude* is functioning in its solidary sense.

Although *dude* is used by almost all the men at some times, some use the term much more than others. As is probably already clear, Pete uses *dude* at least sometimes in many different kinds of speech activities, as does Speed. Hotdog, Mack, and Ram, by contrast, do not use *dude* in meetings, but do use it in in-group narratives. Mack, as we have seen, uses *dude* in the interview, but Hotdog and Ram do not. This pattern is strikingly similar to the patterns for the men's (ING) use I have found (Kiesling 1998), suggesting that there is a similarity in the stances indexed and identities performed by the vernacular variant (-*in*) and *dude*. However, both of these linguistic forms (*dude* and -*in*) can index many kinds of stance while retaining core abstract indexicality of casual, effortless, or non-conformist (in the case of -*in*), and affiliation and "cool" (in the case of *dude*). They overlap in their indexing of effortlessness and cool, and are thus likely to be used by the same men.

In sum, these examples show how the general stances indexed by *dude* can be used as a resource in interaction. By using *dude*, the men are not rigidly encoding a relationship with an addressee, or addressees. Rather, they are using the indexicalities of the term to help create an interpersonal stance, along with many other resources that interact with various parts of context (the nature of the speech event, participants' previous interactions and identities within the institution, etc.). At this point I will thus acknowledge the vagueness with which I have been describing the stance indexed by *dude*, and at the same time argue that this indeterminacy is an aspect of all indexes (see also Silverstein 1996:269). There is no *single* meaning that *dude* encodes without context, and it can be used, it seems, in almost any kind of situation … But we should not confuse flexibility with meaninglessness; rather, the complex of stances indexed by the term—distance, camaraderie, cool, casualness, solidarity—can be made salient through different contexts. *Dude*, then, shows us two important ways indexicality, and meaning more generally, work in language. First, the meaning-making that speakers do when using language in interaction is about stance-taking at least as much as it is about denotation. Neither is this social meaning-making most often focused on signaling group affiliation, or "acts of identity" (LePage and Tabouret-Keller 1985). Rather, it is about *specific* relationships speakers create with each other in *interaction*. Thus (and secondly), we find that meaning is *made* in contextualized interactions; words and sounds are indeterminate *resources* that speakers combine to perform and negotiate stances, which are the primary focus of interaction.

HOW TO SAY DUDE

If context is important to interpretation, then the linguistic- and socio-historical moment in which an utterance takes place is significant. Using *dude* in 2003 is different than using it in 1983, and certainly different than in 1963. This historical view also relates to the manner in which *dude* is pronounced. As shown by Labov (2001:475*ff*), the vowel /u/ is being fronted across North America, especially after coronal onsets. *Dude* is thus a strongly favored environment for this fronting to take place. In fact, *dude* is almost always spoken with a fronted /u/ by the young speakers who use it, especially when it is used in a stylized manner (that is, when someone is performing while using the term, in the sense that they are marking it as not an authentic use of their own). I would suggest that when older speakers pronounce the word with a backed "u," younger speakers identify the token as unauthentic, uncool, or simply "old." There is thus a close connection between the fronted /u/ and *dude*. Phonology and lexis work together in this case to further make *dude*, in its most general sense, indexical of American youth. I would not go so far as to suggest that *dude* is driving this sound change, although Labov does argue that outliers (which are likely to be found in *dude* given its stylized uses) are important in the continuation of a sound change. While *dude* is not causing nor necessarily driving the sound change, it is certainly emblematic of it, and is one of the ways that the sound change has been imbued with social meanings.

DISCUSSION

The casual and cool stance that is the main indexicality of *dude* is an important aspect of men's homosociality in North America. While masculine solidarity is a central cultural Discourse of masculinity in North America, this solidarity is nevertheless ideally performed without much effort or dependence. *Dude* helps men maintain this balance between homosociality and hierarchy. It is not surprising, then, that *dude* has spread so widely among American men, because it encodes a central stance of masculinity. If *dude* use by men is related to the dominant Discourses of masculinity, then why did this term expand significantly in middle-class, European-American youth in the early eighties? What are the cultural currents that made the particular kind of masculinity and stance indexed by *dude* desirable for young men (i.e., for the post-baby-boom generation)?

Youth in general often engage in practices that are meant to express rebellion, or at least differentiate them in some way from older generations (Brake 1985). In language, this nonconformity can be seen in the "adolescent peak"—the rise in non-standard language use by teenagers (see Labov 2001:101*ff*), a peak which flattens out as teenagers become older. The rise of *dude* likely took place because cool solidarity became a valuable non-conformist stance for youth in the 1980s. While I can find no studies analyzing dominant Discourses of masculinity in the 1980s, I would characterize this time—the Reagan years particularly—as one in which 'yuppie consumerism' and wealth accumulation were hegemonic. Edley and Wetherell (1995:141), moreover, comment that

> it could be argued that the 1980s were characterized by the reinstatement of a new form of puritanist philosophy, once again emphasizing hard work and traditional family values (Levitas 1986). Typified in the character played by Michael Douglas in the film *Wall Street*, the

stereotypical or ideal 1980s' man was portrayed as a hard, aggressive person single-mindedly driven by the desire for power and status.

In perhaps the most well-known scenes in *Fast Times at Ridgemont High*, a conflict is set up between Spicoli and his history teacher, Mr. Hand. In the first scene Spicoli is late on the first day of class, and in the second, he has a pizza delivered to class. Mr. Hand is represented as a demanding, uptight teacher who takes stances that could hardly be further from those Spicoli adopts. Mr. Hand, of course, becomes outraged that Spicoli does not even seem to realize his behavior is unacceptable. The conflict between Spicoli and Mr. Hand is an allegory for competing norms of masculinity, from the eyes of a 1980s' teenager, and shows how the stances associated with *dude* are set up in conflict with stances of hard work and other "adult" values.[10] The 'slackers' in the film *Clerks* are also the opposite of Edley and Wetherell's "hard, aggressive person single-mindedly driven by the desire for power and status," but in *Clerks*, the fun-loving of Spicoli has been replaced by nihilism: more "why bother?" than "who cares?" All of these portrayals, which can be connected to the use of *dude*, are part of a general American cultural Discourse which represents the post-baby boom generation as having little or no career ambition—a whole generation of slackers. There is also an aspect of the surfer subculture associated with *dude* that valorizes not just skill and success, but the appearance of *effortless*, yet authentic, achievement. This kind of success is also quite different from the 1980s' image of success based on hard work. So there are many ways in which the stances indexed by *dude* were (and still are) non-conformist and attractive to adolescents.

This view of the motivations for the rise of *dude* in American English shows us that sociolinguistic norms are much more complex than, for example, associating a sound with prestige. The kinds of meanings indexed by language can be numerous, even if connected by a common thread, and change with each use. More importantly, *dude* shows us that it is not just the indexicalities of a form that might change, but that the values and aspirations of the speakers might change as well. What was cool in 1982 is definitely not cool in 2002. In other words, the very definition of prestige changes over time. The casual stance indexed by *dude* is becoming more "prestigious" through the United States, so perhaps it will eventually be used by all ages and in most situations in America. For the time being, it is clear that *dude* is a term that indexes a stance of cool solidarity for everyone, and that it also has second orders of indexicality relating it to young people, young men, and young counter-culture men. It became popular because young men found in *dude* a way to express dissatisfaction with the careerism of the 1980s, and has later been a way of expressing the nihilism of the 1990s. Perhaps we are becoming a nation of skaters and surfers, at least in certain cultural trappings, who only wish for, in Spicoli's words, "tasty waves and cool buds," and *dude* is the harbinger of things to come.

NOTES

1. I use the term *cultural Discourse* in the sense of post-structuralists, following Foucault (1980). Cultural Discourses are similar to ideologies, yet leave open the possibility of contradiction, challenge, and change, and describe more than idea systems, including social practices and structures. For a review of the term, and its relevance to masculinities, see Whitehead (2002). I will always use a capital 'D' with cultural Discourses to distinguish them from the linguistic notion of discourse, or talk-in-interaction.

2. Fraternities are social clubs, with membership typically limited to men, footnotes on college campuses across North America.

3. The corpus results and class assignment are available at http://www.pitt.edu/~kiesling/dude/dude.html. I encourage instructors of linguistics courses to use the survey in their own courses, but please inform me that you have used it and, if possible, the results.

4. 471 out of the total 519 tokens collected, or 91%, were in situations with speakers and addressees under 30. This result may reflect the age population of the class, of course, but it is a relatively valid representation of *dude* use for that age group. In terms of class, most students were middle class or upper working class. Statistics were gathered for ethnicity, with European Americans providing the vast proportion of tokens, but again these results are probably skewed by the predominance of European Americans in the class.

5. These tokens could of course be influenced by who collected them. Both classes had more women than men, however, so if anything women's use of the term has been artificially expanded.

6. Constructed dialogue is more commonly termed *reported speech*, see Tannen 1989 on the motivations for the term constructed dialogue.

7. The survey instrument is included in the appendix. The assignment materials and electronic versions of the survey instrument are available at http://www.pitt.edu/~kiesling/dude/dude.html. I encourage instructors of linguistics, sociolinguistics, and language and gender courses to use the survey in their own courses, but please inform me that you have used it and, if possible, the results.

8. Two of the relationship labels need some explanation. The first is 'Hetero.' This category is heterosexual intimate relationships, labeled on the survey as girlfriend/boyfriend. There were responses for male-male and female-female categories, but it is clear from the students who gathered the data that not all respondents understood the intimate nature of this category for same-sex situations. That is, not all male respondents who gave a rating for 'boyfriend' are homosexual. This confusion makes the response problematic, and so I have removed the same-sex boyfriend/girlfriend data from this, thus making it represent heterosexual relationships only. 'Close' refers to a close friend, and 'Aquaint' is an acquaintance. The rest of the labels should be self-explanatory.

9. Transcription conventions are as follows:
   Each line is roughly a breath group, and unless otherwise noted there is a short pause for breath at the end of each line in the transcripts.

(text)	indicates the accuracy of transcription inside parentheses is uncertain
(?)	indicates an utterance that could be heard but was not intelligible
a:	indicates the segment is lengthened
(# . #)	indicates a pause of #.# seconds
(.)	indicates a pause of less than 0.5 seconds
=	indicates that the utterance continues on the next line without a pause
A|B| | C | D	indicates overlapping speech: B and C are uttered simultaneously, not A nor D.
TEXT	indicates emphasis through amplitude, length, and/or intonation
bu-	indicates an abrupt cutoff of speech
((text))	indicates comments added by the author

10. See http://www.netwalk.com/~truegger/ftrh/ for plot summaries and audio clips of the film, including a "film strip" of the famous scenes (http://www.netwalk.com/~truegger/ftrh/pizza.html).

REFERENCES

Anderson, Gisle. 2001. *Pragmatic Markers and Sociolinguistic Variation: A Relevance-theoretic Approach to the Language of Adolescents*. Amsterdam: John Benjamins.

Bateson, Gregory. 1972. *Steps of an Ecology of Mind*. New York: Ballantine.

Brake, Mike. 1985. *Comparative Youth Culture: The Sociology of Youth Cultures and Youth Subcultures in America, Britain, and Canada*. New York: Routledge and Kegan Paul.

Brown, Penelope and Stephen Levinson. 1987. *Politeness*. New York: Cambridge University Press.

Carrigan, Tim, Robert Connell and John Lee. 1985. "Toward a New Sociology of Masculinity." *Theory and Society* 14:551–604.

Connell, Robert W. 1995. *Masculinities*. Cambridge: Polity Press.

Donald, Ralph R. 2002. "Masculinity and Machismo in Hollywood's War Films." In *The Masculinities Reader*, ed. Stephen M. Whitehead and Frank J. Barrett, 170–83. Cambridge: Polity Press.

Eckert, Penelope. 2000. *Linguistic Variation as Social Practice*. Maiden, MA: Blackwell Publishers.

Edley, Nigel and Margaret Wetherell. 1995. *Men in Perspective*. New York: Prentice Hall/Harvester Wheatsheaf.

Foucault, Michel. 1980. *Power/Knowledge: Selected Interviews and Other Writings 1972–1977*. New York: Pantheon.

Guy, Gregory, Barbara Horvath, Julia Vonwiller, Elaine Daisley, Inge Rogers. 1986. "An Intonational Change in Progress in Australian English." *Language in Society* 15:23–51.

Hill, Richard. 1994. "You've Come a Long Way, Dude—A History." *American Speech* 69:321–7.

Kiesling, Scott F. 1997. "Power and the Language of Men." In *Language and Masculinity*, ed. Ulrike. H. Meinhof and Sally Johnson, 65–85. Maiden, MA: Blackwell Publishers.

Kiesling, Scott F. 1998. "Variation and Men's Identity in a Fraternity." *Journal of Sociolinguistics*, 2: 69–100.

Kiesling, Scott F. 2001a. "Stances of Whiteness and Hegemony in Fraternity Men's Discourse." *Journal of Linguistic Anthropology* 11: 101–15.

Kiesling, Scott F. 2001b. "'Now I Gotta Watch What I Say': Shifting Constructions of Masculinity in Discourse." *Journal of Linguistic Anthropology* 11: 250–73.

Kimmel, Michael. 2002. "Masculinity as Homophobia: Fear, Shame, and Silence in the Construction of Gender Identity." In *The Masculinities Reader*, ed. Stephen M. Whitehead and Frank J. Barrett, 266–287. Cambridge: Polity Press.

Labov, William. 2001. *Principles of Linguistic Change, Volume II: Social Factors*. Maiden, MA: Blackwell Publishers.

LePage, Robert B. and Andrée Tabouret-Keller. 1985. *Acts of Identity: Creole-based Approaches to Language and Ethnicity*. New York: Cambridge University Press.

Levitas, Ruth, ed. 1986. *The Ideology of the New Right*. Cambridge: Polity Press.

McLemore, Cynthia. 1991. "The Pragmatic Interpretation of English Intonation: Sorority Speech." Ph.D. dissertation, University of Texas at Austin.

Morford, Janet. 1997. "Social Indexicality in French Pronominal Address." *Journal of Linguistic Anthropology*. 7: 3–37.

Siegel, Muffy. 2002. "Like: The Discourse Particle and Semantics." *Journal of Semantics* 19:35–71.

Silverstein, Michael. 1996. "Indexical Order and the Dialectics of Sociolinguistic Life." In *SALSA III: Proceedings of the Third Annual Symposium About Language and Society—Austin*, ed. Risako Ide, Rebecca Parker, and Yukako Sunaoshi, 266–95. Austin, TX: University of Texas Department of Linguistics.

Swofford, Anthony. 2003. *Jarhead*. New York: Scribner.

Tannen, Deborah. 1979. "What's in a Frame? Surface Evidence for Underlying Expectations." In *New Directions in Discourse Processing*, ed. Roy Freedle, 137–81. Norwood, NJ: Ablex.

Tannen, Deborah. 1989. *Talking Voices: Repetition, Dialogue, and Imagery in Conversational Discourse*. New York: Cambridge University Press.

Whitehead, Stephen M. 2002. *Men and Masculinities*. Cambridge: Polity Press.

APPENDIX: DUDE SURVEY

Note: This form modified from the original; Yinz has been removed.

Language Survey

Please help me with a survey for a linguistics class. The answers should take you only a few minutes. If you are interested in the topic, I can explain what we are studying after you have taken the survey.

Your answers are anonymous and confidential. No one will know who gave your answers, and the paper will be destroyed at the end of the course.

This survey asks you to answers questions about three words in English. These words are all terms of address. That is, they are used to greet someone or get their attention to talk to them in a sentence like this: "Hey, **sir**, you dropped something!"

The terms are *Dude* and *Babe*.

"Dude"

1. How often do you use this term as an address term (circle one)?

   Many times each day—About once a day—About once a week—Hardly ever—Never

2. What kind of person are you likely to use it to address?
   1 = Not likely at all, will never use it with someone like this
   5 = Very likely, use it all the time with people like this

The person is your ...	The person is also a man	The person is also a woman
Girl/boyfriend	1 2 3 4 5 n/a	1 2 3 4 5 n/a
Close friend	1 2 3 4 5 n/a	1 2 3 4 5 n/a
Acquaintance	1 2 3 4 5 n/a	1 2 3 4 5 n/a
Stranger	1 2 3 4 5 n/a	1 2 3 4 5 n/a
Sibling	1 2 3 4 5 n/a	1 2 3 4 5 n/a
Parent	1 2 3 4 5 n/a	1 2 3 4 5 n/a
Boss	1 2 3 4 5 n/a	1 2 3 4 5 n/a
Professor	1 2 3 4 5 n/a	1 2 3 4 5 n/a

3. Why do you use the term? That is, what do you think it says about you to the person you are talking to?

4. What kind of person do you think uses it frequently?

"Babe"

1. How often do you use this term as an address term (circle one)?

   Many times each day—About once a day—About once a week—Hardly ever—Never

2. What kind of person are you likely to use it to address?
   1 = Not likely at all, will never use it with someone like this
   5 = Very likely, use it all the time with people like this

The person is your ...	The person is also a man	The person is also a woman
Girl/boyfriend	1 2 3 4 5 n/a	1 2 3 4 5 n/a
Close friend	1 2 3 4 5 n/a	1 2 3 4 5 n/a
Acquaintance	1 2 3 4 5 n/a	1 2 3 4 5 n/a
Stranger	1 2 3 4 5 n/a	1 2 3 4 5 n/a
Sibling	1 2 3 4 5 n/a	1 2 3 4 5 n/a
Parent	1 2 3 4 5 n/a	1 2 3 4 5 n/a
Boss	1 2 3 4 5 n/a	1 2 3 4 5 n/a
Professor	1 2 3 4 5 n/a	1 2 3 4 5 n/a

3. Why do you use the term? That is, what do you think it says about you to the person you are talking to?

4. What kind of person do you think uses it frequently?

Now please answer a few questions about yourself:

1. What is you age?

2. What is your ethnicity?

3. What is your gender?

4. In what city did (do) you go to high school?

5. What is your occupation?

6. If you are a college student, what is your major (or school, if undecided):

White English in Blackface, or Who Do I Be?

By Geneva Smitherman

Ain nothin in a long time lit up the English teaching profession like the current hassle over Black English. One finds beaucoup sociolinguistic research studies and language projects for the "disadvantaged" on the scene in nearly every sizable black community in the country.[1] And educators from K–Grad. School bees debating whether: (1) blacks should learn and use only standard white English (hereafter referred to as WE); (2) blacks should command both dialects, i.e., be bi-dialectal (hereafter BD); (3) blacks should be allowed (??????) to use standard Black English (hereafter BE or BI). The appropriate choice having everything to do with American political reality, which is usually ignored, and nothing to do with the educational process, which is usually claimed. I say without qualification that we cannot talk about the Black Idiom apart from Black Culture and the Black Experience. Nor can we specify educational goals for blacks apart from considerations about the structure of (white) American society.

And we black folks is not gon take all that weight, for no one has empirically demonstrated that linguistic/stylistic features of BE impede educational progress in communication skills, or any other area of cognitive learning. Take reading. It's don been charged, but not actually verified, that BE interferes with mastery of reading skills.[2] Yet beyond pointing out the gap between the young brother/sistuh's phonological and syntactical patterns and those of the usually-middle-class-WE-speaking-teacher, this claim has not been validated. The distance between the two systems is, after all, short and is illuminated only by the fact that reading is taught *orally*. (Also get to the fact that preceding generations of BE-speaking folks learned to read, despite the many classrooms in which the teacher spoke a dialect different from that of her students.)

For example, a student who reads *den* for *then* probably pronounces initial /th/ as /d/ in most words. Or the one who reads *doing* for *during* probably deletes intervocalic and final /r/ in most words. So it is not that such students can't read, they is simply employing the black phonological system. In the reading classrooms of today, what we bees needin is teachers with the proper attitudinal orientation who thus can distinguish actual reading problems from mere dialect differences. Or take the writing of an essay. The only percentage in writing a paper with WE spelling, punctuation, and usage is in maybe eliciting a positive *attitudinal* response from a prescriptivist middle-class-aspirant-teacher. Dig on the fact that sheer "correctness" does not a good writer make. And is it any point in dealing with the charge of BE speakers being "non-verbal" or "linguistically deficient" in oral communication skills—behind our many Raps who done disproved that in living, vibrant color?[3]

What linguists and educators need to do at this juncture is to take serious cognizance of the Oral Tradition in Black Culture. The uniqueness of this verbal style requires a language competence/performance model to fit the black scheme of things. Clearly BI speakers possess rich communication skills (i.e., are highly *competent* in using language), but as yet there bees no criteria (evaluative, testing, or other instrument of measurement), based on black communication patterns, wherein BI speakers can demonstrate they competence (i.e., *performance*). Hence brothers and sisters fail on language performance tests and in English classrooms. Like, to amplify on what Nikki said, that's why we always lose, not only cause we don't know the rules, but it ain't even our game.

We can devise a performance model only after an analysis of the components of BI. Now there do be linguists who supposedly done did this categorization and definition of BE.[4] But the descriptions are generally confining, limited as they are to discrete linguistic units. One finds simply ten to fifteen patterns cited, as for example, the most frequently listed one, the use of *be* as finite verb, contrasting with its deletion: (a) *The coffee be cold* contrasts with (b) *The coffee cold,* the former statement denoting a continuing state of affairs, the latter applying to the present moment only. (Like if you the cook, (a) probably get you fired, and (b) only get you talked about.) In WE no comparable grammatical distinction exists and *The coffee is cold* would be used to indicate both meanings. However, rarely does one find an investigation of the total vitality of black expressive style, a style inextricable from the Black Cultural Universe, for after all, BI connects with Black Soul and niggers is more than deleted copulas.[5]

The Black Idiom should be viewed from two important perspectives: linguistic and stylistic. The linguistic dimension is comprised of the so-called nonstandard features of phonology and syntax (patterns like *dis heah* and *The coffee be cold*), and a lexicon generally equated with "slang" or hip talk. The stylistic dimension has to do with *rapping, capping, jiving,* etc., and with features such as cadence, rhythm, resonance, gestures, and all those other elusive, difficult-to-objectify elements that make up what is considered a writer or speaker's "style." While I am separating linguistic and stylistic features, I have done so only for the purpose of simplifying the discussion since the BI speaker runs the full gamut of both dimensions in any given speech event.

I acknowledge from the bell that we's dealing with a dialect structure which is a subsystem of the English language; thus BE and WE may not appear fundamentally different. Yet, though black folks speak English, it do seem to be an entirely different lingo altogether. But wherein lies the uniqueness? Essentially in language, as in other areas of Black Culture, we have the problem of isolating those elements indigenous to black folks from those cultural aspects shared with

FEATURES SHARED WITH MAINSTREAM AMERICA	FEATURES SHARED WITH ALL OPPRESSED PEOPLES	FEATURES UNIQUE TO BLACK AMERICANS
Linguistic	*Linguistic*	*Linguistic*
1. British/American English lexicon	1. Superimposition of dominant culture's language on native language, yielding	Unique meanings attributed to certain English lexical items
2. Most aspects of British/American English phonology and syntax	2. Pidginized form of dominant culture's language, subject to becoming extinct, due to	*Stylistic*
	3. Historical evolution, linguistic leveling out in direction of dominant culture's dialect	Unique communication patterns and rhetorical flourishes

white folks. Anthropologist Johnnetta Cole suggests that Black Culture has three dimensions: (1) those elements shared with mainstream America; (2) those elements shared with all oppressed peoples; (3) those elements peculiar to the black condition in America.[6] Applying her concepts to language, I propose the accompanying schematic representation.

Referring to the first column, contemporary BE is simply one of the many dialects of contemporary American English, and it is most likely the case that the linguistic patterns of BE differ from those of WE in surface structure only. There's no essential linguistic difference between *dis heah* and *this here,* and from a strictly linguistic point of view, *God don't never change* can be written *God doesn't ever change* (though definitely not from a socio-cultural/political perspective, as Baraka quite rightly notes).[7] Perhaps we could make a case for deep structure difference in the BE use of *be* as finite verb (refer to *The coffee be cold* example above), but we be hard pressed to find any other examples, and even in this case, we could posit that the copula exists in the deep structure, and is simply deleted by some low-level phonological deletion rule, dig: The coffee is cold … The coffee's cold … The coffee cold. My conclusion at this point is that despite the claims of some highly respected Creole linguists (with special propers to bad Sistuh Beryl Bailey),[8] the argument for deep structure differences between contemporary BE and WE syntax can not pass the test of rigorous transformational analysis.

Referring to the second column, we note the psychological tendency of oppressed people to adopt the modes of behavior and expression of their oppressors (also, during the African slave trade, the functional necessity of pidginized forms of European language). Not only does the conqueror force his victims into political subjugation, he also coerces them into adopting his language and doles out special rewards to those among the oppressed who best mimic his language and cultural style. In the initial language contact stage, the victims attempt to assemble the new language into their native linguistic mold, producing a linguistic mixture that is termed *pidgin.* In the next stage, the pidgin may develop into a Creole, a highly systematic, widely used mode of communication among the oppressed, characterized by a substratum of patterns from the victim's language with an overlay of forms from the oppressor's language. As the oppressed people's identification with the victor's culture intensifies, the pidgin/Creole begins to lose its linguistic currency and naturally evolves in the direction of the victor's language. Reconstructing the linguistic history of BE, we theorize that it followed a similar pattern, but due to the radically different condition of black oppression in America, the process of *de-creolization* is nearly complete and has been for perhaps over a hundred years.

The most important features of BI are, of course, those referred to in column three, for they point us toward the linguistic uniqueness and cultural significance of the Oral Tradition in the Black Experience. It should be clear that all along I been talkin bout that Black Experience associated with the grass-roots folks, the masses, the sho-nuff niggers—in short, all those black folks who do not aspire to white middle-class American standards.

Within this tradition, language is used as a teaching/socializing force and as a means of establishing one's reputation via his verbal competence. Black talk is never meaningless cocktail chit-chat but a functional dynamic that is simultaneously a mechanism for acculturation and information-passing and a vehicle for achieving group recognition. Black communication is highly verbal and highly stylized; it is a performance before a black audience who become both observers and participants in the speech event. Whether it be through slapping of hands ("giving five" or "giving skin"), Amen's, or Right on's, the audience influences the direction of a given rap and at the same time acknowledges or withholds its approval, depending on the linguistic skill and stylistic ingenuity of the speaker. I mean like a Brother is only as bad as his rap bees.

I. TOWARD A BLACK LANGUAGE MODEL: LINGUISTIC

While we concede that black people use the vocabulary of the English language, certain words are always selected out of that lexicon and given a special black semantic slant. So though we rappin bout the same language, the reality referents are different.

As one linguist has suggested, the proper question is not what do words mean but what do the users of the words mean? These words may be associated with and more frequently used in black street culture but not necessarily. *Muthafucka* has social boundaries, but not *nigger*.

Referring to the lexicon of BI, then, the following general principles obtain:

1. The words given the special black slant exist in a dynamic state. The terms are discarded when they move into the white mainstream. (Example: One no longer speaks of a "hip" brother; now he is a "togetha" brother.) This was/is necessitated by our need to have a code that was/is undecipherable by foreigners (i.e., whites).
2. In BI, the concept of denotation vs. connotation does not apply.
3. What does apply is shades of meaning along the connotative spectrum. For example, depending on contextual environment, the word *bad* can mean extraordinary; beautiful; good; versatile; or a host of other terms of positive value. Dig it: after watching a Sammy Davis performance, a BI speaker testified: "Sammy sho did some *bad* stuff," i.e., extraordinary stuff. Or upon observing a beautiful sister: "She sho is *bad*" i.e., beautiful, pretty, or good-looking. Or, noticing how a brother is dressed: "You sho got on some *bad* shit," i.e., *good* shit = attractively dressed.
   Note that the above examples are all in the category *of approbation*. It is necessary to rap bout *denigration* as well, since certain words in the black lexicon can frequently be used both ways. Consider the word *nigger*, for instance. "He's my main nigger" means my best friend (hence, approbation); "The nigger ain't shit," means he's probably lazy, trifling, scheming, wrong-doing, or a host of other *denigrative* terms, depending on the total context of the utterance.
4. Approbation and denigration relate to the semantic level; we can add two other possible functions of the same word on the grammatical level: *intensification* and *completion*. Slide back to *nigger* for a minute, and dig that often the word is void of real meaning and simply supplies the sentence

SACRED	SECULAR
Political rap style	*Political rap style*
EXAMPLES: Jesse Jackson	EXAMPLES: Malcolm X
Martin Luther King	Rap Brown
Political literary style	*Political literary style*
EXAMPLES: Barbara Ann Teer's	EXAMPLES: Don Lee
National Black Theatre	Last Poets
Nikki Giovanni's	
"Truth Is on Its Way"	

with a subject. "Niggers was getting out of there left and right, then the niggers was running, and so the niggers said … " etc., etc., my point being that a steady stream of overuse means neither denigration nor approbation. Some excellent illustrations of this function of the word are to be found in *Manchild in the Promised Land,* where you can observe the word used in larger contexts. To give you a most vivid illustration, consider the use of what WE labels "obscenities." From the streets of Detroit: (a) "That's a bad *muthafucka.*" Referring to a Cadillac Eldorado, obviously indicating approval, (b) "He's a no-good *muthafucka.*" Referring to a person who has just "put some game" on the speaker, obviously indicating disapproval, (c) "You *muthafuckin* right I wasn't gon let him do that." Emphasizing how correct the listener's assessment is, obviously using the term as a grammatical intensifier, modifying "right." (d) "We wasn't doin nothing, just messin round and *shit.*" Though a different "obscenity," the point is nonetheless illustrated, "shit" being used neutrally, as an expletive (filler) to complete the sentence pattern; semantically speaking, it is an empty word in this contextual environment.

Where I'm comin from is that the lexicon of BI, consisting of certain specially selected words, requires a unique scheme of analysis to account for the diverse range and multiplicity of meanings attributed to these words. While there do be some dictionaries of Afro-American "slang," they fail to get at the important question: what are the psycho-cultural processes that guide our selection of certain words out of the thousands of possible words in the Anglo-Saxon vocabulary? Like, for instance, Kochman[9] has suggested that we value action in the black community, and so those words that have action implied in them, we take and give positive meanings to, such as *swing, game, hip, hustle,* etc.; whereas words of implied stasis are taken and given negative connotations, such as *lame, square, hung-up, stiffin and jivin,* etc. At any rate, what I've tried to lay here are some suggestions in this particular linguistic dimension; the definitive word on black lexicon is yet to be given.

I shall go on to discuss the stylistic dimension of black communication patterns, where I have worked out a more definitive model.

II. TOWARD A BLACK LANGUAGE MODEL: STYLISTIC

Black verbal style exists on a sacred-secular continuum, as represented by the accompanying scheme. The model allows us to account for the many individual variations in black speech, which can all be located at some point along the continuum.

The sacred style is rural and Southern. It is the style of the black preacher and that associated with the black church tradition. It tends to be more emotive and highly charged than the secular style. It is also older in time. However, though I've called it "sacred," it abounds in secularisms. Black church service tends to be highly informal, and it ain nothin for a preacher to get up in the pulpit and, say, show off what he's wearing: "Y'all didn't notice the new suit I got on today, did y'all? Ain the Lord good to us? … "

The secular style is urban and Northern, but since it probably had its beginnings in black folk tales and proverbs, its *roots* are Southern and rural. This is the street culture style; the style found in barbershops and on street corners in the black ghettos of American cities. It tends to be more cool, more emotionally restrained than the sacred style. It is newer and younger in time and only fully evolved as a distinct style with the massive wave of black migration to the cities.

Both sacred and secular styles share the following characteristics:

1. *Call and response.* This is basic to black oral tradition. The speaker's solo voice alternates or is intermingled with the audience's response. In the sacred style, the minister is urged on by the congregation's Amen's, That's right, Reverend's, or Preach Reverend's. One also hears occasional Take your time's when the preacher is initiating his sermon, the congregation desiring to savor every little bit of this good message they bout to hear. (In both sacred and secular political rap styles, the "Preach Reverend" is transposed to "Teach Brother.") In the secular style, the response can take the form of a back-and-forth banter between the speaker and various members of the audience. Or the audience might manifest its response in giving skin (fives) when a really down verbal point is scored. Other approval responses include laughter and phrases like "Oh, you mean, nigger," "Get back, nigger," "Git down, baby," etc.

2. *Rhythmic pattern.* I refer to cadence, tone, and musical quality. This is a pattern that is lyrical, sonorous, and generally emphasizing sound apart from sense. It is often established through repetition, either of certain sounds or words. The preacher will get a rhythm going, conveying his message through sound rather than depending on sheer semantic import. "I-I-I-I-I-Oh-I-I-Oh, yeah, Lord-I-I-heard the voice of Jesus saying. … " Even though the secular style is characterized by rapidity, as in the toasts (narrative tales of bad niggers and they exploits, like Stag-O-Lee, or bad animals and they trickeration, like the Signifying Monkey), the speaker's voice tone still has that rhythmic, musical quality, just with a faster tempo.

3. *Spontaneity.* Generally, the speaker's performance is improvisational, with the rich interaction between speaker and audience dictating and/or directing the course and outcome of the speech event. Since the speaker does not prepare a formal document, his delivery is casual, nondeliberate, and uncontrived. He speaks in a lively, conversational tone, and with an ever-present quality of immediacy. All emphasis is on process, movement, and creativity of the moment. The preacher says "Y'all don wont to hear dat, so I'm gon leave it lone," and his audience shouts, "Naw, tell it Reverend, tell it!," and he does. Or, like, once Malcolm mentioned the fact of his being in prison, and sensing the surprise of his audience, he took advantage of the opportunity to note that all black people were in prison: "That's what America means: prison."

4. *Concreteness.* The speaker's imagery and ideas center around the empirical world, the world of reality, and the contemporary Here and Now. Rarely does he drift off into esoteric abstractions; his metaphors and illustrations are commonplace and grounded in everyday experience. Perhaps because of this concreteness, there is a sense of identification with the event being described or narrated, as in the secular style where the toast-teller's identity merges with that of the protagonist of his tale, and he becomes Stag-O-Lee or Shine; or when the preacher assumes the voice of God or the personality of a Biblical character. Even the experience of being saved takes on a presentness and rootedness in everyday life: "I first met God in 1925. … "

5. *Signifying.* This is a technique of talking about the entire audience or some member of the audience either to initiate verbal "war" or to make a point hit home. The interesting thang bout this rhetorical device is that the audience is not offended and realizes—naw, expects—the speaker to launch this offensive to achieve his desired effect. "Pimp, punk, prostitute, Ph.D.—all the P's—you still in slavery!" announces the Reverend Jesse Jackson. Malcolm puts down the non-violent movement with: "In a revolution, you swinging, not singing." (Notice the characteristic rhythmic pattern in the above examples—the alliterative poetic effect of Jackson's statement and the rhyming device in Malcolm's.)

An analysis of black expressive style, such as presented here, should facilitate the construction of a performance instrument to measure the degree of command of the style of any given BI speaker. Linguists and educators sincerely interested in black education might be about the difficult, complex business of devising such a "test," rather than establishing linguistic remediation programs to correct a nonexistent remediation. Like in any other area of human activity, some BI rappers are better than others, and today's most effective black preachers, leaders, politicians, writers are those who rap in the black expressive style, appropriating the ritual framework of the Oral Tradition as vehicle for the conveyance of they political ideologies. Which brings me back to what I said from Jump Street. The real heart of this language controversy relates to/is the underlying political nature of the American educational system. Brother Frantz Fanon is highly instructive at this point. From his "Negro and Language," in *Black Skins, White Masks*:

> I ascribe a basic importance to the phenomenon of language. ... To speak means ... above all to assume a culture, to support the weight of a civilization. ... Every dialect is a way of thinking. ... And the fact that the newly returned [i.e., from white schools] Negro adopts a language different from that of the group into which he was born is evidence of a dislocation, a separation. ...

In showing why the "Negro adopts such a position ... with respect to European languages," Fanon continues:

> It is because he wants to emphasize the rupture that has now occurred. He is incarnating a new type of man that he imposes on his associates and his family. And so his old mother can no longer understand him when he talks to her about his *duds*, the family's *crummy joint*, the *dump* ... all of it, of course, tricked out with the appropriate accent.
>   In every country of the world, there are climbers, 'the ones who forget who they are,' and in contrast to them, 'the ones who remember where they came from.' The Antilles Negro who goes home from France expresses himself in the dialect if he wants to make it plain that nothing has changed.[10]

As black people go moving on up toward separation and cultural nationalism, the question of the moment is not which dialect, but which culture, not whose vocabulary but whose values, not *I am vs. I be,* but WHO DO I BE?

NOTES

1. For examples of such programs, see *Non-Standard Dialect,* Board of Education of the City of New York (National Council of Teachers of English, 1968); San-Su C. Lin, *Pattern Practices in the Teaching of Standard English to Students with a Non-Standard Dialect* (USOE Project 1339, 1965); Arno Jewett, Joseph Mersand, Doris Gunderson, *Improving English Skills of Culturally Different Youth in Large Cities* (U.S. Department of Health, Education and Welfare, 1964); *Language Programs for the Disadvantaged* (NCTE, 1965).

2. See, for example, Joan Baratz and Roger Shuy, ed., *Teaching Black Children to Read* (Center for Applied Linguistics, 1969); A. L. Davis, ed., *On the Dialects of Children* (NCTE, 1968); Eldonna L. Evertts, ed., *Dimensions of Dialect* (NCTE,1967).

3. For the most racist and glaring of these charges, see Fred Hechinger, ed., *Pre-School Education Today* (Doubleday, 1966); for an excellent rebuttal, see William Labov, *Nonstandard English* (NCTE 1970); for a complete overview of the controversy and issues involved as well as historical perspective and rebuttal to the non-verbal claim, see my "Black Idiom and White Institutions," *Negro American Literature Forum,* Fall 1971.

4. The most thorough and scholarly of these, though a bit overly technical, is Walter Wolfram, *Detroit Negro Speech* (Center for Applied Linguistics, 1969).

5. Kochman is one linguist who done gone this route; see for instance his "Rapping in the Black Ghetto," *Trans-action,* February 1969. However, he makes some black folks mad because of what one of my students called his "superfluity," and others shame cause of his exposure of our "bad" street elements. Kochman's data: jam up with muthafuckas and pussy-copping raps collected from Southside Chicago.

6. Johnnetta B. Cole, "Culture: Negro, Black and Nigger," *The Black Scholar,* June 1970.

7. Imamu Baraka, "Expressive Language," *Home,* pp. 166–172.

8. See her "Toward a New Perspective in Negro English Dialectology," *American Speech* (1965) and "Language and Communicative Styles of Afro-American Children in the United States," *Florida FL Reporter* 7 (Spring/Summer 1969).

9. See Thomas Kochman, "The Kinetic Element in Black Idiom," paper read at the American Anthropological Association Convention, Seattle, Washington, 1968; also his *Rappin' and Stylin' Out: Communication in Urban Black America.*

10. Frantz Fanon, *Black Skin, White Masks,* trans. Charles Lamm Markmann (New York, 1967), pp. 17–40.

How to Tame a Wild Tongue

By Gloria Anzaldúa

We're going to have to control your tongue," the dentist says, pulling out all the metal from my mouth. Silver bits plop and tinkle into the basin. My mouth is a mother lode. The dentist is cleaning out my roots, I get a whiff of the stench when I gasp, "I can't cap that tooth yet, you're still draining," he says.

"We're going to have to do something about your tongue," I hear the anger rising in his voice. My tongue keeps pushing out the wads of cotton, pushing back the drills, the long thin needles. "I've never seen anything as strong or as stubborn," he says. And I think, how do you tame a wild tongue, train it to be quiet, how do you bridle and saddle it? How do you make it lie down?

"Who is to say that robbing a people of its language is less violent than war?"

—Ray Gwyn Smith

I remember being caught speaking Spanish at recess—that was good for three licks on the knuckles with a sharp ruler. I remember being sent to the corner of the classroom for "talking back" to the Anglo teacher when all I was trying to do was tell her how to pronounce my name. "If you want to be American, speak 'American.' If you don't like it, go back to Mexico where you belong."

"I want you to speak English. *Pa' hallar buen trabajo tienes que saber hablar el inglés bien. Qué vale toda tu educación si todavía hablas inglés con an* 'accent,'" my mother would say, mortified that I spoke English like a Mexican. At Pan American University, I, and all Chicano students were required to take two speech classes. Their purpose: to get rid of our accents.

Attacks on one's form of expression with the intent to censor are a violation of the First Amendment. *El Anglo con cara de inocente nos arrancó la lengua.* Wild tongues can't be tamed, they can only be cut out.

OVERCOMING THE TRADITION OF SILENCE

Abogadas, escupimos el oscuro.
Peleando con nuestra propia sombra
el silencio nos sepulta.

En boca cerrada no entran moscas. "Flies don't enter a closed mouth" is a saying I kept hearing when I was a child. *Ser habladora* was to be a gossip and a liar, to talk too much. *Muchachitas bien criadas,* well-bred girls don't answer back. *Es una falta de respeto* to talk back to one's mother or father. I remember one of the sins I'd recite to the priest in the confession box the few times I went to confession: talking back to my mother, *hablar pa' 'trás, repelar. Hocicona, repelona, chismosa,* having a big mouth, questioning, carrying tales are all signs of being *mal criada.* In my culture they are all words that are derogatory if applied to women—I've never heard them applied to men.

The first time I heard two women, a Puerto Rican and a Cuban, say the word *"nosotras,"* I was shocked. I had not known the word existed. Chicanas use *nosotros* whether we're male or female. We are robbed of our female being by the masculine plural. Language is a male discourse.

> And our tongues have become
> dry   the wilderness has
> dried out our tongues   and
> we have forgotten speech.
>
> —Irena Klepfisz

Even our own people, other Spanish speakers *nos quieren poner candados en la boca.* They would hold us back with their bag of *reglas de academia.*

OYÉ COMO LADRA: EL LENGUAJE DE LA FRONTERA

Quien tiene boca se equivoca.   —Mexican saying

"*Pocho,* cultural traitor, you're speaking the oppressor's language by speaking English, you're ruining the Spanish language," I have been accused by various Latinos and Latinas. Chicano Spanish is considered by the purist and by most Latinos deficient, a mutilation of Spanish.

But Chicano Spanish is a border tongue which developed naturally. Change, *evolución, enriquecimiento de palabras nuevas por invención o adopción* have created variants of Chicano Spanish, *un nuevo lenguaje. Un lenguaje que corresponde a un modo de vivir.* Chicana Spanish is not incorrect, it is a living language.

For a people who are neither Spanish nor live in a country in which Spanish is the first language; for a people who live in a country in which English is the reigning tongue but who are not Anglo; for a people who cannot entirely identify with either standard (formal, Castillian) Spanish nor standard English, what recourse is left to them but to create their own language? A language which they can connect their identity to, one capable of communicating the realities and values true to themselves—a language with terms that are neither *español ni inglés*, but both. We speak a patois, a forked tongue, a variation of two languages.

Chicano Spanish sprang out of the Chicanos' need to identify ourselves as a distinct people. We needed a language with which we could communicate with ourselves, a secret language. For some of us, language is a homeland closer than the Southwest—for many Chicanos today live in the Midwest and the East. And because we are a complex, heterogeneous people, we speak many languages. Some of the languages we speak are:

1. Standard English
2. Working class and slang English
3. Standard Spanish
4. Standard Mexican Spanish
5. North Mexican Spanish dialect
6. Chicano Spanish (Texas, New Mexico, Arizona and California have regional variations)
7. Tex-Mex
8. *Pachuco* (called *caló*)

My "home" tongues are the languages I speak with my sister and brothers, with my friends. They are the last five listed, with 6 and 7 being closest to my heart. From school, the media and job situations, I've picked up standard and working class English. From Mamagrande Locha and from reading Spanish and Mexican literature, I've picked up Standard Spanish and Standard Mexican Spanish. From *los recién llegados*, Mexican immigrants, and *braceros*, I learned the North Mexican dialect. With Mexicans, I'll try to speak either Standard Mexican Spanish or the North Mexican dialect. From my parents and Chicanos living in the Valley, I picked up Chicano Texas Spanish, and I speak it with my mom, younger brother (who married a Mexican and who rarely mixes Spanish with English), aunts and older relatives.

With Chicanas from *Nuevo México* or *Arizona* I will speak Chicano Spanish a little, but often they don't understand what I'm saying. With most California Chicanas I speak entirely in English (unless I forget). When I first moved to San Francisco, I'd rattle off something in Spanish, unintentionally embarrassing them. Often it is only with another Chicana *tejana* that I can talk freely.

Words distorted by English are known as anglicisms or *pochismos*. The *pocho* is an anglicized Mexican or American of Mexican origin who speaks Spanish with an accent characteristic of North Americans and who distorts and reconstructs the language according to the influence of English. Tex-Mex, or Spanglish, comes most naturally to me. I may switch back and forth from English to Spanish in the same sentence or in the same word. With my sister and my brother Nune and with Chicano *tejano* contemporaries I speak in Tex-Mex.

From kids and people my own age I picked up *Pachuco*. *Pachuco* (the language of the zoot suiters) is a language of rebellion, both against Standard Spanish and Standard English. It is a secret language. Adults of the culture and outsiders cannot understand it. It is made up of slang words from both English and Spanish. *Ruca* means girl or woman, *vato* means guy or dude, *chale* means no, *simón* means yes, *churo* is sure, talk *is periquiar, pigionear* means petting, *que gacho* means how nerdy, *ponte águila* means watch out, death is called *la pelona.*

Through lack of practice and not having others who can speak it, I've lost most of the *Pachuco* tongue.

CHICANO SPANISH

Chicanos, after 250 years of Spanish/Anglo colonization have developed significant differences in the Spanish we speak. We collapse two adjacent vowels into a single syllable and sometimes shift the stress in certain words such as *maíz/maiz, cohete/cuete.* We leave out certain consonants when they appear between vowels: *lado/lao, mojado/mojao.* Chicanos from South Texas pronounce *f* as *j* as in *jue* (*fue*). Chicanos use "archaisms," words that are no longer in the Spanish language, words that have been evolved out. We say *semos, truje, haiga, ansina,* and *naiden.* We retain the "archaic" *j,* as in *jalar* that derives from an earlier *h,* (the French *halar* or the Germanic *halon* which was lost to standard Spanish in the 16th century), but which is still found in several regional dialects such as the one spoken in South Texas. (Due to geography, Chicanos from the Valley of South Texas were cut off linguistically from other Spanish speakers. We tend to use words that the Spaniards brought over from Medieval Spain. The majority of the Spanish colonizers in Mexico and the Southwest came from Extremadura—Hernán Cortés was one of them—and Andalucía. Andalucians pronounce *ll* like a *y,* and their *d*'s tend to be absorbed by adjacent vowels: *tirado* becomes *tirao.* They brought *el lenguaje popular, dialectos y regionalismos.*)

Chicanos and other Spanish speakers also shift *ll* to *y* and *z* to *s.* We leave out initial syllables, saying *tar* for *estar, toy* for *estoy, hora* for *ahora* (*cubanos* and *puertorriqueños* also leave out initial letters of some words.) We also leave out the final syllable such as *pa* for *para.* The intervocalic *y,* the *ll* as in *tortilla, ella, botella,* gets replaced by *tortia* or *tortiya, ea, botea.* We add an additional syllable at the beginning of certain words: *atocar* for *tocar, agastar* for *gastar.* Sometimes we'll say *lavaste las vacijas,* other times *lavates* (substituting the *ates* verb endings for the *aste*).

We use anglicisms, words borrowed from English: *bola* from ball, *carpeta* from carpet, *máchina de lavar* (instead of *lavadora*) from washing machine. Tex-Mex argot, created by adding a Spanish sound at the beginning or end of an English word such as *cookiar* for cook, *watchar* for watch, *parkiar* for park, and *rapiar* for rape, is the result of the pressures on Spanish speakers to adapt to English.

We don't use the word *vosotros/as* or its accompanying verb form. We don't say *claro* (to mean yes), *imagínate,* or *me emociona,* unless we picked up Spanish from Latinas, out of a book, or in a classroom. Other Spanish-speaking groups are going through the same, or similar, development in their Spanish.

LINGUISTIC TERRORISM

Deslenguadas. Somos los del español deficiente. We are your linguistic nightmare, your linguistic aberration, your linguistic *mestizaje,* the subject of your *burla.* Because we speak with tongues of fire we are culturally crucified. Racially, culturally and linguistically *somos huérfanos*—we speak an orphan tongue.

Chicanas who grew up speaking Chicano Spanish have internalized the belief that we speak poor Spanish. It is illegitimate, a bastard language. And because we internalize how our language has been used against us by the dominant culture, we use our language differences against each other.

Chicana feminists often skirt around each other with suspicion and hesitation. For the longest time I couldn't figure it out. Then it dawned on me. To be close to another Chicana is like looking into the mirror. We are afraid of what we'll see there. *Pena.* Shame. Low estimation of self. In childhood we are told that our language is wrong. Repeated attacks on our native tongue diminish our sense of self. The attacks continue throughout our lives.

Chicanas feel uncomfortable talking in Spanish to Latinas, afraid of their censure. Their language was not outlawed in their countries. They had a whole lifetime of being immersed in their native tongue; generations, centuries in which Spanish was a first language, taught in school, heard on radio and TV, and read in the newspaper.

If a person, Chicana or Latina, has a low estimation of my native tongue, she also has a low estimation of me. Often with *mexicanas y latinas* we'll speak English as a neutral language. Even among Chicanas we tend to speak English at parties or conferences. Yet, at the same time, we're afraid the other will think we're *agringadas* because we don't speak Chicano Spanish. We oppress each other trying to out-Chicano each other, vying to be the "real" Chicanas, to speak like Chicanos. There is no one Chicano language just as there is no one Chicano experience. A monolingual Chicana whose first language is English or Spanish is just as much a Chicana as one who speaks several variants of Spanish. A Chicana from Michigan or Chicago or Detroit is just as much a Chicana as one from the Southwest. Chicano Spanish is as diverse linguistically as it is regionally.

By the end of this century, Spanish speakers will comprise the biggest minority group in the U.S., a country where students in high schools and colleges are encouraged to take French classes because French is considered more "cultured." But for a language to remain alive it must be used. By the end of this century English, and not Spanish, will be the mother tongue of most Chicanos and Latinos.

So, if you want to really hurt me, talk badly about my language. Ethnic identity is twin skin to linguistic identity—I am my language. Until I can take pride in my language, I cannot take pride in myself. Until I can accept as legitimate Chicano Texas Spanish, Tex-Mex and all the other languages I speak, I cannot accept the legitimacy of myself. Until I am free to write bilingually and to switch codes without having always to translate, while I still have to speak English or Spanish when I would rather speak Spanglish, and as long as I have to accommodate the English speakers rather than having them accommodate me, my tongue will be illegitimate.

I will no longer be made to feel ashamed of existing. I will have my voice: Indian, Spanish, white. I will have my serpent's tongue—my woman's voice, my sexual voice, my poet's voice. I will overcome the tradition of silence.

> My fingers
> move sly against your palm
> Like women everywhere, we speak in code. …
>
> —Melanie Kaye/Kantrowitz

"VISTAS," CORRIDOS, Y COMIDA: MY NATIVE TONGUE

In the 1960s, I read my first Chicano novel. It was *City of Night* by John Rechy, a gay Texan, son of a Scottish father and a Mexican mother. For days I walked around in stunned amazement that a Chicano could write and could get published. When I read *I Am Joaquín* I was surprised to see a bilingual book by a Chicano in print. When I saw poetry written in Tex-Mex for the first time, a feeling of pure joy flashed through me. I felt like we really existed as a people. In 1971, when I started teaching High School English to Chicano students, I tried to supplement the required texts with works by Chicanos, only to be reprimanded and forbidden to do so by the principal. He claimed that I was supposed to teach "American" and English literature. At the risk of being fired, I swore my students to secrecy and slipped in Chicano short stories, poems, a play. In graduate school, while working toward a Ph.D., I had to "argue" with one advisor after the other, semester after semester, before I was allowed to make Chicano literature an area of focus.

Even before I read books by Chicanos or Mexicans, it was the Mexican movies I saw at the drive-in—the Thursday night special of $1.00 a carload—that gave me a sense of belonging. *"Vámonos a las vistas,"* my mother would call out and we'd all—grandmother, brothers, sister and cousins—squeeze into the car. We'd wolf down cheese and bologna white bread sandwiches while watching Pedro Infante in melodramatic tear-jerkers like *Nosotros los pobres,* the first "real" Mexican movie (that was not an imitation of European movies). I remember seeing *Cuando los hijos se van* and surmising that all Mexican movies played up the love a mother has for her children and what ungrateful sons and daughters suffer when they are not devoted to their mothers. I remember the singing-type "westerns" of Jorge Negrete and Miguel Aceves Mejía. When watching Mexican movies, I felt a sense of homecoming as well as alienation. People who were to amount to something didn't go to Mexican movies, or *bailes* or tune their radios to *bolero, rancherita,* and *corrido* music.

The whole time I was growing up, there *was norteño* music sometimes called North Mexican border music, or Tex-Mex music, or Chicano music, or *cantina* (bar) music. I grew up listening *to conjuntos,* three- or four-piece bands made up of folk musicians playing guitar, *bajo sexto,* drums and button accordion, which Chicanos had borrowed from the German immigrants who had come to Central Texas and Mexico to farm and build breweries. In the Rio Grande Valley, Steve Jordan and Little Joe Hernández were popular, and Flaco Jiménez was the accordion king. The rhythms of Tex-Mex music are those of the polka, also adapted from the Germans, who in turn had borrowed the polka from the Czechs and Bohemians.

I remember the hot, sultry evenings when *corridos*—songs of love and death on the Texas-Mexican borderlands—reverberated out of cheap amplifiers from the local *cantinas* and wafted in through my bedroom window,

Corridos first became widely used along the South Texas/Mexican border during the early conflict between Chicanos and Anglos. The *corridos* are usually about Mexican heroes who do valiant deeds against the Anglo oppressors. Pancho Villa's song, *"La cucaracha,"* is the most famous one. *Corridos* of John F. Kennedy and his death are still very popular in the Valley. Older Chicanos remember Lydia Mendoza, one of the great border *corrido* singers who was called *la Gloria de Tejas.* Her *"El tango negro,"* sung during the Great Depression, made her a singer of the people. The ever-present *corridos* narrated one hundred years of border history, bringing news of events as well as entertaining. These folk musicians and folk songs are our chief cultural myth-makers, and they made our hard lives seem bearable.

I grew up feeling ambivalent about our music. Country western and rock-and-roll had more status. In the 50s and 60s, for the slightly educated and *agringado* Chicanos, there existed a sense of shame at being caught listening to our music. Yet I couldn't stop my feet from thumping to the music, could not stop humming the words, nor hide from myself the exhilaration I felt when I heard it.

There are more subtle ways that we internalize identification, especially in the forms of images and emotions. For me food and certain smells are tied to my identity, to my homeland. Woodsmoke curling up to an immense blue sky; wood smoke perfuming my grandmother's clothes, her skin. The stench of cow manure and the yellow patches on the ground; the crack of a .22 rifle and the reek of cordite. Homemade white cheese sizzling in a pan, melting inside a folded *tortilla*. My sister Hilda's hot, spicy *menudo, chile colorado* making it deep red, pieces of *panza* and hominy floating on top. My brother Carito barbecuing *fajitas* in the backyard. Even now and 3,000 miles away, I can see my mother spicing the ground beef, pork and venison with chile. My mouth salivates at the thought of the hot steaming *tamales* I would be eating if I were home.

SI LE PREGUNTAS A MI MAMÁ, "¿QUÉ ERES?"

> "Identity is the essential core of who
> we are as individuals, the conscious
> experience of the self inside."
> —Kaufman

Nosotros los Chicanos straddle the borderlands. On one side of us, we are constantly exposed to the Spanish of the Mexicans, on the other side we hear the Anglos' incessant clamoring so that we forget our language. Among ourselves we don't say *nosotros los americanos, o nosotros los españoles, o nosotros los hispanos.* We say *nosotros los mexicanos* (by *mexicanos* we do not mean citizens of Mexico; we do not mean a national identity, but a racial one). We distinguish between *mexicanos del otro lado* and *mexicanos de este lado.* Deep in our hearts we believe that being Mexican has nothing to do with which country one lives in. Being Mexican is a state of soul—not one of mind, not one of citizenship. Neither eagle nor serpent, but both. And like the ocean, neither animal respects borders.

> *Dime con quien andas y te diré quien eres.*
> (Tell me who your friends are and I'll tell you who you are.)
> —Mexican saying

Si le preguntas a mi mamá "¿Qué eres?" te dirá, "Soy mexicana." My brothers and sister say the same. I sometimes will answer *"soy mexicana"* and at others will say *"soy Chicana" o "soy tejana."* But I identified as *"Raza"* before I ever identified as *"mexicana"* or "Chicana."

As a culture, we call ourselves Spanish when referring to ourselves as a linguistic group and when copping out. It is then that we forget our predominant Indian genes. We are 70–80% Indian. We call ourselves Hispanic or Spanish-American or Latin American or Latin when linking ourselves to other Spanish-speaking peoples of the Western hemisphere and when copping out. We call ourselves Mexican-American to signify we are neither Mexican nor American, but more the noun "American" than the adjective "Mexican" (and when copping out).

Chicanos and other people of color suffer economically for not acculturating. This voluntary (yet forced) alienation makes for psychological conflict, a kind of dual identity—we don't identify with the Anglo-American cultural values and we don't totally identify with the Mexican cultural values. We are a synergy of two cultures with various degrees of Mexicanness or Angloness. I have so internalized the borderland conflict that sometimes I feel like one cancels out the other and we are zero, nothing, no one. *A veces no soy nada ni nadie. Pero hasta cuando no lo soy, lo soy.*

When not copping out, when we know we are more than nothing, we call ourselves Mexican, referring to face and ancestry; *mestizo* when affirming both our Indian and Spanish (but we hardly ever own our Black ancestry); Chicano when referring to a politically aware people born and/or raised in the U.S.; *Raza* when referring to Chicanos; *tejanos* when we are Chicanos from Texas.

Chicanos did not know we were a people until 1965 when Cesar Chavez and the farm workers united and *I Am Joaquín* was published and *la Raza Unida* party was formed in Texas. With that recognition, we became a distinct people. Something momentous happened to the Chicano soul—we became aware of our reality and acquired a name and a language (Chicano Spanish) that reflected that reality. Now that we had a name, some of the fragmented pieces began to fall together—who we were, what we were, how we had evolved. We began to get glimpses of what we might eventually become.

Yet the struggle of identities continues, the struggle of borders is our reality still. One day the inner struggle will cease and a true integration take place. In the meantime, *tenemos que hacerla lucha. ¿Quién está protegiendo los ranchos de mi gente? ¿Quién está tratando de cerrar la fisura entre la india y el blanco en nuestra sangre? El Chicano, sí, el Chicano que anda como un ladrón en su propia casa.*

Los Chicanos, how patient we seem, how very patient. There is the quiet of the Indian about us. We know how to survive. When other races have given up their tongue, we've kept ours. We know what it is to live under the hammer blow of the dominant *norteamericano* culture. But more than we count the blows, we count the days the weeks the years the centuries the eons until the white laws and commerce and customs will rot in the deserts they've created, lie bleached. *Humildes* yet proud, *quietos* yet wild, *nosotros los mexicanos-Chicanos* will walk by the crumbling ashes as we go about our business. Stubborn, persevering, impenetrable as stone, yet possessing a malleability that renders us unbreakable, we, the *mestizas* and *mestizos,* will remain.

Subculture

The Meaning of Style

By Dick Hebdige

INTRODUCTION: SUBCULTURE AND STYLE

I managed to get about twenty photographs, and with bits of chewed bread I pasted them on the back of the cardboard sheet of regulations that hangs on the wall. Some are pinned with bits of brass wire which the foreman brings me and on which I have to string coloured glass heads. Using the same beads with which the prisoners next door make funeral wreaths, I have made star-shaped frames for the most purely criminal. In the evening, as you open your window to the street, I turn the hack of the regulation sheet towards me. Smiles and sneers, alike inexorably enter me by all the holes I offer. ... They watch over my little routines.

(Genet, 1966a)

N the opening pages of *The Thief's Journal*, Jean Genet describes how a tube of vaseline, found in his possession, is confiscated by the Spanish police during a raid. This 'dirty, wretched object', proclaiming his homosexuality to the world, becomes for Genet a kind of guarantee—'the sign of a secret grace which was soon to save me from contempt'. The discovery of the vaseline is greeted with laughter in the record-office of the station, and the police 'smelling of garlic, sweat and oil, but ... strong in their moral assurance' subject Genet to a tirade of hostile innuendo. The author joins in the laughter too ('though painfully') but later, in his cell, 'the image of the tube of vaseline never left me'.

I was sure that this puny and most humble object would hold its own against them; by its mere presence it would be able to exasperate all the police in the world; it would draw down upon itself contempt, hatred, white and dumb rages. (Genet, 1967)

I have chosen to begin with these extracts from Genet because he more than most has explored in both his life and his art the subversive implications of style. I shall be returning again and again to Genet's major themes: the status and meaning of revolt, the idea of style as a form of Refusal, the elevation of crime into art (even though, in our case, the 'crimes' are only broken codes). Like Genet, we are interested in subculture—in the expressive forms and rituals of those subordinate groups—the teddy boys and mods and rockers, the skinheads and the punks—who are alternately dismissed, denounced and canonized; treated at different times as threats to public order and as harmless buffoons. Like Genet also, we are intrigued by the most mundane objects—a safety pin, a pointed shoe, a motor cycle—which none the less, like the tube of vaseline, take on a symbolic dimension, becoming a form of stigmata, tokens of a self-imposed exile. Finally, like Genet, we must seek to recreate the dialectic between action and reaction which renders these objects meaningful. For, just as the conflict between Genet's 'unnatural' sexuality and the policemen's 'legitimate' outrage can be encapsulated in a single object, so the tensions between dominant and subordinate groups can be found reflected in the surfaces of subculture—in the styles made up of mundane objects which have a double meaning. On the one hand, they warn the 'straight' world in advance of a sinister presence—the presence of difference—and draw down upon themselves vague suspicions, uneasy laughter, 'white and dumb rages'. On the other hand, for those who erect them into icons, who use them as words or as curses, these objects become signs of forbidden identity, sources of value. Recalling his humiliation at the hands of the police, Genet finds consolation in the tube of vaseline. It becomes a symbol of his 'triumph'—'I would indeed rather have shed blood than repudiate that silly object' (Genet, 1967).

The meaning of subculture is, then, always in dispute, and style is the area in which the opposing definitions clash with most dramatic force. Much of the available space in this book will therefore be taken up with a description of the process whereby objects are made to mean and mean again as 'style' in subculture. As in Genet's novels, this process begins with a crime against the natural order, though in this case the deviation may seem slight indeed—the cultivation of a quiff, the acquisition of a scooter or a record or a certain type of suit. But it ends in the construction of a style, in a gesture of defiance or contempt, in a smile or a sneer. It signals a Refusal. I would like to think that this Refusal is worth making, that these gestures have a meaning, that the smiles and the sneers have some subversive value, even if, in the final analysis, they are, like Genet's gangster pin-ups, just the darker side of sets of regulations, just so much graffiti on a prison wall.

Even so, graffiti can make fascinating reading. They draw attention to themselves. They are an expression both of impotence and a kind of power—the power to disfigure [Norman Mailer calls graffiti—'Your presence on their Presence … hanging your alias on their scene' (Mailer, 1974)]. In this book I shall attempt to decipher the graffiti, to tease out the meanings embedded in the various post-war youth styles. But before we can proceed to individual subcultures, we must first define the basic terms. The word 'subculture' is loaded down with mystery. It suggests secrecy, masonic oaths, an Underworld. It also invokes the larger and no less difficult concept 'culture'. So it is with the idea of culture that we should begin.

ONE

From culture to hegemony
Culture

> Culture: cultivation, tending, in Christian authors, worship; the action or practice of cultivating the soil; tillage, husbandry; the cultivation or rearing of certain animals (e.g. fish); the artificial development of microscopic organisms, organisms so produced; the cultivating or development (of the mind, faculties, manners), improvement or refinement by education and training; the condition of being trained or refined; the intellectual side of civilization; the prosecution or special attention or study of any subject or pursuit. (*Oxford English Dictionary*)

Culture is a notoriously ambiguous concept as the above definition demonstrates. Refracted through centuries of usage, the word has acquired a number of quite different, often contradictory, meanings. Even as a scientific term, it refers both to a process (artificial development of microscopic organisms) and a product (organisms so produced). More specifically, since the end of the eighteenth century it has been used by English intellectuals and literary figures to focus critical attention on a whole range of controversial issues. The 'quality of life', the effects in human terms of mechanization, the division of labour and the creation of a mass society have all been discussed within the larger confines of what Raymond Williams has called the 'Culture and Society' debate (Williams, 1961). It was through this tradition of dissent and criticism that the dream of the 'organic society'—of society as an integrated, meaningful whole—was largely kept alive. The dream had two basic trajectories. One led back to the past and to the feudal ideal of a hierarchically ordered community. Here, culture assumed an almost sacred function. Its 'harmonious perfection' [Arnold, 1868] was posited against the Wasteland of contemporary life.

The other trajectory, less heavily supported, led towards the future, to a socialist Utopia where the distinction between labour and leisure was to be annulled. Two basic definitions of culture emerged from this tradition, though these were by no means necessarily congruent with the two trajectories outlined above. The first one—which is probably most familiar to the reader—was essentially classical and conservative. It represented culture as a standard of aesthetic excellence: 'the best that has been thought and said in the world' (Arnold, 1868), and it derived from an appreciation of 'classic' aesthetic form (opera, ballet, drama, literature, art). The second, traced back by Williams to Herder and the eighteenth century (Williams, 1976), was rooted in anthropology. Here the term 'culture' referred to a

> … particular way of life which expresses certain meanings and values not only in art and learning but also in institutions and ordinary behaviour. The analysis of culture, from such a definition, is the clarification of the meanings and values implicit and explicit in a particular way of life, a particular culture. (Williams, 1965)

This definition obviously had a much broader range. It encompassed, in T. S. Eliot's words,

> … all the characteristic activities and interests of a people. Derby Day, Henley Regatta, Cowes, the 12th of August, a cup final, the dog races, the pin table, the dartboard, Wensleydale cheese,

boiled cabbage cut into sections, beetroot in vinegar, 19th Century Gothic churches, the music of Elgar. …(Eliot, 1948)

As Williams noted, such a definition could only he supported if a new theoretical initiative was taken. The theory of culture now involved the 'study of relationships between elements in a whole way of life' (Williams, 1965). The emphasis shifted from immutable to historical criteria, from fixity to transformation:

> … an emphasis [which] from studying particular meanings and values seeks not so much to compare these, as a way of establishing a scale, but by studying their modes of change to discover certain general causes or 'trends' by which social and cultural developments as a whole can be better understood. (Williams, 1965)

Williams was, then, proposing an altogether broader formulation of the relationships between culture and society, one which through the analysis of 'particular meanings and values' sought to uncover the concealed fundamentals of history; the 'general causes' and broad social 'trends' which lie behind the manifest appearances of an 'everyday life'.

In the early years, when it was being established in the Universities, Cultural Studies sat rather uncomfortably on the fence between these two conflicting definitions—culture as a standard of excellence, culture as a 'whole way of life'—unable to determine which represented the most fruitful line of enquiry. Richard Hoggart and Raymond Williams portrayed working-class culture sympathetically in wistful accounts of pre-scholarship boyhoods (Leeds for Hoggart [1958], a Welsh mining village for Williams [1960]) but their work displayed a strong bias towards literature and literacy and an equally strong moral tone. Hoggart deplored the way in which the traditional working-class community—a community of tried and tested values despite the dour landscape in which it had been set—was being undermined and replaced by a 'Candy Floss World' of thrills and cheap fiction which was somehow bland *and* sleazy. Williams tentatively endorsed the new mass communications but was concerned to establish aesthetic and moral criteria for distinguishing the worthwhile products from the 'trash': the jazz—'a real musical form'—and the football—'a wonderful game'—from the 'rape novel, the Sunday strip paper and the latest Tin Pan drool' (Williams, 1965). In 1966 Hoggart laid down the basic premises upon which Cultural Studies were based:

> First, without appreciating good literature, no one will really understand the nature of society, second, literary critical analysis can be applied to certain social phenomena other than 'academically respectable' literature (for example, the popular arts, mass communications) so as to illuminate their meanings for individuals and their societies. (Hoggart, 1966)

The implicit assumption that it still required a literary sensibility to 'read' society with the requisite subtlety, and that the two ideas of culture could lie ultimately reconciled was also, paradoxically, to inform the early work of the French writer, Roland Barthes, though here it found validation in a method—semiotics—a way of reading signs (Hawkes, 1977).

Barthes: Myths and signs

Using models derived from the work of the Swiss linguist Ferdinand de Saussure, Barthes sought to expose the *arbitrary* nature of cultural phenomena, to uncover the latent meanings of an everyday life which, to all intents and purposes, was 'perfectly natural'. Unlike Hoggart, Barthes was not concerned with distinguishing the good from the bad in modern mass culture, but rather with showing how *all* the apparently spontaneous forms and rituals of contemporary bourgeois societies are subject to a systematic distortion, liable at any moment to be dehistoricized, 'naturalized', converted into myth:

> The whole of France is steeped in this anonymous ideology: our press, our films, our theatre, our pulp literature, our rituals, our Justice, our diplomacy, our conversations, our remarks about the weather, a murder trial, a touching wedding, the cooking we dream of, the garments we wear, everything in everyday life is dependent on the representation which the bourgeoisie *has and makes us have* of the relations between men and the world. (Barthes, 1972)

Like Eliot, Barthes' notion of culture extends beyond the library, the opera-house and the theatre to encompass the whole of everyday life. But this everyday life is for Barthes overlaid with a significance which is at once more insidious and more systematically organised. Starting from the premise that 'myth is a type of speech', Barthes set out in *Mythologies* to examine the normally hidden set of rules, codes and conventions through which meanings particular to specific social groups (i.e. those in power) are rendered universal and 'given' for the whole of society, He found in phenomena as disparate as a wrestling match, a writer on holiday, a tourist-guide book, the same artificial nature, the same ideological core. Each had been exposed to the same prevailing rhetoric (the rhetoric of common sense) and turned into myth, into a mere element in a 'second-order semiological system' (Barthes, 1972). (Barthes uses the example of a photograph in *Paris-Match* of a Negro soldier saluting the French flag, which has a first and second order connotation: (1) a gesture of loyalty, but also (2) 'France is a great empire, and all her sons, without colour discrimination, faithfully serve under her flag'.)

Barthes' application of a method rooted in linguistics to other systems of discourse outside language (fashion, film, food, etc.) opened up completely new possibilities for contemporary cultural studies. It was hoped that the invisible seam between language, experience and reality could be located and prised open through a semiotic analysis of this kind: that the gulf between the alienated intellectual and the 'real' world could be rendered meaningful and, miraculously, at the same time, be made to disappear. Moreover, under Barthes' direction, semiotics promised nothing less than the reconciliation of the two conflicting definitions of culture upon which Cultural Studies was so ambiguously posited—a marriage of moral conviction (in this case, Barthes' Marxist beliefs) and popular themes: the study of a society's total way of life.

This is not to say that semiotics was easily assimilable within the Cultural Studies project. Though Barthes shared the literary preoccupations of Hoggart and Williams, his work introduced a new Marxist 'problematic' which was alien to the British tradition of concerned and largely untheorized 'social commentary'. As a result, the old debate seemed suddenly unlimited. In E. P. Thompson's words it appeared to reflect the parochial concerns of a group of 'gentlemen amateurs'. Thompson sought to replace Williams' definition of the theory of culture as 'a theory of relations between elements in a whole way of life' with his own more rigorously Marxist formulation: 'the study of relationships in a whole way of *conflict*'. A more analytical framework was required; a new vocabulary had to he learned. As part of this process of theorization, the word 'ideology' came to acquire a much wider range of meanings than had previously been the case. We have seen how Barthes found an 'anonymous ideology' penetrating every possible level of social life, inscribed in the most mundane of rituals, framing the most casual social encounters. But how can ideology be 'anonymous', and how can it assume such a broad significance? Before we attempt any reading of subcultural style, we must first define the term 'ideology' more precisely.

Ideology: A lived relation

In the German Ideology, Marx shows how the basis of the capitalist economic structure (surplus value, neatly defined by Godelier as 'Profit ... is unpaid work' [Godelier, 1970]) is hidden from the consciousness of the agents of production. The failure to see through appearances to the real relations which underlie them does not occur as the direct result of some kind of masking operation consciously carried out by individuals, social groups or institutions. On the contrary, ideology by definition thrives *beneath* consciousness. It is here, at the level of 'normal common sense', that ideological frames of reference are most firmly sedimented and most effective, because it is here that their ideological nature is most effectively concealed. As Stuarl Hall puts it:

> It is precisely its 'spontaneous' quality, its transparency, its 'naturalness', its refusal to be made to examine the premises on which it is founded, its resistance to change or to correction, its effect of instant recognition, and the closed circle in which it moves which makes common sense, at one and the same time, 'spontaneous', ideological and *unconscious*. You cannot learn, through common sense, *how things are*: you can only discover *where they fit* into the existing scheme of things. In this way, its very taken-for-grantedness is what establishes it as a medium in which its own premises and presuppositions are being rendered *invisible* by its apparent transparency. (Hall, 1977)

Since ideology saturates everyday discourse in the form of common sense, it cannot be bracketed off from everyday life as a self-contained set of 'political opinions' or 'biased views'. Neither can it he reduced to the abstract dimensions of a 'world view' or used in the crude Marxist sense to designate 'false consciousness". Instead, as Louis Althusser has pointed out:

> ... ideology has very little to do with 'consciousness"' ... It is profoundly *unconscious*. ... Ideology is indeed a system of representation, but in the majority of cases these representations have nothing to do with 'consciousness': they are usually images and occasionally concepts, but it is above all as *structures* that they impose on the vast majority of men, not via their 'consciousness'. They are perceived-accepted-suffered cultural objects and they act functionally on men via a process that escapes them. (Althusser, 1969)

Although Althusser is here referring to structures like the family, cultural and political institutions, etc., we can illustrate the point quite simply by taking as our example a physical structure. Most modern institutes of education, despite the apparent neutrality of the materials from which they are constructed (red brick, white tile, etc.) carry within themselves implicit ideological assumptions which are literally structured into the architecture itself. The categorization of knowledge into arts and sciences is reproduced in the faculty system which houses different disciplines in different buildings, and most colleges maintain the traditional divisions by devoting a separate floor to each subject. Moreover, the hierarchical relationship between teacher and taught is inscribed in the very lay-out of the lecture theatre where the seating arrangements—benches rising in tiers before a raised lectern—dictate the flow of information and serve to 'naturalize' professorial authority. Thus, a whole range of decisions about what is and what is not possible within education have been made, however unconsciously, before the content of individual courses is even decided.

These decisions help to set the limits not only on what is taught but on *how* it is taught. Here the buildings literally *reproduce* in concrete terms prevailing (ideological) notions about what education *is* and it is through this process that the educational structure, which can, of course, be altered, is placed beyond question and appears to us as a 'given' (i.e. as immutable). In this case, the frames of our thinking have been translated into actual bricks and mortar.

Social relations and processes are then appropriated by individuals only through the forms in which they are represented to those individuals. These forms are, as we have seen, by no means transparent. They are shrouded in a 'common sense' which simultaneously validates and mystifies them. It is precisely these 'perceived-accepted-suffered cultural objects' which semiotics sets out to 'interrogate' and decipher. All aspects of culture possess a semiotic value, and the most taken-for-granted phenomena can function as signs: as elements in communication systems governed by semantic rules and codes which are not themselves directly apprehended in experience. These signs are, then, as opaque as the social relations which produce them and which they re-present. In other words, there is an ideological dimension to every signification:

> A sign does not simply exist as part of reality—it reflects and refracts another reality. Therefore it may distort that reality or be true to it, or may perceive it from a special point of view, and so forth. Every sign is subject to the criteria of ideological evaluation. … The domain of ideology coincides with the domain of signs. They equate with one another. Whenever a sign is present, ideology is present too. Everything ideological possesses a semiotic value. (Volosinov, 1973)

To uncover the ideological dimension of signs we must final try to disentangle the codes through which meaning is organized. 'Connotative' codes are particularly important. As Stuart Hall has argued, they '… cover the face of social life and render it classifiable, intelligible, meaningful' (Hall. 1977). He goes on to describe these codes as 'maps of meaning' which are of necessity the product of selection. They cut across a range of potential meanings, making certain meanings available and ruling others out of court. We tend to live inside these maps as surely as we live in the 'real' world: they 'think' us as much as we 'think' them, and this in itself is quite 'natural'. All human societies *reproduce* themselves in this way through a process of 'naturalisation'. It is through this process—a kind of inevitable reflex of all social life—that *particular* sets of social relations, *particular* ways of organizing the world appear to us as if they were universal and timeless. This is what Althusser (1971) means when he says that 'ideology has no history' and that ideology in this general sense will always be an 'essential element of every social formation' (Althusser and Balibar, 1968).

However, in highly complex societies like ours, which function through a finely graded system of divided (i.e. specialised) labour, the crucial question has to do with which specific ideologies, representing the interests of which specific groups and classes will prevail at any given moment, in any given situation. To deal with this question, we must first consider how power is distributed in our society. That is, we must ask which groups and classes have how much say in defining, ordering and classifying out the social world. For instance, if we pause to reflect for a moment, it should be obvious that access to the means by which ideas are disseminated in our society (i.e. principally the mass media) is *not* the same for all classes. Some groups have more say, more opportunity to make the rules, to organize meaning, while others are less favorably placed, have less power to produce and impose their definitions of the world on the world.

Thus, when we come to look beneath the level of ideology in general at the way in which specific ideologies work, how some gain dominance and others remain marginal, we can see that in advanced Western democracies the ideological field is by no means neutral. To return to the 'connotative' codes to which Stuart Hall refers we can see that these 'maps of meaning' are charged with a potentially explosive significance because they are traced and re-traced along the lines laid down by the *dominant* discourses about reality, the *dominant* ideologies. They thus tend to represent, in however obscure and contradictory a fashion, the interests of the *dominant* groups in society.

To understand this point we should refer to Marx:

> The ideas of the ruling class are in every epoch the ruling ideas, i.e. the class which is the ruling *material* force of society is at the same time its ruling *intellectual* force. The class which has the means of material production at its disposal, has control at the same time over the means of mental production, so that generally speaking, the ideas of those who lack the means of mental production are subject to it. The ruling ideas are nothing more than the ideal expression of the dominant material relationships grasped as ideas; hence of the relationships which make the one class the ruling class, therefore the ideas of its dominance. (Marx and Engels, 1970)

This is the basis of Antonio Gramsci's theory of *hegemony* which provides the most adequate account of how dominance is sustained in advanced capitalist societies.

Hegemony: The moving equilibrium
'Society cannot share a common communication system so long as it is split into warring classes' (Brecht, *A Short Organum for the Theatre*).

The term hegemony refers to a situation in which a provisional alliance of certain social groups can exert 'total social authority' over other subordinate groups, not simply by coersion or by the direct imposition of ruling ideas, but by 'winning and shaping consent so that the power of the dominant classes appears both legitimate and natural' (Hall, 1977). Hegemony can only be maintained so long as the dominant classes 'succeed in framing all competing definitions within their range' (Hall, 1977), so that subordinate groups are, if not controlled; then at least contained within an ideological space which does not seem at all 'ideological': which appears instead to be permanent and 'natural', to lie outside history, to be beyond particular interests (see *Social Trends*, no. 6. 1975).

This is how, according to Barthes, 'mythology' performs its vital function of naturalization and normalization and it is in his book *Mythologies* that Barthes demonstrates most forcefully the full extension of these normalized forms and meanings. However, Gramsci adds the important proviso that hegemonic power, precisely *because* it requires the consent of the dominated majority, can never be permanently exercised by the same alliance of 'class fractions'. As has been pointted out, 'Hegemony ... is not universal and "given" to the continuing rule of a particular class. It has to he won, reproduced, sustained. Hegemony is, as Gramsci said, a "moving equilibrium" containing relations of forces favourable or unfavourable to this or that tendency' (Hall *et al.*, 1976a).

In the same way, forms cannot be permanently normalized. They can always be deconstructed, demystified, hy a 'mythologist' like Barthes. Moreover commodities can he symbolically 'repossessed' in every day life, and endowed with implicitly oppositional meanings, by the very groups who originally produced them. The symbiosis in which ideology and social order, production and reproduction, are linked is then neither fixed nor guaranteed. It can be prised open. The consensus can be fractured, challenged, overruled, and resistance to the groups in dominance cannot always be lightly dismissed or automatically incorporated. Although, as Lefebvre has written, we live in a society where '... objects in practice become signs and signs objects and a second nature takes the place of the first the initial layer of perceptible reality' Lefebvre, 1971), there are, as he goes on to affirm, always 'objections and contradictions which hinder the closing of the circuit' between sign and object, production and reproduction.

We can now return to the meaning of youth subcultures, for the emergence of such groups has signalled in a spectacular fashion the breakdown of consensus in the post-war period. In the following chapters we shall see that it is precisely objections and contradictions of the kind which Lefebvre has described that find expression in subculture. However, the challenge to hegemony which subcultures represent is not issued directly by them. Rather it is expressed obliquely, in style. The objections are lodged, the contradictions displayed (and, as we shall see, 'magically resolved') at the profoundly superficial level of appearances: that is, at the level of signs. For the sign-eommunity, the community of myth-consumers, is not a uniform body, As Volosinov has written, it is cut through by class:

> Class does not coincide with the sign community, i.e. with the totality of users of the same
> set of signs of ideological communication. Thus various different classes will use one and the
> same language. As a result, differently oriented accents intersect in every ideological sign. Sign
> becomes the arena of the class struggle. (Volosinov, 1973)

The struggle between different discourses, different definitions and meanings within ideology is therefore always, at the same time, a struggle within signification: a struggle for possession of the sign which extends to even the most mundane areas of everyday life. To turn once more to the examples used in the Introduction, to the safety pins and tubes of vaseline, we can see that such commodities are indeed open to a double inflection: to 'illegitimate' as well as 'legitimate' uses. These 'humble objects' can be magically appropriated; 'stolen' by subordinate groups and made to carry 'secret' meanings: meanings which express, in code, a form of resistance to the order which guarantees their continued subordination.

Style in subculture is, then, pregnant with significance. Its transformations go 'against nature', interrupting the process of 'normalisation'. As such, they are gestures, movements towards a speech which offends the 'silent majority', which challenges the principle of unity and cohesion, which contradicts the myth of consensus. Our task becomes, like Barthes', to discern the hidden messages inscribed in code on the glossy surfaces of style, to trace them out as 'maps of meaning' which obscurely re-present the very contradictions they are designed to resolve or conceal.

Academics who adopt a semiotic approach are not alone in reading significance into the loaded surfaces of life. The existence of spectacular subcultures continually opens up those surfaces to other potentially subversive readings. Jean Genet, the archetype of the 'unnatural' deviant, again exemplifies the practice of resistance through style. He is as convinced in his own way as is Roland Barthes of the ideological character of cultural signs. He is equally oppressed by the seamless web of forms and meanings which encloses and yet excludes him. His reading is equally partial. He makes his own list and draws his own conclusions:

> I was astounded by so rigorous an edifice whose details were united against me. Nothing in the world is irrelevant: the stars on the general's sleeve, the stockmarket quotations, the olive harvest, the style of the judiciary, the wheat exchange, the flower-beds. … Nothing. This order … had a meaning—my exile. (Genet, 1967)

It is this alienation from the deceptive 'innocence' of appearances which gives the teds, the mods, the punks and no doubt future groups of as yet unimaginable 'deviants' the impetus to move from man's second 'false nature' (Barthes, 1972) to a genuinely expressive artifice; a truly subterranean style. As a symbolic violation of the social order, such a movement attracts and will continue to attract attention, to provoke censure and to act, as we shall see, as the fundamental bearer of significance in subculture.

No subculture has sought with more grim determination than the punks to detach itself from the taken-for-granted landscape of normalized forms, nor to bring down upon itself such vehement disapproval. We shall begin therefore with the moment of punk and we shall return to that moment throughout the course of this hook. It is perhaps appropriate that the punks, who have made such large claims for illiteracy, who have pushed profanity to such startling extremes, should be used to test some of the methods for 'reading' signs evolved in the centuries-old debate on the sanctity of culture.

TWO

April 3, 1989, Marrakech
The chic thing is to dress in expensive tailor-made rags and all the queens are camping about in wild-boy drag. There are Bowery suits that appear to he stained with urine and vomit which on closer inspection turn out to be intricate embroideries of fine gold thread. There are clochard suits of the finest linen, shabby gentility suits … felt hats seasoned by old junkies … Joud cheap pi nip suits that turn out to be ziot so elicap the loudness is a subtle harmony of colours only the very hest Poor Boy shops can turn out. … It is the double take and many carry it much further to as many as six takes (William Burroughs, 1969)

Holiday in the sun: Mister Rotten makes the grade

THE British summer of 1976 was extraordinarily hot and dry: there were no recorded precedents. From May through to August, London parched and sweltered under luminous skies and the inevitable fog of exhaust fumes. Initially hailed as a Godsend, and a national 'tonic' in the press and television (was Britain's 'curse' finally broken?) the sun provided seasonal relief from the dreary cycle of doom-laden headlines which had dominated the front pages of the tabloids throughout the winter. Nature performed its statutory ideological function and 'stood in' for all the other 'bad news', provided tangible proof of 'improvement' and pushed aside the strikes and the dissension. With predictable regularity, 'bright young things' were shown flouncing along Oxford Street in harem bags and beach shorts, bikini tops and polaroids in that last uplifting item for the *News at Ten*. The sun served as a 'cheeky' postscript to the crisis: a light hearted addendum filled with tropical promise. The crisis, too, could have its holiday. But as the weeks and months passed and the heatwave continued, the old mythology of doom and disaster was reasserted with a vengeance. The 'miracle' rapidly became a commonplace, an everyday affair, until one morning in mid-July it was suddenly re-christened a 'freak disorder': a dreadful, last, unlooked-for factor in Britain's decline.

The heatwave was officially declared a drought in August, water was rationed, crops were failing, and Hyde Park's grass burned into a delicate shade of raw sienna. The end was at hand and Last Days imagery began to figure once more in the press. Economic categories, cultural and natural phenomena were confounded with more than customary abandon until the drought took on an almost metaphysical significance. A Minister for Drought was appointed. Nature had now been officially declared 'unnatural', and all the age-old inferences were drawn with an obligatory modicum of irony to keep within the hounds of common sense. In late August, two events of completely different mythical stature coincided to confirm the worst forebodings: it was demonstrated that the excessive heat was threatening the very structure of the nation's houses (cracking the foundations) and the Notting Hill Carnival, traditionally a paradigm of racial harmony, exploded into violence. The Caribbean festival, with all its Cook's Tours con-notations of happy, dancing coloured folk, of jaunty bright calypsos and exotic costumes, was suddenly, unaccountably, transformed into a menacing congregation of angry black youths and embattled police. Hordes of young black Britons did the Soweto dash across the nation's television screens and conjured up fearful images of other Negroes, other confrontations, other 'long, hot summers'. The humble dustbin lid, the staple of every steel band, the symbol of the 'carnival spirit', of Negro ingenuity and the resilience of ghetto culture, took on an altogether more ominous significance when used by white-faced policemen as a desperate shield against an angry rain of bricks.

It was during this strange apocalyptic summer that punk made its sensational debut in the music press. In London, especially in the south west and more specifically in the vicinity of the King's Road, a new style was being generated combining elements drawn from a whole range of heterogeneous youth styles. In fact punk claimed a dubious parentage. Strands from David Bowie and glitter-rock were woven together with elements from American proto-punk (the Ramones, the Heartbreakers, Iggy Pop, Richard Hell), from that faction within London pub-rock (the 101-ers, the Gorillas, etc.) inspired by the mod subculture of the 60s, from the Canvey Island 40s revival and the Southend r & b bands (Dr Feelgood, Lew Lewis, etc.), from northern soul and from reggae.

Not surprisingly, the resulting mix was somewhat unstable: all these elements constantly threatened to separate and return to their original sources. Glam rock contributed narcissism, nihilism and gender confusion. American punk offered a minimalist aesthetic (e.g. the Ramones' 'Pinhead' or Crime's 'I Stupid'), the cult of the Street and a penchant for self-laceration. Northern Soul (a genuinely secret subculture of working-class youngsters dedicated to acrobatic dancing and fast American soul of the 60s, which centres on clubs like the Wigan Casino) brought its subterranean tradition of fast, jerky rhythms, solo dance styles and amphetamines: reggae its exotic and dangerous aura of forbidden identity, its conscience, its dread and its cool. Native rhythm 'n blues reinforced the brashness and the speed of Northern Soul, took rock back to the basics and contributed a highly developed iconoclasm, a thoroughly British persona and an extremely selective appropriation of the rock 'n roll heritage.

This unlikely alliance of diverse and superficially incompatible musical traditions, mysteriously accomplished under punk, found ratification in an equally eclectic clothing style which reproduced the same kind of cacophony on the visual level. The whole ensemble, literally safety-pinned together, became the celebrated and highly photogenic phenomenon known as punk which throughout 1977 provided the tabloids with a fund of predictably sensational copy and the quality press with a welcome catalogue of beautifully broken codes. Punk reproduced the entire sartorial history of post-war working-class youth cultures in 'cut up' form, combining elements which had originally belonged to completely different epochs. There was a chaos of quiffs and leather jackets, brothel creepers and winkle pickers, plimsolls and paka macs, moddy crops and skinhead strides, drainpipes and vivid socks, bum freezers and bovver boots—all kept 'in place' and 'out of time' by the spectacular adhesives: the safety pins and plastic clothes pegs, the bondage straps and bits of string which attracted so much horrified and fascinated attention. Punk is therefore a singularly appropriate point of departure for a study of this kind because punk style contained distorted reflections of all the major post-war subcultures. But before we can interpret the significance of these subcultures, we must first unscramble the sequence in which they occurred.

Boredom in Babylon

> Ordinary life is so dull that I get out of it as much as possible. (Steve Jones, a Sex Pistol, quoted in *Melody Maker*)

It seems entirely appropriate that punk's 'unnatural' synthesis should have hit the London streets during that bizarre summer. Apocalypse was in the air and the rhetoric of punk was drenched in apocalypse: in the stock imagery of crisis and sudden change. Indeed, even punk's epiphanies were hybrid affairs, representing the awkward and unsteady confluence of the two radically dissimilar languages of *reggae* and *rock*. As the shock-haired punks began to gather in a shop called Sex on a comer of the King's Road, aptly named the Worlds End, David Bowie's day of the *Diamond Dogs* (R.C.A. Victor, 1974) and the triumph of the 'super-alienated humanoid' was somehow made to coincide with reggae's Day of Judgement, with the overthrow of Babylon and the end of alienation altogether.

It is here that we encounter the first of punk's endemic contradictions, for the visions of apocalypse superficially fused in punk came from essentially antagonistic sources. David Bowie and the New York punk hands had pieced together from a variety of acknowledged 'artistic' sources—from the literary *avant-garde* and the underground cinema—a self-consciously profane and terminal aesthetic. Patti Smith, an American punk and ex-art student, claimed to have invented a new form, 'rock poetry', and incorporated readings from Rimbaud and William Burroughs into her act. Bowie, too, cited Burroughs as an influence and used his famous cut-up technique of random juxtapositions to 'compose' lyrics. Richard Hell drew on the writings of Lautréamont and Huysmans. British punk hands, generally younger and more self-consciously proletarian, remained largely innocent of literature. However, for better or worse, the literary sources turned out to be firmly although implicitly inscribed hi the aesthetics of British punk too. Similarly, there were connections (via Warhol and Wayne County in America, via the art school hands like the Who and the Clash in Britain) with underground cinema and *avant-garde* art.

By the early 70s these tendencies had begun to cohere into a fully fledged nihilist aesthetic and the emergence of this aesthetic together with its characteristic focal concerns (polymorphous, often wilfully perverse sexuality, obsessive individualism, fragmented sense of self, etc.) generated a good deal of controversy amongst those interested in rock culture (see Melly, 1972; Taylor and Wall, 1976). From Jagger in *Performance* (Warner Bros, 1969) to Bowie as the 'thin white duke', the spectre of the dandy 'drowning in his own opera' (Sartre, 1968) has haunted rock from the wings as it were, and in the words of Ian Taylor and Dave Wall 'plays back the alienation of youth onto itself' (1976). Punk represents the most recent phase in this process. In punk, alienation assumed an almost tangible quality. It could almost be grasped. It gave itself up to the cameras in 'blankness', the removal of expression (see any photograph of any punk group), the refusal to speak and be positioned. This trajectory—the solipsism, the neurosis, the cosmetic rage—had its origins in rock.

But at almost every turn the dictates of this profane aesthetic were countermanded by the righteous imperatives of another musical form: reggae. Reggae occupies the other end of that wide spectrum of influences which bore upon punk. As early as May 1977 Jordan, the famous punk shop assistant of Sex and Seditionaries was expressing a preference for reggae over 'new wave' on the pages of the *New Musical Express* (7 May 1977). 'It's the only music we [i.e. Jordan and J. Rotten] dance to.' Although Rotten himself insisted on the relative autonomy of punk and reggae, he displayed a detailed knowledge of the more esoteric reggae numbers in a series of interviews throughout 1977. Most conspicuously amongst punk groups, the Clash were heavily influenced not only by the music, but also by the visual iconography of black Jamaican street style. Khaki battle dress stencilled with the Caribbean legends DUB and HEAVY MANNERS, narrow 'sta-prest' trousers, black brogues and slip ons, even the pork pie hat, were all adopted at different times by various members of the group. In addition, the group played 'White Riot', a song inspired directly by the '76 Carnival, against a screen-printed backdrop of the Notting Mill disturbances, and they toured with a reggae discotheque presided over by Don Letts, the black Kastafarian d-j who shot the documentary film *Punk* while working at the Roxy Club in Covent Garden.

As we shall see, although apparently separate and autonomous, punk and the black British subcultures with which reggae is associated were connected at a deep structural level. But the dialogue between the two forms cannot properly be decoded until the internal composition and significance of both reggae and the British working-class youth cultures which preceded punk are fully understood. This involves two major tasks. First reggae must be traced back to its roots in the West Indies, and second the history of post-war British youth culture must be reinterpreted as a succession of differential responses to the black immigrant presence in Britain from the 1950s onwards. Such a reassessment demands a shift of emphasis away from the normal areas of interest—the school, police, media and parent culture (which have anyway been fairly exhaustively treated by other writers, see, e.g. Hall *et al.*, 1976)—to what I feel to be the largely neglected dimension of race and race relations.

The Technology and the Society

By Raymond Williams

I t is often said that television has altered our world. In the same way, people often speak of a new world, new society, a new phase of history, being created—'brought about'—by this or that new technology: the steam-engine, he automobile, the atomic bomb. Most of us know what is generally implied when such things are said. But this may be the central difficulty: that we have got so used to statements of this general kind, in our most ordinary discussions, that we can fail to realise their specific meanings.

For behind all such statements lie some of the most difficult and most unresolved historical and philosophical questions. Yet the questions are not posed by the statements; indeed they are ordinarily masked by them. Thus we often discuss, with animation, this or that 'effect' of television, or the kinds of social behaviour, the cultural and psychological 'conditions, which television has 'led to', without feeling ourselves obliged to ask whether it is reasonable to describe any technology as a cause, or, if we think of it as a cause, as what kind of cause, and in what relations with other kinds of causes. The most precise and discriminating local study of 'effects' can remain superficial if we have not looked into the notions of use and effect, as between a technology and a society, a technology and a culture, a technology and a psychology, which underlie our questions and may often determine our answers.

It can of course be said that these fundamental questions are very much too difficult; and that they are indeed difficult is very soon obvious to anyone who tries to follow them through. We could spend our lives trying to answer them, whereas here and now, in a society in which television is important, there is immediate and practical work to be done: surveys to be made, research undertaken; surveys and research, moreover, which we know how to do. It is an appealing position, and it has the advantage, in our kind of society, that it is understood as practical, so that it can then be supported and funded. By contrast, other kinds of question seem merely theoretical and abstract.

Yet all questions about cause and effect, as between a technology and a society, are intensely practical. Until we have begun to answer them, we really do not know, in any particular case, whether, for example, we are talking about a technology or about the uses of a technology; about necessary institutions or particular and changeable institutions; about a content or about a form. And this is not only a matter of intellectual uncertainty; it is a matter of social practice. If the technology is a cause, we can at best modify or seek to control its effects. Or if the technology, as used, is an effect, to what other kinds of cause, and other kinds of action, should we refer and relate our experience of its uses? These are not abstract questions. They form an increasingly important part of our social and cultural arguments, and they are being decided all the time in real practice, by real and effective decisions.

It is with these problems in mind that I want to try to analyse television as a particular cultural technology, and to look at its development, its institutions, its forms and its effects, in this critical dimension. In the present chapter, I shall begin the analysis under three headings: (a) versions of cause and effect in technology and society; (b) the social history of television as a technology; (c) the social history of the uses of television technology.

A. VERSIONS OF CAUSE AND EFFECT IN TECHNOLOGY AND SOCIETY

We can begin by looking again at the general statement that television has altered our world. It is worth setting down some of the different things this kind of statement has been taken to mean. For example:

(i) Television was invented as a result of scientific and technical research. Its power as a medium of news and entertainment was then so great that it altered all preceding media of news and entertainment.

(ii) Television was invented as a result of scientific and technical research. Its power as a medium of social communication was then so great that it altered many of our institutions and forms of social relationships.

(iii) Television was invented as a result of scientific and technical research. Its inherent properties as an electronic medium altered our basic perceptions of reality, and thence our relations with each other and with the world.

(iv) Television was invented as a result of scientific and technical research. As a powerful medium of communication and entertainment it takes its place with other factors—such as greatly increased physical mobility, itself the result of other newly invented technologies—in altering the scale and form of our societies.

(v) Television was invented as a result of scientific and technical research, and developed as a medium of entertainment and news. It then had unforeseen consequences, not only on other entertainment and news media, which it reduced in viability and importance, but on some of the central processes family, cultural and social life.

(vi) Television, discovered as a possibility technical research, was selected for investment and development to meet the needs of a new kind of society, especially in the provision of centralised entertainment and in the centralised formations of opinions and styles of behaviour.

(vii) Television, discovered as a possibility by scientific and technical research, was selected for investment and promotion as a new and profitable phase of a domestic consumer economy; it is then one of the characteristic 'machines for the home'.

(viii) Television became available as a result of scientific and technical research, and in its character and uses exploited and emphasised elements of a passivity, a cultural and psychological inadequacy, which had always been latent in people, but which television now organised and came to represent.

(ix) Television became available as a result of scientific and technical research, and in its character and uses both served and exploited the needs of a new kind of large-scale and complex but atomised society.

These are only some of the possible glosses on the ordinary bald statement that television has altered our world. Many people hold mixed versions of what are really alternative opinions, and in some cases there is some inevitable overlapping. But we can distinguish between two broad classes of opinion.

In the first—(i) to (v)—the technology is in effect accidental. Beyond the strictly internal development of the technology there is no reason why any particular invention should have come about. Similarly it then has consequences which are also in the true sense accidental, since they follow directly from the technology itself. If television had not been invented, this argument would run, certain definite social and cultural events would not have occurred.

In the second—(vi) to (ix)—television is again, in effect, a technological accident, but its significance lies in its uses, which are held to be symptomatic of some order of society or some qualities of human nature which are otherwise determined. If television had not been invented, this argument runs, we would still be manipulated or mindlessly entertained, but in some other way and perhaps less powerfully.

For all the variations of local interpretation and emphasis, these two classes of opinion underlie the overwhelming majority of both professional and amateur views of the effects of television. What they have in common is the fundamental form of the statement: 'television has altered our world'.

It is then necessary to make a further theoretical distinction. The first class of opinion, described above, is usually known, at least to its opponents, as *technological determinism*. It is an immensely powerful and now largely orthodox view of the nature of social change. New technologies are discovered, by an essentially internal process of research and development, which then sets the conditions for social change and progress. Progress, in particular, is the history of these inventions, which 'created the modern world'. The effects of the technologies, whether direct or indirect, foreseen or unforeseen, are as it were the rest of history. The steam engine, the automobile, television, the atomic bomb, have *made* modern man and the modern condition.

The second class of opinion appears less determinist. Television, like any other technology, becomes available as an element or a medium in a process of change that is in any case occurring or about to occur. By contrast with pure technological determinism, this view emphasises other causal factors in social change. It then considers particular technologies, or a complex of technologies, as *symptoms* of change of some other kind. Any particular technology is then as it were a by-product of a social process that is otherwise determined. It only acquires effective status when it is used for purposes which are already contained in this known social process.

The debate between these two general positions occupies the greater part of our thinking about technology and society. It is a real debate, and each side makes important points. But it is in the end sterile, because each position, though in different ways, has abstracted technology from society. In *technological determinism*, research and development have been assumed as self-generating. The new technologies are invented as it were in an independent sphere, and then create new societies or new human conditions. The view of *symptomatic technology*, similarly, assumes that research and development are self-generating, but in a more marginal way. What is discovered in the margin is then taken up and used.

Each view can then be seen to depend on the isolation of technology. It is either a self-acting force which creates new ways of life, or it is a self-acting force which provides materials for new ways of life. These positions are so deeply established, in modern social thought, that it is very difficult to think beyond them. Most histories of technology, like most histories of scientific discovery, are written from their assumptions. An appeal to 'the facts', against this or that interpretation, is made very difficult simply because the histories are usually written, consciously or unconsciously, to illustrate the assumptions. This is either explicit, with the consequential interpretation attached, or more often implicit, in that the history of technology or of scientific development is offered as a history on its own. This can be seen as a device of specialisation or of emphasis, but it then necessarily implies merely internal intentions and criteria.

To change these emphases would require prolonged and cooperative intellectual effort. But in the particular case of television it may be possible to outline a different kind of interpretation, which would allow us to see not only its history but also its uses in a more radical way. Such an interpretation would differ from technological determinism in that it would restore intention to the process of research and development. The technology would be seen, that is to say, as being looked for and developed with certain purposes and practices already in mind. At the same time the interpretation would differ from symptomatic technology in that these purposes and practices would be seen as direct: as known social needs, purposes and practices to which the technology is not marginal but central.

B. THE SOCIAL HISTORY OF TELEVISION AS A TECHNOLOGY

The invention of television was no single event or series of events. It depended on a complex of inventions and developments in electricity, telegraphy, photography and motion pictures, and radio. It can be said to have separated out as a specific technological objective in the period 1875–1890, and then, after a lag, to have developed as a specific technological enterprise from 1920 through to the first public television systems of the 1930s. Yet in each of these stages it depended for parts of its realisation on inventions made with other ends primarily in view.

Until the early nineteenth century, investigations of electricity, which had long been known as a phenomenon, were primarily philosophical: investigations of a puzzling natural effect. The technology associated with these investigations directed towards isolation and concentration of clearer study. Towards the end of the eighteen century there began to be applications, characteristically in relation to other known natural effects (lightning conductors). But there is then a key transitional period in a cluster of invention between 1800 and 1831, ranging from Volta's battery to Faraday's demonstration of electro-magnetic induction, leading quickly to the production of generators. This can be properly trace as a scientific history, but it is significant that the key period of advance coincides with an important stage of the development of industrial production.

The advantages of electric power were closely related to new industrial needs: for mobility and transfer in the location of power sources, and for flexible and rapid controllable conversion. The steam engine had been well suited to textiles, and its industries had been based in local sitting. A more extensive development, both physically and in the complexity of multiple-part processes, such as engineering, could be attempted with other power sources but could only be fully realised with electricity. There was a very complex interaction between new needs and new inventions, at the level of primary production, of new applied industries (plating) and of new social needs which were themselves related to industrial developments (city and house lighting). From 1830 to large-scale generation in the 1880s there was this continuing complex of need and invention and application.

In telegraphy the development was simpler. The transmission of messages by beacons and similar primary devices had been long established. In the development of navigation and naval warfare the flag-system had been standardised in the course of the sixteenth and seventeenth centuries. During the Napoleonic wars there was a marked development of land telegraphy, by semaphore stations, and some of this survived into peacetime. Electrical telegraphy had been suggested as a technical system as early as 1753, and was actually demonstrated in several places in the early nineteenth century. An English inventor in 1816 was told that the Admiralty was not interested. It is interesting that it was the development of the railways, themselves a response to the development of an industrial system and the related growth of cities, which clarified the need for improved telegraphy. A complex of technical possibilities was brought to a working system from 1837 onwards. The development of international trade and transport brought rapid extensions of the system, including the transatlantic cable in the 1850s and the 1860s. A general system of electric telegraphy had been established by the 1870s, and in the same decade the telephone system began to be developed, in this case as a new and intended invention.

In photography, the idea of light-writing had been suggested by (among others) Wedgwood and Davy in 1802, and the *camera obscura* had already been developed. It was not the projection but the fixing of images which at first awaited technical solution, and from 1816 (Niepce) and through to 1839 (Daguerre) this was worked on, together with the improvement of camera devices. Professional and then amateur photography spread rapidly, and reproduction and then transmission, in the developing newspaper press, were achieved. By the 1880s the idea of a 'photographed reality'—still more for record than for observation—was familiar.

The idea of moving pictures had been similarly developing. The magic lantern (slide projection) had been known from the seventeenth century, and had acquired simple motion (one slide over another) by 1736. From at latest 1826 there was a development of mechanical motion-picture devices, such as the wheel-of-life, and these came to be linked with the effect of persistence in human vision—that is to say, our capacity to hold the 'memory' of an image through an interval to the next image, thus allowing the possibility of a sequence built from rapidly succeeding units—had been known since classical times. Series of cameras photographing stages of a sequence were followed (Marey, 1882) by multiple-shot cameras. Friese-Greene and Edison worked on techniques of filming and projection, and celluloid was substituted for paper reels. By the 1890s the first public motion-picture shows were being given in France, America and England.

Television, as an idea, was involved with many of these developments. It is difficult to separate it, in its earliest stages, from photo-telegraphy. Bain proposed a device for transmitting pictures by electric wires in 1842; Bakewell in 1847 showed the copying telegraph; Caselli in 1862 transmitted pictures by wire over a considerable distance. In 1873, while working at a terminal of the Atlantic telegraph cable, May observed the light-sensitive properties of selenium (which had been isolated by Berzelius in 1817 and was in use for resistors). In a host of ways, following an already defined need, the means of transmitting still pictures and moving pictures were actively sought and to a considerable extent discovered. The list is long even when selective: Carey's electric eye in 1875; Nipkow's scanning system in 1884; Elster and Geitel's photoelectric cells in 1890; Braun's cathode-ray tube in 1897; Rosing's cathode-ray receiver in 1907; Campbell Swinton's electronic camera proposal in 1911. Through this whole period two facts are evident: that a system of television was foreseen, and its means were being actively sought; but also that, by comparison with electrical generation and electrical telegraphy and telephony, there was very little social investment to bring the scattered work together. It is true that there were technical blocks before 1914—the thermionic valve and the multi-stage amplifier can be seen to have been needed and were not yet invented. But the critical difference between the various spheres of applied technology can be stated in terms of a social dimension: new systems of production and of business or transport communication were already organised, at an economic level; the new systems of social communication were not. Thus when motion pictures were developed, their application was characteristically in the margin of established social forms—the sideshows—until their success was capitalised in a version of an established form, the motion-picture *theatre*.

The development of radio, in its significant scientific and technical stages between 1885 and 1911, was at first conceived, within already effective social systems, as an advanced form of telegraphy. Its application as a significantly new social form belongs to the immediate post-war period, in a changed social situation. It is significant that the hiatus in technical television development then also ended. In 1923 Zworykin introduced the electronic television camera tube. Through the early 1920s Baird and Jenkins, separately and competitively, were working on systems using mechanical scanning. From 1925 the rate of progress was qualitatively changed, through important technical advances but also with the example of sound broadcasting systems as a model. The Bell System in 1927 demonstrated wire transmission through a radio link, and the pre-history of the form can be seen to be ending. There was great rivalry between systems—especially those of mechanical and electronic scanning—and there is still great controversy about contributions and priorities. But this is characteristic of the phase in which the development of a technology moves into the stage of a new social form.

What is interesting throughout is that in a number of complex and related fields, these systems of mobility and transfer in production and communication, whether in mechanical and electric transport, or in telegraphy, photography, motion pictures, radio and television, were at once incentives and responses within a phase of general social transformation. Though some of the crucial scientific and technical discoveries were made by isolated and unsupported individuals, there was a crucial community of selected emphasis and intention, in a society characterised at its most general levels by a mobility and extension of the scale of organisations: forms of growth which brought with them immediate and longer-term problems of operative communication. In many different countries, and in apparently unconnected ways, such needs isolated and technically defined. It is especially of the communications systems that *all were forseen—not in utopian but in technical ways—before the crucial components of the developed systems had been discovered and refined.* In no way is this a history of communications systems creating a new society or new social conditions. The decisive and earlier transformation of industrial production, and its new social forms, which had grown out of a long history of capital accumulation and working technical improvements, created new needs but also new possibilities, and the communications systems, do were their intrinsic outcome.

C. THE SOCIAL HISTORY OF THE USES OF TECHNOLOGY

It is never quite true to say that in modem societies, when a social need has been demonstrated, its appropriate technology will be found. This is partly because some real needs, in any particular period, are beyond the scope of existing or foreseeable scientific and technical knowledge. It is even more because the key question, about technological response to a need, is less a question about the need itself than about its place in an existing social formation. A need which corresponds with the priorities of the real decision-making groups will, obviously, more quickly attract the investment of resources and the official permission, approval or encouragement on which a working technology, as distinct from available technical devices, depends. We can see this clearly in the major developments of industrial production and, significantly, in military technology. The social history of communications technology is interestingly different from either of these, and it is important to try to discover what are the real factors of this variation.

The problem must be seen at several different levels. In the very broadest perspective, there is an operative relationship between a new kind of expanded, mobile and complex society and the development of a modern communications technology. At one level this relationship can be reasonably seen as causal, in a direct way. The principal incentives to first-stage improvements in communications technology came from problems of communication and control in expanded military and commercial operations. This was both direct, arising from factors of greatly extending distance and scale, and indirect, as a factor within the development of transport technology, which was for obvious reasons the major direct response. Thus telegraphy and telephony, and in its early stages radio, were secondary factors within a primary communications system which was directly serving the needs of an established and developing military and commercial system. Through the nineteenth and into the twentieth century this was the decisive pattern.

But there were other social and political relationships and needs emerging from this complex of change. Indeed it is a consequence of the particular and dominant interpretation of these changes that the complex was at first seen as one requiring improvement in *operational* communication. The direct priorities of the expanding commercial system, and in certain periods of the military system, led to a definition of needs within the terms of these systems. The objectives and the consequent technologies were operational within the structures of these systems: passing necessary specific information, or maintaining contact and control. Modern electric technology, in this phase, was thus oriented to uses of person to person, operator and operative to operator and operative, within established specific structures. This quality can best be emphasised by contrast with the electric technology of the second phase, which was properly and significantly called *broadcasting*. A technology of specific messages to specific persons was complemented, but only relatively late, by a technology of varied messages to a general public.

Yet to understand this development we have to look at a wider communications system. The true basis of this system had preceded the developments in technology. Then as now there was a major, indeed dominant, area of social communication, by word of mouth, within every kind of social group. In addition, then as now, there were specific institutions of that kind of communication which involves or is predicated on social teaching and control: churches, schools, assemblies and proclamations, direction in places of work. All these interacted with forms of communication within the family.

What then were the new needs which led to the development of a new technology of social communication? The development of the press gives us the evidence for our first major instance. It was at once a response to the development of an extended social, economic and political system and a response to crisis within that system. The centralisation of political power led to a need for messages from that centre along other than official lines. Early newspapers were a combination of that kind of message—political and social information—and the specific messages —classified advertising and general commercial news—of an expanding system of trade. In Britain development of the press went through its major formative stages in periods of crisis: the Civil War and Commonwealth, when the newspaper form was defined; the Industrial Revolution, when new forms of popular journalism were successively established; the major wars of the twentieth century, when the newspaper became a universal social form. For the transmission of simple orders, a communications system already existed. For the transmission of an ideology, there were specific traditional institutions. But for the transmission of news and background—the whole orienting, predictive and updating process which the fully developed press represented—there was an evident need for a new form, which the largely traditional institutions of church and school could not meet. And to the large extent that the crises of general change provoked both anxiety and controversy, this flexible and competitive form met social needs of a new kind. As the struggle for a share in decision and control became sharper, in campaigns for the vote and then in competition for the vote, the press became not only a new communications system but, centrally, a new social institution.

This can be interpreted as response to a political need and a political crisis, and it was certainly this. But a wider social need and social crisis can also be recognised. In a changing society, and especially after the Industrial Revolution, problems of social perspective and social orientation became more acute. New relations between men, and between men and things, were being intensely experienced, and in this area, especially, the traditional institutions of church and school, or of settled community and persisting family, had very little to say. A great deal was of course said, but from positions defined within an older kind of society. In a number of ways, and drawing on a range of impulses from curiosity to anxiety, new information and new kinds of orientation were deeply required: more deeply, indeed, than any specialisation to political, military or commercial information can account for. An increased awareness of mobility and change, not just as abstractions but as lived experiences, led to a major redefinition, in practice and then in theory, of the function and process of social communication.

What can be seen most evidently in the press can be seen also in the development of photography and the motion picture. The photograph is in one sense a popular extension of the portrait, for recognition and for record. But in a period of great mobility, with new separations of families and with internal and external migrations, it became more centrally necessary as a form of maintaining, over distance and through time, certain personal connections. Moreover, in altering relations to the physical world, the photograph as an object became a form of the photography of objects: moments of isolation and stasis within an experienced rush of change; and then, in its technical extension to motion, a means of observing and analysing motion itself, in new ways—a dynamic form in which new kinds of recognition were not only possible but necessary.

Now it is significant that until the period after the First World War, and in some ways until the period after the Second World War, these varying needs of a new kind of society and a new way of life were met by what were seen as specialised means: the press for political and economic information the photograph for community, family and personal life; the motion picture for curiosity and entertainment; telegraphy and telephony for business information and some important personal messages. It was within this complex of specialised forms that broadcasting arrived.

The consequent difficulty of defining its social uses, and the intense kind of controversy which has ever since surrounded it, can then be more broadly understood. Moreover, the first definitions of broadcasting were made for sound radio. It is significant and perhaps puzzling that the definitions and institutions then created were those within which television developed.

We have now become used to a situation in which broadcasting is a major social institution, about which there is always controversy but which, in its familiar form, seems to have been predestined by the technology. This predestination, however, when closely examined, proves to be no more than a set of particular social decisions, in particular circumstances, which were then so widely if imperfectly ratified that it is now difficult to see them as decisions rather than as (retrospectively) inevitable results.

Thus, if seen only in hindsight, broadcasting can be diagnosed as a new and powerful form of social integral and control. Many of its main uses can be seen as socially, commercially and at times politically manipulative. Moreover, this viewpoint is rationalised by its description as 'mass communication', a phrase used by almost all its agents and advisers as well, curiously, as by most of its radical critics. 'Masses' had been the new nineteenth-century term of contempt for what was formerly described as 'the mob'. The physical 'massing' of the urban and industrial revolution underwrote this. A new radical class-consciousness adopted the term to express the material of new social formations: 'mass organisations'. The 'mass meeting' was an observable physical effect. So pervasive was this description that in the twentieth century multiple serial production was called, falsely but significantly, 'mass production': mass now meant large numbers (but within certain assumed social relationships) rather than any physical or social aggregate. Sound radio and television, for reasons we shall look at, were developed for transmission to *individual* homes, though there was nothing in the technology to make this inevitable. But then this new form of social communication—broadcasting—was obscured by its definition as 'mass communication': an abstraction to its most general characteristic, that it went to many people, 'the masses', which obscured the fact that the means chosen was the offer of individual sets, a method much better described by the earlier word 'broadcasting'. It is interesting that the only developed 'mass' use of radio was in Nazi Germany, where under Goebbels' orders the Party organised compulsory public listening groups and the receivers were in the streets. There has been some imitation of this by similar regimes, and Goebbels was deeply interested in television for the same kind of use. What was developed within most capitalist societies, though called 'mass communication', was significantly different.

There was early official intervention in the development of broadcasting, but in form this was only at a technical level. In the earlier struggle against the development of the press, the State had licensed and taxed newspapers, but for a century before the coming of broadcasting the alternative idea of an independent press had been realised both in practice and in theory.

State intervention in broadcasting had some real and some plausible technical grounds: the distribution of wavelengths. But to these were added, though always controversially, more general social directions or attempts at direction. This social history of broadcasting can be discussed on its own, at the levels of practice and principle. Yet it is unrealistic to extract it from another and perhaps more decisive process, through which, In particular economic situations, a set of scattered technical devices became an applied technology and then a social technology.

A Fascist regime might quickly see the use of broadcasting for direct political and social control. But that, in any case, was when the technology had already been developed elsewhere. In capitalist democracies, the thrust for conversion from scattered techniques to a technology was not political but economic. The characteristically isolated inventors, from Nipkow and Rosing to Baird and Jenkins and Zwyorkin, found their point of development, if at all, in the manufacturers and prospective manufacturers of the technical apparatus. The history at one level is of these isolated names, but at another level it is of EMI, RCA and a score of similar companies and corporations. In the history of motion pictures, capitalist development was primarily in production; large-scale capitalist distribution came much later, as a way of controlling and organising a market for given production. In broadcasting, both in sound radio and later in television, the major investment was in the means of distribution, and was devoted to production only so far as to make the distribution technically possible and then at active. Unlike all previous communications technologies, radio and television were *systems primarily devised for transmission and reception as abstract processes, with little or no definition of preceding content.* When the question of content was raised, it was resolved, in the main, parasitically. There were state occasions, public sporting events, theatres and so on, which would be communicatively distributed by these new technical means. *It not only that the supply of broadcasting facilities preceded the demand; it is that the means of communication preceded their content.*

The period of decisive development in sound broadcasting was the 1920s. After the technical advances in sound telegraphy which had been made for military purposes during the war, there was at once an economic opportunity and the need for a new social definition. No nation or manufacturing group held a monopoly of the technical means of broadcasting, and there was a period of intensive litigation followed by cross-licensing of the scattered basic components of successful transmission and reception (the vacuum tube or valve, developed from 1904 to 1913; the feedback circuit, developed from 1912; the neutrodyne and heterodyne circuits, from 1923). Crucially, in the mid-1920s, there was a series of investment-guided technical solutions to the problem of building a small and simple domestic receiver, on which the whole qualitative transformation from wireless telegraphy to broadcasting depended. By the mid-1920s—1923 and 1924 are especially decisive years—this breakthrough had happened in the leading industrial societies: the United States, Britain, Germany and France. By the end of the 1920s the radio industry had become a major sector of industrial production, within a rapid general expansion of the new kinds of machines which were eventually to be called 'consumer durables'. This complex of developments included the motorcycle and motorcar, the box camera and its successors, home electrical appliances, and radio sets. Socially, this complex is characterised by the two apparently paradoxical yet deeply connected tendencies of modem urban industrial living: on the one hand mobility, on the other hand the more apparently self-sufficient family home. The earlier period of public technology, best exemplified by the railways and city lighting, was being replaced by a kind of technology for which no satisfactory name has yet been found: that which served an at once mobile and home-centred way of living: a form of mobile privatisation. Broadcasting in its applied form was a social product of this distinctive tendency.

The contradictory pressures of this phase of industrial capitalist society were indeed resolved, at a certain level, by the institution of broadcasting. For mobility was only in part the impulse of an independent curiosity: the wish to go out and see new places. It was essentially an impulse formed in the breakdown and dissolution of older and smaller kinds of settlement and productive labour. The new and larger settlements and industrial organisations required major internal mobility, at a primary level, and this was joined by secondary consequences in the dispersal of extended families and in the needs of new kinds of social organisation. Social processes long implicit in the revolution of industrial capitalism were then greatly intensified: especially an increasing distance between immediate living areas and the directed places of work and government. No effective kinds of social control over these transformed industrial and political processes had come anywhere near being achieved or even foreseen. Most people were living in the fall-out area of processes determined beyond them. What had been gained, nevertheless, in intense social struggle, had been the improvement of immediate conditions, within the limits and pressures of these decisive large-scale processes. There was some relative improvement in wages and working conditions, and there was a qualitative change in the distribution of the day, the week and the year between work and off-work periods. These two effects combined in a major emphasis on improvement of the small family home. Yet this privatisation, which was at once an effective achievement and a defensive response, carried, as a consequence, an imperative need for new kinds f contact. The new homes might appear private and 'self-sufficient' but could be maintained only by regular funding and supply from external sources, and these, over a range from employment and prices to depressions and wars, had a decisive and often a disrupting influence on what was nevertheless seen as a separable 'family' project. This relationship created both the need and the form of a new kind of 'communication': news from 'outside', from otherwise inaccessible sources. Already in the drama of the 1880s and 1890s (Ibsen, Chekhov) this structure had appeared: the centre of dramatic interest was now for the first time the family home, but men and women stared from its windows anxiously for messages, to learn about forces, 'out there', which would determine the conditions of their lives. The new 'consumer' technology which reached its first decisive stage in the 1920s served this complex of needs within just these limits and pressures. There were immediate improvements of the condition and efficiency of the privatised home; there were new facilities, in private transport, for expeditions and then, in radio, there was a facility for a new kind of social input—news and entertainment brought into the home. Some people spoke of the new machines as gadgets, but they were always much more than this. They were the applied technology of a set of emphases and responses within the determining limits and pressures of industrial capitalist society.

The cheap radio receiver is then a significant index of a general condition and response. It was especially welcomed by all those who had least social opportunities of other kinds; who lacked independent mobility or access to the previously diverse places of entertainment and information. Broadcasting could also come to serve, or seem to serve, as a form of *unified* social intake, at the most general levels. What had been intensively promoted by the radio manufacturing companies thus interlocked with this kind of social need, itself defined within general limits and pressures. In the early stages of radio manufacturing, transmission was conceived before content. By the end of the 1920s the network was there, but still at a low level of content-definition. It was in the 1930s, in the second phase of radio, that most of the significant advances in content were made. The transmission and reception networks created, *as a by-product*, the facilities of primary broadcasting production. But the general social definition of 'content' was already there.

This theoretical model of the general development of broadcasting is necessary to an understanding of the particular development of television. For there were, in the abstract, several different ways in which television as a technical means might have been developed. After a generation of universal domestic television it is not easy to realise this. But it remains true that, after a great deal of intensive research and development, the domestic television set is in a number of ways an inefficient medium of visual broadcasting. Its visual inefficiency by comparison with the cinema is especially striking, whereas in the case of radio there was by the 1930s a highly efficient sound broadcasting receiver, without any real competitors in its own line. Within the limits of the television home-set emphasis it has so far not been possible to make more than minor qualitative improvements. Higher-definition systems, and colour, have still only brought the domestic television set, as a machine, to the standard of a very inferior kind of cinema. Yet most people have adapted to this inferior visual medium, in an unusual kind of preference for an inferior immediate technology, because of the social complex—and especially that of the privatised home—within which broadcasting, as a system, is operative. The cinema had remained at an earlier level of social definition; it was and remains a special kind of theatre, offering specific and discrete works of one general kind. Broadcasting, by contrast, offered a whole social intake: music, news, entertainment, sport. The advantages of this general intake, within the home, much more than outweighed the technical advantages of visual transmission and reception in the cinema, confined as this was to specific and discrete works. While broadcasting was confined to sound, the powerful visual medium of cinema was an immensely popular alternative. But when broadcasting became visual, the option for its social advantages outweigh the immediate technical deficits.

The transition to television broadcasting would have occurred quite generally in the late 1930s and early 1940s, if the war had not intervened. Public television services had begun in Britain in 1936 and in the United States in 1939, but with still very expensive receivers. The full investment in transmission and reception facilities did not occur until the late 1940s and early 1950s, but the growth was thereafter very rapid. The key social tendencies which had led to the definition of broadcasting were by then even more pronounced. There was significantly higher investment in the privatised home, and the social and physical distances between these homes and the decisive political and productive centres of the society had become much greater. Broadcasting, as it had developed in radio, seemed an inevitable model: the central transmitters and the domestic sets.

Television then went through some of the same phases as radio. Essentially, again, the technology of transmission and reception developed before the content, and important parts of the content were and have remained by-products of the technology rather than independent enterprises. As late as the introduction of colour, 'colourful' programmes were being devised to persuade people to buy colour sets. In the earliest stages there was the familiar parasitism on existing events: a coronation, a major sporting event, theatres. A comparable parasitism on the cinema was slower to show itself, until the decline of the cinema altered the terms of trade; it is now very widespread, most evidently in the United States. But again, as in radio, the end of the first general decade brought significant independent television production. By the middle and late 1950s, as in radio in the middle and late 1930s, new kinds of programme were being made for television and there were very important advances in the productive use of the medium, including, as again at a comparable stage in radio, some kinds of original work.

Yet the complex social and technical definition of broadcasting led to inevitable difficulties, especially in the productive field. What television could do relatively cheaply was to transmit something that was in any case happening or had happened. In news, sport, and some similar areas it could provide a service of transmission at comparatively low cost. But in every kind of new work, which it had to produce, it became a very expensive medium, within the broadcasting model. It was never as expensive as film, but the cinema, as a distributive medium, could directly control its revenues. It was, on the other hand, implicit in broadcasting that given the tunable receiver all programmes could be received without immediate charge. There could have been and can still be a socially financed system of production and distribution within which local and specific charges would be unnecessary; the BBC, based on the licence system for domestic receivers, came nearest to this. But short of monopoly, which still exists in some state-controlled systems, the problems of investment for production, in any broadcasting system, are severe.

Thus within the broadcasting model there was this deep contradiction, of centralised transmission and privatised reception. One economic response was licensing. Another, less direct, was commercial sponsorship and then supportive advertising. But the crisis of production control and financing has been endemic in broadcasting precisely because of the social and technical model that was adopted and that has become so deeply established. The problem is masked, rather than solved, by the fact that as a transmitting technology—its functions largely limited to relay and commentary on other events—some balance could be struck; a limited revenue could finance this limited service. But many of the creative possibilities of television have been frustrated precisely by this apparent solution, and this has far more than local effects on producers and on the balance of programmes. When there has been such heavy investment in a particular model of social communications, there is a restraining complex of financial institutions, of cultural expectations and of specific technical developments, which though it can be seen, superficially, as the effect of a technology is in fact a social complex of a new and central kind.

It is against this background that we have to look at the development of broadcasting institutions, at their uses of the media, and at the social problems of the new technical phase which we are about to enter.

Television, Representation and Gender

By Julie D'Acci

I F I ASKED PEOPLE THE WORLD OVER to tell me what immediately sprang to mind when they heard the phrase "television and gender representations" I would undoubtedly be deluged with wildly different responses. Different because different cultures and countries and different people within them conceive of these terms in widely divergent ways; different also because right now the terms themselves are in tremendous flux. But I would also surely get a flood of similar responses, because these three terms have come to achieve a kind of common-sense understanding in many areas of the globe. It is in the spaces among these similarities and differences surrounding gender, television and representations, among the persistence of particular meanings and the struggles over new ones, that I want to situate this essay. I could plunge in with an exploration of any of the three terms, but because this book is devoted to television, let me begin there.[1]

TELEVISION

It is clear that television not only means different things but has different functions and uses in societies all over the world. From the perspective of a cultural critic working within a Cultural Studies perspective in the United States, I have come to understand TV and analyze it in some very specific ways. On a most general level, I conceive of it as a technology, and as a social, economic, cultural, and ideological institution. As a technology (and at a most rudimentary level), I see it as producing electronic images and sounds; as a social institution, as producing viewers and citizens; as an economic institution (in some societies), as producing consumers; as a cultural institution, as producing programs and schedules; and as an ideological institution, as producing norms and rules that tell viewers what's okay and what's not in any given society.

In other words, television's electronic sounds and images, its programs and its regular schedules of news, commercials, announcements, and so forth, gather viewers (often for many hours every week) and give them a sense of who and what they are, where they are, and when (morning, late-night, holiday seasons, for instance), if they are safe or in danger (from threatening weather, hostile attacks, economic recessions, and so forth), and how they ought to feel and be. Television's schedule, its information, and its stories, therefore, have active roles in shaping the ways TV viewers think about themselves and feel about themselves and their worlds, including how they think and feel about themselves as gendered human beings.

As a cultural institution that produces programming (or more basically televised content), TV continuously represents gender to its viewers. It also, of course, represents race, ethnicity, age, class, sexuality, nationality, religion—all of the categories that humans and their social institutions have developed in order to classify and regulate the chaos of their universe. While this particular essay focuses on television and gender, other essays of its kind could focus (and have focused) on the other categories (also called markers, axes, identities, and social representations) listed above. We can see, in fact, from the articles collected in this volume that many scholars the world over have turned their attention, from many different points of view, to the analysis of TV and these (among other) various dimensions.

Even though we may come to agree that TV is a technology and a social, economic, cultural, and ideological institution, it exists as such within a whole range of different relationships to the countries in which it is produced and/or consumed, and to the economic, religious, and ideological frameworks of those countries. Television's infrastructure and programming, for example, may be controlled and shaped by national governments, private corporations, religious entities, or local communities (to name some arrangements), and the various beliefs and interests—including those pertaining to gender—that impel and motivate them. But as is abundantly clear the world over, television is also in the throes of radical change, transmogrifying into digital signals, and satellite, cable and Internet delivery systems; becoming more interactive and in some countries (such as the US) more oriented to niche programming; and holding out, in these changes, the promise (however tenuous) of more viewer negotiations over gender representations (and all representations for that matter), as well as more alternatives to conventional depictions of gender and the other social categories.

REPRESENTATION

If television is a term with multiple meanings and is currently caught up in revolutionary changes (many the result of technological and geopolitical shifts), "representation" too has many meanings and is itself undergoing conceptual transformations. Recently, a number of philosophical and theoretical debates, as well as scientific advances (in, for example, the field of physics) have revolved around the notion of representation and its presumed correlate, reality.

As a term, "representation" has typically been defined as referring to signs, symbols, images, portrayals, depictions, likenesses, and substitutions; and we have tended to think of representation as the primary function that television performs. "Television representation," therefore, conjures up notions of one thing standing in for something else; and we typically contrast this representation to reality, believing, for example, that the electronic image of a man on the TV screen is a portrayal, a substitute, or a reproduction of a flesh and blood man out there in the world of empirical reality. But, as much recent writing has argued, it may not be as simple as that.[2]

Recognizing that there are raging debates about this issue, with radically different positions espoused, let me take a particular stance and ask: What if the *truth* of nature, the world, the universe, *reality*, is fundamentally unknowable by human beings? What if it is the human being that imposes order and categories on the world within the limits of human perceptual capabilities (eyes, ears, brain and so forth)? What if reality is truly a swirl of molecules (or some other unknown substances or non-substances), and if we were able to perceive differently we would see it, hear it, feel it in a totally different way than we do with our human senses and brains? What if nature actually does present some repeated patterns, some similarities and differences (amidst the wildness), but what if nonetheless we, as human beings, are still fundamentally bound by our own limited ways of processing, interpreting, making meaning out of them? What if, in other words, reality really is construed by humans, really is humanly constructed? What if, furthermore, different human societies train (even inadvertently) their humans to perceive and interpret reality in particular ways? And what if this humanly produced social reality passes in most societies lor natural reality, the common sense understanding about the world, the truth? And what if the constant generation of *representations* of this social reality enforces over and over again the notion that this human, social construction is really the real thing?

It is in the spirit of these questions that we may speak (among many other things) of representations as human constructs and as social representations. Speaking of them as human constructs emphasizes that representations are produced by the human brain and other human perceptual systems. It emphasizes that representations are mediations—that is, they are formed in the human mind and are human interpretations of some exterior realm. Speaking of representations in this way also emphasizes that they are distinct from reality, a step (at least) removed from it. Representations in this sense are also spoken of as "social representations" to underscore the fact that they don't spring up in isolated human minds, but rather they come into being, exist, and do their work in the social realm (in groups of human minds and bodies), in the realm of particular, empirical, human societies.

To take a gender-related example, in many societies a boy, at a particular point in his life, may start to dress like the men in his family or region or country. He may then represent to himself and to those around him something like young manhood or masculinity. He may start to talk and move and adopt the behaviors of the men around him, again representing masculinity. Pretty soon, these representations come to seem to him (as they have before to those around him) natural. He's a boy who is becoming a man and this is how men are, this is how they represent a masculinity that's out there in nature. The point, of course, that needs to be made here (and will be discussed more later) is that there is no real manhood out there in nature of which this enactment is a re-presentation. The representation, the social construction, has come to stand in tor an imaginary original reality.

Whereas representations such as the one involving this boy are referred to by some as social representations, other representations such as those involving the spheres of television, film, literature, art, and so forth, often get referred to as *cultural* representations, representations that exist and do their work in the cultural realm—the realm of language, art, entertainment; the realm specific to ideas, thoughts, and the mind. In making this distinction some people have intended to imply that the difference between cultural representations and social representations is a fundamental one, with cultural representations usually serving to shore up, buttress, or reinforce the more primary and more important social representations. (More important because, within the terms of this distinction, social representations may be thought to be more directly connected to the material existence of the empirical human body, and more directly connected to actual societies and their various economies).

The notion of nation may serve here as an example of a cultural representation, because in many ways, nation is a representation that primarily derives from what have traditionally been called cultural spheres. We read about nations (our own and others') in newspapers, magazines, and books; we see a nation's boundaries and its geographical relationship to the rest of the world on maps and atlases; we learn about the culture, politics, and symbols of nations from television Prime Minister Tony Blair argues his case before British Parliament, the British royal family is profiled in a documentary, the Beatles are mobbed by British teens in a TV retrospective. Or we see that Pakistan is comprised of three major ethnic groups (Punjabi, Sindhi, and Pashtun), that tensions with India are ongoing over the disputed state of Kashmir, that President General Pervez Musharraf seeks to present a picture of a strong and unified country. Some Pakistani and English citizens may come to see the "imagined communities" portrayed on TV as commensurate with their own notions of their nations, in the same ways that many of us have come to imagine our own and other nations based on what we've watched on TV, read in newspapers, or seen on maps. The main point to be made here is that we don't really see nations out there in our everyday social reality. We derive a sense of them from our exposure to various cultural representations, often over the course of our lifetimes. We then come to see our everyday social (and national) worlds through the lens of these cultural representations. But it is completely clear that these cultural representations have the same power and effects as what I described earlier as social representations.

It is, then, a contention of this essay that the distinction between the social and the cultural (although often useful for the purposes of analysis) is too arbitrary and too artificial to be ultimately sustained. One of the main points I want to argue is that television representations of gender (like television representations of nation and other categories) indeed have very profound effects on very real human bodies, societies, and economies. For example, most of us come to have at least an inkling of what the normative ideal of a woman or man from our own nation is supposed to look like, behave like, think like, and feel like. And this inkling is absolutely tied up with the rules of the gender and nationality game that govern the societies in which we live, and which we, in one way or another, come to live by (or not).

To tie some of these remarks about representation even more tightly to television, it may be useful to ponder for a moment the often heard truisms that "television holds a mirror up to nature" or "television reflects society." It is probably clear already that my position on television and representation does not support these metaphors. Although it seems natural tor us to think about TV in these terms and hard to extricate ourselves completely from their grip, it may be productive now to pry them apart, to consolidate some of the points we've already covered, and to look toward a couple of new ones. First, TV can't hold a mirror up to "nature" because, as I've already suggested, nature is not simply waiting out there to be reflected, it is not simply knowable, it is already humanly and socially constructed. Second, TV can't even hold a mirror up to (or reflect) society's or the human being's version of nature (or reality or society) because TV *itself*, for a whole range of reasons, is utterly selective about what it chooses to represent and how. The reasons it is selective have everything to do with the countries or regions in which it is produced and the types of institutional arrangements (government, public, community, commercial, religious, local, and so forth) that fund or support it. In the commercial US system, for instance, it is possible to trace direct relationships between television representations and television's economic imperatives.

For example, with regard to one aspect of gender, US television in its early history (1950s–1970s when US TV was dominated by three commercial networks), repeatedly produced representations of young, white, middle-class, heterosexual, conventionally attractive (according to US standards), domesticated women, as the norm of femininity. One of the obvious reasons it did this was to attract the largest possible audience of young upscale mothers who would then go out and buy the home and beauty-related products advertised on screen. Another reason (which also continues to this day) is that particular representations of femininity (and masculinity) have long been used by commercial culture to associate heterosexual desirability with consumer products and consumerism in general—to encourage consumption by linking it to images of idealized objects of heterosexual desire. But we can see from this example that, in its earliest years, US TV didn't even hold up a mirror to the social representations of femininity in the country in which it was produced—many US women were not middle class, white, young, or heterosexual. Perhaps it could be said, using the words of advertising historian Roland Marchand, that what TV held up was a distortional fun-house mirror to society.[3] But actually it was even worse than that, because US television's "mirror" was selective not only in the sense of distorting what was there for the sake of its own economic exigencies, it was selective in the sense of largely ignoring (particularly in those early years) whole segments of the society that it purportedly reflected. For most of its early history, US TV rarely depicted the people of color, the poor, the citizens with handicaps, the lesbians, and so forth that also constituted the category of US femininity. But television's selective, distorted, and constrained representations of femininity came, for many years and for many people, to constitute the truth or reality of femininity, what femininity out there in the world of the US was actually about. It came, moreover, to figure as a *universal* ideal of femininity for many in the (myopic) United States because US television was after all simply reflecting all reality, mirroring nature, in another of its defining metaphors, simply being a "window on the world."

However, as US TV has changed dramatically since the mid-1980s (with the break-up of three network hegemony, the proliferation of cable and satellite services, the marketing to niche audiences, the competition from the more adventurous cable channels, the more daring forays of the older three networks in the face of cable's competition, and so forth), the representations of femininity have changed in a number of ways. For example, a special on HBO (Home Box Office, a premium and costly cable channel) called *Queens of Comedy*, featured a large black comedienne named Monique who is ruthless in her overt critique of conventional white femininity; and the network program, *Ellen*, featured a lesbian character and an out lesbian star. It cannot be denied that these new venues and practices are offering up representations that complicate the more conventional ones; and they also hold out the hope of more and more alternative representations. Nonetheless, we are constantly reminded when looking at US TV (and TV from many other nations, for that matter) that *particular* ideals of beauty and femininity are still held up as the norms against which these other more innovative manifestations are positioned. And this is the tension in which some television and its representations of gender are currently caught.

GENDER

Gender, like representation, has been the topic of much theoretical and scientific debate in the past thirty years and its meanings are also hotly contested. It has, over the years, been defined as the social and cultural meanings or representations assigned to biologically sexed bodies; with the terms "masculine" and "feminine" usually referring to socially and culturally-produced gender, and "male" and "female" referring to biologically-produced sex (with "man" and "woman" floating in between, but often closer to the social/cultural side). When we look at the writing that has grappled with television and gender representations, we notice that some of it, particularly in the earlier days of the research (in the 1970s and early 1980s), studied the depictions of male and female fictional characters or personalities (such as news people), and perpetuated (inadvertently, perhaps) the binary divisions of gender into the hard and fast categories of male/female, masculinity/femininity.[4] We see, however, that a good deal of later work approached television representations of gender in many broader ways.[5] The binaries of male/female, masculinity/femininity, and the conventional ways of thinking about and enacting gender that they legislate, perpetuate, and underwrite are nonetheless hard to dislodge.

In the last few years, a number of scholarly articles and books, including Judith Butler's, *Gender Trouble and Bodies that Matter*, have taken on the task of breaking the binaries, of shaking up the conventional notions and definitions of gender, and have argued, in Butler's words, that "the sexes" are not "unproblematically binary in their morphology and constitution;" and further that if, "the immutable character of sex is contested, perhaps this construct called 'sex' is as culturally constructed as gender; indeed, perhaps it was always already gender. ..."[6] Butler here makes reference to the fact (alluded to above) that over the past few decades, the term gender has been used to designate the social and cultural construction of sex; and the term sex has been used to designate the seemingly obvious and uncontested biological difference between males and females. She argues explicitly that not only gender but sex itself is a social and cultural construction, that the binaries male/female (as well as the binaries masculine/feminine) do not hold.

Butler and others, for one tiling, can point to enormous ranges of hormone distributions in individuals we typically call male and female, ranges of secondary sex characteristics such as facial and body hair and muscle mass; more instances of sexual dimorphism (babies born with both penises and vaginas) than we realize, more instances of transgenderism—individuals with one sex organ who feel like members of the other gender, and so forth. There are enough actual instances, in other words, to call into question the binary division of two sexes, and, given what seems to be incontrovertible evidence of a wide range and breadth of gender manifestations, surely enough evidence to call the division of two genders into question. In this respect (and in addition to a range of other arguments), Butler advocates a radical reconception of both gender and sex as cultural constructions, as performances, enactments, iterations of regulatory norms that *make bodies matter* according to laws of human history rather than those of nature.[7]

Without going into the details of the argument here, and without saying much more about culture and biology, nurture and nature, or some combinations thereof, it is important to recognize that work like Butler's has made the investigations of gender and its television-based representations an ever more pressing pursuit, and has expanded the boundaries of gender's definition and potential power. And even though people still want to argue that hormones or genes are the primary (and sometimes sole) determinants of behavior, of gender, or of sexuality, there is, I contend, no way of finally settling this question. The closest, it seems, we can come to adjudicating the debate is to say that both biology and nurture, both nature and social construction figure in the formation of what we call gender (and sex). How, in lieu of raising a control group of children in hermetically sealed environments (and even that, of course, wouldn't yield incontrovertible findings), could we ever prove that one side or other of the debate is right?

Having said all of this, it is still crushingly clear that even though on an intellectual, and perhaps even an ethical, level many people believe in gender as a continuum rather than gender as two binaries, it is also extraordinarily hard to actually live out those beliefs. Whether one is involved in raising children, forging new ways of enacting gender, or simply negotiating the affairs of an ordinary day, one is continually confronted with the regulatory norms of gender (with the I written and unwritten rules) and what it means or could mean to transgress them. For example, some, but not many, people are comfortable encouraging their children to be as fluid with gender as possible, or are comfortable letting their sexually dimorphic babies forego surgery. The consequences, for many, however, seem far too great; and the courage of those who break the binaries should never be ignored or underestimated.

This, of course, brings us squarely up against the question of why. Why is the maintenance on these gender norms deemed so crucial? Why does the blurring or the crossing of the gender binary cause such discomfort, indeed such panic? Why does it promote such atrocities? Why were two cross-dressing US adolescent males (Deon Davis and Wilbur Thomas) killed (as have other cross-dressing and transgendered teens been killed) in August 2002? Something as devastating charged as this thing called gender is obviously in need of a great deal more thought and study.

STUDYING TELEVISION AND REPRESENTATIONS OF GENDER

As we will see more below, television scholars have moved the study of gender well beyond examining the depictions of male and female characters. But early research on gender and television had its beginnings in the worldwide second-wave feminist movements, and initially (primarily in the early 1970s) focused on representations of femininity—images of female characters or personalities in television fiction or news programs.[8] Such was the case because feminism was initially bent on illuminating the egregious inequalities caused by worldwide gender systems in constructing woman as the subservient category to man in the gender binary. This research art writing on images of women on television was soon criticized for being too atomistic, that is, for plucking the women characters in fictional programs out of their contexts and neglecting, for example, the ways in which women were portrayed in the overall narrative; and, furthermore, for focusing on particular limited dimensions of the characters, such as their professional statuses (were women portrayed as physicians or as housewives, etc.?) or their personality traits (were they active or passive, etc.?).[9]

Soon also, and spurred mainly by the work of women of color, it was made apparent that to study gender in isolation was to replicate what the category itself excludes or represses—the myriad other social representations (or identities) upon which and against which notions of gender are produced—identities involving race, ethnicity, class, age, sexuality, nationality, and religion, for example. It became apparent that future work on the representations of gender would have to take into account the ways the categories masculinity and femininity depended on such exclusions and repressions, the ways, for example, that normative femininity on early United States television was not only represented as white, middle-class, young, maternal, heterosexual and American, but was utterly dependent on the excluded categories of black, ethnic, working-class, old, non-maternal, lesbian, and non-American as its repressed others. It became clear, in other words, that scholars could not continue to speak of the category gender without recognizing its dependence on its formative exclusions.[10]

Research and writing on representations of masculinity soon followed the initial work on femininity. Here scholars sought to stress that even though femininity was the devalued term of the masculinity/femininity binary, masculinity's representation was also severely constrained and circumscribed in its conventional deployment. In the words of John Fiske in *Television Culture*, "Masculinity is a paradox of power and discipline. The privilege of authority is bought by the discipline of duty and service."[11] Fiske and other scholars wanted to drive home the point that masculinity was not the unmarked term of the gender binary, that is, not a natural unsocialized manifestation of gender, but was, in fact, just as thoroughly constructed as femininity. They were trying to stress that although femininity may be more readily understood as a constructed category (because of its association with things like make-up, hairstyles, clothing, body standards, plastic surgery, particular ways of moving and talking—artifice of all kinds), masculinity (which is often seen as just plain natural in, for example, its rugged outdoorsy unkemptness) was equally socially constructed. Masculinity, in other words, was shown to be a marked category in the same way that whiteness (which seems to some Americans completely free of marking—pure, plain, normal, and natural) has been shown to be as wrapped up in ethnicity as blackness, Native American, Latino American, Asian American, and so forth.[12]

Soon, writing on what some refer to as non-normative sexualities, and some call queerness, including gayness, lesbianism, bisexuality, and transgenderism, followed the initial research on femininity and television. This writing illuminated, among many other things, how the conventional binary of masculinity/femininity worked to limit the depiction of multiple sexualities and genders on television; and to enforce the notion that the two categories in the conventional binary were universally accepted and have clear inviolable boundaries. To the contrary, as Alexander Doty demonstrated in *Making Things Perfectly Queer*, television representations of masculinity and femininity could be interpreted by scholars and by everyday TV viewers for all the queerness they actually mobilize but that society and culture works so hard to repress and contain. For Doty (following Judith Butler and Sue Ellen Case), queerness:

> is something that is ultimately beyond gender it is an attitude, a way of responding, that begins in a place not concerned with, or limited by, notions of a binary opposition of male and female or the homo versus hetero paradigm usually articulated as an extension of this gender binarism.

If we looked at television with new eyes, we could see, for example, all the repressed homoeroticism in traditional TV depictions of men police teams or of women's friendship. In Doty's words, we could see the queerness contained within what we thought were obvious examples of heterosexual women and heterosexual men in relationships of just plain friendship. We could, as Doty does, interpret the US program *Laverne and Shirley* (a show about two heterosexual women friends) as a lesbian or a queer program.[13]

In other words, we could try to unleash the multiplicities in gender that are bound up in the conventional binaries of male/female, masculinity/femininity, man/woman. We could try to see gender (and sexuality) as a continuum (of multiple genders and sexualities), with innumerable possibilities for individuals and for relationships.[14]

Also in the history of studying representations of gender on television, scholars began to argue that TV needed to be studied for its representations of gender that were not confined to characters or TV personalities alone. They argued that we needed to study gender as it was manifested in, or at least associated with, whole genres—talk shows, soap operas, melodramas, soft news could be seen as feminine; sports, hard news, financial facts and figures reporting could be seen as masculine, and so forth. Others argued that we needed to see gender as it was manifested in and associated with particular narrative structures—open-ended serials could be seen as more feminine, whereas closed narratives (ones that achieved final resolution) could be seen as more masculine. Yet others believed that television itself manifested or was associated with the feminine because it was domestic, passive, and generally oriented to consumption rather than production. As might be imagined, these arguments continue to be debated in the overall field, with different scholars taking various and conflicting positions.[15]

All in all, and as I think we have seen, the study of the relationships between gender and television from a Cultural Studies position brings us squarely up against some tricky imperatives. On the one hand, we face the importance of demonstrating exactly how the conventional masculine/feminine binary gets produced and reproduced by television, and of demonstrating exactly how the representation of variations in terms of gender get tamped down. Similarly we face the importance of championing new, alternative representations of gender (the multiple representations of gender that are actually lived in the social sphere, representations that may foster new and unimagined possibilities, and representations that might hasten the demise of the gender category altogether). But on the other hand, we face the importance of not replicating (even inadvertently) the gender binary while we demonstrate its cultural construction, or while we fight against the injustices it fosters. Similarly, we face the importance of not underestimating the ways the conventional gender binary structures most people's everyday lives even as we speak out against the atrocities committed in its service. And finally, we face the importance of recognizing the need for groups forged within the terms of the binary's inequalities (women's movements, lor example), at the same time as we try to break the binary apart.

AN INTEGRATED APPROACH TO THE STUDY OF TELEVISION REPRESENTATIONS OF GENDER

Let me now advocate a particular approach to the study of television's representations of gender, an approach that many scholars working in a Cultural Studies tradition have used in one way or another, and an approach that I believe greatly aids research and analysis. In other places I have used the phrase, the "integrated approach" to the study of television to refer to this approach, one that conceives of its field of study as involving four interrelated sites or spheres: television production, television reception, television programming (or overall content), and television's social/historical context. The approach is solidly based in Cultural Studies, and draws on Stuart Hall's *encoding/decoding* model (1980), Richard Johnson's *circuit of production, circulation, and consumption of cultural products* (1986), and the Open University's *circuit of culture* (1997/99). I have elaborated my own take on this model in an article called "Cultural Studies, Television Studies, and the Crisis in the Humanities."[16] The point I want to make here is that each of these four sites (not simply programming) is involved in generating or constructing representations of gender, and each needs to be examined and analyzed for the ways it does so. This is not to say that every individual study of gender and television needs to include an investigation of each of the four sites—it would be virtually impossible to do this. It is simply to say that the specific activities of each site and the potential interactions among them should be considered when conceiving a particular research project involving television and gender, when posing the questions that impel the research, and when drawing the final conclusions. In any actual study, an investigation into one or two of the sites may virtually eclipse the others.

As I think we have seen, when we think of gender representations and television, we may initially tend to think of the ways men and women are represented in programs (news, commercials, fictional forms, and so forth) and how those representations constitute the norms up against which actual people enact, or do not enact, culturally legitimated femininity and masculinity. We will return to a discussion of programming shortly, but at this point we have to remember a few things: (1) Representations of gender are continually constructed and very much operative not only in the site of programming but in the other three sites as well. (2) Representations of gender (even when one is focusing on the site of programming) should not simply be equated with TV depictions of male/female or masculine/feminine characters or personalities. As mentioned above, we have to look at the position of characters in plots, at narrative structures as a whole, at genres, at the overall television enterprise, among potentially many other things. (3) Representations of the conventional binaries of male/female, masculinity/femininity, man/woman need to be studied not only for how they get constructed, reproduced, and enforced, but also for how they already are and can continue to be broken apart. (4) Representations and constructions of gender variations need to be studied as much as representations of conventional masculinity and femininity; and we need to figure out how to forge ahead with such studies without minimizing the repressive and oftentimes horrific power that accompanies the enforcement of the conventional binary.

Let me turn to US television for some general examples, but let me add that each national television system may be analyzed along similar lines. Let me also say that even though I will be using a commercial system to provide examples, public service systems could equally be mined for the many illustrations of the "integrated approach" they would provide. Finally, let me also say that my following remarks on the four sites are only meant to suggest a few of the ways this approach may be put into action when examining any individual site or the numerous interactions among them.

Production

If we turn to the site of *production* and US television, for example, we find that there are a number of levels on which gender is constructed and needs much more investigation. First, at the general structural level of the corporate capitalist enterprise, the way gender is imagined and represented in the mind's eye of the television industry, has everything to do with the historical distribution of jobs, money, and power—with the functioning of the industry as an economic and social sector. This, of course, has everything to do with the ways in which the binary male/female has structured US society and specifically the ways it has structured the distribution of jobs in the news and entertainment industries, where jobs have been distributed primarily (but not always) according to traditional gender lines. For much of its early history, the television industry, for example, directed women to such professions as "continuity girls" (the people responsible for the continuity from shot to shot is the actor's hair parted on the same side in every shot of the scene, is the glass of bourbon at a consistent level from shot to shot, is the actress wearing the same shoes in every shot of the scene, and so forth). This assertion does not mean to imply that individual women in early US TV could not or did not hold jobs in the upper echelons of the industry (soap opera creator/writers, Irna Phillips and Agnes Nixon, come to mind, as do Lucille Ball, and producer, writer, actress, Gertrude Berg). It is simply to point out the inequities in the television workplace that have structured the sphere of production. Today, the barriers to women in many areas of TV production, although by no means as rigid as in earlier years, are nonetheless still in evidence. The action group, Women in Film, founded by women working in the film and television industries in the 1970s and still active today, sprang up to specifically combat the discrimination these conditions perpetuate.

Such conditions, moreover, have countless repercussions for not only the division of labor and wages but for what actually ends up on the home screen as well. More scholarly attention needs to be paid here because the issue is an enormously complex one. But as we have seen, the gender binary has structured many people's notions about what is and should be associated with masculinity and what with femininity. To turn for a moment to an example from British television, research indicates that in the sphere of factual entertainment, more women have become involved in key stages of production (filming, directing, editing, producing), especially in independent production. However, they have typically been associated with "reality TV" and have come under criticism for "feminizing" documentary practices—for focusing on everyday life, gossip, and so forth. What we see here, then, is an example of the complexities involving gender in this situation. The women from the outset may have been assigned to reality TV because for some in the television institution, that may be the genre most immediately and traditionally associated with females (soft rather than hard news). Also, the women's own culturally-constructed femininity may, in fact, have influenced the ways they grappled with the news material (zeroing in on the personal, the private, rather than the public, details of life). But, furthermore, the television they produced was received by the wider professional community in conventional gender-based ways (others in television production judged the women's work as too "feminine" and as working to "feminize" television documentary).[17]

Conversely, the point has been made in the US that even if women are a fundamental part of a production team, their presence in and of itself cannot have a large effect on changing what actually gets produced in the heavily routinized and constrained commercial system. The women, this argument runs, necessarily become swallowed up by the commercial exigencies of industrial practices and don't have the leeway to introduce much change.[18] From yet another point of view, criticisms of Lifetime Television demonstrate the ways that one of the US cable channels dedicated specifically to programming for women (and employing a number of women), produces very conflicted representations of femininity, representations that draw on some of the most egregious dimensions of the conventional binary.[19] Each of these criticisms is illuminating and each needs to be more fully pursued. None, however, may be viewed as the definitive analysis of the situation. It is difficult, for example, to predict what would happen on the level of programming if large numbers of women and men with critical views and analyses of the conventional gender binary were part of the television work force.

The work of some scholars on race and television representations, however, may point us in the right direction. Herman Gray's writing on the US program *Frank's Place*, for example, demonstrates the influence of black producers and writers (who had well-developed critiques of white society and white television culture) on the production of innovative and complex representations of blackness on the program. Crystal Zook's study, chronicling the appearance of black writers at FOX entertainment television in the late 1980s and 1990s, does the same. Zook additionally underscores the dearth of black women writers who she feels (because of their formulated critiques of white society and gender) could have and would have introduced significant differences with regard to both representations of race and gender onto the home-screens.[20]

Within US TV production, gender is also produced at the level of the overall production process—in the myriad imperatives that directly govern the construction of audiences and programs. A majority of these imperatives are tightly tied up with conventional gender, such as the ways the industry has consistently fashioned its market and programs according to gender: the ways it has developed formulaic programs that it thinks and hopes will appeal to conventionally-produced and identified males and females; and the ways it has divided its programming and scheduling according to the formulaic genres and times of day that it thinks will draw large numbers of respective male and female viewers (for example, sports on weekends to attract men, soaps during weekdays to attract women and so forth).

Target audience analyses may also illuminate not only how conventional gender representations get produced but also how variations regarding gender and sexuality make it onto television. For example, Ron Becker's work on the spate of gay-themed television programs in the 1990s demonstrates the ways that both new representations of gender and sexuality were introduced to US home screens, attracting gay, lesbian, and bi-sexual audiences along the way; but also how these representations were used to attract and shore up a particular segment of the mainstream heterosexual audience.[21]

The sphere of production needs also to be studied for the other ways that differences with regard to gender and sexuality may be seen to function. Sean Griffin's work on Disney, for example, examines gay professionals who work at Disney, gay-inflected films and programs, and gay interpretations by audience members. Although this study is directed more specifically toward the film industry, it points the way to other such studies for television.[22]

Only these few specific instances with regard to studying the site of TV production and gender can be suggested here. But the key point is that the sphere of production (whether it is commercial, public, community, religious, cable access, or state-controlled) needs to be rigorously examined for all the ways it depends upon conventional gender demarcations for its functioning and its production of audiences and programs; and consequently for how it contributes to, draws on, and circulates particular representations and conceptions of gender as opposed to others. It must also be studied, however, for the ways it may produce variations, differences, and innovations in the representations of gender and sexuality.

Reception

The sphere of reception is replete with its own gender dimensions that need intensive examination. They involve, first, the overall institution of viewing -the social and environmental factors that comprise viewing situations and revolve around gender, such as traditional family hierarchies and the venue of home viewing documented in the work of David Morley, Ann Gray and others. Likewise conventional gender roles and their enactments in out-of-home public venues such as bars, community centers, and so forth also call for further investigation. Anna McCarthy's work on television in public places is particularly instructive in relation to these.[23]

Reception also involves the gender dimensions of the actual viewer/program interactions. How, for example, do meaning, pleasure, and other forms of affect actually get produced? How exactly do audience members absorb, reject, or negotiate the norms of gender offered up by programs? How and why do particular groups (teenagers, for example) choose programs based on conventional gender designations? How do audiences use cultural representations to rally lor changes in conventional social assumptions about gender? How do fans become avidly identified with programming in gender-based ways? How do gay, lesbian, bisexual, and trans-gendered viewers interpret the gender-based dimensions of particular programs in different ways than the programs were intended? How do particular women's audiences (and so forth) do the same? How do shows with a marked difference of subject matter and dramatic innovations in the portrayal of sexualities and gender (such as US Showtime's and British Channel 4's *Queer as Folk*, for instance) forge their own new situations of viewing as well as new relationships between viewers and programs?[24]

It must, furthermore, be remembered when talking about reception, that scholars have debated over TV's role in shaping our identities. On the one hand, scholars have argued that because of television's continual shifts in point of view, in genres, in subject matter; because of its overall structure of fragmentation and distraction, it may indeed contribute to the construction of human beings that are not structured as solidly within the terms of conventional binaries, including the binary of gender. According to this argument, television may, in fact, be contributing to the formation of new types of human beings—ones less forged by all the conventional binaries (male/female, white/black, rich/poor, young/old, etc.), simply because TV viewers, in a variety of global systems, are continuously bombarded with all sorts of different points of view, modes of address, enactments of gender, race, nation and so forth.[25] On the other hand, other scholars have continued to argue that TV works to construct a generic feminized viewer, a passive, consumption-oriented, domesticated being—a consumer rather than a citizen. And although the conventional binary-based import of these designations is not lost on the proponents of this position, it is one that we must be careful to interrogate more completely than we have to date.

Programming

If we turn to the sphere of programming itself, we recognize the complexity of gender representations in actual television fare. First let me make clear that I am using the term programming here to refer to all televised content, including commercials, voice-overs, channel announcements, promos, written slogans, weather reports, and so forth, everything that we see or hear on the screen. Needless to say, each of these facets needs to be studied more from the point of view of gender.

When we turn to examine the fictional programs in this sphere, we see, as the feminist critics in the late 1970s and 1980s came to see, that gender cannot be analyzed in isolated images alone, but must be seen as it is produced in all of its specificity, in and through all the formal dimensions of television. We see that gender is represented in the unfolding of the narrative, in the genre, and in each of the techniques such as camera work (close ups and soft focus, for example); editing (romantic dissolves, for example); sound (authoritative speech or voice overs, for example); and mise en scene (which includes lighting, makeup, costumes, sets, props, and the way the characters move, and might, for example, generate a figure of typical "macho" dimensions—a large white body, toting a gun, and jumping over roof tops).

We also see, when examining this sphere, and as discussed before, the ways some forms and genres of television, not to mention television itself, have been considered gendered. Especially given the fact that recent writing on television points to the gendered nature of the medium itself (as well as the viewers it produces) this contention too needs a lot more investigation.

Social/historical context

Finally, the social and historical context is the major sphere that demarcates the ways general social events, movements, beliefs, and changes, produce or represent particular notions about gender in and for the society at-large. Here, for example, we see how, among many other things, social movements such as the women's movements, the gay and civil rights movements, and the fundamentalist religious movements, introduced different and conflicting representations of gender into US society during the last half of the twentieth century, representations that influenced the television industry, its programming, and reception, and in turn further influenced the social/ historical context. We also see here how philosophical and theoretical debates may have a real influence on the ways in which gender, among other categories is actually conceived and lived.

It is in social and cultural institutions like television that specific representations of gender get generated day in and day out and circulated as tacit and not so tacit norms to millions of viewers the world over (based, of course, on the different beliefs and interests that undergird both the norms and the shaping of the television programs). And it is for this reason that gender, representation, and television need to be thought together and examined ever more fully for their specific interrelations in all television systems throughout the world.

NOTES

1. Thanks to Bobby Allen, Annette Hill and Ron Becker for their astute comments on earlier drafts of this essay.
2. See Stuart Hall, ed., *Representation*, London: Sage and the Open University, 1997, for a synopsis of these issues.
3. Roland Marchand, *Advertising the American Dream*, Berkeley: University of California Press, 1985, p. xvii.
4. For some examples see Gaye Tuchman, Arlene Kaplan Daniels, and James Benet, eds, *Hearth and Home: Images of Women in the Mass Media*, New York: Oxford University Press, 1978; Matilda Butler and William Paisley, *Women and the Mass Media*, New York: Human Sciences Press, 1980; Diana M. Meehan, *Ladies of the Evening: Women Characters of Prime-Time Television*, New York: Scarecrow Press, 1983. Most of this early research came from a liberal or sociological feminist perspective and was published before the rash of socialist, materialist, and poststructuralist feminist writing that interrogated the masculine/feminine binaries.
5. For overviews of this literature see Charlotte Brunsdon, Julie D'Acci, Lynn Spigel, eds, *Feminist Television Criticism*, London: Oxford University Press, 1997; Laura Stempel Mumford, "Feminist Theory and Television Studies," in Christine Geraghty and David Lusted, eds, *The Television*

Studies Book, London: Edward Arnold, 1998; Lisbet Van Zoonen, *Feminist Media Studies*, London: Sage, 1994.

6. Judith Butler, *Gender Trouble*, New York: Routledge, 1990, p. 6 and 7; Judith Butler, *Bodies That Matter*, New York: Routledge, 1993.

7. Judith Butler, *Gender Trouble*, New York: Routledge, 1990; Judith Butler, *Bodies That Matter*, New York: Routledge, 1993. See also Elizabeth Grosz's *Space, Time and Perversion*, New York, Routledge, 1995.

8. See notes 4 arid 5 above.

9. Diane Waldman, "There's More to a Positive Image than Meets the Eye," in Patricia Erens, ed., *Issues in Feminist Film Criticism*, Bloomington: Indiana University Press, 1990, pp. 13–18. Newer work began to focus on the place of women characters in overall narrative structures, on genres, and on broader questions of gender and representation. See Charlotte Brunsdon, "*Crossroads*: Notes on a Soap Opera," *Screen*, 22/4, 1981, pp. 32–7; Tania Modleski, *Loving with a Vengeance: Mass Produced Fantasies for Women*, Hamden CT.: Shoestring Press, 1982; Serafina Bathrick, "The Mary Tyler Moore Show: Women at Home and at Work," in Jane Feuer, Paul Kerr, and Tise Vahimagi, *MTM: "Quality Television,"* London: British Film Institute, 1984, pp. 91–131; Robert C. Allen, *Speaking of Soap Operas*, Chapel Hill: University of North Carolina Press, 1985; Helen Baehr and Gillian Dyer, eds, *Boxed In: Women and Television*, London: Pandora, 1987; Lorraine Gamman and Margaret Marshment, *The Female Gaze*, London: The Women's Press, 1988; E. Deidre Pribram, ed., F*emale Spectators: Looking at Film and Television*, London: Verso, 1988; Lynn Spigel and Densie Mann, eds, *Private Screenings*, Minneapolis: University of Minnesota Press, 1992.

10. See Michele Wallace, *Invisibility Blues: From Pop to Theory*, London: Verso, 1990; Jacqueline Bobo and Ellen Seiter, "Black Feminism and Media Criticism: *The Women of Brewster Place*," *Screen*, 32/3. 1991, 286–302; bell hooks, *Black Looks: Race and Representation*, Boston: South End Press, 1992; Toni Morrison, *Playing in the Dark: Whiteness and the Literary Imagination*, Cambridge, MA: Harvard University Press, 1992, Gail Dines and Jean M. Humez, *Gender, Race and Class in Media*, Thousand Oaks, CA: Sage, 1995; Sasha Torres, ed., *Living Color: Race and Television in the United States*, Durham and London: Duke University Press, 1998. For gender representations and class considerations see Andrea L. Press, *Women Watching Television*, Philadelphia: University of Pennsylvania Press, 1991.

11. John Fiske, *Television Culture*, London and New York: Methuen, 1987, p. 208.

12. See John Fiske, *Television Culture*, London and New York: Methuen, 1987; Constance Penley and Sharon Willis, eds, *Male Trouble*, Minneapolis: University of Minnesota Press, 1993; Maurice Berger, Brian Wallis, and Simon Watson, eds, *Constructing Masculinity*, New York: Routledge, 1995; Mark Simpson, *Male Impersonators: Men Performing Masculinity*: New York, Routledge, 1994.

13. Alexander Doty, *Making Things Perfectly Queer*, Minneapolis: University of Minnesota, 1993, pp. xv and 39–62.

14. As television began to portray more diversity regarding gender and sexuality, more scholars focused on gay and lesbian representations. For some examples see Hilary Hinds, "Fruitful Investigations: The Case of the Successful Lesbian Text," in Sally Munt, ed., *New Lesbian Criticism*, New York: Columbia University Press, pp. 153–72; Rosanne Kennedy, "The Gorgeous Lesbian in LA Law: The Present Absence?" in Diane Hamer and Belinda Budge, eds, *The Good, the Bad, and the Gorgeous*, London: Pandora Press, 1994, pp. 132–41 (both articles also reprinted

in Brunsdon, D'Acci and Spigel, eds, *Feminist Television Criticism*, London: Oxford University Press, 1997).

15. Andreas Huyssen, "Mass Culture as Woman: Modernism's Other," in *After the Great Divide: Modernism, Mass Culture, Postmodernism*, Bloomington: Indiana University Press, 1986, pp. 44–62. Lynne Joyrich, "All that Television Allows: TV Melodrama, Postmodernism and Consumer Culture," *Camera Obscura* 16, 1988, pp. 129–54. John Fiske, *Television Culture*, London and New York: Methuen, 1987; Lynne Joyrich, *Re-Viewing Reception: Television, Gender, and Postmodern Culture*, Bloomington: Indiana University Press, 1996.

16. Stuart Hall, "Encoding/Decoding," in Stuart Hall, Dorothy Hobson, Andrew Lowe, and Paul Willis, eds, *Culture, Media, Language* (London: Hutchinson, 1980). The essay had previously circulated as a Centre for Contemporary Cultural Studies stenciled paper (in a longer form) as "Encoding and Decoding in Television Discourse." See also Stuart Hall, Ian Angus, Jon Cruz, James Der Derian, Sut Jhally, Justin Lewis, and Cathy Schwichtenberg, "Reflections upon the Encoding/Decoding Model: An Interview with Stuart Hall," in Jon Cruz and Justin Lewis, eds, *Viewing, Reading, Listening: Audiences and Cultural Reception* (Boulder, Colorado: Westview Press, 1994) pp. 253–74. Richard Johnson, "What Is Cultural Studies Anyway?" *Social Text*, 16, Winter 1986/7, pp. 38–80. Julie D'Acci, "Cultural Studies, Television Studies and the Crisis in the Humanities," in *The Persistence of Television*, Lynn Spigel and Jan Olsen eds, Duke University Press, forthcoming. Julie D'Acci, "Television Genres" in the *International Encyclopedia of Social and Behavioral Sciences*, Oxford: Elsevier Science Ltd., 2002, pp. 15574–8.

17. See Dover, C. J. (2001) British documentary television production: tradition, change and "crisis" within a practitioner community. Unpublished thesis: Goldsmiths College, University of London.

18. Hollywood producer, writer and network executive, Barbara Corday, personal conversation, 1996, University of Southern California.

19. Special issue on Lifetime Television, ed. Julie D'Acci, *Camera Obscura*, 3.3 4, 1994–95.

20. Herman Gray, *Watching Race: Television and the Struggle for "Blackness,"* Minneapolis: University of Minnesota Press, 1995; Kristal Brent Zook, *Color by FOX: The Fox Network and the Revolution in Black Television*, New York: Oxford University Press, 1999.

21. Ronald Becker, "Prime Time Television in the Gay Nineties: Network Television, Quality Audiences and Gay Politics," *Velvet Light Trap*, Fall 1998, pp. 36–47.

22. Sean Griffin, *Tinker Belles and Evil Queens: The Walt Disney Company from the Inside Out*, New York, New York University Press, 1999.

23. Morlev, David, *Family Television: Cultural Power and Domestic Leisure*, London: Comedia, 1986; Gray, Ann, *Video Playtime: The Gendering of a Leisure Technology*, London: Routledge, 1992; McCarthy, Anna, *Ambient Television: Visual Culture and Public Space*, Durham: NC Duke University Press, 2001.

24. In the UK, *Queer as Folk* (shown on Channel 4) raised quite a stir in the British tabloids. See Annette Hill and Katarina Thomson's work for the British Social Attitudes Survey detailing how the British press used the program as a marker for extreme gender representations. Hill, Annette and Thomson, Katarina (2001) "Sex and the Media: a Shifting Landscape" in R. Jowell, J. Curtice, A. Park, K. Thomson, L. Jarvis, C, Bromley, N. Stratford, eds, *British Social Attitudes the 17th Report: Focusing on Diversity*, London: Sage: 71–99.

25. See E. Ann Kaplan, *Rocking Around the Clock: Music Television, Postmodernism, and Consumer Culture*, London: Methuen, 1987; Jim Collins, "Television and Postmodernism," in Robert C. Allen, ed., *Channels of Discourse Reassembled*, second edition, pp. 327–53.

Bibliography

Allen, R. C. (1985) *Speaking of Soap Operas*, Chapel Hill: University of North Carolina Press.

Baehr, H. and Dyer, G. (eds) (1987) *Boxed In: Women and Television*, London: Pandora.

Bathrick, S. (1984) "The Mary Tyler Moore Show: Women at Home and at Work", in Jane Feuer, Paul Kerr, and Tise Vahimagi, *MTM: "Quality Television"*, London: British Film Institute: pp. 91–131.

Becker, R. (1998) "Prime Time Television in the Gay Nineties: Network Television, Quality, Audiences and Gay Politics", *Velvet Light Trap*, Fall, pp. 36–47.

Bobo, J., and Seiter, F. (1991) "Black Feminism and Media Criticism: *The Women of Brewster Place*," *Screen*, 32/3: pp. 286–302.

Brunsdon, C. "Crossroads: Notes on a Soap Opera", *Screen*, 22/4: pp. 32–37.

——D'Acci, J. and Spigel, L. (eds) (1997) *Feminist Television Criticism*, London: Oxford University Press.

Butler, J. (1990) *Gender Trouble*, New York: Routledge.

——(1993) *Bodies That Matter*, New York: Routledge.

Butler, M. and Paisley, W. (1983) *Women and the Mass Media*, New York: Human Sciences Press.

Collins, J. (1992) "Television and Postmodernism", in Robert C. Allen (ed.) *Channels of Discourse Reassembled* (2nd edn), London: Routledge: pp. 327–53.

D'Acci, J. (2002) "Television Genres", in the *International Encyclopedia of Social and Behavioral Sciences*, Oxford: Elsevier Science Ltd: pp. 15574–8.

——(forthcoming) "Cultural Studies, Television Studies and the Crisis in the Humanities," in Lynn Spigel and Jan Olsen (eds) *The Persistence of Television*, Durham, NC: Duke University Press.

Deidre Pribram, E. (ed.) (1988) *Female Spectators: Looking at Film and Television*, London: Verso.

Dines, G. and Humez, J. M. (1995) *Gender, Race and Class in Media*, Thousand Oaks, CA: Sage.

Doty, A. (1993) *Making Things Perfectly Queer*, Minneapolis: University of Minnesota.

Dover, C. J. (2001) "British Documentary Television Production: Tradition, Change and 'Crisis' Within a Practitioner Community", Unpublished Thesis: Goldsmiths College, University of London.

Fiske, F. (1987) *Television Culture*, London and New York: Methuen.

Gamman, L. and Marshment, M. (1988) *The Female Gaze*, London: The Women's Press.

Gray, A. (1992) *Video Playtime: The Gendering of a Leisure Technology*, London: Routledge.

Gray, H. (1995) *Watching Race: Television and the Struggle for "Blackness"*, Minneapolis: University of Minnesota Press.

Griffin, S. (1999) *Tinker Belles and Evil Queens: The Walt Disney Company from the Inside Out*, New York, New York University Press.

Grosz, E. (1995) *Space, Time and Perversion*, New York, Routledge.

Hall, S. et al. (1994) "Reflections upon the Encoding/Decoding Model: An Interview with Stuart Hall," in Jon Cruz and Justin Lewis (eds) *Viewing, Reading, Listening: Audiences and Cultural Reception*, Boulder, Colorado: Westview Press: pp. 253–74.

——(1980) "Encoding/Decoding," in Stuart Hall, Dorothy Hobson, Andrew Lowe, and Paul Willis (eds) *Culture, Media*, Language, London: Hutchinson.

——(ed.) (1997) *Representation*, London: Sage and the Open University.

Hill, A., and Thomson, K. (2001) "Sex and the Media: a Shifting Landscape," in R. Jowell, J. Curtice, A. Park,

K. Thomson, L. Jarvis, C. Bromley, N. Stratford (eds) *British Social Attitudes the 17th Report: Focusing on Diversity*, London: Sage: 71–99.

Hinds, H. (1990) "Fruitful Investigations: The Case of the Successful Lesbian Text," in Sally Munt (ed.) *New Lesbian Criticism*, New York: Columbia University Press: pp. 153–72.

hooks, b. (1992) *Black Looks: Race and Representation*, Boston: South End Press.

Huvssen, A. (1986) "Mass Culture as Woman: Modernism's Other", in *After the Great Divide: Modernism, Mass Culture, Postmodernism*, Bloomington: Indiana University Press: 44–62.

Johnson, R. (1986) "What Is Cultural Studies Anyway?", *Social Text*, 16, Winter 1986/7, pp. 38–80.

Jovrich, L. (1988) "All that Television Allows: TV Melodrama, Postmodernism and Consumer Culture", *Camera Obscura* 16: 129–54.

The Culture Industry

Enlightenment as Mass Deception

By Theodor Adorno and Max Horkheimer

INTRODUCTION

Adorno and Horkheimer's essay, published in the mid-1940s, remains the classic denunciation of the 'culture industry'. It offers a vision of a society that has lost its capacity to nourish true freedom and individuality—as well as the ability to represent the real conditions of existence. Adorno and Horkheimer believe this loss results from the fact that cultural production has moved from an artisanal stage, which depended on individual effort and required little or no investment, to an industrial stage. For them, the modern culture industry produces safe, standardized products geared to the larger demands of the capitalist economy. It does so by representing 'average' life for purposes of pure entertainment or distraction as seductively and realistically as possible. Thus, for them, Hollywood movies, radio, mass-produced journalism, and advertising are only different at the most superficial level. Furthermore, the culture industry has become so successful that 'art' and 'life' are no longer wholly separable—which is the theme later theorists of postmodernity took from the essay. (See Jameson 1990; and the Lyotard essay in this volume.) Of course, 'high' art still exists as 'mass culture's opposite, but for Adorno, in a famous phrase, these are two halves of a whole that do not add up.

Debate about the essay continues, but it is important to remember the situation in which it was written. The Second World War had not quite ended, and Adorno and Horkheimer were refugees from Nazi Germany living in the U.S.A. Hitler's totalitarianism (with its state control of cultural production) and the American market system are fused in their thought—all the more easily because, for them as members of the German (or rather the secularized German Jewish) bourgeoisie, high culture, particularly drama and music, is a powerful vehicle of civil values. It is also worth emphasizing that when this essay was written the cultural industry was less variegated than it was to become, during the 1960s in particular. Hollywood, for instance,

Theodor Adorno and Max Horkheimer, "The Culture Industry: Enlightenment as Mass Deception," from *The Cultural Studies Reader*, pp. 29–43. Published by Routledge.

was still 'vertically integrated' so that the five major studios owned the production, distribution, and exhibition arms of the film business between them; television was still in its infancy; the LP and the single were unknown; the cultural market had not been broken into various demographic sectors—of which, in the 1950s, the youth segment was to become the most energetic. This helps explain how Adorno and Horkheimer neglect what was to become central to cultural studies: the ways in which the cultural industry, while in the service of organized capital, also provides the opportunities for all kinds of individual and collective creativity and decoding.

Further reading: Adorno 1991; Berman 1989; Connerton 1980; Jameson 1990; Jay 1984a. S.D.

The sociological theory that the loss of the support of objectively established religion, the dissolution of the last remnants of precapitalism, together with technological and social differentiation or specialization, have led to cultural chaos is disproved every day; for culture now impresses the same stamp on everything. Films, radio and magazines make up a system, which is uniform as a whole and in every part. Even the aesthetic activities of political opposites are one in their enthusiastic obedience to the rhythm of the iron system. The decorative industrial management buildings and exhibition centres in authoritarian countries are much the same as anywhere else. The huge gleaming towers that shoot up everywhere are outward, signs of the ingenious planning of international concerns, toward which the unleashed entrepreneurial system (whose monuments are a mass of gloomy houses and business premises in grimy, spiritless cities) was already hastening. Even now the older houses just outside the concrete city centres look like slums, and the new bungalows on the outskirts are at one with the flimsy structures of world fairs in their praise of technical progress and their built-in demand to be discarded after a short while like empty food cans. Yet the city housing projects designed to perpetuate the individual as a supposedly independent unit in a small hygienic dwelling make him all the more subservient to his adversary—the absolute power of capitalism. Because the inhabitants, as producers and as consumers, are drawn into the centre in search of work and pleasure, all the living units crystallize into well-organized complexes. The striking unity of microcosm and macrocosm presents men with a model of their culture: the false identity of the general and the particular. Under monopoly all mass culture is identical, and the lines of its artificial framework begin to show through. The people at the top are no longer so interested in concealing monopoly; as its violence becomes more open, so its power grows. Movies and radio need no longer pretend to be art. The truth that they are just business is made into an ideology in order to justify the rubbish they deliberately produce. They call themselves industries; and when their directors' incomes are published, any doubt about the social utility of the finished products is removed.

Interested parties explain the culture industry in technological terms. It is alleged that because millions participate in it, certain reproduction processes are necessary that inevitably require identical needs in innumerable places to be satisfied with identical goods. The technical contrast between the few production centres and the large number of widely dispersed consumption points is said to demand organization and planning by management. Furthermore, it is claimed that standards were based in the first place on consumers' needs, and for that reason were accepted with so little resistance. The result is the circle of manipulation and retroactive need in which the unity of the system grows ever stronger. No mention is made of the fact that the basis on which technology acquires power over society is the power of those whose economic hold over society is greatest. A technological rationale is the rationale of domination itself. It is the coercive nature of society alienated from itself. Automobiles, bombs, and movies keep the whole thing together until their leveling element shows its strength in the very wrong which it furthered. It has made the technology of the culture industry no more than the achievement of standardization and mass production, sacrificing whatever involved a distinction between the logic of the work and that of the social system. This is the result not of a law of movement in technology as such but of its function in today's economy. The need, which might resist central control, has already been suppressed by the control of the individual consciousness. The step from the telephone to the radio has clearly distinguished the roles. The former still allowed the subscriber to play the role of subject, and was liberal. The latter is democratic: it turns all participants into listeners and authoritatively subjects them to broadcast programmers which are all exactly the same. No machinery of rejoinder has been devised, and private broadcasters are denied any freedom. They are confined to the apocryphal field of the 'amateur', and also have to accept organization from above. But any trace of spontaneity from the public in official broadcasting is controlled and absorbed by talent scouts, studio competitions and official programmes of every kind selected by professionals. Talented performers belong to the industry long before it displays them, otherwise they would not be so eager to fit in. The attitude of the public, which ostensibly and actually favours the system of the culture industry, is a part of the system and not an excuse for it. If one branch of art follows the same formula as one with a very different medium and content; if the dramatic intrigue of broadcast soap operas becomes no more than useful material for showing how to master technical problems at both ends of the scale of musical experience—real jazz or a cheap imitation; or if a movement from a Beethoven symphony is crudely 'adapted' for a film sound-track in the same way as a Tolstoy novel is garbled in a film script: then the claim that this is done to satisfy the spontaneous wishes of the public is no more than hot air. We are closer to the facts if we explain these phenomena as inherent in the technical and personnel apparatus, which, down to its last cog, forms part of the economic mechanism of selection itself. In addition there is the agreement—or at least the determination—of all executive authorities not to produce or sanction anything that in any way differs from their own rules, their own ideas about consumers, or above all themselves.

In our age the objective social tendency is incarnate in the hidden subjective purposes of company directors, the foremost among whom are in the most powerful sectors of industry— steel, petroleum, electricity, and chemicals. Culture monopolies are weak and dependent in comparison. They cannot afford to neglect their appeasement of the real holders of power if their sphere of activity in mass society (a sphere producing a specific type of commodity which anyhow is still too closely bound up with easygoing liberalism and Jewish intellectuals) is not to undergo a series of purges. The dependence of the most powerful broadcasting company on the electrical industry, or of the motion picture industry on the banks, is characteristic of the whole sphere, whose individual branches are themselves economically interwoven. All are in such close contact that the extreme concentration of mental forces allows demarcation lines between different firms and technical branches to be ignored. The ruthless unity in the culture industry is evidence of what will happen in politics. Marked differentiations such as those of A and B films, or of stories in magazines in different price ranges, depend not so much on subject matter as on classifying, organizing, and labeling consumers. Something is provided for all so that none may escape; the distinctions are emphasized and extended. The public is catered for with a hierarchical range of mass-produced products of varying quality, thus advancing the rule of complete quantification. Everybody must behave (as if spontaneously) in accordance with his previously determined and indexed level, and choose the category of mass product turned out for his type. Consumers appear as statistics on research organization charts, and are divided by income groups into red, green, and blue areas; the technique is that used for any type of propaganda.

How formalized the procedure is can be seen when the mechanically differentiated products prove to be all alike in the end. That the difference between the Chrysler range and General Motors products is basically illusory strikes every child with a keen interest in varieties. What connoisseurs discuss as good or bad points serve only to perpetuate the semblance of competition and range of choice. The same applies to the Warner Brothers and Metro Goldwyn Mayer productions. But even the differences between the more expensive and cheaper models put out by the same firm steadily diminish: for automobiles, there are such differences as the number of cylinders, cubic capacity, details of patented gadgets; and for films there are the number of stars, the extravagant use of technology, labor, and equipment, and the introduction of the latest psychological formulas. The universal criterion of merit is the amount of 'conspicuous production', of blatant cash investment. The varying budgets in the culture industry do not bear the slightest relation to factual values, to the meaning of the products themselves. Even the technical media are relentlessly forced into uniformity. Television aims at a synthesis of radio and film, and is held up only because the interested parties have not yet reached agreement, but its consequences will be quite enormous and promise to intensify the impoverishment of aesthetic matter so drastically, that by tomorrow the thinly veiled identity of all industrial culture products can come triumphantly out into the open, derisively fulfilling the Wagnerian dream of the *Gesamtkunstwerk*—the fusion of all the arts in one work. The alliance of word, image, and music is all the more perfect than in *Tristan* because the sensuous elements which all approvingly reflect the surface of social reality are in principle embodied in the same technical process, the unity of which becomes its distinctive content. This process integrates all the elements of the production, from the novel (shaped with an eye to the film) to the last sound effect. It is the triumph of invested capital, whose title as absolute master is etched deep into the hearts of the dispossessed in the employment line; it is the meaningful content of every film, whatever plot the production team may have selected.

The whole world is made to pass through the filter of the culture industry. The old experience of the movie-goer, who sees the world outside as an extension of the film he has just left (because the latter is intent upon reproducing the world of everyday perceptions), is now the producer's guideline. The more intensely and flawlessly his techniques duplicate empirical objects, the easier it is today for the illusion to prevail that the outside world is the straightforward continuation of that presented on the screen. This purpose has been furthered by mechanical reproduction since the lightning takeover by the sound film.

Real life is becoming indistinguishable from the movies. The sound film, far surpassing the theatre of illusion, leaves no room for imagination or reflection on the part of the audience, who is unable to respond within the structure of the film, yet deviate from its precise detail without losing the thread of the story; hence the film forces its victims to equate it directly with reality. The stunting of the mass-media consumer's powers of imagination and spontaneity does not have to be traced back to any psychological mechanisms; he must ascribe the loss of those attributes to the objective nature of the products themselves, especially to the most characteristic of them, the sound film. They are so designed that quickness, powers of observation, and experience are undeniably needed to apprehend them at all; yet sustained thought is at of the question if the spectator is not to miss the relentless rush of acts. Even though the effort required for his response is semiautomatic, no scope is left for the imagination. Those who are so absorbed by the world of the movie—by its images, gestures, and words—that they are unable to supply what really makes it a world, do not have to dwell on particular points of its mechanics during a screening. All the other films and products of the entertainment industry which they have seen have taught them what to expect; they react automatically. The might of industrial society is lodged in men's minds. The entertainments manufacturers know that their products will be consumed with alertness even when the customer is distraught, for each of them is a model of the huge economic machinery which has always sustained the masses, whether at work or at leisure—which is akin to work. From every sound film and every broadcast programme the social effect can be inferred which is exclusive to none but is shared by all alike. The culture industry as a whole has moulded men as a type unfailingly reproduced in every product. All the agents of this process, from the producer to the women's clubs, take good care that the simple reproduction of this mental state is not nuanced or extended in any way.

The art historians and guardians of culture who complain of the extinction in the West of a basic style—determining power are wrong. The stereotyped appropriation of everything, even the inchoate, for the purposes of mechanical reproduction surpasses the rigour and general currency of any 'real style', in the sense in which cultural *cognoscenti* celebrate the organic precapitalist past. No Palestrina could be more of a purist in eliminating every unprepared and unresolved discord than the jazz arranger in suppressing any development, which does not conform to the jargon. When jazzing up Mozart he changes him not only when he is too serious or too difficult but when he harmonizes the melody in a different way, perhaps more simply, than is customary now. No medieval builder can have scrutinized the subjects for church windows and sculptures more suspiciously than the studio hierarchy scrutinizes a work by Balzac or Hugo before finally approving it. No medieval theologian could have determined the degree of the torment to be suffered by the damned in accordance with the *ordo* of divine love more meticulously than the producers of shoddy epics calculate the torture to be undergone by the hero or the exact point to which the leading lady's hemline shall be raised. The explicit and implicit exoteric and esoteric catalogue of the forbidden and tolerated is so extensive that it not only defines the area of freedom but is all-powerful inside it. Everything down to the last detail is shaped accordingly.

Like its counterpart, avant-garde art, the entertainment industry determines its own language, down to its very syntax and vocabulary, by the use of anathema. The constant pressure to produce new effects (which must conform to the old pattern) serves merely as another rule to increase the power of the conventions when any single effect threatens to slip through the net. Every detail is so firmly stamped with sameness that nothing can appear which is not marked at birth, or does not meet with approval at first sight. And the star performers, whether they produce or reproduce, use this jargon as freely and fluently and with as much gusto as if it were the very language, which it silenced long ago. Such is the ideal of what is natural in this field of activity, and its influence becomes all the more powerful, the more technique is perfected and diminishes the tension between the finished product and everyday life. The paradox of this routine, which is essentially travesty, can be detected and is often predominant in everything that the culture industry turns out. A jazz musician who is playing a piece of serious music, one of Beethoven's simplest minuets, syncopates it involuntarily and will smile superciliously when asked to follow the normal divisions of the beat. This is the 'nature' which, complicated by the ever-present and extravagant demands of the specific medium, constitutes the new style and is a 'system of non-culture, to which one might even concede a certain "unity of style" if it really made any sense to speak of stylized barbarity'.

The universal imposition of this stylized mode can even go beyond what is quasi-officially sanctioned or forbidden; today a hit song is more readily forgiven for not observing the 32 beats or the compass of the ninth than for containing even the most clandestine melodic or harmonic detail which does not conform to the idiom. Whenever Orson Welles offends against the tricks of the trade, he is forgiven because his departures from the norm are regarded as calculated mutations, which serve all the more strongly to confirm the validity of the system. The constraint of the technically conditioned idiom, which stars and directors have to produce as 'nature' so that the people can appropriate it, extends to such fine nuances that they almost attain the subtlety of the devices of an avant-garde work as against those of truth. The rare capacity minutely to fulfill the obligations of the natural idiom in all branches of the culture industry becomes the criterion of efficiency. What and how they say it must be measurable by everyday language, as in logical positivism. The producers are experts. The idiom demands an astounding productive power, which it absorbs and squanders. In a diabolical way it has overreached the culturally conservative distinction between genuine and artificial style. A style might be called artificial which is imposed from without on the refractory impulses of a form. But in the culture industry every element of the subject matter has its origin in the same apparatus as that jargon whose stamp it bears. The quarrels in which the artistic experts become involved with sponsor and censor about a lie going beyond the bounds of credibility are evidence not so much of an inner aesthetic tension as of a divergence of interests. The reputation of the specialist, in which a last remnant of objective independence sometimes finds refuge, conflicts with the business politics of the Church, or the concern which is manufacturing the cultural commodity. But the thing itself has been essentially objectified and made viable before the established authorities began to argue about it. Even before Zanuck acquired her, Saint Bernadette was regarded by her latter-day hagiographer as brilliant propaganda for all interested parties. That is what became of the emotions of the character. Hence the style of the culture industry, which no longer has to test itself against any refractory material, is also the negation of style. The reconciliation of the general and particular, of the rule and the specific demands of the subject matter, the achievement of which alone gives essential, meaningful content to style, is futile because there has ceased to be the slightest tension between opposite poles: these concordant extremes are dismally identical; the general can replace the particular, and vice versa.

Nevertheless, this caricature of style does not amount to something beyond the genuine style of the past. In the culture industry the notion of genuine style is seen to be the aesthetic equivalent of domination. Style considered as mere aesthetic regularity is a romantic dream of the past. The unity of style not only of the Christian Middle Ages but of the Renaissance expresses in each case the different structure of social power, and not the obscure experience of the oppressed in which the general was enclosed. The great artists were never those who embodied a wholly flawless and perfect style, but those who used style as a way of hardening themselves against the chaotic expression of suffering, as a negative truth. The style of their works gave what was expressed that force without which life flows away unheard. Those very art forms, which are known as classical, such as Mozart's music, contain objective trends, which represent something different to the style which they incarnate. As late as Schonberg and Picasso, the great artists have retained a mistrust of style, and at crucial points have subordinated it to the logic of the matter. What Dadaists and Expressionists called the untruth of style as such triumphs today in the sung jargon of a crooner, in the carefully contrived elegance of a film star, and even in the admirable expertise of a photograph of a peasant's squalid hut. Style represents a promise in every work of art. That which is expressed is subsumed through style into the dominant forms of generality, into the language of music, painting, or words, in the hope that it will be reconciled thus with the idea of true generality. This promise held out by the work of art that it will create truth by lending new shape to the conventional social forms is as necessary as it is hypocritical. It unconditionally posits the real forms of life as it is by suggesting that fulfillment lies in their aesthetic derivatives. To this extent the claim of art is always ideology too. However, only in this confrontation with tradition of which style is the record can art express suffering. That factor in a work of art which enables it to transcend reality certainly cannot be detached from style; but it does not consist of the harmony actually realized, of any doubtful unity of form and content, within and without, of individual and society; it is to be found in those features in which discrepancy appears: in the necessary failure of the passionate striving for identity. Instead of exposing itself to this failure in which the style of the great work of art has always achieved self-negation, the inferior work has always relied on its similarity with others—on a surrogate identity.

In the culture industry this imitation finally becomes absolute. Having ceased to be anything but style, it reveals the latter's secret: obedience to the social hierarchy. Today aesthetic barbarity completes what has threatened the creations of the spirit since they were gathered together as culture and neutralized. To speak of culture was always contrary to culture. Culture as a common denominator already contains in embryo that schematization and process of cataloguing and classification which bring culture within the sphere of administration. And it is precisely the industrialized, the consequent, subsumption which entirely accords with this notion of culture. By subordinating in the same way and to the same end all areas of intellectual creation, by occupying men's senses from the time they leave the factory in the evening to the time they clock in again the next morning with matter that bears the impress of the labour process they themselves have to sustain throughout the day, this subsumption mockingly satisfies the concept of a unified culture which the philosophers of personality contrasted with mass culture.

The culture industry perpetually cheats its consumers of what it perpetually promises. The promissory note which, with its plots and staging, it draws on pleasure is endlessly prolonged; the promise, which is actually all the spectacle consists of, is illusory: all it actually confirms is that the real point will never be reached, that the diner must be satisfied with the menu. In front of the appetite stimulated by all those brilliant names and images there is finally set no more than a commendation of the depressing everyday world it sought to escape. Of course works of art were not sexual exhibitions either. However, by representing deprivation as negative, they retracted, as it were, the prostitution of the impulse and rescued by mediation what was denied. The secret of aesthetic sublimation is its representation of fulfillment as a broken promise. The culture industry does not sublimate; it represses. By repeatedly exposing the objects of desire, breasts in a clinging sweater or the naked torso of the athletic hero, it only stimulates the unsublimated forepleasure which habitual deprivation has long since reduced to a masochistic semblance. There is no erotic situation, which, while insinuating and exciting, does not fail to indicate unmistakably that things can never go that far. The Hays Office merely confirms the ritual of Tantalus that the culture industry has established anyway. Works of art are ascetic and unashamed; the culture industry is pornographic and prudish. Love is downgraded to romance. And, after the descent, much is permitted; even license as a marketable speciality has its quota bearing the trade description 'daring'. The mass production of the sexual automatically achieves its repression. Because of his ubiquity, the film star with whom one is meant to fall in love is from the outset a copy of himself. Every tenor voice comes to sound like a Caruso record, and the 'natural' faces of Texas girls are like the successful models by whom Hollywood has typecast them. The mechanical reproduction of beauty, which reactionary cultural fanaticism wholeheartedly serves in its methodical idolization of individuality, leaves no room for that unconscious idolatry which was once essential to beauty. The triumph over beauty is celebrated by humour—the *Schadenfreude* that every successful deprivation calls forth. There is laughter because there is nothing to laugh at. Laughter, whether conciliatory or terrible, always occurs when some fear passes. It indicates liberation either from physical danger or from the grip of logic. Conciliatory laughter is heard as the echo of an escape from power; the wrong kind overcomes fear by capitulating to the forces, which are to be feared. It is the echo of power as something inescapable. Fun is a medicinal bath. The pleasure industry never fails to prescribe it. It makes laughter the instrument of the fraud practiced on happiness. Moments of happiness are without laughter; only operettas and films portray sex to the accompaniment of resounding laughter. But Baudelaire is as devoid of humour as Holderlin. In the false society, laughter is a disease, which has attacked happiness and is drawing it into its worthless totality. To laugh at something is always to deride it, and the life that, according to Bergson, in laughter breaks through the barrier, is actually an invading barbaric life, self-assertion prepared to parade its liberation from any scruple when the social occasion arises. Such a laughing audience is a parody of humanity. Its members are monads, all dedicated to the pleasure of being ready for anything at the expense of everyone else. Their harmony is a caricature of solidarity. What is fiendish about this false laughter is that it is a compelling parody of the best, which is conciliatory. Delight is austere: *res severa verum gaudium*. The monastic theory that not asceticism but the sexual act denotes the renunciation of attainable bliss receives negative confirmation in the gravity of the lover who with foreboding commits his life to the fleeting moment. In the culture industry, jovial denial takes the place of the pain found in ecstasy and in asceticism. The supreme law is that they shall not satisfy their desires at any price; they must laugh and be content with laughter. In every product of the culture industry, the permanent denial imposed by civilization is once again unmistakably demonstrated and inflicted on its victims. To offer and to deprive them of something is one and the same. This is what happens in erotic films. Precisely because it must never take place, everything centres upon copulation. In films it is more strictly forbidden for an illegitimate relationship to be admitted without the parties being punished than for a millionaire's future son-in-law to be active in the labour movement. In contrast to the liberal era, industrialized as well as popular culture may wax indignant at capitalism, but it cannot renounce the threat of castration. This is fundamental. It outlasts the organized acceptance of the uniformed seen in the films that are produced to that end, and in reality. What is decisive today is no longer Puritanism, although it still asserts itself in the form of women's organizations, but the necessity inherent in the system not to leave the customer alone, not for a moment to allow him any suspicion that resistance is possible. The principle dictates that he should be shown all his needs as capable of fulfilment, but that those needs should be so predetermined that he feels himself to be the eternal consumer, the object of the culture industry. Not only does it make him believe that the deception it practices is satisfaction, but it goes further and implies that, whatever the state of affairs, he must put up with what is offered. The escape from everyday drudgery, which the whole culture industry promises may be compared to the daughter's abduction in the cartoon: the father is holding the ladder in the dark. The paradise offered by the culture industry is the same old drudgery. Both escape and elopement are predesigned to lead back to the starting point. Pleasure promotes the resignation, which it ought to help to forget.

Amusement, if released from every restraint, would not only be the antithesis of art but its extreme role. The Mark Twain absurdity with which the American culture industry flirts at times might be a corrective of art. The more seriously the latter regards the incompatibility with life, the more it resembles the seriousness of life, its antithesis; the more effort it devotes to developing wholly from its own formal law, the more effort it demands from the intelligence to neutralize its burden. In some revue films, and especially in the grotesque and the funnies, the possibility of this negation does glimmer for a few moments. But of course it cannot happen. Pure amusement in its consequence, relaxed self-surrender to all kinds of associations and happy nonsense, is cut short by the amusement on the market: instead, it is interrupted by a surrogate overall meaning which the culture industry insists on giving to its products, and yet misuses as a mere pretext for bringing in the stars. Biographies and other simple stories patch the fragments of nonsense into an idiotic plot. We do not have the cap and bells of the jester but the bunch of keys of capitalist reason, which even screens the pleasure of achieving success. Every kiss in the revue film has to contribute to the career of the boxer, or some hit song expert or other whose rise to fame is being glorified. The deception is not that the culture industry supplies amusement but that it ruins the fun by allowing business considerations to involve it in the ideological clichés of a culture in the process of self-liquidation. Ethics and taste cut short unrestrained amusement as 'naïve'—naïveté is thought to be as bad as intellectualism—and even restrict technical possibilities. The culture industry is corrupt, not because it is a sinful Babylon but because it is a cathedral dedicated to elevated pleasure. On all levels, from Hemingway to Emil Ludwig, from Mrs. Miniver to the Lone Ranger, from Toscanini to Guy Lombardo, there is untruth in the intellectual content taken ready-made from art and science. The culture industry does retain a trace of something better in those features, which bring it close to the circus, in the self-justifying and nonsensical skill of riders, acrobats and clowns, in the 'defence and justification of physical as against intellectual art'. But the refuges of a mindless artistry, which represents what is human as opposed to the social mechanism are being relentlessly hunted down by a schematic reason which compels everything to prove its significance and effect. The consequence is that the nonsensical at the bottom disappears as utterly as the sense in works of art at the top.

In the culture industry the individual is an illusion not merely because of the standardization of the means of production. He is tolerated only so long as his complete identification with the generality is unquestioned. Pseudo individuality is rife: from the standardized jazz improvization to the exceptional film star whose hair curls over her eye to demonstrate her originality. What is individual is no more than the generality's power to stamp the accidental detail so firmly that it is accepted as such. The defiant reserve or elegant appearance of the individual on show is mass-produced like Yale locks, whose only difference can be measured in fractions of millimetres. The peculiarity of the self is a monopoly commodity determined by society; it is falsely represented as natural. It is no more than the moustache, the French accent, the deep voice of the woman of the world, the Lubitsch touch: finger prints on identity cards which are otherwise exactly the same, and into which the lives and faces of every single person are transformed by the power of the generality. Pseudo individuality is the prerequisite for comprehending tragedy and removing its poison: only because individuals have ceased to be themselves and are now merely centres where the general tendencies meet, is it possible to receive them again, whole and entire, into the generality.

In this way mass culture discloses the fictitious character of the 'individual' in the bourgeois era, and is merely unjust in boasting on account of this dreary harmony of general and particular. The principle of individuality was always full of contradiction. Individuation has never really been achieved. Self-preservation in the shape of class has kept everyone at the stage of a mere species being. Every bourgeois characteristic, in spite of its deviation and indeed because of it, expressed the same thing: the harshness of the competitive society. The individual who supported society bore its disfiguring mark; seemingly free, he was actually the product of its economic and social apparatus. Power based itself on the prevailing conditions of power when it sought the approval of persons affected by it. As it progressed, bourgeois society did also develop the individual. Against the will of its leaders, technology has changed human beings from children into persons. However, every advance in individuation of this kind took place at the expense of the individuality in whose name it occurred, so that nothing was left but the resolve to pursue one's own particular purpose. The bourgeois whose existence is split into a business and a private life, whose private life is split into keeping up his public image and intimacy, whose intimacy is split into the surly partnership of marriage and the bitter comfort of being quite alone, at odds with himself and everybody else, is already virtually a Nazi, replete both with enthusiasm and abuse; or a modern city-dweller who can now only imagine friendship as a 'social contact': that is, as being in social contact with others with whom he has no inward contact. The only reason why the culture industry can deal so successfully with individuality is that the latter has always reproduced the fragility of society. On the faces of private individuals and movie heroes put together according to the patterns on magazine covers vanishes a pretence in which no one now believes; the popularity of the hero models comes partly from a secret satisfaction that the effort to achieve individuation has at last been replaced by the effort to imitate, which is admittedly more breathless. It is idle to hope that this self-contradictory, disintegrating 'person' will not last for generations, that the system must collapse because of such a psychological split, or that the deceitful substitution of the stereotype for the individual will of itself become unbearable for mankind. Since Shakespeare's *Hamlet,* the unity of the personality has been seen through as a pretence. Synthetically produced physiognomies show that the people of today have already forgotten that there was ever a notion of what human life was. For centuries society has been preparing for Victor Mature and Mickey Rooney. By destroying they come to fulfill.

The Whole World Is Watching

By Todd Gitlin

INTRODUCTION

This book is about the mass media, the New Left, and their complex relations in historical time. It tells of one fateful conflict over control of the public cultural space in a society saturated with mass media.

Since the advent of radio broadcasting half a century ago, social movements have organized, campaigned, and formed their social identities on a floodlit social terrain. The economic concentration of the media and their speed and efficiency in spreading news and telling stories have combined to produce a new situation for movements seeking to change the order of society. Yet movements, media, and sociology alike have been slow to explore the meanings of modern cultural surroundings.

People directly know only tiny regions of social life; their beliefs and loyalties lack deep tradition. The modern situation is precisely the common vulnerability to rumor, news, trend, and fashion: lacking the assurances of tradition, or of shared political power, people are pressed to rely on mass media for bearings in an obscure and shifting world. And the process is reciprocal: pervasive mass media help pulverize political community, thereby deepening popular dependence on the media themselves. The media bring a manufactured public world into private space. From within their private crevices, people find themselves relying on the media for concepts, for images of their heroes, for guiding information, for emotional charges, for a recognition of public values, for symbols in general, even for language. Of all the institutions of daily life, the media specialize in orchestrating everyday consciousness—by virtue of their pervasiveness, their accessibility, their centralized symbolic capacity. They name the world's parts, they certify reality *as* reality—and when their certifications are doubted and opposed, as they surely are, it is those same certifications that limit the terms of effective opposition. To put it simply: the mass media have become core systems for the distribution of ideology.

That is to say, every day, directly or indirectly, by statement and omission, in pictures and words, in entertainment and news and advertisement, the mass media produce fields of definition and association, symbol and rhetoric, through which ideology becomes manifest and concrete. One important task for ideology is to define—and also define away—its opposition. This has always been true, of course. But the omnipresence and centralization of the mass media, and their integration into the dominant economic sector and the web of the State, create new conditions for opposition. The New Left of the 1960s, facing nightly television news, wire service reports, and a journalistic ideology of "objectivity," inhabited a cultural world vastly different from that of the Populist small farmers' movement of the 1890s, with its fifteen hundred autonomous weekly newspapers, or that of the worker-based Socialist Party of the early 1900s, with its own newspapers circulating in the millions. By the sixties, American society was dominated by a *consolidated* corporate economy, no longer by a *nascent* one. The dream of Manifest Destiny had become realized in a missile-brandishing national security state. And astonishingly, America was now the first society in the history of the world with more college students than farmers. The social base of radical opposition, accordingly, had shifted—from small farmers and immigrant workers to blacks, students, youth, and women. What was transformed was not only the dominant *structures* of capitalist society, but its *textures*. The whole quality of political movements, their procedures and tones, their cultural commitments, had changed. There was now a mass market culture industry, and opposition movements had to reckon with it—had to operate on its edges, in its interstices, and against it. The New Left, like its Populist and Socialist Party predecessors, had its own scatter of "underground" newspapers, with hundreds of thousands of readers, but every night some twenty million Americans watched Walter Cronkite's news, an almost equal number watched Chet Huntley's and David Brinkley's, and over sixty million bought daily newspapers which purchased most of their news from one of two international wire services. In a floodlit society, it becomes extremely difficult, perhaps unimaginable, for an opposition movement to define itself and its world view, to build up an infrastructure of self-generated cultural institutions, outside the dominant culture.[1] Truly, the process of making meanings in the world of centralized commercial culture has become comparable to the process of making value in the world through labor. Just as people *as workers* have no voice in what they make, how they make it, or how the product is distributed and used, so do people *as producers of meaning* have no voice in what the media make of what they say or do, or in the context within which the media frame their activity. The resulting meanings, now mediated, acquire an eery substance in the real world, standing outside their ostensible makers and confronting them as an alien force. The social meanings of intentional action have been deformed beyond recognition.

In the late twentieth century, political movements feel called upon to rely on large-scale communications in order to *matter,* to say who they are and what they intend to publics they want to sway; but in the process they become "newsworthy" only by submitting to the implicit rules of newsmaking, by conforming to journalistic notions (themselves embedded in history)

---

1   This point is made by Walter Adamson, "Beyond Reform and Revolution: Notes on Political Education in Gramsci, Habermas and Arendt," *Theory and Society* 6 (November 1978): 429–460.

of what a "story" is, what an "event" is, what a "protest" is. The processed image then tends to *become* "the movement" for wider publics and institutions who have few alternative sources of information, or none at all, about it; that image has its impact on public policy, and when the movement is being opposed, what is being opposed is in large part a set of mass-mediated images. Mass media define the public significance of movement events or, by blanking them out, actively deprive them of larger significance. Media images also become implicated in a movement's self-image; media certify leaders and officially noteworthy "personalities"; indeed, they are able to convert leadership into *celebrity,* something quite different. The forms of coverage accrete into systematic framing, and this framing, much amplified, helps determine the movement's fate.

For what defines a movement as "good copy" is often flamboyance, often the presence of a media-certified celebrity-leader, and usually a certain fit with whatever frame the newsmakers have construed to be "the story" at a given time; but these qualities of the image are not what movements intend to be their projects, their identities, their goals. Yet while they constrict and deform movements, the media do amplify the issues which fuel these same movements; as I argue at length in Part III, they expose scandal in the State and in the corporations, while reserving to duly constituted authority the legitimate right to remedy evils. The liberal media quietly invoke the need for reform—while disparaging movements that radically oppose the system that needs reforming.

The routines of journalism, set within the economic and political interests of the news organizations, normally and regularly combine to select certain versions of reality over others. Day by day, *normal* organizational procedures define "the story," identify the protagonists and the issues, and suggest appropriate attitudes toward them. Only episodically, in moments of political crisis and large-scale shifts in the overarching hegemonic ideology, do political and economic managers and owners intervene directly to re-gear or reinforce the prevailing journalistic routines. But most, of the time the taken-for-granted code of "objectivity" and "balance" presses reporters to seek out scruffy-looking, chanting, "Viet Cong" flag-waving demonstrators and to counterpose them to reasonable-sounding, fact-brandishing authorities. Calm and cautionary tones of voice affirm that all "disturbance" is or should be under control by rational authority; code words like *disturbance* commend the established normality; camera angles and verbal shibboleths ("and that's the way it is") enforce the integrity and authority of the news anchorman and commend the inevitability of the established order. Hotheads carry on, the message connotes, while wiser heads, officials and reporters both, with superb self-control, watch the unenlightened ones make trouble.

Yet these conventions originate, persist, and shift in historical time. The world of news production is not self-enclosed; for commercial as well as professional reasons, it cannot afford to ignore big ideological changes. Yesterday's ignored or ridiculed kook becomes today's respected "consumer activist," while at the same time the mediated image of the wild sixties yields to the image of the laid-back, apathetic, self-satisfied seventies. Yesterday's revolutionary John Froines of the Chicago Seven, who went to Washington in 1971 to shut down the government, goes to work for it in 1977 at a high salary; in 1977, Mark Rudd surfaces from the Weather Underground, and the sturdy meta-father Walter Cronkite chuckles approvingly as he reports that Mark's father thinks the age of thirty is "too old to be a revolutionary"—these are widely publicized signs of presumably calmer, saner times. Meanwhile, movements for utility rate reform, for unionization in the South, for full employment, for disarmament, and against nuclear power—movements which are not led by "recognized leaders" (those whom the media selectively acknowledged as celebrities in the first place) and which fall outside the prevailing frames ("the New Left is dead," "America is moving to the right")—are routinely neglected or denigrated—until the prevailing frame changes (as it did after the accident at Three Mile Island). An activist against nuclear weapons, released from jail in May 1978 after a series of demonstrations at the Rocky Flats, Colorado, factory that manufactures plutonium triggers for all American H-bombs, telephoned an editor he knew in the *New York Times*' Washington bureau to ask whether the *Times* had been covering these demonstrations and arrests. No, the editor said, adding: "America is tired of protest. America is tired of Daniel Ellsberg." Blackouts do take place; the editorial or executive censor rationalizes his expurgation, condescendingly and disingenuously, as the good shepherd's fair-minded act of professional news judgment, as his service to the benighted, homogenized, presumably sovereign audience. The closer an issue is to the core interests of national political elites, the more likely is a blackout of news that effectively challenges that interest. That there is safety in the country's nuclear weapons program is, to date, a core principle; and so news of its menace is extremely difficult to get reported—far more difficult, for example, than news about dangers of nuclear power after Three Mile Island. But if the issue is contested at an elite level, or if an elite position has not yet crystallized, journalism's more regular approach is to *process* social opposition, to control its image and to diffuse it at the same time, to absorb what can be absorbed into the dominant structure of definitions and images and to push the rest to the margins of social life.

The processed message becomes complex. To take a single example of a news item: on the CBS Evening News of May 8, 1976, Dan Rather reported that the FBI's burglaries and wiretaps began in the thirties and continued through World War II and the Cold War; and he concluded the piece by saying that these activities reached a peak "during the civil disturbances of the sixties." In this piece we can see some of the contradictory workings of broadcast journalism—and the limits within which contradictory forces play themselves out. First of all, Rather was conveying the information that a once sacrosanct sector of the State had been violating the law for decades. Second, and more subtly—with a clipped, no-nonsense manner and a tough-but-gentle, trustworthy, Watergate-certified voice of technocracy—he was deploring this law-breaking, lending support to those institutions within the State that brought it to the surface and now proposed to stop it, and affirming that the media are integral to this self-correcting system as a whole. Third, he was defining a onetime political opposition *outside* the State as "civil disturbance." The black and student opposition movements of the sixties, which would look different if they were called, say, "movements for peace and justice," were reduced to nasty little things. Through his language, Rather was inviting the audience to identify with forces of reason within the State: with the very source of the story, most likely. In a single news item, with (I imagine) no deliberate forethought, Rather was (a) identifying an abuse of government, (b) legitimating reform within the existing institutions, and (c) rendering illegitimate popular or radical opposition outside the State. The news that man has bitten dog carries an unspoken morality: it proposes to coax men to stop biting those particular dogs, so that the world can be restored to its essential soundness. In such quiet fashion, not deliberately, and without calling attention to this spotlighting process, the media divide movements into legitimate main acts and illegitimate sideshows, so that these distinctions appear "natural," matters of "common sense."[2]

What makes the world beyond direct experience look natural is a media *frame*.[3] Certainly we cannot take for granted that the world depicted is simply the world that exists. Many things exist. At each moment the world is rife with events. Even within a given event there is an infinity of noticeable details. Frames are principles of selection, emphasis, and presentation composed of little tacit theories about what exists, what happens, and what matters. In everyday life, as Erving Goffman has amply demonstrated, we frame reality in order to negotiate it, manage it, comprehend it, and choose appropriate repertories of cognition and action.[4] *Media* frames, largely unspoken and unacknowledged, organize the world both for journalists who report it and, in some important degree, for us who rely on their reports. *Media frames are persistent patterns of cognition, interpretation, and presentation, of selection, emphasis, and exclusion, by which symbol-handlers routinely organize discourse, whether verbal or visual.* Frames enable journalists to process large amounts of information quickly and routinely: to recognize it as information, to assign it to cognitive categories, and to package it for efficient relay to their audiences. Thus, for organizational reasons alone, frames are unavoidable, and journalism is organized to regulate their production. Any analytic approach to journalism—indeed, to the production of any mass-mediated content—must ask: What is the frame here? Why this frame and not another? What patterns are shared by the frames clamped over this event and the frames clamped over that one, by frames in different media in different places at different moments? And how does the news-reporting institution regulate these regularities?

And then: What difference do the frames make for the larger world?

The issue of the influence of mass media on larger political currents does not, of course, emerge only with the rise of broadcasting. In the Paris of a century and a half ago, when the commercial press was young, a journalistic novice and littérateur-around-town named Honoré de Balzac was already fascinated by the force of commercialized images. Central to his vivid semi-autobiographical novel, *Lost Illusions,* was the giddy, corroded career of the journalist. Balzac saw that the press degraded writers into purveyors of commodities. Writing in 1839 about the wild and miserable spectacle of "A Provincial Great Man in Paris," Balzac in one snatch of dinner-party dialogue picked up the dispute aborning over political consequences of a mass press; he was alert to the fears of reactionaries and the hopes of Enlightenment liberals alike:

> "The power and influence of the press are only at their dawn," said Finot. "Journalism is in its infancy, it will grow and grow. Ten years hence everything will be subjected to publicity. Thought will enlighten everything, it—"
> "Will blight everything," interposed Blondet.
> "That's a *bon mot*," said Claude Vignon.

---

2   For further analysis of the meaning of this and other television news items, see Todd Gitlin, "Spotlights and Shadows: Television and the Culture of Politics," *College English* 38 (April 1977): 791–796.

3   On media frames, see Gaye Tuchman, *Making News* (New York: The Free Press, 1978); and Stuart Hall, "Encoding and Decoding in the Television Discourse," mimeographed paper, Centre for Contemporary Cultural Studies, University of Birmingham, England, 1973.

4   Erving Goffman, *Frame Analysis: An Essay on the Organization of Experience* (New York: Harper and Row, 1974), pp. 10–11 and passim.

"It will make kings," said Lousteau.

"It will unmake monarchies," said the diplomat.

"If the press did not exist," said Blondet, "we could get along without it; but it's here, so we live on it."

"You will die of it," said the diplomat. "Don't you see that the superiority of the masses, assuming that you enlighten them, would make individual greatness the more difficult of attainment; that, if you sow reasoning power in the heart of the lower classes, you will reap revolution, and that you will be the first victims?"[5]

Balzac's ear for hopes and fears and new social tensions was acute; he was present at the making of a new institution in a new social era. Since then, of course, radio and now television have become standard home furnishings. And in considerable measure broadcast content has become part of the popular ideological furniture as well. But while researchers debate the exact "effects" of mass media on the popularity of presidential candidates and presidents, or the "effects" on specific patterns of voting or the salience of issues, evidence quietly accumulates that the texture of political life has changed since broadcasting became a central feature of American life. Media certainly help set the agendas for political discourse; although they are far from autonomous, they do not passively reflect the agendas of the State, the parties, the corporations, or "public opinion."[6] The centralization and commercialization of the mass media of communication make them instruments of cultural dominance on a scale unimagined even by Balzac. In some ways the very ubiquity of the mass media removes media *as a whole system* from the scope of positivist social analysis; for how may we "measure" the "impact" of a social force which is omnipresent within social life and which has a great deal to do with constituting it? I work from the assumption that the mass media are, to say the least, a significant social force in the forming and delimiting of public assumptions, attitudes, and moods—of ideology, in short. They sometimes generate, sometimes amplify a field of legitimate discourse that shapes the public's "definitions of its situations," and they work through selections and omissions, through emphases and tones, through all their forms of treatment.

Such ideological force is central to the continuation of the established order. While I defer a fuller statement of this position until Part III, I take it for now that the central command structures of this order are an oligopolized, privately controlled corporate economy and its intimate ally, the bureaucratic national security state, together embedded within a capitalist world complex of nation-states. But the economic and political powers of twentieth-century capitalist society, while formidable, do not by themselves account for the society's persistence, do not secure the dominant institutions against the radical consequences of the system's deep and enduring conflicts. In the language of present-day social theory, why does the population

---

5 Honore de Balzac, *Lost Illusions*, trans. G. Burnham Ives (Philadelphia: George Barrie, 1898), Vol. 2, p. 112.

6 Least of all, public opinion. Evidence is accumulating that the priorities conveyed by the media in their treatment of political issues lead public opinion rather than following it. See Maxwell E. McCombs and Donald L. Shaw, "The Agenda-Setting Function of Mass Media," *Public Opinion Quarterly* 36 (1972): 176–187; Jack M. McLeod, Lee B. Becker, and James E. Byrnes, "Another Look at the Agenda-Setting Function of the Press," *Communication Research* 1 (April 1974): 131–166; Lee B. Becker, Maxwell E. McCombs, and Jack M. McLeod, "The Development of Political Cognitions," in Steven H. Chaffee, ed., *Political Communication* (Beverly Hills, Calif.: Sage Publications, 1975), pp. 21–63, especially pp. 38–53; and Jay G. Blumler and Denis McQuail, *Television in Politics: Its Uses and Influence* (London: Faber, 1968).

accord legitimacy to the prevailing institutions? The goods are delivered, true; but why do citizens agree to identify themselves and to behave as consumers, devoting themselves to labor in a deteriorating environment in order to acquire private possessions and services as emblems of satisfaction? The answers are by no means self-evident. But however we approach these questions, the answers will have to be found in the realm of ideology, of culture in the broadest sense. Society is not a machine or a thing; it is a coexistence of human beings who do what they do (including maintaining or changing a social structure) as sentient, reasoning, moral, and active beings who experience the world, who are not simply "caused" by it. The patterned experiencing of the world takes place in the realm of what we call ideology. And any social theory of ideology asks two interlocking questions: How and where are ideas generated in society? And why are certain ideas accepted or rejected in varying degrees at different times?

In the version of Marxist theory inaugurated by Antonio Gramsci, *hegemony* is the name given to a ruling class's domination through ideology, through the shaping of popular consent.[7] More recently, Raymond Williams has transcended the classical Marxist base-superstructure dichotomy (in which the "material base" of "forces and relations of production" "gives rise" to the ideological "superstructure"). Williams has proposed a notion of hegemony as "not only the articulate upper level of 'ideology,'" but "a whole body of practices and expectations" which "constitutes a sense of reality for most people in the society."[8] The main economic structures, or "relations of production," set limits on the ideologies and commonsense understandings that circulate as ways of making sense of the world—without mechanically "determining" them. The fact that the networks are capitalist corporations, for example, does not automatically decree the precise frame of a report on socialism, but it does preclude continuing, emphatic reports that would embrace socialism as the most reasonable framework for the solution of social problems. One need not accept all of Gramsci's analytic baggage to see the penetrating importance of the notion of hegemony—uniting persuasion from above with consent from below—for comprehending the endurance of advanced capitalist society. In particular, one need not accept a strictly Marxist premise that the "material base" of "forces of production" *in any* sense (even "ultimately") precedes culture.[9] But I retain Gramsci's core conception: those who rule the dominant institutions secure their power in large measure directly *and indirectly*, by impressing their definitions of the situation upon those they rule and, if not usurping the whole of ideological space, still significantly limiting what is thought throughout the society. The notion of hegemony that I am working with is an active one: hegemony operating through a complex web of social activities and institutional procedures. Hegemony is done by the dominant and collaborated in by the dominated.

Hegemonic ideology enters into everything people do and think is "natural"—making a living, loving, playing, believing, knowing, even rebelling. In every sphere of social activity, it meshes with the "common sense" through which people make the world seem intelligible; it

---

7   Antonio Gramsci, *Selections from the Prison Notebooks*, ed. and trans. Quintin Hoare and Geoffrey Nowell Smith (New York: International, 1971).

8   Raymond Williams, "Base and Superstructure in Marxist Cultural Theory," *New Left Review,* No. 82 (1973), pp. 3–16. See also Williams, *Marxism and Literature* (New York: Oxford University Press, 1977), especially pp. 108–114.

9   For a brilliant demonstration of ways in which culture helps constitute a given society's "material base," and in particular the way in which the bourgeois concept of utility conditions capitalism's claims to efficiency, see Marshall Sahlins, *Culture and Practical Reason* (Chicago: University of Chicago Press, 1976), Part 2.

tries to *become* that common sense. Yet, at the same time, people only partially and unevenly accept the hegemonic terms; they stretch, dispute, and sometimes struggle to transform the hegemonic ideology. Indeed, its contents shift to a certain degree, as the desires and strategies of the top institutions shift, and as different coalitions form among the dominant social groups; in turn, these desires and strategies are modified, moderated by popular currents. In corporate capitalist society (and in state socialism as well), the schools and the mass media specialize in formulating and conveying national ideology. At the same time, indirectly, the media—at least in liberal capitalist society—take account of certain popular currents and pressures, symbolically incorporating them, repackaging and distributing them throughout the society. That is to say, groups out of power—radical students, farm workers, feminists, environmentalists, or homeowners groaning under the property tax—can contest the prevailing structures of power and definitions of reality. One strategy which insurgent social movements adopt is to make "news events."

The media create and relay images of order. Yet the social reality is enormously complex, fluid, and self-contradictory, even in its own terms. Movements constantly boil up out of the everyday suffering and grievance of dominated groups. From their sense of injury and their desire for justice, movements assert their interests, mobilize their resources, make their demands for reform, and try to find space to live their alternative "lifestyles." These *alternative visions* are not yet *oppositional*—not until they challenge the main structures and ideas of the existing order the preeminence of the corporate economy, the militarized State, and authoritarian social relations as a whole. In liberal capitalist society, movements embody and exploit the fact that the dominant ideology enfolds contradictory values: liberty versus equality, democracy versus hierarchy, public rights versus property rights, rational claims to truth versus the arrogations and mystifications of power.[10] Then how does enduring ideology find its way into the news, absorbing and ironing out contradictions with relative consistency? How, in particular, are rather standardized frames clamped onto the reporting of insurgent movements? For the most part, through journalists' routines.

These routines are structured in the ways journalists are socialized from childhood, and then trained, recruited, assigned, edited, rewarded, and promoted on the job; they decisively shape the ways in which news is defined, events are considered newsworthy, and "objectivity" is secured. News is managed routinely, automatically, as reporters import definitions of news worthiness from editors and institutional beats, as they accept the analytical frameworks of officials even while taking up adversary positions. When reporters make decisions about what to cover and how, rarely do they deliberate about ideological assumptions or political consequences.[11] Simply by doing their jobs, journalists tend to serve the political and economic elite definitions of reality.

But there are disruptive moments, critical times when the routines no longer serve a coherent hegemonic interest. The routines produce news that no longer harmonizes with the

---

10   I adapt this argument from my "Prime Time Ideology: The Hegemonic Process in Television Entertainment," *Social Problems* 26 (February 1979): 264–265.

11   As Gaye Tuchman writes, "news both draws upon and reproduces institutional structures" (*Making News*, p. 210). For particulars, see Leon V. Sigal, *Reporters and Officials: The Organization and Politics of Newsmaking* (Lexington, Mass.: D. C. Heath, 1973); Bernard Roshco, *Newsmaking* (Chicago: University of Chicago Press, 1975); and most fully, Herbert Gans, *Deciding What's News* (New York: Pantheon, 1979).

hegemonic ideology, or with important elite interests as the elites construe them; or the elites are themselves so divided as to quarrel over the content of the news. (In the extreme case, as in Chile in 1973, the hegemonic ideology is pushed to the extremity of its self-contradiction, and snaps; the dominant frame then shifts dramatically, in that case toward the Right.) At these critical moments, political and economic elites (including owners and executives of media corporations) are more likely to intervene directly in journalistic routine, attempting to keep journalism within harness. To put it another way, the cultural apparatus normally maintains its own momentum, its own standards and procedures, which grant it a certain independence from top political and economic elites. In a liberal capitalist society, this bounded but real independence helps legitimate the institutional order as a whole and the news in particular. But the elites prefer not to let such independence stretch "too far." It serves the interests of the elites as long as it is "relative," as long as it does not violate core hegemonic values or contribute too heavily to radical critique or social unrest. (It is the elites who determine, or establish routines to determine, what goes "too far.") Yet when elites are themselves at odds in important ways, and when core values are deeply disputed—as happened in the sixties—journalism itself becomes contested. Opposition groups pressing for social and political change can exploit self-contradictions in hegemonic ideology, including its journalistic codes. Society-wide conflict is then carried into the cultural institutions, though in muted and sanitized forms. And then ideological domestication plays an important part—along with the less visible activities of the police[12]—in taming and isolating ideological threats to the system.

The test of such a line of argument, of course, is whether it makes sense of evidence, whether it comprehends historical truth. Most of this book sorts out evidence in the course of telling the particular story of major media and the New Left in the 1960s. One set of questions I ask addresses *the nature of media coverage.* Just how did major media respond to the emergence of student radicalism? Which events and rhetorical gestures were considered newsworthy, and what were the reasons? What were the major themes and tones of this coverage, and how did they shift over time? To what extent were these shifts determined by shifts in the actual policies and actions of the movement? (Methodological difficulties notwithstanding, there is no avoiding the attempt to discover and describe *what actually happened.*) I try first to locate the central emphases in coverage of the movement, and then to reach behind them to grasp the media's central—usually unspoken—assumptions about the political world and about political opposition in particular.[13] For before messages can have "effects" on audiences, they must emanate

---

12 Very little has been written on direct relations between police agencies and the mass media. Gans (*Deciding What's News*, p. 121) makes the valuable point that "perhaps the most able sources are organizations that carry out the equivalent of investigative reporting, offer the results of their work as 'exclusives,' and can afford to do so anonymously, foregoing the rewards of publicity." For a survey of the FBI's COINTELPRO media operations, especially active in New York, Chicago, Los Angeles, and Milwaukee, at least between 1956 and 1971, and a few extant details of direct cooperation between the FBI and reporters, see Chip Berlet, "COINTELPRO: What the (Deleted) Was It? Media Op," *The Public Eye* 1 (April 1978): 28–38. I know of no evidence of cooperation between the FBI and either CBS News or the *New York Times*, but this entire field is *terra incognita.*

13 A fine precedent for thematically analyzing media coverage of a movement's activities, and the sources of this coverage in the organizational activities and assumptions of news-gatherers, is James D. Halloran, Philip Elliott, and Graham Murdock, *Demonstrations and Communication: A Case Study* (Harmondsworth, England: Penguin Books,

outward from message-producers and then into the audience's minds, there to be interpreted. The recent flurry of concern with "the effects of television" selects out certain aspects of the message (violence, say) as *the* content, then masks this selectivity with the trappings of quantitative methodology. Since the media aim at least to influence, condition, and reproduce the activity of audiences by reaching into the symbolic organization of thought, the student of mass media must pay attention to the symbolic content of media messages before the question of effects can even be sensibly posed. These questions about how the media treated the movement constitute the agenda of Part I, tested on the case of Students for a Democratic Society (SDS)—and, for comparison, other segments of the antiwar movement—in the year SDS first became public, 1965. I organize this discussion chronologically to call attention to both regularities and shifts of journalistic frame.

But the movement was far from the passive object of media attentions. The study of mass communications effects has had quite enough of Pavlovian stimulus-response psychology, along with its pluralist opposite. Although I may sometimes adopt the convenient language of a single cause producing a single effect, I am talking not about determined objects "having impacts" on each other, as if movements and media were billiard balls, but about an *active* movement and *active* media pressing on each other, sometimes deliberately, sometimes not, in a process rich with contradiction and self-contradiction, a process developing in historical time.

A second set of questions, then, concerns *what the New Left did about media treatment.* Once floodlit, from 1965 on, the New Left found it necessary to take the media into account in planning actions, choosing leaders, responding to those leaders, and articulating positions. What tensions developed within the movement about how to approach the media, and how were they resolved or surpassed? How did the New Left's approach to the media change over time, and from leadership generation to leadership generation?

And here we fade into a third set of questions. *What were the consequences of media coverage for the movement—for its structure, its leadership, its politics, its strategy and tactics—for the*

1970), which closely follows British newspaper and television coverage of the giant October 1968 anti-Vietnam War demonstration in London. Also relevant is Stanley Cohen's study of the media-aided "social construction" of Mod and Rocker teenage gangs in the early sixties, *Folk Devils and Moral Panics* (London: MacGibbon and Kee, 1972). Several of the essays in Stanley Cohen and Jock Young, eds., *The Manufacture of News: A Reader* (London: Constable, 1973; and Beverly Hills, Calif.: Sage Publications, 1973) give useful informal textual analyses of media frames for deviant activities; see also Charles Winick, ed., *Deviance and Mass Media* (Beverly Hills, Calif.: Sage Publications, 1978). The existence of systematic news frames for political events is demonstrated empirically in Harvey Molotch and Marilyn Lester, "News as Purposive Behavior: On the Strategic Use of Routine Events, Scandals, and Rumors," *American Sociological Review* 39 (1974): 101–112, and is extended to media treatment of opposition movements in Molotch's "Media and Movements," unpublished paper, 1977. Several essays by Stuart Hall also contain rich semiological "readings" of media programs, especially in television; see especially his "Encoding and Decoding in the Television Discourse," and Stuart Hall, Ian Connell, and Lidia Curti, "The 'Unity' of Public Affairs Television," *Working Papers in Cultural Studies* 9 (Spring 1976): 51–93, both forthcoming in Stuart Hall, *Reproducing Ideologies* (London: Macmillan). An attempt at a more systematic interpretive scheme for television programs may be found in John Fiske and John Hartley, *Reading Television* (London: Methuen, 1978); see also my review in *Theory and Society,* forthcoming. My earlier discussions of television's frames for the New Left may be found in Gitlin, "Fourteen Notes on Television and the Movement," *Leviathan* 1 (July–August 1969): 3–9; "Sixteen Notes on Television and the Movement," in George Abbott White and Charles Newman, eds., *Literature in Revolution* (New York: Holt, Rinehart and Winston, 1972) pp. 335–366; and "Spotlights and Shadows" (note 2, above).

history, the texture, and the feeling tone of the New Left? This second and third set of questions, applied mostly to SDS between 1965 and 1970, constitute the agenda for Part II.

Two general questions hover beneath the surface of these particular accounts. First, *why did the media do what they did?* In reporting the movement, how important were routine journalistic practices, organizational arrangements, the specific (and changing) institutional interests of the news media, the society's wider (and also changing) political and economic structures, and the ideological surroundings, needs, and consequences of those structures? How was the media treatment of movements like, and how unlike, their treatment of any other social happening accorded the dignity of a continuing story? These issues filter back into the question of structure: What is the place of the cultural apparatus and its ideological constructions among the major social institutions in ensemble?

And no less important: *Why did the movement do what it did?* Just how important was media treatment in turning the movement in this or that political direction, and how important were class identity, ideology, organizational structure, State repression, and the play of political events and deliberate choices? All these shaped the New Left, and each mattered in the context of the others. I am most emphatically not propounding a new single-factor political analysis; but I am scrutinizing one feature of a whole history in order to cast light on the whole. I want to ask, finally: How far can the SDS experience with the media be generalized to other movements at other times? These questions are the business of Part III.

This is a study of the nature, sources, and consequences of news. It is also one point of entry into a rethinking of the New Left's moment in history. I aim to contribute to a new reckoning with the much-mythologized sixties, already fast receding either into oblivion or into convenient distortion. For neo-conservative historiography and the unreconstructed Nixonian Right, the New Left was a catastrophic upsurge of adversary culture gone anti-American and wild. For fashionable popular writers, it was a moment of puerility, adolescent enthusiasm, and naivete, a fad at last discarded. For the current generation of Marxist-Leninists, it was a petit bourgeois adventure needing to be purged of its "moralistic," "idealist," "reformist" elements before the true road to revolution could emerge into clean, hard, twentieth-century light. For many who participated, and their younger brothers and sisters, it was perhaps a noble crusade that failed, perhaps a vaguely interesting or dangerous tumult. For the younger still, nothing remains but the shadow of a reputation, a rumor conditioned by media images of something that mysteriously came, made trouble, and went. Without writing a memoir, a collective biography, or a political chronicle, I hope to show something of the New Left as a movement, a motion in history: that is, a coherent process wherein organizations and individuals, making choices in specific situations, mattered. I approach this history as the story of a movement in its lived richness; at the same time, I distill from this story analytic categories which extend beyond the particular events of a particular decade.

I cannot do justice to the whole of the movement. Since my point of entry is the movement's collision with the large-scale commercial media, there are very important dimensions of the movement's history and cultural identity which I do not discuss at all. Not least, there are the movement's *own* media, the hundreds of weekly photo-offset "underground" papers that sprang up in the later sixties and early seventies. Nor do I discuss the role of other cultural and communication institutions that served the movement: its own internal newspapers and magazines; political weeklies like *The Guardian;* monthlies like *Ramparts;* the Liberation News Service; or Newsreel filmmaking and film distributing collectives. I do not trace the movement's ideological career in much detail, nor many of its political choices and settings, nor the contingencies of political developments outside the largely white, largely youthful sector of the New Left. *I never mean to suggest that the movement's interior culture was purely the creature of media images, or that movement people were wholly or even largely dependent on them for information and bearings.* I offer *one* approach to a recomprehending of the New Left's experience; and I would like it to take its place among others, together to give the sixties their due.

In looking at the movement-media dance, of course, I had to limit my attention within each domain. The reader who wishes fuller information about my choices and procedures should consult the Appendix. But briefly: as for the movement, I've drawn most of my particulars from the history of Students for a Democratic Society during the half-decade it operated under the media spotlight. At points I've supplemented this history with information about other New Left groups during the same period. SDS was the main national organization of the white New Left during most of this period; it was also the major field of my own political work in the mid-sixties. Much reflected upon and reconsidered, my experience in SDS primed me to ask questions about the movement-media relation, about the nature of media coverage, and about its consequences for the movement. I participated in demonstrations—and helped organize them—and then followed the television and newspaper and newsmagazine versions; the disjuncture, the shock of nonrecognition, raised wrenching questions about media frames. I worked in a movement and watched it construed as something quite other than what I thought it was. Living with the discrepancy became one characteristic experience of my generation; we had, after all, grown up to take on faith what was in the newspapers, and to believe with Walter Cronkite that "that's the way it is." This continuing experience of disjuncture gave me my agenda for research; it did not give me answers.

As for the media, I was also compelled to make choices. As is usually the case in social research, theoretical considerations and practical exigencies intertwined to create my field of exploration, my "data base." For several reasons I centered on CBS News and the *New York Times:* they were influential in powerful circles *and* inside the movement, they were in some sense the best of the mainstream media (and we expected the best of them), and their archives are relatively accessible. So most of my reflections on the sources of news treatment concern these institutions in particular. I take up the reasons, the limits of my samples and conclusions, and the problems of extending them in the Appendix.

One more prefatory note. I study news here, except for brief digressions into TV documentary and film. News is one component of popular culture; the study of news should ultimately be enfolded within a more ample study of all the forms of cultural production and their ideology. Television entertainment is also an ideological field, and must have played a part in formulating and crystallizing the cultural tendencies of the sixties; surely it deserves extensive treatment of its own.[14] So do other cultural forms, including popular songs, popular fiction (genre novels

---

14 Considering the great amount of time Americans and others spend watching TV entertainment, there is a great imbalance in sociological attention: many more studies have been done of the production and meanings of news, which is more transparently available for political understandings, than of everyday fiction. I have sketched some preliminary categories for the analysis of TV entertainment conventions in "Prime Time Ideology," (note 10, above). On TV entertainment and its evolution in general, there is abundant material in Erik Barnouw's *The Image Empire* (New York: Oxford University Press, 1970), *Tube of Plenty* (New York: Oxford University Press, 1975), and *The Sponsor* (New York: Oxford University Press, 1978); in Fiske and Hartley, *Reading Television*, and Hall, "Encoding and Decoding in the

as well as magazine stories), jokes, and popular films (which are not necessarily the acclaimed films which critics prefer to see and to analyze); so do the careers of pop stars like Bob Dylan and Joan Baez, the San Francisco bands and hip heroes who stood somewhere on the thin and fluid boundary between the New Left and the counterculture. Let popular culture have its analytic due: we live in it.

MEDIA ROUTINES AND POLITICAL CRISES

THEORIES OF THE NEWS

Where do news frames come from? How are they fixed into the appearance of the stable, the natural, the taken-for-granted? And how, despite this, are the prevailing frames disputed and changed? How are we to understand the systematic denigration of the New Left?

Herbert Gans has recently put forward a list of theories that purport to explain how certain stories are selected as news, a list that will serve as a starting point.[1] First, there are *journalist-centered* theories, which explain the news as a product of professional news judgments. In the extreme form of this viewpoint, journalism is a profession with autonomous criteria for training, recruitment, and promotion, serving the public interest by following its own stated and unstated rules concerning objectivity. Like any other profession, journalism is—or ought to be (there is this tension in thought about the professions generally)—insulated from extrinsic considerations, whether from political pressures, pressures from publishers, news executives, or advertisers, pressures from outside interest groups, or, indeed, conscious or unconscious ideological screens operating within journalists themselves. In less extreme form, such theories are commonly held by journalists, and also by politicians like Nixon and Agnew who hold journalists guilty of a special ideological bias.

A second group of theories stresses *the inertia, the sheer habit of news organization*. Some of the organizational theories emphasize commercial imperatives; others, the organizational structure of the news operations themselves.[2] Compatible with these theories, and not sharply demarcated from them, are the more recent *phenomeological* approaches to news as a social construct, which emphasize the human agency of news, the informal rules which Journalists adopt to enable them to process vast amount of information and to select and repackage it in a form that audiences will accept as The News.[3]

Television Discourse," both cited in note 13, above; and in Rose K. Goldsen, *The Show and Tell Machine* (New York: Dial Press, 1977), though many analytic questions remain. On the content and history of specific shows and types of show, see Danny Czitrom, "Bilko: A Sitcom for All Seasons," *Cultural Correspondence* 4 (Spring 1977): 16–19; Todd Gitlin, "The Televised Professional," *Social Policy*, November–December 1977, pp. 94–99; Pete Knutson, "Dragnet: The Perfect Crime?" *Liberation* 18 (May 1974): 28–31; Michael R. Real, *Mass-Mediated Culture* (Englewood Cliffs, N.J.: Prentice-Hall, 1977), pp. 118–139 (on medical shows); and Bob Schneider, "Spelling's Salvation Armies," *Cultural Correspondence*, No. 4 (Spring 1977): 27–36 (on police shows). On soap operas, see Dennis Porter, "Soap Time: Thoughts on a Commodity Art Form," *College English* 38 (April 1977): 782–788. On the production process, see Muriel G. Cantor, *The Hollywood TV Producer* (New York: Basic Books, 1971); Les Brown, *Television; The Business Behind the Box* (New York: Harcourt Brace Jovanovich, 1971); and Gaye Tuchman, "Assembling a Network Talk-Show," in Tuchman, ed., *The TV Establishment* (Englewood Cliffs, N.J.: Prentice-Hall, 1974), pp. 119–135.

The third approach is *event-centered*: it argues that news "mirrors" or "reflects" the actual nature of the world. From this point of view, if media treatment of the New Left changed between 1965 and 1969, it must have been because the movement, and the events it was involved in, changed. The mirror metaphor, as Edward Jay Epstein showed, was common among news executives in the late sixties.[4] Although it has waned in credibility as critics from the first two groups have pointed to the systematic selectivities of news, mirror theory retains a commonsense standing among many journalists and news executives; it is reproduced in Walter Cronkite's nightly closing, "And that's the way it is."

There are also theories which locate the causes of story selection *in institutions or social conditions outside the news organization*: in technological factors, national culture, economics, the audience, the most powerful news sources, and/or the ideologies of the dominant social powers. As Gans points out, each of these theories has something to recommend it, and each falls short of completeness. Professional, organizational, directly economic and political and ideological forces *together* constitute, from the traces of events in the world, images of The News which are limited in definite ways and tilted toward the prevailing frames. Gans himself composes a synthesis of these approaches, viewing "news as information which is transmitted from sources to audiences, with journalists—who are both employees of bureaucratic commercial organizations and members of a profession—summarizing, refining, and altering what becomes available to them from sources in order to make the information suitable for their audiences. Because news has consequences, however, journalists are susceptible to pressure from groups and individuals (including sources and audiences) with power to hurt them, their organizations, and their firms. ... [S]ources, journalists, and audiences coexist in a system, although it is closer to being a tug of war than a functionally interrelated organism." These "tugs of war" are in the end "resolved by power," and news is therefore, among other things, in the words of Philip Schlesinger, "the exercise of power over the interpretation of reality."[5]

Gans is right to look both inside and outside news organizations for explanations of the news, and right to conclude that the production of news is a system of power. These conclusions are irresistible; they help comprehend the framing patterns I have demonstrated in Parts I and II. What I seek here is not so much an alternative as a more ample theoretical domain within which to understand the framing process and the media-movement relationship. For this purpose I want an approach attuned to the particular procedures of journalism, yet sensitive to the fact that journalism exists alongside—and interlocked with—a range of other professions and institutions with ideological functions within an entire social system. I want an approach which is both structural and historical—that is, which can account for regularities in journalistic procedure and product, yet which at the same time can account for historical changes in both. Such an approach should encompass not only news and its frames, but movements and their identities, goals, and strategies; it should comprehend both news and movements as contending conveyors of ideas and images of what the world is and should be like. As I suggested in the Introduction, the most comprehensive theoretical approach can be found in recent developments of the Gramscian idea of hegemony. After briefly canvassing the Gramscian territory, we can draw together some of this book's themes and explore the specific question of the sources of news frames for the New Left and opposition movements in general.

IDEOLOGICAL HEGEMONY AS A PROCESS

There exists no full-blown theory of hegemony, specifying social-structural and historical conditions for its sources, strengths, and weaknesses.[6] But a certain paradigm has been developing during the seventies, after the collapse of the New Left and the translation of Antonio Gramsci's prison writings,[7] and it is this paradigm—a domain of concerns, sensitivities, and conclusions—that can help situate the history of media-movement relations. Unfortunately, Gramsci, who was the first to specify the concept in a modern Marxist context,[8] wrote ambiguously and in fragments: he was isolated in a Fascist prison, he was at pains to pass censorship, and he was at times gravely ill. Condemned to prison between 1926 and his death in 1937, Gramsci filled notebook after notebook trying to understand, among other things, why the working-class uprising in Northern Italy after World War I had failed; why the working class was not necessarily revolutionary; why most of it could be defeated by Fascism. Without neglecting the role of force in securing State power, Gramsci centered on the limits of working-class consciousness, on the issue of whether and when the working class could successfully challenge the prevailing bourgeois conception of its place in the world.

Gramsci's concept can be defined this way: hegemony is a ruling class's (or alliance's) domination of subordinate classes and groups through the elaboration and penetration of ideology (ideas and assumptions) into their common sense and everyday practice; it is the systematic (but not necessarily or even usually deliberate) engineering of mass consent to the established order. No hard and fast line can be drawn between the mechanisms of hegemony and the mechanisms of coercion; the hold of hegemony rests on elements of coercion, just as the force of coercion over the dominated both presupposes and reinforces elements of hegemony.[9] In any given society, hegemony and coercion are interwoven. Recently, Raymond Williams[10] to and Stuart Hall[11] have elaborated the notion of hegemony and begun to use it in the analysis of popular culture. In Hall's words, drawing on Gramsci's terminology:

> "hegemony" exists when a ruling class (or, rather, an alliance of ruling class fractions, a "historical bloc") is able not only to coerce a subordinate class to conform to its interests, but exerts a "total social authority" over those classes and the social formation as a whole. "Hegemony" is in operation when the dominant class fractions not only dominate but *direct*—lead: when they not only possess the power to coerce but actively organize so as to command and win the consent of the subordinated classes to their continuing sway. "Hegemony" thus depends on a combination of force and consent. But—Gramsci argues—in the liberal-capitalist state, consent is normally in the lead, operating behind "the armour of coercion."[12]

Further, hegemony is, in the end, a process that is entered into by both dominators and dominated.[13] Both rulers and ruled derive psychological and material rewards in the course of confirming and reconfirming their inequality. The hegemonic sense of the world seeps into popular "common sense" and gets reproduced there; it may even appear to be generated *by* that common sense.

In liberal capitalist societies, no institution is devoid of hegemonic functions, and none does hegemonic work only. But it is the cultural industry as a whole, along with the educational system, that most coherently specializes in the production, relaying, and regearing of hegemonic ideology. The media of the culture industry are ordinarily controlled by members of top corporate and political elites, and by individuals they attempt (with varying success) to bring into their social and ideological worlds. At the same time, the ruling coalitions of "class fractions" are to a great extent dependent on these ideology-shaping institutions (1) to formulate the terms of their own unity, and (2) to certify the limits within which all competing definitions of reality will contend. They structure the ideological field within which, as Hall says, "subordinate classes 'live' and make sense of their subordination in such a way as to sustain the dominance of those ruling over them."[14] Because at any given moment there is not a unitary functioning "ruling class," but rather an alliance of powerful groups in search of an enduring basis for legitimate authority, the particular hegemonic ideology will not be simple; "the content of dominant ideology will reflect this complex interior formation of the dominant classes."[15]

The hegemonic ideology will be complex for a deeper structural reason as well. The dominant economic class does not, for the most part, produce and disseminate ideology directly. That task is left to writers and journalists, producers and teachers, bureaucrats and artists organized for production within the cultural apparatus as a whole—the schools and mass media as a whole, advertising and show business, and specialized bureaucracies within the State and the corporations. Thus the corporate owners stand, as Alvin W. Gouldner points out, in marked contrast to previous ruling classes: "Unlike the slave-owners of antiquity or the ruling nobility of feudalism, the dominant class under capitalism is actively and routinely engaged in the conduct of economic affairs."[16] By itself it cannot directly command the political or the administrative or the cultural apparatus that conditions the consent of the governed, even should it desire to do so. Rather, distinct strata have emerged and solidified, charged with specialized responsibilities for the administration of the entire social order. The liberal capitalist political economy is layered as an economy and a polity which meet and interpenetrate at many levels but remain organized separately; the executives and owners of the cultural apparatus—the press, mass entertainment, sports, and arts—are also interlocked at high levels with the managers of corporate and political sectors. But these sectors operate according to different principles. What Gouldner writes about the differentiation of political and economic sectors might then be extended, *mutatis mutandis*, to the cultural order:

> In consequence of these developments, the system of stratification under capitalism differs profoundly from that of previous societies. … With the growing differentiation between the economic, political, and bureaucratic *orders*, and with the growing specialization among different *personnel* each of the newly differentiated spheres develops a measure of *autonomy*; and, we might add, of "slippage" from the other. The operating personnel of the administrative, the political, and the ruling classes, each develop specialized standards and skills for dealing with their own spheres, thereby taking the latter less intelligible and less accessible to the direct supervision of the dominant economic class.[17]

The fact that power and culture in a modern social system are to some considerable degree segmented and specialized makes ideology essential: ideology comes to the fore as a potentially cohesive force—especially in a society segmented in all the realms of life experience, ethnically and geographically as well as politically and occupationally. At the same time, the relative autonomy of the different sector legitimates the system as a whole. And crucially, as Gouldner pOints out, the economic elite now becomes dependent on other sectors for securing the allegiance of the whole society. Specifically:

Ideology assumes special importance as a symbolic mechanism through which the interests of these diverse social strata may be integrated; through the sharing of it the several dominant strata are enabled to make compatible responses to changing social conditions.[18]

But the need for unifying ideology is also a vulnerability for the system as a whole:

It is precisely because the hegemonic elite is *separated from* the means of culture, including the production of ideologies, that ideologies developed in capitalist society may often be discomforting to the hegemonic elite, so that they prefer other mechanisms of dominance and integration more fully and routinely accessible to them.[19]

Indeed, the hegemonic ideology of bourgeois culture is extremely complex and absorptive; only by absorbing and domesticating conflicting values, definitions of reality, and demands on it, in fact, does it remain hegemonic.[20] In this way the hegemonic ideology of liberal, democratic capitalism is dramatically different from the ideologies of pre-capitalist societies and from the dominant ideology of authoritarian socialist or Fascist regimes. What permits it to absorb and domesticate criticism is not something accidental to liberal capitalist ideology, but rather its core. The hegemonic ideology of liberal, democratic capitalist society is deeply and essentially conflicted in a number of ways. At the center of liberal capitalist ideology there coils a tension between the affirmation of patriarchal authority currently enshrined in the national security State—and the affirmation of individual worth and self-determination. Bourgeois ideology in all its incarnations has been from the first a contradiction in terms, affirming the once revolutionary ideals of "life, liberty, and the pursuit of happiness," or "liberty, equality, and fraternity," as if these ideas were compatible, or even mutually dependent, at all times in all places. More recently, the dominant ideology has strained to enfold a second-generation set of contradictory values: liberty versus equality, democracy versus hierarchy, public rights versus property rights, rational claims to truth versus the arrogations of power. All opposition movements in bourgeois society whether for liberation or for domination—wage their battles precisely in terms of liberty, equality, or fraternity (or, recently, sorority)—on behalf of one set of bourgeois values against another. They press on the dominant ideology in its own name.

And, indeed, the economic system routinely generates, encourages, and tolerates ideologies which challenge and alter its own rationale, for example, as corporate capitalism became dependent on an indefinite expansion of consumer goods and consumer credit, it began to commend and diffuse hedonist values which conflicted with the older values of thrift, craft, and productivity. Workers are now told to be self-sacrificing and disciplined for eight hours a day and to relish their pleasurable selves for the next eight: to give themselves over to the production interests of the company or the office during the week and to express their true, questing, consuming selves over the weekend. Inevitably, hedonism and self-affirmation spill over from the realm of consumption into the realm of production, disrupting workplace efficiency and provoking managerial response: this whole process is central to what Daniel Bell rightly calls "the cultural contradictions of capitalism."[21]

But contradictions of this sort operate within a hegemonic framework which bounds and narrows the range of actual and potential contending world views. Hegemony is an historical process in which one picture of the world is systematically preferred over others: usually through practical routines and at times through extraordinary measures. Its internal structures, as Raymond Williams writes, "have continually to be renewed, recreated and defended; and by he same token … they can be continually challenged and in certain respects modified."[22] Normally the dominant frames are taken for granted by media practitioners, and reproduced and defended by them for reasons, and via practices, which the practitioners do not conceive to be hegemonic. Hegemony operates effectively—it does deliver the news—yet outside consciousness; it is exercised by self-conceived professionals working with a great deal of autonomy within institutions that proclaim the neutral goal of informing the public.[23] Yet we have seen in Part I that the news frame applied to the New Left was not neutral: it held reporting within definite limits. Specifically how was this possible? How, more generally, does hegemony take place within journalism as a totality of techniques, assumptions, and choices?

THE WORKINGS OF HEGEMONY IN JOURNALISM

As Ben Bagdikian puts it, news outside regular beats usually results from three stages in selection: (1) an editor decides that a certain scene should be looked at as the site of a newsworthy event; (2) a reporter decides what is worthy of notice on that scene; and (3) editors decide how to treat and place the resulting story.[24] Behind this process stands the institutional structure of the media, and above all the managers who set overall corporate policy, though hardly with utter freedom. (In the argument to come, I shall single out national commercial television, but the argument about print media would not be essentially different.) By socialization, by the bonds of experience and relationships—in other words, by direct corporate and class interest—the owners and managers of the major media are committed to the maintenance of the going system in its main outlines: committed, that is to say, to private property relations which honor the prerogatives of capital; committed to a national security State; committed to reform of selected violations of the moral code through selective action by State agencies; and committed to approving individual success within corporate and bureaucratic structures.

The media elite want to honor the political-economic system as a whole; their very power and prestige deeply presuppose that system. At the same time, they are committed, like members of any other Corporate elite, to their own particular economic and political advantage. The networks above all—far more than prestigious newspapers like the *New York Times*—play for high profit stakes. The resulting conflicts between particular corporate interests and what the networks take to be the interests of the corporate system as a whole constitute one irreducible source of strain within the system as a whole. Even a news organization's methods for legitimizing the system as a whole, its code of objectivity and balance, pull it in conflicting directions: at one moment toward the institutions of political and economic power, and at another toward alternative, and even, at times, oppositional movements, depending on political circumstance. Organized as a distinct pyramid of power, he network develops the strategy of neutralization, incorporating the competing forces in such a way as to maximize its audiences and thus its profits, its legitimacy, and its stature. It claims and earns legitimacy (Harris Polls show TV news to be the most credible of *all* American institutions, though it shares in the general relative decline) in part by sanctioning reliable routines of objectivity; yet those very routines of objectivity sometimes permit—indeed, may insist on—the entry of challenging social movements into the public ideological space. The network's claim to legitimacy, embodied in the professional ideology of objectivity, requires it, in other words, to take a certain risk of undermining the legitimacy of the social system as a whole. The network's strategy for managing this contradiction is to apply the whole apparatus of techniques that we have examined in Part I, precisely to tame, to contain, the opposition that it dares not ignore.

After all, the legitimacy of a news operation rests heavily on the substantial—if bounded—autonomy of its employees. The audience must believe that what they are viewing is not only interesting but true, and the reporters must be permitted to feel that they have professional prerogatives to preserve. To avoid a reputation for having an ax to grind, the top media managers endow their news operations with the appearance, and a considerable actuality, of autonomy; their forms of social control must be indirect, subtle, and not at all necessarily conscious. Their standards flow through the processes of recruitment and promotion, through policy, reward, and the sort of social osmosis that flows overwhelmingly in one direction: downward. The editors and reporters they hire are generally upper-middle-class in origin, and although their personal values may be liberal by the conventional nomenclature of American politics, they tend to share the *core* hegemonic assumptions of their class: that is, of their managers as well as their major sources.[25] Their salaries are handsome (in 1976, CBS News paid its correspondents between $35,000 and $80,000 a year, not counting fringe benefits and perquisites), and they share tastes and vacation spots and circulate at dinner parties with many of their sources. In the essentially impersonal operations of the newsroom, their relatively homogenized outlook ordinarily overwhelms any discordant personal opinions they might harbor, at least when it comes to defining a story and selecting its essential themes. Their common approach to the world infuses their homogenized cadence and tone: the news voice conveys the impression that the world is unruly because of deviations from a normally adequate and well-managed social order.[26]

The network chiefs want to maximize both audience size and prestige: size determines the rates they may charge advertisers, and prestige, desirable for its own sake, also boosts the upper-middle-class audience for whose attention advertisers will pay more. In working to maximize the audience and to report the news "as it is," the networks must operate, of course, under the (ordinarily glazed) eye of the Federal Communications Commission, Congress, and whatever interventions the White House may attempt. The FCC is charged by 1934 law with ensuring that local stations serve "the public interest, convenience, and necessity." Since in practice this empty phrase is interpreted to mean that the local channels must run a certain amount of news and "public affairs" programs, and since it is cheapest and most profitable by far for the affiliates to meet this requirement by broadcasting what the networks have to offer (along with local news), the FCC is in effect constraining not only the local stations but the networks. In effect, through the so-called Fairness Doctrine, the FCC is requiring the networks to provide response time for interests—but not all interests—offended by their coverage. (Consider this boundary to the permissible: It is not "the Commission's intention to make time available to Communists or to the Communist viewpoints.")[27] But how much do the networks actually fear FCC regulation, and how much does their fear explain the timidity of news departments in their habit of imposing "balance" upon each news story? Probably not very much. CBS, at least, wants to repeal the Fairness Doctrine, to "deregulate" broadcasting, arguing that the balance requirement violates their First Amendment rights and that deregulation would permit more aggressive, freewheeling journalism.[28] On the other hand, ABC News, early in 1979, defended the Fairness Doctrine. How unconstrained the networks want their journalism may be doubted. Skepticism comes easily when the FCC has placed only the lightest of hands on programming at large, and no restraint at all on the vast profits in broadcasting. For all the broadcasters' hue and cry, the FCC has never lifted a station license for violations of the Fairness Doctrine, and continued violations have only once played a part in a decision not to renew.[29] The networks' top commands are probably more concerned about the possibility of congressional investigations and constricting laws, about losing profits to cable and satellite systems, about direct protests from offended political powers, and about vaguely anticipated regulation and repression in a hypothetical future. (One top CBS producer exclaimed to me in November 1976, "We're weak as hell. The First Amendment is a frail reed. Look what Mme. Gandhi did in India—she closed down the press just like that.") In any case, the conventions about objectivity, balance, legitimate sources, and the rest are all derived from newspaper journalism: and no Fairness Doctrine applies there.

In the force field of intersecting political pressures—from the White House, the FCC, Congress, and the affiliates—the networks test the boundaries of the permissible; they carve out an ideological sphere in which they are free to move as they please. With documentaries especially, where the total air time and budget are so limited to start with, choices of subject and slant will depend most directly on the larger interests (in both the economic and the ideological sense) of the media elites. These interests, in turn, will of course take into account larger ideological currents in the society, and decisions will be made to amplify some and to dampen others. With the network's mass market mentality, "controversial" decisions—that is, decisions to broadcast anything of political substance—are not taken lightly. For example, CBS's "The Selling of the Pentagon" in 1971 capitalized on a rising tide of antimilitarist sentiment, expressed CBS's desire to declare independence from the military propaganda apparatus, and pointed the finger at a strictly limited, isolable sector of Pentagon operations. For all its limits, though, "Selling" drew complaints of bias—and congressional subpoenas for top executives. In a glare of First Amendment publicity, CBS stood fast against releasing outtakes to Congress, but subsequently failed to give the "Selling" producer, Peter Davis, new assignments; nor did it broadcast another documentary critical of the military until mid-1976, when the Vietnam war and the Nixon administration itself had ended. Early in 1977, likewise, CBS broadcast Bill Moyers's dramatic two-hour exposé of CIA sponsored military actions against Cuba. It is hard to believe that such a broadcast would have been made under an administration that was not moving toward *détente* with Cuba. Yet Moyers shortly thereafter left CBS, saying that there was no room there for serious documentaries; and the top CBS Evening News producer, Ron Bonn, argues that "the most serious damage done to our branch of the free press by Mr. Agnew" was to "make it possible to think the formerly unthinkable—that maybe television *didn't* have [the obligation to provide a steady flow of news and public affairs]—that maybe it should just shut up and run some more game shows. I date the decline of the serious documentary, of tough, controversial television from that time, from that administration, and from that man."[30] One need not rue the loss of a Golden Age of "tough, controversial television" to observe a loss of luster: a decline from the sixties, when network news conventions were fresher and more fluid and had not yet quite hardened into bureaucratically fixed patterns.

But day to day, political and corporate pressures have not changed much: they go on setting unspoken outer limits for the routines that journalists are trained for and believe in. Once hired and assigned, reporters customarily from strong bonds with the sources (especially in Washington) on whom they depend for stones. They absorb the world views of the powerful. They may also contest them: when one institutional Source disputes another (the General Accounting Office against the White House, say, or the Environmental Protection Agency against the Department of Energy); or when they come to believe that the powerful are violating the going code of conduct;[31] or when they develop, consciously or not, their own interest (as when their spouses and children actively opposed the Vietnam war); or, on occasion, when they resent, and organize to protest, one of their publishers' more outspoken editorial opinions.

But even when there are conflicts of policy between reporters and sources, or reporters and editors, or editors and publishers, thee conflicts are played out within a field of terms and premises which does not overstep the hegemonic boundary. Several assumptions about news value serve, for the most part, to secure that boundary that news involves the novel event, not the underlying, enduring condition; the person, not the group; the visible conflict, not the deep consensus; the fact that "advances the story," not the one that explains or enlarges it.[32] Only where coverage under these rules flies in the face of immediate institutional interest, or might be construed to be at odds with it, or wanders into some neutral zone where interests have not yet been clearly defined, is there ground for conflict between reporters and media elites over the integrity of the news operation. When outside political powers complain, top news executives mediate between them and the reporters; they may ask the staff to document their factual claims, for example. In newspaper rooms, national and foreign editors mediate between the top editors who are their superiors and the reporters who work beneath them.[33] CBS personnel almost universally say that the news executives insulate them from direct political pressures with great skill and reliability (with the important exception of the censored Watergate takeout; see p. 278, below)—which is not, of course, to deny the indirect pressures and understandings that one way or another find their way into the preconscious stuff of news policy.

Finally, there are organizational factors that in a lesser way constrain the news. Budget ceilings, for example, lead to shortages of bureaus, correspondents, and crews, all of which increase television news's dependence on a few big stories, preferably the *dramatic* and the *metropolitan*.[34] For the same reasons, many major newspapers have been shutting down their expensive out-of-town bureaus, especially abroad, and increasing their dependence on the wire services and on the *New York Times* and *Los Angeles Times–Washington Post* services.

The work of hegemony, all in all, consists of Imposing standardized assumptions over events and conditions that must be "covered" by the dictates of the prevailing news standards. On television especially, this work is fairly routine. It *is* work: effort is expended on it. But certain conventions make the effortless burdensome to news processors. One such convention is the ritualized news story format. The correspondent identifies the problem; there is a rising curve of narrative which establishes the situation, identifies protagonists, and sets them against one another; whatever complication emerges from this conflict then dissolves as the correspondent wraps up the package as neatly as possible. (The term *wrap-up* is well chosen.) Meanwhile, on the screen, the pictures stereotypically illustrate the package. Despite the industry's rhetoric about the value it places on TV pictures as such, the regular format is actually what one perceptive cameraman calls the "illustrated lecture."[35] The ratio of film (or tape) shot to film used is very high, often twenty or thirty to one; the film used must be *selected* to illustrate the verbal story. It is the correspondent's narration that situates the story, identifies its components, and names the point. Television's reputation as a visual medium for news is based disproportionately on some extraordinary pictures (e.g., Jack Ruby shooting Lee Harvey Oswald), on routine disaster coverage, on "shooting bloody" in war; but in the bulk of stories most actual pictures are decorative and illustrative—shots of coal shovels gouging coal out of a seam, with the "natural sound" of gouging, as the reporter talks about the energy crisis; and so on. If, at times, the words and pictures are slightly discrepant, this discrepancy may be one index of friction in the work of hegemonic superimposition. Aspects of the pictures may imperfectly, inadvertently, or weakly testify to the existence of a discordant reality which the correspondent is working to assimilate into a conventional framework. Battlefield footage in Vietnam, for example, might in its bloodiness fight against the government's we-can-see-the-light-at-the-end-of-the-tunnel frame, which is relayed, however skeptically, by the correspondent's voice-over narrative. The closer to air time the story breaks, the fewer hands and minds may intervene to process the film into the dominant frames. But most of the discrepancies are flattened out by producers and editors splicing the piece together in New York (or another major bureau). Commonly the lecture is unitary and controlling. The lecture format enables the correspondent and the producer to clamp a rather definite frame onto a minute or two of film—selected from footage which itself has been shot selectively from amidst a complex and contradictory reality.

So stereotyping does result in part—as network people often admit and complain—from their simple shortage of time. The network news runs to some 22½ minutes of reporting every evening: that is what is left after commercials take their bite from the half-hour. But stereotyping also results from the organization's desire for easy ways of transmitting and manipulating bits of information—bits which, moreover, need to be easily interchangeable and easily edited, re-edited, or reorganized at the last minute, usually by producers and editors who have been nowhere near the scene of the story. If the network is to "cover the day's news," it has to simplify stories so that they can be processed and covered in one-and-a-half or two minutes; even a "long" takeout may be only three or four minutes. (Probably on average it is even shorter in the seventies than in the sixties, though, in 1977, NBC News installed one major takeout each evening as "Segment 3.") The imperative of finding "good pictures" (usually vivid illustrations) adds to the premium on simplification.

But although the length of a day or an hour is fixed, the way in which time pressure is experienced is not a neutral, technologically determined, ineradicable feature of a world of scarcity. What is experienced as time pressure actually flows from a combination of immediate economic imperatives and the more general imperatives of the commercial system as a whole. In the first place, the affiliate makes considerably more money on locally originated programs where it sells advertising time directly—than it does on network programs; thus the affiliates resisted the networks' move from fifteen to thirty minutes of national news, starting with CBS in 1963, and they have so far successfully resisted the CBS news executives' desire to expand from thirty to forty-five or sixty minutes.[36] The more general imperative is that the network must sell a reliable audience to the sponsors, and a reliable audience is usually (though not always) one that can be counted on to tune in at a given time every day (or, in the case of an entertainment, every week). Although the weekliness of entertainment has broken down, at least temporarily, with the success of "Roots" in early 1977, and although the networks are now liable to cancel series with greater alacrity than ever before, the dailiness of news remains a commercial necessity. And this regularity is not simply concocted by network elites: *it makes good sense to an audience conditioned to a regular existence by regularity in its school schedules and regularity in its working schedules.* A regularly programmed life-world conditions, an is partly reconditioned by, the orderliness of the news and entertainment formats.

The orderly format ends up promoting social stability, which is what much of the audience longs for: a sense that whatever is wrong in the world, it can be put right by authoritative (almost always official) agencies. Even if the story is about disorder, it likely turns to the restoration of order under benign official aegis.[37] Content that starts out seeming destabilizing and threatening—a mass demonstration, a riot, a new style of political deviance—may thus end up confirming the inherent rightness and necessity of the core hegemonic principles. The same process operates after news of scandal of disaster. After Watergate and Nixon's resignation, the new media frame was: "The system works." Official folk heroes such as Senator Sam Ervin, or Harold Denton of the Nuclear Regulatory Commission after the accident at Three Mile Island, are elevated as new mass-mediated fountainheads of authoritative moral and technical excellence, to replace the fallen gods.

In general, then, stereotyping solves an enormous number of practical problems for journalism. But why should time pressure and the desire of networkers and audiences for regular stories, rhythms, and authoritative *dramatis personae* lead to *particular* stereotypes? To process news from the campuses in the sixties, journalists had to reify a category of "student activists"; but why *this* stereotyped version and not *that*? As Harvey Molotch and Marilyn Lester point out, the imperative of building a large audience cannot, by itself, explain any specific frame; in strictly market terms, how could executives be sure in advance that their ratings would suffer from this news treatment rather than that?[38] Reporters hear little from their actual audience, tend to have a low opinion of the audiences knowledge and attention span, and form images of this abstract audience compounded of wish, fact, and indifference. Abstractions of market and audience explain little indeed. Rather, the stereotypes usually derive from editors' and reporters' immediate work and social circles, and from premises that filter through the organizational hierarchy: from sources, peers, and superiors, on occasion from friends and Spouses, and from the more prestigious media reports, especially those of the *New York Times* and the wire services.[39] Journalists and executives may justify these images in terms of audience Interest ("America is tired of protest," as the *Times* editor said about uncovered demonstrations against nuclear weapons In Colorado; see p. 5 above), but they perceive that audience through a frame, darkly.

At the same time, news stereotypes are not frozen. As Harvey Molotch points out, "news" is a rather undefined state of affair.[40] Anything *could* be news, for news is what news-gatherers working in news-processing organizations say is news. Therefore, it is historical and contestable; all deep social conflicts are in part conflicts over what is news. Despite the widespread claim that objectivity in news is possible, any attempt to exact a general definition of news—a routine, universalizable definition—comes to naught. Ask a reporter what is news and one is likely to elicit vague references to "what is important" or "what is interesting" or "what is new." As one probes these notions, posing examples and counterexamples, the general criteria dissolve. Reporters finally acknowledge that "what is important" depends on who is asking, or on "the situation," or on "news judgment." These notions have to be just clear and specific enough to justify the claim that journalism is a profession, and then to justify the naming of a particular beat that can be relied upon to produce news (the police beat, for example); and just general enough to allow for the "unlikely" story that is to say, for "news."

The professional insistence that objective journalism is desirable, and that objective determinations of newsworthiness are possible, arose during the nineteenth century, albeit fitfully, as part of the sweeping intellectual movement toward scientific detachment and the culturewide separation of fact from value.[41] From time to time, as in the sixties, the value of objectivity gets questioned; it always returns, virtually by default. "Opinion" will be reserved to editorials, "news" to the news columns; whatever was in the minds of the ideologues of objectivity, generations of jouralists have aspired to that value, even enshrined it. And the aspiration does have the effect of insulating reporters greatly—though far from perfectly—from the direct political pressures of specific advertisers, politicians, and interest groups, and even in the more prestigious news institutions, from the prerogatives of interfering publishers.[42] Journalists are trained to be desensitized to the voices and life-worlds of working-class and minority people;[43] they are also trained in locating and treating "the news" so that it is "credible" and, by their own lights, "important." "Credibility," "importance," "objectivity"—these elusive categories are neither arbitrary nor fixed. They are flexible enough to shift with the expectations and experience of news executives and high-level sources, yet definite enough to justify journalists' claims to professional status and standards. A top TV producer told Herbert Gans: "They can order me to do something on big or small issues, for after all this is a company and a business, but they rarely exert that influence. *I am as autonomous as I could expect to be.*"[44] I stress the final sentence. Journalists' ideals are fluid enough to protect them from seeing that their autonomy is bounded: that by going about their business in a professional way, they systematically frame the news to be compatible with the main institutional arrangements of the society. Journalists thus sustain the dominant frames through the banal, everyday momentum of their routines. Their autonomy keeps within the boundaries of the hegemonic system.

THE LIMITS OF HEGEMONIC ROUTINE

Still, traditional methods of news-gathering often contradict the demands that interested publics make for "credibility" and "responsibility" as their needs and expectations develop and shift. As oppositional groups and movements make claims for coverage, reporters may change their images of their audience or even of the world, and, too, their "instincts" about what is "newsworthy," "interesting," or "important." These changes may be more or less subtle, more or less conscious: reporters may be influenced even as they resist overt pressures to report an issue in this or that way. Their vulnerability depends on many things: personal life-experience, specific organizational arrangements, and the shifting boundaries of the ideologically permissible in the wider society as well as within the newsroom. But this vulnerability also begins with the fact that reporters have only sparse contacts with their actual readers and viewers; their everyday sense of audience cannot be strong enough to insulate them against specific, focused pressures. And media managements cannot entirely overcome the symbiosis between reporters and their movement beats, even when they wish to, since the organization's ability to generate the commodity called "news" depends on the reporter's ability to achieve rapport with a client group. Management's worry about reporter source rapport is suggested, for example, in the *New York Times*'s practice of rotating reporters out of a foreign country every year, on the theory that within a few years familiarity will obstruct their critical distance.[45]

When movements mobilize, then, reporters may be pulled into the magnetic fields generated by their alternative or oppositional world views. Now the routines of objectivity prove somewhat adaptable. For normally, in the course of gathering news, reporters tend to be pulled into the cognitive worlds of their sources. Whatever their particular *opinions*, for example, Pentagon correspondents define military issues as generals, admirals, and Pentagon bureaucrats define them: as a choice between this missile system and that, not as a choice between the arms race and disarmament. When movements become newsworthy, reporters who cover them steadily are subject to a similar pull. Indeed, they may use the rhetoric and practices of objectivity to justify covering the movement sympathetically and to protect their work from editorial dampening.[46] Or further: when opposition is robust and compelling, reporter's may even go so far as to jeopardize their mainstream careers. Thus, in 1970, Earl Caldwell of the *New York Times* refused to turn over to a grand jury his notes on the Black Panther Party, arguing that he could only do his job of covering them objectively if the Panthers could trust him. For although the main sources of news are official, the media also need other sources: they must survey the society for signs of instability, they must produce dramatic news, and thus they are vulnerable to the news-making claims of unofficial groups. Because the idea of "objectivity" and the standards of "newsworthiness" are loose, the hegemonic routines of news coverage are vulnerable to the demands of oppositional and deviant groups. *Through the everyday workings of journalism, large-scale social conflict is imported into the news institution and reproduced there: reproduced, however, in terms derived from the dominant ideology.* Discrepant statements about reality are acknowledged—but muffled, softened, blurred, fragmented, *domesticated* at the same time.

That is, the vulnerability of the news system is not neutrality. The news routines are skewed toward representing demands, individuals, and frames which do not fundamentally contradict *the dominant hegemonic principles: the legitimacy of private control of commodity production; the legitimacy of the national security State; the legitimacy of technocratic experts; the right and ability of authorized agencies to manage conflict and make the necessary reforms; the legitimacy of the social order secured and defined by the dominant elites; and the value of individualism as the measure of social existence.* The news routines do not easily represent demands, movements, and frames which are inchoate, subtle, and most deeply subversive of these core principles. Political news is treated as if it were crime news—what went wrong today, not what goes wrong every day. A demonstration is treated as a potential or actual disruption of legitimate order, not as a statement about the world. These assumptions automatically divert coverage away from critical treatment of the institutional, systemic, and everyday workings of property and the State. (In 1977, for example, the *New York Times* hired its first investigative reporter assigned to business.) And secondly, the needs and values of sources, constituencies, and journalists alike are structured within the dominant ideology as a whole. Journalists and audiences collaborate in preferring media products which ratify the established order of commodity production and State power. Within these real limits, and only within them, the media may work out a limited autonomy from the expressed interests of political and corporate command posts; they may even affect the ways in which the elites understand their own immediate choices.

When the *New York Times* published parts of the Pentagon Papers in 1971, it risked legal penalties for relaying evidence that several administrations had lied about what they were doing in Vietnam. It did not report that the Papers confirmed some of what antiwar activists had been saying about the war for years. Editorial Page Editor Max Frankel told me that he compared the Pentagon Papers and the *Times*'s war coverage, and "discovered we didn't do so badly. If you read the papers carefully, the press didn't do all that badly, given what we knew. Though true, it was hard for the general reader to put it all together."[47] The antiwar movement, researching and writing outside the *Times*'s conventions for objectivity, had presented over the years a range of views that rather successfully "put it all together," amassing a strong case that American policy was systematically neocolonial, racist, and criminally targeted on the civilian population; but the *Times* did not cover these revelations and analyses at the time, and it would not have been seemly, in 1971 or since, for the *Times* to endorse the world view of the radical opposition, even retroactively. The solution to these unfortunate matters had to be left in the hands of duly constituted authorities; the *Times* could not criticize its own conventions or comprehend its own blind spots.

A news item like Dan Rather's routine report on FBI lawbreaking (discussed in the Introduction, pp. 5–6, above) illustrate how a certified social problem and a legitimate solution are ordinarily framed together. The FBI has been committing burglaries and illegal wiretaps for forty years, the story says. These illegalities continued through the period of "civil disturbances of the Sixties." Thus, by implication, popular movements—responsible for "civil disturbances"—are not to be looked to as ways of keeping the FBI in line. Or, by the same token, a report on the landing of the first two Concordes at Dulles Airport (on both CBS and ABC News, May 24, 1976) becomes (1) a certification that the "controversy" over the plane's noise is legitimate controversy, (2) a certification that noise-detecting machines placed by the Federal Aviation Authority will determine ("objectively") whether the noise is "excessive," and (3) a deprecation of what ABC called "almost unnoticed" demonstrators, who were, in their leaflets and signs, asserting their own right to say what is excessive noise. The complete message is: when there is legitimate ground for "controversy," it will be defined and taken care of by authorities, not by marginal disruptors.[48] And yet, at the same time, those demonstrators lurking in the margins for a few seconds of film may suggest—to viewers primed to receive this alternative layer of the message—a different model of social action. The FBI's and Air France's views of the world do not totally fill the ideological space; but their definitions of problems ("civil disturbance," noise levels whose seriousness can be certified only by officially monitored machines) are preferred and relayed, while conflict between these and alternative views is denatured, managed, and contained.

Thus, in brief: sources are segmented and exist in history; journalists' values are anchored in routines that are at once *steady* enough to sustain hegemonic principles and *flexible* enough to absorb many new facts; and these routines are bounded by perceptions of the audience's common sense and are finally accountable to the world views of top managers and owners. These factors shape the news; even centralized manipulations by the State have to respect these limits. Everyday frames and procedures suffice to sustain the legitimacy of the economic-political system as a whole.

Yet the hegemonic system for regulating conflict through judgments of newsworthiness presupposes a certain minimum of political stability. When political crises erupt in the real world, they call to question whether the hegemonic routines, left to themselves, an go on contributing to social stability. Now some of the opposition movement's claims about reality seem to be verified by what mainstream reporters and editors discover about the world. *Then the hegemonic frame begins to shift.* Thus, in 1968, editors at the *New York Times* and other establishment news organizations turned sympathetic to moderate antiwar activity. The Tet offensive shattered the official rationale that the war should be pursued because It was not only just but winnable. The observed and reported facts of Tet subverted the Johnson administration's own claims—precisely the claims which had structured the media's dominant frame. At the same time, amidst what they experienced as economic and political crisis, the foreign policy elite (the "Wise Men") began to turn against Johnson's war policy. The elite media amplified their critique of the war—a critique itself lodged within the hegemonic assumption that the United States had a right to intervene against revolutions everywhere—just as business and political authorities influenced media executives to shift positions on the war. But the political crisis was not confined to a back-and-forth process between sealed-off elites; the elite experienced political crisis precisely because of the upwelling of opposition—both radical-militant and liberal-moderate—throughout the society. That opposition made its way simultaneously into the newsrooms. Younger reporters had already begun to share in their generation's rejection of the war. And crucially, editors, like other members of their class, worried about their sons' draftability and were influenced by their antiwar children and spouses (wives, mostly). Ben Bagdikian, former national editor of the *Washington Post*, remembers this complaint by Executive Editor Ben Bradlee: "We tell reporters not to march in a demonstration. But what can you do when their wives march in demonstrations?"[49] Reporters wheeling around to see the war differently were obviously more inclined to frame the anti-war movement differently. After the Chicago police riot of August 1968, they were still less inclined to assume that the police were the legitimate enforcers of a reasonable social order.

If editors had not shifted away from administration war policy—if elite authorities had not turned against the war—it is hard to know how far the journalists would have been able to stretch their frames for antiwar activity. Frames are in effect negotiated among sources, editors, and reporters; how they will emerge in practice is not preordained. But as the antiwar frame changed, the formulae for denigrating New Left actions remained in force; now they were clamped onto the *illegitimate* movement. As we saw in Chapter 7, the media were now at pains to distinguish acceptable from unacceptable opposition. Respectful treatment of the moderate antiwar activists, including the Moratorium, was clamped within the newly adjusted hegemonic frame: the war is unsuccessful, perhaps wrong; but ending it is the task of responsible authorities, not radical movements.

This adjusted frame presented problems for the media, the State, and the movement alike. The hegemonic routines had been amplifying—and distorting—an opposition movement. Legitimate authorities were not coping smoothly with the economic and political crisis; willy-nilly, they were firing up opposition; they were now widely seen as incompetent managers. At this point, *the normal routines for constructing news and reproducing hegemony became, from the point of view of much of the political elite, unreliable.* Opposition seemed to dominate the news and to contest routine management of the frames for war and antiwar news. Top media managers bridled at the normal results of hegemonic routines; therefore, from 1968 through 1973, and especially (but not only) under pressure from the Nixon White House, they interfered more directly in the news-gathering process. The forms of direct intervention are hard to smoke out. They are singular (by definition they are not routine), they may be idiosyncratic, and news of them is embarrassing: after all, they fly in the face of the hegemonic claim to professional journalistic autonomy. But a few examples of executive intervention have surfaced. During the Columbia University uprising in the spring of 1968, for example, Managing Editor A. M. Rosenthal of the *New York Times*—an organization deeply entangled with the Columbia administration—went to the unprecedented length of filing a front-page story under his own by-line, focusing on how brutish the occupying radicals had been in messing up Columbia President Grayson Kirk's office.[50] The *Times* Magazine that spring ran two pieces inspired by the Columbia rebellion: one a general alarm by Harvard neo-conservative James Q. Wilson, the other a critique of militant nonviolence by Supreme Court Justice and Johnson advisor Abe Fortas. Herbert Gans writes that *Newsweek* killed its own reporter's story, which was sympathetic to the radicals, after its top editors saw the *Times* account.[51] In crisis, the normally hegemonic routines threatened to undermine hegemonic ideology; caught in a bind between class loyalties and strict professionalism, executives were now more likely to intervene in the news process in order to sustain their deepest principles.

But precisely because the media have established some independence from the State, top political officials may feel threatened enough by amplified dissidence, however domesticated, to crack down directly. The State can intervene in media operations most subtly by withholding interviews, by preferring competitors, or by feeding false information to reliable reporters. The President can reward compliant editors and writers with prestigious political jobs (thus, for example, Johnson appointed pro-war *Washington Post* editor J. Russell Wiggins to a lame-duck term as Ambassador to the United Nations);[52] or the President and other officials can alternately scold and cajole insufficiently docile media powers, or try to intimidate them directly. In October 1963, John F. Kennedy tried to convince *Times* publisher Arthur Ochs ("Punch") Sulzberger to transfer David Halberstam out of Vietnam.[53] Lyndon Johnson preferred to phone reporters with his complaints; he also liked to go over low-level heads, calling his friends Frank Stanton and Robert Kintner, the presidents of CBS and NBC, respectively, appealing to them in the name of old ties and patriotic duties. Stanton above all had been Johnson's friend and counselor since 1938, when Johnson had acquired CBS affiliate status for his wife's Austin radio station. Former CBS News General Manager and Vice-President Blair Clark told me that while covering the presidential campaign of 1956, he had shared a plane ride with Johnson, who had asked him: "How well do you know Frank Stanton?" and then advised:. "You better know Frank better. He's one of the finest men in America. Why, he and Ruth were down on the ranch doe-shooting last week."[54] During the mid-sixties, Johnson was regularly infuriated by CBS's war coverage, and Stanton, as chairman of the Board of Trustees of the RAND Corporation, a top military research think tank, was in any event no critic of the main thrust of Cold War an interventionist politics. So Stanton regularly relayed Johnson's anger—in Chairman Paley's presence, no less—at weekly lunches of CBS News executives. At one point in 1964, according to David Halberstam, Johnson complained to Stanton about Dan Rather's work—nothing radical here—and Stanton relayed the complaint to News President Fred Friendly, who, violating the norm (news executives are supposed to insulate reporters from high-level intervention), chewed out Rather for irresponsible reporting.[55]

Johnson's style was mostly person-to-person; he was the master of arm-twisting. But he could go further when pressed: In August 1965, CBS correspondent Morley Safer—a Canadian y birth—covered the U.S. Marines setting fire to Vietnamese huts in the village of Cam Ne. Simply as film, Safer's piece was so strong and so shocking that, as David Halberstam says, the news executives "simply could not fail to use it." They ran the piece. Early the next morning, according to CBS officials whom Halberstam interviewed, Johnson called Stanton and woke him up. "Frank," said the President of the United States, "are you trying to fuck me?" "Who is this?" asked the sleepy Stanton. "Frank, this is your President, and yesterday your boys shat on the American flag." Johnson insisted that Safer must be a Communist, got the Royal Canadian Mounted Police to investigate him, and, when informed later that Safer was not a Communist, only a Canadian, insisted: "Well, I knew he wasn't an American."[56]

But for all this, Johnson kept his fury at CB behind closed doors. Beginning late in 1969, by contrast, the Nixon Oval Office launched a public crusade, a protracted campaign against not only the media but the Wall Street-Council on Foreign Relations establishment as a whole. Johnson had to keep face with Frank Stanton; Nixon owed no such debts. He was blunter and more sweeping; he had a Vice-President who specialized in threatening rhetoric; and he orchestrated years of attacks, including, not least, threats to regulate the networks more closely. Only in retrospect are we entitled to say that he paid a price for overstepping; he might have succeeded.

For most of the Nixon years, the media strained to occupy a middle ground between the Nixon White House and the newly legitimized antiwar movement. Nixon had campaigned in 1968 as a "peace" candidate, and the media relayed that frame unskeptically. He had campaigned to "bring us together," and the media shared that objective as well. In fact, at the beginning of Nixon's first term in office, the media processed antiwar coverage into a frame that legitimated his administration as the agency to end the war. With all due respect to Vice-President Agnew and the White House's critique of network "instant analysis," both NBC and ABC had gone so far toward the presidential frame as to have promulgated the policy that the "story" in Vietnam was now the negotiations, not the battles. In March 1969, as Edward Epstein discovered, the executive producer of the ABC Evening News, Av Westin, sent a telex message to the Saigon bureau:

> I think the time has come to shift some of our focus from the battlefield, or more specifi- cally American military involvement with the enemy, to themes and stories under the general heading: We Are On Our Way Out of Vietnam. …

And as Epstein writes: "Quite predictably, a radical change from combat stories to 'We Are On Our Way Out'-type stories followed in ABC's coverage of the Vietnam war."[57] NBC decided likewise. The air bombardment of Cambodia and Laos was down played to the vanishing point. Such decisions admirably suited the purposes of the Nixon administration, which wanted not so much to extricate America from the war as to create an *image* of extrication ("Vietnamization").

Nonetheless, Nixon was unplacated: he found the incoherent, superficial, halting, unre- flective media version of the war, and its amplifying of the moderate antiwar movement, an obstacle still. And so came the heavy hand. The new chairman of the FCC, Dean Burch, phoned the three network heads on the morning after Nixon's "Vietnamization" speech of November 3, 1969, asking for transcripts of the networks' "instant analyses." After Vice-President Agnew's anti-media speeches of November 13 and 20, the White House mobilized the local affiliates against the networks. Nixon and his staff orchestrated a campaign to manage the news dur- ing the Mobilization and Moratorium of November 15. In 1971, Nixon went to court seeking to restrain the *New York Times* and other newspapers from publishing some of the Pentagon Papers. In 1972, Charles Colson of the White House staff called and visited CBS's Paley and Stanton, complaining about the first part of Stanhope Gould's takeout on Watergate; as a result, CBS News President Salant ordered the second installment cut from fifteen to seven minutes.[58] Salant has denied that Colson's intervention was the direct immediate cause,[59] but the overall impact of the Nixon campaign against the media is deniable only at the cost of common sense. Even a top CBS producer acknowledges that Agnew's crusade "made us more cautious," though he is quick to add: "That might not have been a bad thing: where we would have double-checked a fact before, we would triple-check it now."[60] A CBS cameraman remembers considerably more apprehension: "Everybody was running scared. Everybody was being incredibly cautious. And [correspondents] would make jokes about it to us. Like, 'We can't offend Mr. Agnew,' or 'We have to be careful because Agnew's watching.'"[61] A few months later, Walter Cronkite said: "I think the industry as a whole has been intimidated."[62] Everyone I spoke to who was connected with CBS at the time is at pains to deny there was any direct management interference with reporters after November 1969; but documentaries, news specials, and "instant analyses" suffered. The Nixonian chill was felt—and resisted.[63]

Yet the power of *direct* political intervention is still easily exaggerated. In this case, *TV Guide* was announcing on September 27, 1969—fully six weeks before Agnew's opening barrage in Des Moines—that the networks were going to be retrenching in their coverage of the left, that they would be shifting toward "exploring middle and lower-middle-class Americans."[64] "Middle America" and the "silent majority" were the new shibboleths. Thus did the networks strive to maintain a political equilibrium in which their corporate position was secure. They do not need to be chided in public to know that their room for maneuver is limited. The low-background potential threat of the State is a constant. Political crises may disrupt the normal equilibrium of institutions. Yet between crises and normal situations—between situations requiring extraordinary State or corporate interventions into the news, and situations in which the routine procedures are left to take their course—there is no hard-and-fast line. Indeed, the late sixties were a time when political crisis itself became routine—Tet, the antiwar campaigns within the Democratic Party, the intervention of the Wise Men, the balance-of-payments and gold crises, Johnson's abdication, the King and Kennedy assassinations, black uprisings, student rebellion, Chicago, the November 1969 Mobilization, and the killings at Kent State and Jackson State. Extraordinary interventions into news policy became more ordinary.

The media, finally, are corporations of a peculiar type. It is not only that broadcasters are regulated, directly and not, by the State; so are many other industries. (In any event, newspapers and newsmagazines are not directly regulated, and their framing procedures and the frames that result are not vastly different from those of the networks.) More to the point, the product that the networks sell is the attention of audiences; their primary market is the advertisers themselves. (Newspapers, too, draw the bulk of their income from advertising.) To assemble the largest and richest possible audiences, for whose attention advertisers will pay the highest rates, the media may risk offending particular corporate interests. They see themselves exercising a general steering function for the entire political economy. As CBS President Stanton said in 1960: "Since we are advertiser-supported we must take into account the general objectives and desires of advertisers as a whole."[65] But the networks' profit interests are, in general, perfectly compatible with their journalists' routines for achieving objectivity. The "good story" in traditional journalistic terms is also appealing to a mass audience: "common sense" ratifies the hegemonic frames. The news organization therefore has two reasons to reward the production of "good stories": for the network, good journalism is good business; but more, the media have a general interest in stabilizing the liberal capitalist order as a whole, and it is this interest, played out through all the hegemonic routines, which stands behind the dominant news frames. The whole hegemonic process in journalism operates in a reformist key: it exposes particular business and State violations of the core hegemonic principles. Precisely for that reason, the relations among media, corporations, and the State are intrinsically thick with conflict.[66]

So it is hardly surprising that businessmen regularly complain that the networks are biased against them.[67] In the first issue of a closed-circulation magazine called *Chief Executive*, for example, Walter Cronkite urges businessmen to make themselves more available to reporters in order to respond to charges against corporate practice. Cronkite argues that businesses need a reliable press to satisfy their own intelligence function, and he tries to enlist them in the networks' contest with the State over press freedoms and the First Amendment. He defends the bond between business and the news media as "something known in the biological sciences as symbiosis":

> It's a word that may have been sullied and discredited in your minds by that group of ill-fated young fanatics who called themselves the "Symbionese Liberation Army," but it remains a valid concept. Symbiosis is a curious relationship. It is defined as the intimate living together of two kinds of organisms whereby such association is advantageous to each. It seems to me that journalists and business leaders are bound together in just such a relationship. Newspapers, broadcasting outlets and networks survive on the advertising revenues that come from business. Journalism can thrive only so long as the business community remains healthy enough to provide these funds. Business, on the other hand, depends upon journalism to foster its own growth—through the dissemination of information through news and advertising.[68]

This is what the "Dean of the World's Broadcast Journalists" (the magazine's blurb) urges upon an audience of top business, government, and other executives. Campaigning for symbiosis, as other top media people have also been doing, Cronkite acknowledges implicitly that it is far from an accomplished fact. On the other hand, the fact that he takes the trouble to spell out the goal reveals that the media elite is defensive. It is media strategy to *accomplish* symbiosis with the corporations as a whole, to guide that symbiosis, and in the process to guide the whole society toward a stable environment in which the media corporations may flourish. Just as the networks must be careful not to offend core interests of the State, so they must take care not to violate the most central premises of the business system as a whole: they must sanction the right of private control over investment and production, just as they sanctify their own right to control the space within which public communication takes place. The business practices exposed in the news—bribes, sudden health hazards, damage to the environment—are precisely the exceptional; and the frames generally cushion the impact of these reports by isolating exceptional corporations, by blaming "the public," by speaking from the angle of consumers and not workers, and by refraining from attempts at general explanation and radical solution. Yet, in this weakly reformist process, the media set terms for discourse which, corporations believe, threaten the legitimacy of the corporate system as a whole. *The media seek symbiosis with the corporate system precisely through the bounded routines of "objective" journalism.* This drive is utopian; it does not cease, though it is always, in the end, unconsummated.

ENDNOTES

1. I adapt the following discussion from Herbert Cans, *Deciding What's News* (New York: Pantheon, 1979), pp. 78–80. The typology of theories is essentially Gans's, but I have altered his capsule descriptions considerably.
2. The major organizational studies are Warren Breed, "Social Control in the Newroom," *Social Forces* 33 (May 1955): 467–477; Edward Jay Epstein, *News from Nowhere: Television and the News* (New York: Random House 1973); Leon V. Sigal: *Reporters and Officials: The Organization and Politics of Newsmaking.* (Lexngton, Mass.: D. C. Heath, 1973); Bernard Roshco, *Newsmaking* (Chicago: University of Chicago Press 1975); and Robert Darnton, "Writing News and Telling

Stories, *Daedalus* 4 (Sprig 1975): 175–194. Also see the excellent survey of this literature by Philip Elliott "Media Organizations and Occupations: An Overview, In James Curran, Michael Gurevitch, and Janet Woollacott, eds., *Mass Comunication and Society* (London: Edward Arnold, 1977), pp. 142–173, and Elliott's bibliography.

3. The major phenomenological studies are Gale Tuchman, "Objectivity as Strategic Ritual: An Examination of Newsmen's Notions of Objectivity," *American Journal of Sociology* 77 (1972): 660–679; Tuchman, "Making News by Doing Work: Routinizing the Unexpected," *American Journal of Sociology* 79 (July 1974). 110–131, Tuchman, *Making News* (New York: The Free Press, 1978); Harvey L. Molotch and Marilyn J. Lester, "News as Purposive Behavior: On the Strategic Use of Routine Events, Accidents, and Scandals," *American Sociological Review* 39 (February 1974) 101–112; and Molotch and Lester, "Accidental News: The Great Oil Spill as Local Occurrence and National Event," *American Journal of Sociology* 81 (September 1974). 235–260.

4. Epstein, News from Nowhere, pp. 13–18.

5. Gans, *Deciding What's News*, p. 80, quoting Philip Schlesinger, "The Sociology of Knowledge" (paper presented at the 1972 meeting of the British Sociological Association, March 24, 1972), p. 4.

6. The following paragraph is based on p. 251 of my "Prime Time Ideology: The Hegemonic Process in Television Entertainment," *Social Problems* 26 (February 1979): 251–266.

7. Antonio Gramsci, *Selections from the Prison Notebooks*, ed. and trans. Quintin Hoare and Geoffrey Nowell Smith (New York: International Publishers, 1971). There is no single passage in which Gramsci unequivocally defines and applies the concept of hegemony; rather, it is a leitmotif throughout his entire work. But see especially pp. 12, 52, 175–182.

8. But note that his distinction between hegemony and coercion corresponds in some ways to Machiavelli's distinction between force and fraud in the operations of the State. See Sheldon S. Wolin's commentary *In Politics and Vision: Continuity and Innovation in Western Political Thought* (Boston: Little, Brown, 1), pp. 22–24, and Wolin's references to Machiavelli in notes on p. 470. Gramsci honored his intellectual lineage by writing eighty pages of commentary on Machiavelli's *The Prince* under the heading *The Modern Prince* (pp. 125–205 in the *Prison Notebooks*).

9. In an astute essay, Perry Anderson has shown with a close reading of Gramsci's *Prison Notebooks* that various major inconsistencies were built into Gramsci's now original usage of his term: specifically that Gramsci was ambiguous in how he positioned culture and hegemony vis-à-vis the State and force in his diagraming of society. (Perry Anderson, "The Antinomies of Antonio Gramsci," *New Left Review*, No. 100 [November 1976–January 1977], pp. 5–78, especially pp.12–44.) These issues are not at the center of my current concern, but further development of the theory of ideological hegemony should not overlook the clarifications of Anderson's essay.

10. "Base and Superstructure in Marxist Cultural Theory," *New Left Review*, No. 82 (1973), pp. 3–16; later reworked and extended in *Marxism and Literature* (New York: Oxford University Press, 1977), pp. 108–114.

11. Stuart Hall, "Culture, the Media and the 'Ideological Effect,'" in Curran, Gurevitch, and Woollacott, *Mass Communication and Society*, pp. 315–348.

12. Ibid., p. 332.

13. See, by contrast, Georg Simmel's notion of domination as "a form of interaction" in which the dominant "will draws its satisfaction from the fact that the acting or suffering of the other … offers itself to the dominator as the product of *his* will" (Simmel, "Domination," trans. Kurt H.

Wolff, in Donald N. Devine, ed., *Georg Simmel: On Individuality and Social Forms* [Chicago: University of Chicago Press, 1971], p. 96). In this sense, hegemony differs from domination: in hegemony, dominator and dominated alike believe that the dominated is consenting *freely*. I am grateful to Mark Osiel for calling my attention to Simmel's discussion.

14. Hall, "Culture, the Media and the 'Ideological Effect,'" p. 333.

15. Ibid.

16. Alvin W. Gouldner, *The Dialectic of Ideology and Technology: The Origin, Grammar, and Future of Ideology* (New York: Seabury Press, 1976), p. 229. A similar approach to relations between economic and political structures is contained in Anthony Giddens, *The Class Structure of the Advanced Societies* (New York: Harper and Row, 1973).

17. Gouldner, *Dialectic of Ideology and Technology*, p. 230 (emphasis in the original).

18. Ibid., pp. 230–231.

19. Ibid., p. 232 (emphasis in the original).

20. I have drawn much of this paragraph from my "Prime Time Ideology", pp. 264–265.

21. Daniel Bell, *The Cultural Contradictions of Capitalism* (New York: Basic Books, 1976). On deliberate corporate attempts to define popular happiness as the consumption of mass-produced goods and to bring workers to identify themselves as consumers, see Stuart Ewen, *Captains of Consciousness: Advertising and the Roots of the Consumer Culture* (New York: McGraw-Hill. 1976).

22. Williams, "Base and Superstructure," p. 8.

23. In a 1971 national survey of over four thousand journalists (including editors), a little over three-quarters said that they had "almost complete freedom in deciding which aspects of a news story should be emphasized"; 60 percent, said that they had "almost complete freedom in selecting the stories they work on (though only 48 percent of editorial employees in the larger organizations, those employing over 100 persons, claimed freedom of selection); and 46 percent said that they made their own story assignments (as opposed to only 36 percent in the larger news organizations). See John W. C. Johnstone, Edward J. Slawski, and William W. Bowman, *The News People: A Sociological Portrait of American Journalists and Their Work* (Urbana: University of Illinois Press, 1976), p. 222. Asked to rank aspects of their jobs in importance the journalists in this sample placed public service first, followed, in descending order, by autonomy, freedom from supervision: job security, pay, and fringe benefits (p. 229). Such ordering is roughly what sociologists find among the professionals generally, though journalists differ from other professionals in lacking a generally agreed-upon training program and credential (chap. 6).

24. Interview, Ben H. Bagdikian, May 2, 1979.

25. Gans, *Deciding What's News*, p. 209; Johnstone et al., *The News People*, pp.25–28.

26. There has not been much discussion of the meanings and impact of style and format in television news. See my "Spotlights and Shadows: Television and the Culture of Politics," *College English* 38 (April 1977): 789–801; Tuchman, *Making News*, chap. 6; and Gans, *Deciding What's News*, Part 1.

27. FCC, "Application of the Fairness Doctrine in the Handling of Controversial Issues of Public Importance," *Federal Register* 29, Part 2 (July 25, 1%4): 10416, cited in Epstein, *News from Nowhere*, pp. 64–65.

28. See, for example, William Small, *To Kill a Messenger: Television News and the Real World* (New York: Hastings House, 1970), pp. 267–270. Small was head of CBS News's Washington Bureau,

then Senior Vice-President and Director of News of CBS News, and is at this writing a high executive at NBC News.

29. Nicholas Johnson, "Audience Rights," *Columbia Journalism Review* 18 (May-June 1979): 63.

30. Ron Bonn, letter to the author, May 1,1979.

31. Gans, *Deciding What's News*, p. 60.

32. Some of the historical constancies throughout the 150 years of mass commercial newspapers are underscored in Helen M. Hughes, *News and the Human Interest Story* (Chicago: University of Chicago Press, 1940), and Darnton, "Writing News and Telling Stories." The concept of "advancing the story" comes from Cindy Samuels, Assistant Manager of the New York Bureau of CBS News, who defines it qualitatively: "If you have a story, and it gets bigger, then something else happens that moves it forward, you say it moved forward and it got bigger, you don't say it got bigger and it moved forward" (interview, November 13, 1976).

33. Sigal, *Reporters and Officials*, p. 19.

34. See Epstein, *News from Nowhere*, pp. 105–112, and Gould, "The Trials of Network News," *More* 3 (May 1973): 8–11. For example, in November 1976, the Northeast bureau of CBS News, located in New York and responsible for the territory from Maryland through Maine, had a total of five camera crews.

35. Interview, Stephen Lighthill, June 16,1977. In a systematic study of British television news, the Glasgow University Media Group makes the same point: "In most newsfilm the shots do not directly relate to one another in the ways we are used to from the feature cinema. Rather they are used to illustrate the audiotext and the rules governing their juxtapositioning come not from the visual but from the audio track—indeed largely from the commentary. … It is because the journalistic logic dominates the film logic that common professional opinion of television news journalists as film makers is a low one" (*Bad News* [London: Routledge and Kegan Paul, 19761, p. 29).

36. CBS and NBC News went from fifteen to thirty minutes of evening news in September 1963. According to Godfrey Hodgson, whose theories of the importance of the media in the American sixties overlap mine somewhat, one reason for the expansion was that the networks had forfeited a good deal of legitimacy in the quiz show scandals of 1959–60, and were seeking to make good [on] their losses. See Godfrey Hodgson, *America in Our Time* (Garden City, N.Y.: Doubleday, 1976), pp. 142–145.

37. Gitlin, "Spotlights and Shadows," p. 792; Gans, *Deciding What's News*, p. 54. In a study that Gans cites (p. 226), Mark R. Levy concludes that many television news viewers "watched to be reassured that the world both near and far was safe and secure, and that … it demanded no immediate action on their part" (Levy, "The Audience Experience With Television News" *Journalism Monographs* No. 55 [April 1978], p. 13).

38. Molotch and Lester, "Accidental News," p. 254.

39. See Gans, *Deciding What's News*, p. 201 and chap. 7.

40. Molotch, "Media and Movements," unpublished paper, 1977.

41. Michael Schudson, *Discovering the News: A Social History of American Newspapers* (New York: Basic Books, 1978).

42. Of course, publishers went on ensuring that their immediate economic interests would be protected. Newspapers do not ordinarily cover antitrust suits against themselves, for example, and their coverage of downtown business developments tilts toward the downtown businesses

that are their advertising mainstays. The closer to home the affected interest, the greater the strictures on news coverage.

43. Thelma McCormack, "Establishment Media and the Backlash," paper read to meetings of the American Sociological Association, Washington, D.C., 1970, pp. 32–33.

44. Gans, *Deciding What's News*, p. 96 (emphasis added).

45. Damton, "Writing News and Telling Stories."

46. Tuchman, *Making News*, pp. 100 ff.

47. Telephone interview, Max Frankel, March 23, 1979.

48. I draw these examples from my "Spotlights and Shadows," pp. 792 and 795, where I discuss them in more detail.

49. Interview, Ben Bagdikian, May 2, 1979.

50. See Gay Talese, *The Kingdom and the Power* (New York: World, 1969), pp. 513–515, and Richard Pollak, "Abe Rosenthal Presents the *New* New York Times," *Penthouse*, September 1977, p. 50. *Times* publisher Sulzberger was a Columbia trustee.

51. Gans, *Deciding What's News*, p. 347, n. 32.

52. David Halberstam, *The Powers That Be* (New York: Alfred A. Knopf, 1979), pp. 545–546.

53. Ibid., pp. 445–446.

54. Interview, Blair Clark, November 10, 1976.

55. Ibid., pp. 432–442.

56. Ibid., pp. 486–492. Quotations from p. 490.

57. Epstein, *News from Nowhere*, pp. 17–18; Hodgson, *America in Our Time*, p. 378.

58. On Colson's intervention and CBS's response, see Timothy Crouse, *The Boys on the Bus* (New York: Random House, 1973), pp. 174–175; Robert Cirino, *Power to Persuade* (New York: Bantam Books, 1974), p. 35; William S. Paley, *As It Happened* (Garden City, N.Y.: Doubleday, 1979), pp. 318–327; Daniel Schorr, *Clearing the Air* (Boston: Houghton Mifflin, 1977), pp. 52–58; and Halberstam, *Powers That Be*, pp. 651–661. On the Nixon White House and its campaign against the networks generally, see Jeb Stuart Magruder, *An American Life* (New York: Atheneum, 1974), pp. 81 ff. and 105 ff., and my discussion above, pp. 224–229; the extremely thorough account in William J. Porter, *Assault on the Media: The Nixon Years* (Ann Arbor: University of Michigan Press, 1976); Thomas Whiteside, "Shaking the Tree," *The New Yorker*, March 17, 1975, pp. 41–91; and Schorr, *Clearing the Air*, pp. 14–120.

59. Salant twice refused my attempts to interview him about CBS coverage of the New Left, in the fall of 1976 and again in the spring of 1977, claiming that "I have the world's worst memory and can't remember what happened yesterday, let alone the sixties." He did insist, however, that "the way we work here at CBS News, the choices were never mine." (Letter to the author, October 18, 1976.)

60. Interview, Ron Bonn, November 19, 1976. See Bonn's further remark, above, p. 262.

61. Interview, Stephen Lighthill, June 16, 1977.

62. Cronkite was speaking on March 3, 1970, as quoted in James Aronson, *Deadline for the Media* (Indianapolis: Bobbs-Merrill, 1972), p. 9.

63. According to Daniel Schorr (interview, May 10, 1977), when Chairman Paley, in June 1973, discontinued all vestiges of "instant analysis," even the bland summaries that CBS had instituted in late 1969, correspondents in the Washington bureau "were all rocked by that; we were all very angry." Several, including Schorr, wrote a letter of protest to Salant, who acted as if he welcomed

it as ammunition against Paley's decision. And indeed the decision was rescinded in November. See also Schorr, *Clearing the Air*, pp. 61–64.

64. Cited in Hogdson, *America in Our Time*, pp. 382–383. Hodgson's interesting discussion of the 1968–69 media retrenchment (pp. 369–377) emphasizes the conservative force of public opinion and the media elite's fear of finding itself too far ahead of the mass audience. There is no question that the media managers felt this fear. But their fear of the public reaction was inextricably entangled with their fear of the potentially regulating State. These were experienced as a single fear.

65. *Television Network Program Procurement: Report of the Committee on Interstate and Foreign Commerce, House of Representatives, 88th Cong., 1st sess.* (Washington, D.C.: Government Printing Office, 1963), p. 335, as quoted in Erik Barnouw, *The Sponsor* (New York: Oxford University Press, 1978), p. 57.

66. See Gans, *Deciding What's News*, pp. 68–69, 203–206, on the muckraking Progressivism of American journalism.

67. Business critiques of the news media are legion. Among the more articulate versions are "Business and the Press-Independent or Interdependent?" a speech by Donald S. MacNaughton, Chairman and Chief Executive Officer, the Prudential Insurance Company of America, November 4, 1975, excerpted in the *New York Times*, Business Section, March 7, 1976, p. 12; "The Values That Can Serve Mankind," Remarks by David Rockefeller, Chairman of the Board, the Chase Manhattan Bank, before the Northern California Region of the National Conference of Christians and Jews, April 7, 1976; and the discussion in Leonard Silk and David Vogel, *Ethics and Profits* (New York: Simon and Schuster, 1976), pp. 104–116, drawing on comments from many executives who are members of the Conference Board. Media responses include "Business and the Press: Who's Doing What to Whom and Why?" Remarks of Arthur R. Taylor, President, CBS Inc., before the Financial Executives Institute, October 21, 1975; and "Businessmen Can Look Better If They Try," by Dan Cordtz, economics editor at ABC, in the *New York Times*, Business Section, July 18, 1976, p. 12. The tone of these latter two articles is strikingly similar to Cronkite's appeal, below, for a symbiotic division of labor: the media have their jobs to do, business has its job to do, and businessmen should learn how to make more effective use of the existing media system. In other words, the media spokesmen are defending a functional division of labor between economic and cultural-legitimation spheres.

68. *Chief Executive 1* (July-September 1977): 26. Weirdly enough, the role of the young heiress-terrorist in the film *Network* was played by Walter Cronkite's daughter, Kathy.

The Visibility of Race and Media History

By Jane Rhodes

The Negro, never so much a Negro as since he has been dominated by the whites, when he decides to prove that he has a culture and to behave like a cultured person, comes to realize that history points out a well-defined path to him: he must demonstrate that a Negro culture exists.

—Frantz Fanon
The Wretched of the Earth (1963)

The psychiatrist and black revolutionary from Martinque, Frantz Fanon, used the experience of Africans under colonial rule—in this case Algeria—as his model for understanding the racialization of thought and history. But he could just as easily have been describing how American society responded to the existence of Africans, Asians, and indigenous people by erasing their cultures and substituting images that supported a system of racial dominance and control. Over time, these representations of America's subordinate groups nourished the nation's popular culture and helped fuel the rise of mass media. Members of these groups responded, when they could, with images of their own creation, and alternative media to disseminate them. Yet, they could do little to counteract the prevailing definitions of race.

This struggle between the transmission of racist ideology and dogma, and the efforts of oppressed groups to claim control over their own image, is part of the legacy of the American mass media. Racial identity has been—and continues to be—a crucial factor in determining who can produce popular culture, and what messages are created. Yet this story has received minimal attention in a historiography that has focused on the celebration of technological achievement and financial success. This is the darker side of media history; the tale of a national institution encumbered by a racist past. Contemporary discussions about the politics of identity in media production lack relevance unless they are placed in the context of this history.

Jane Rhodes, "The Visibility of Race and Media History," from *Critical Studies in Media Communication*, Vol. 10, No. 2; June 1993, pp. 184–190. Published by National Communication Association, 1993. Copyright by Taylor & Francis. Permission to reprint granted by the rights holder.

Twenty years ago, a noted scholar of African-American history proclaimed that "a racist society breeds and needs a racist historiography" to support and reinforce the ideologies of racial superiority (Aptheker, 1971, p. 9). We might extend that concept to suggest that a racist society also requires a racist media to disseminate these values and beliefs to a mass audience. Recent historical studies have begun to explore the manifestations of race in popular novels, the press, and early motion pictures, and they tell us a great deal about the role of the media in American social formation (for example, see Fredrickson, 1971; Saxton, 1990; Van Deburg, 1984). Media historians have lagged far behind in this process, and students of mass communication receive little exposure to this legacy. In this essay I will explore two points of juncture in media history: the emergence of the penny press and the coinciding development of the black press, and the development of early motion pictures and the efforts to form an independent black film movement. Each example demonstrates the centrality of race to media production.

Race has been a popular text of the American mass media since the eighteenth century. Racism, which maintained the superiority of white European settlers over the continent's indigenous people, African slaves, and Asian immigrant workers, was equal to the ideologies of manifest destiny and free enterprise in their impact on the developing nation. Racist stereotypes were an important political and sociological tool for presenting this ideology.

Winthrop Jordan locates the origins of American racial ideas in seventeenth century Britain, where whites sought to account for the physical and cultural differences between themselves and Africans by employing explanations based on religion and mythology. Thus, Negroes were the forever-cursed sons of Ham. Just as the industrial revolution and colonialism fueled British expansionism, religion provided a rationale for the growth of slavery: "… to be Christian was to be civilized rather than barbarous, English rather than African, white rather than black" (Jordan, 1974, p. 51). Reginald Horsman finds the beginnings of modern racism in eighteenth-century British intellectuals' claim to an Anglo-Saxon tradition, which explained England's quests for land, power, and cultural superiority. A century later these notions were widely disseminated in books and the press by influential authors such as Thomas Carlyle, who published a tract titled "Occasional Discourse on the Nigger Question." In Carlyle's view, "The Saxons were a race destined for greatness and accomplishment; other races could be viewed as obstacles to progress" (Horsman, 1981, p. 65).

This ideology profoundly influenced American colonists, who sought political independence from Britain but clung to the cultural and ethnic heritage of their forebears. The burgeoning popular culture of the new republic served as a powerful agent of control, encouraging the dominant group to assert their authority and constantly reminding the subordinate groups of their fragile and oppressed status in society. For example, the newly-formed American musical theater of the late eighteenth century created a host of characters that lampooned and stereotyped free and enslaved blacks. One of the most enduring of these images, introduced in 1795, was Sambo, the vain, pompous, and ignorant darkie whose life revolved around song and dance (Van Deburg, 1984). Sambo was effective in perpetuating the myth that blacks were happy with their slave status.

While the nation's cultural discourse reinforced the inferiority of blacks with highly visible stereotypes, the political discourse of early newspapers rendered them invisible except as commodities. Publications both before and after the Revolutionary War relied heavily on advertisements for the sale of slaves, or for the return of runaway slaves, as a source of revenue. Amid the discussions of liberty, free speech, and Jeffersonian democracy there was little consideration of the plight of blacks or Indians in the republic. Indeed, as the penny newspapers took hold in the early nineteenth century, they frequently served the agenda of asserting racial superiority. Alexander Saxton argues that the press almost universally portrayed Indians as savage and barbaric in order to justify westward expansion. The same papers, however, showed ambivalence about slavery, perhaps in response to the growing impact of abolitionism. Yet some of the earliest and most famous newspaper publishers were equally hostile to blacks and frequently employed racist invective. Benjamin Day, founder of *The New York Sun*, constantly fought with his partner because he "was always sticking his damned little Abolitionist articles" in the paper (Saxton, 1990, p. 103). James Gordon Bennett, publisher of the New York Herald, regularly used racial stereotypes in his attacks on competitors, one of whom he likened to "a small, decrepit, dying penny paper, owned and controlled by a set of woolly-headed and thick-lipped Negroes" (Kluger, 1986, p. 45). There were opposing voices, of course, such as Horace Greeley, publisher of the *New York Tribune* and an outspoken abolitionist. But his was a minority view in American journalism of the period.

Even the African-American's champion, the abolitionist press, was deeply paternalistic and relied on racist mythologies. While white-owned newspapers such as *The Liberator* provided an early forum for African-American writers, their voice was buried within the rhetoric of abolitionism which cast the slave as childlike and dependent. The image of the slave supplicant, kneeling, pleading for freedom, and looking to benevolent whites for salvation, was popularized in abolitionist periodicals (Van Deburg, 1984; Yellin, 1989).

The first African-American newspaper, *Freedom's Journal*, emerged in response to the racist discourse of the nation's press and sought to present a distinct racial identity and agenda. In 1827, after a series of especially vituperative anti-black attacks by several New York City editors, John B. Russwurm and Samuel E. Cornish collaborated to produce their newspaper in which they hoped to counter the stereotypes that prevailed in American popular culture. "We wish to plead our own cause. Too long have others spoken for us. Too long has the publick been deceived by misrepresentations …" they wrote in the first issue. But their efforts at counter-discourse were only marginally successful in ameliorating American racism. The impulse to establish an alternative medium in response to oppression from the mainstream served to improve communication to a smaller audience—in this case, other blacks and white abolitionist supporters. Nordin (1977–1978) suggests *Freedom's Journal* functioned primarily as a medium to develop a sense of fraternity and consciousness for freeborn African-Americans. I have come to similar conclusions in my own research on the black press that published in Canada during the 1850s: A prime function of these newspapers was to establish community ties among a fragmented population, and to foster a black nationalist identity (Rhodes, 1989).

Despite their tenacity and courage, black journalists of the antebellum era had little power to transform the racist content of the mainstream media, or to influence public opinion on any large scale. Few whites who were not already converted to the abolitionist cause were persuaded by the black press' efforts to show the best intellectual and social accomplishments of the race. The black press was responsible, in part, for elevating a handful of black activists such as Frederick Douglass to a visible position in the national debate on slavery. But Douglass' success also was due to his ability as an orator and his skill as a power broker in the anti-slavery movement.

Meanwhile, most black newspapers struggled against harassment, financial insolvency, illiteracy, and intergroup squabbles. Of the 40-odd newspapers founded by African-Americans before the Civil War, only a handful survived more than two years. And the few that lived on, including *Frederick Douglass' Paper* and *The Christian Recorder*, relied heavily on philanthropic aid or support from larger institutions. Antebellum African-American voices could be heard, on a limited basis, through literature, the press, and the lecture hall. But theirs was a small chorus amid the thunder of American racism.

Racist stereotypes shifted throughout the nineteenth century to coincide with the nation's political and social mood. Scientific theories, particularly social Darwinism, replaced earlier justifications for American racism as separation of the races became codified into law (Saxton, 1990, pp. 369–377). By the 1890s, Jim Crow segregation was reinforced by a system of economic exploitation, political disenfranchisement, and violence targeted at the black population. The motion picture industry was born in an era when the full effects of Redemption—the white southern response to blacks' gains during Reconstruction—had taken hold.

Thus, the pre-Civil War images of the benign and happy slave, such as Sambo, were replaced in popular culture by the more sinister coon or the black brute whose sole aim was raping white women. Black women often were characterized as the complacent servant mammy whose matriarchal loyalty compensated for the black male's lasciviousness and irresponsibility. But promiscuous black women also could be found in the role of a scheming and wicked Jezebel casting her spell over vulnerable men. The sexualization of black stereotypes, especially the preoccupation with black male sexual prowess, fueled the practice of lynching, which rose to epidemic proportions in the early twentieth century (see Wiegman, 1993). These, and other representations, illustrated whites' irrational fears of miscegenation and black liberation, and were employed liberally in early motion pictures.

Silent films borrowed heavily from the racial narratives of the Jim Crow south and the hostile north. Movies such as *The Watermelon Contest* (1890s), *The Wedding and Wooing of a Coon* (1905), and *The Nigger* (1915), ridiculed and debased black life in the crude, slapstick form that had been inherited from minstrel shows and vaudeville (Cripps, 1977). Another tradition inherited from the stage was the use of white actors in blackface to parody black characters; the growing film industry had no intention of employing blacks to portray themselves, even in demeaning roles. Filmmakers joined historians at the turn of the century to produce a particularly racist revision of history that portrayed slavery as a benign institution which befit the black character. For example, Edwin Porter, considered a film pioneer by media historians, brought Harriet Beecher Stowe's novel *Uncle Tom's Cabin* to the screen in 1903. One scholar notes the movie diluted the horrors of slavery, and depicted slaves as "grinning, singing and dancing blacks who apparently love their masters and are even made to appear grateful when sold" (Silk & Silk, 1990, p. 122).

No film in this racist tradition has received more attention than *Birth of a Nation*. In this context, it is useful to consider the legacy of D.W. Griffith's notorious film and the way it is presented in the historiography of mass media (Emery & Emery, 1988; Folkerts & Teeter, 1989). An early film history described Griffith as "the admitted master of the art of the screen" and argued that protests against the film by the NAACP and others actually contributed to its popularity and box-office receipts, rather than causing it any serious injury (Ramsaye, 1926/1986). Today, basic textbooks often gloss over the racist content of the film, while extolling Griffith's excellence as a filmmaker and technical innovator. A new edition of one textbook refers to *Birth of a Nation* as "his brilliant Civil War drama," using terms such as "masterful" to describe Griffith's accomplishments (Dominick, 1993). One video documentary I have used in my introductory classes shows clips from the film that often cause students to gasp and shake their heads in horror at Griffith's sympathetic portrayal of the KKK, and his gross stereotypes of African-Americans. In the next breath, however, this teaching aid demonstrates the editing, directing, and other techniques that Griffith is credited with developing. The student is left to decide what Griffith's legacy should be, and his racism is seen as an aberration. The underlying message is that Griffith's contributions to the film industry override his "horrible little prejudices," which are blamed on the fact that he was an unreconstructed Southerner.

Griffith's racism is also presented as an individualized phenomenon—as a solitary interpretation of events that had little relationship to the structures of meaning in American society. In fact, *Birth of a Nation* was part of an era in which historians, led by William Archibald Dunning, reinforced the image of blacks as inferior, slavery as benevolent, and Reconstruction as a failure. It is not surprising, then, that Griffith selected Thomas Dixon's popular novel *The Clansmen*, published in 1905, as the subject for his first epic film. In the novel's introduction, Dixon explained the historical vision that he sought to dramatize:

> How the young South, led by the reincarnated souls of the Clansmen of Old Scotland, went forth under this cover and against overwhelming odds, daring exile, imprisonment, and a felon's death, and saved the life of a people, forms one of the most dramatic chapters in the history of the Aryan race. (1905/1970, p. 2)

Despite the film's financial success, Griffith was frustrated by what he saw as affronts to his right to free speech, and his next major film, *Intolerance* (1916), was an "endeavor to expose the absurdities of public opinion" (Ramsaye, 1926/1986, p. 644).

The African-American response to *Birth of a Nation* helped to launch a campaign to counter Griffith's representations. Black newspapers and periodicals, led by *The Crisis*, which was edited by W.E.B. DuBois, urged their readers to boycott the film and encouraged investment in an independent black film industry. By the 1920s several small black film companies were cranking out low-budget products for both black and white audiences (Bogle, 1973; Cripps, 1977). These companies succeeded in giving black performers their entrée into the movies, but like the antebellum black press, they were hampered by insufficient funds and competition from an established and cut-throat film industry. A handful of black producers, perhaps the best known being Oscar Micheaux, fed the "race movie" business through the Depression. But in their clumsy attempts to overcome the racist discourse of American society, these films often relied on trivial or stereotyped themes such as the black gangster, and reinforced white standards of beauty with their use of light-skinned performers. Once again, the structures of racism prevented the broad dissemination of messages contradicting the dominant ideology. Not until World War II was there any concerted effort on the part of the motion picture industry to temper its racial content.

When a historical perspective is applied to the examination of the race, gender, or sexual identity of media producers, it becomes readily apparent that the patterns of earlier generations continue to replicate themselves. Today, the cultural products of African-Americans and other subordinate groups are routinely appropriated and commodified by the mainstream, while the originators struggle for an autonomous voice. African-American newspapers falter while hip-hop and rap become part of the middle-class, white American practice. Only one African-American woman, Julie Dash, has produced and directed a full-length feature film that received critical (but not financial) success. These media producers shoulder the burden of satisfying the need for alternative representations in a racist society while being true to their art. But many hold on to the belief in the empowerment and healing that can be accomplished with their work. Says Dash, "I like telling stories and controlling worlds. In my world, black women can do anything. They ride horses and fly from trapezes; they are in the future as well as in the past" (Rule, 1992). Media scholars, take heed; learn this history and incorporate it into the dominant narratives of our discipline before another generation is lost.

REFERENCES

Aptheker, H. (1971). *Afro-American History: The Modern Era*. New York: Citadel Press.

Bogle, D. (1973). *Toms, Coons, Mulattoes, Mammies, and Bucks: An Interpretive History of Blacks in American Films*. New York: Viking.

Cripps, T. (1977). *Slow Fade to Black: The Negro in American Film, 1900–1942*. New York: Oxford University Press.

Dixon, T. (1970). *The Clansman: An Historical Romance of the Ku Klux Klan*. Lexington: University of Kentucky Press. (Original work published 1905)

Dominick, J. R. (1993). *The Dynamics of Mass Communication* (3rd ed.). New York: McGraw-Hill.

Emery, M., & Emery, E. (1988). *The Press and America: An Interpretive History of the Mass Media* (6th ed.). Englewood Cliffs, NJ: Prentice Hall.

Fanon, F. (1963). *The Wretched of the Earth*. New York: Grove.

Folkerts, J., & Teeter, D. L. (1989). *Voices of a Nation: A History of the Media in the United States*. New York: Macmillan.

Fredrickson, G. M. (1971). *The Black Image in the White Mind: The Debate on Afro-American Character and Destiny, 1817–1914*. New York: Harper & Row.

Horsman, R. (1981). *Race and Manifest Destiny: The Origins of American Racial Anglo-Saxonism*. Cambridge, MA: Harvard University Press.

Jordan, W. D. (1974). *The White Man's Burden: Historical Origins of Racism in the United States*. New York: Oxford University Press.

Kluger, R. (1986). *The Paper: The Life and Death of the* New York Herald Tribune. New York: Knopf.

Nordin, K. D. (1977–1978). "In Search of Black Unity: An Interpretation of the Content and Function of 'Freedom's Journal.'" *Journalism History*, 4(4), 123–128.

Ramsaye, T. (1986). *A Million and One Nights: A History of the Motion Picture Through 1925*. New York: Simon & Schuster. (Original work published 1926)

Rhodes, J. (1989, August). *Fugitives and Freemen: The Role of the Abolitionist Press in the Building of a Black Community in Canada West*. Paper presented at the Association for Education in Journalism and Mass Communication Conference, Washington, DC.

Rule, S. (1992, February 12). Director Defies the Odds, and Wins. *New York Times*, pp. C15, C17.

Saxton, A. (1990). *The Rise and Fall of the White Republic: Class, Politics and Mass Culture in Nineteenth-Century America*. London: Verso.

Silk, C., & Silk, J. (1990). *Racism and Anti-racism in American Popular Culture*. Manchester, UK: Manchester University Press.

Van Deburg, W. L. (1984). *Slavery and Race in American Popular Culture*. Madison: University of Wisconsin Press.

Wiegman, R. (1993). "The Anatomy of Lynching." *Journal of the History of Sexuality*, 3, 445–467.

Yellin, J. F. (1989). *Women and Sisters: The Antislavery Feminists in American Culture*. New Haven, CT: Yale University Press.

Visual Pleasure and Narrative Cinema

By Laura Mulvey

*A*s working methodologies, psychoanalysis and semiotics can be used to different ends. Both have attracted the attention of feminists as ways of helping to understand how women are represented in the cinema. They have helped feminist critics to extend critiques stressing the limited, stereotypical roles assigned to most female characters to a broad examination of how the formal organization of a film is a function of ideology as well as of aesthetics. One particularly significant aspect of this examination has been inquiry into the ways in which formal organization—the textual system—promotes certain states of mind among viewers. This line of reasoning has received extended treatment in the writings of Laura Mulvey, as well as by Claire Johnston, Pam Cook, and many other writers whose works are in included Further Readings.

In this seminal article, which was written in 1975, Mulvey gives a sharply feminist twist to psychoanalytic theory. Taking Freud's account of sexuality and the unconscious as a basically accurate description of the place of women in a phallocentric order, Mulvey asks how the unconscious of patriarchal society has structured film form. Many would disagree with this premise as an unnecessary endorsement of Freud's essentialism and as an undervaluation of the social experience of mothering as a major determinant of both gender roles and the psychic internalizations that support them. See, for example, Nancy Chodorow's The Reproduction of Mothering (Berkeley: University of California Press, 1978), which cites a wealth of psychoanalytic and sociological literature to support the contrary position. The most direct critique is Julia Lesage's "The Human Subject—You, He, or Me?" Or, "The Case of the Missing Penis" (originally published in Jump Cut, no. 4 [1974]: 26–27), which engendered an extended debate. Written prior to publication of Mulvey's article and directed expressly at points made in Screen 15, no. 2 (Summer 1974), an issue devoted to Brecht, Lesage's article reminds us that Freud's and Lacan's conception that the body of the woman is a threat to men because it signifies that lack or castration is not the *only reading of woman's body available, even in psychoanalytic literature. The critique seemed to go unheard until recently. D. N. Rodowick's "The Difficulty of Difference" (Wide Angle 5, no. 1 [1982]: 4–15) broaches the topic of masochism, which Mulvey's essay suppresses, but it fails to make a radical break with Mulvey's assumptions. In Part 5, Gaylyn Studlar's article, "Masochism and the Perverse Pleasures of the Cinema," carries this critique further by arguing that visual pleasure derives primarily from masochistic sources. Thus, she overturns the basic premises of Mulvey's article and of others who have followed her lead. Studlar's article and the section of* Jump Cut, *no 29 (1984) on women and representation (see in particular Jane Gaines's introduction) indicate that, after a period of remarkably strong influence, Mulvey's perspective is being displaced or contextualized by alternatives that are only now being heard.*

Mulvey's view of patriarchy and film form is seductively direct. Assuming that male visual pleasure is the controlling pleasure in cinema, she describes its two central forms: scopophilic pleasure that is linked to sexual attraction (voyeurism in extremis) and scopophilic pleasure that is linked to narcissistic identification (the introjection of ideal egos). Within the assumptions of the heterosexual orientation which Mulvey does not contest, narcissistic identification works to strengthen the ego through same-sex identification (between boys and male stars, for example), while sexual attraction is of a different order, since it can weaken the ego in the interests of instinctual gratification. Mulvey then considers the consequences of the erotic attraction of male viewers for female characters, arguing that the attraction is ambivalent, since the feminine is seen not only as a lure but as a threat: the threat of sinking into the "half-light of the imaginary," the threat of castration conveyed by the "real absence of a penis" from the body of the woman. The reality of that absence has often been called into question by those who point out that absence is itself a conceptual and symbolic category. The existence of female genitalia must be denied in order to see the "lack" that Freud and our phallocentric culture proclaim. See the "Critique of Phallocentrism" in Anthony Wilden's System and Structure 2nd *ed. (London: Tavistock, 1980, 278–301).*

For Mulvey, male ambivalence toward the image of woman propels the film text and the viewer toward non-mutually exclusive extremes: either to devalue, punish, or save woman, the guilty object, as Hitchcock's films do, or to make her a pedestal figure, a fetish, as von Sternberg and sometimes Hitchcock films do. These extremes leave no place for the female viewer. (In a later article, Mulvey describes how the female viewer must accept identification with a female heroine on the impossible terms of an aggressive, preoedipal sexuality or a passive, postoedipal one.) The possibilities for female sexual attraction (voyeuristic instead of narcissistic scopophilia) remain to be explored in comparable detail, See Mulvey's "Afterthoughts ... Inspired by Duel in the Sun" in Framework, *nos. 15–17 (Summer 1981): 12–15.*

The alternative that Mulvey proposes is the refusal of visual pleasure as structured by a patriarchal order. Mulvey's own filmmaking work may be seen as an indication of the directions that such a refusal might take, while Claire Johnston's references in the next article to Chantal Akerman's work suggest another. (Mulvey's films include Penthesilea *[1974],* Riddles of the Sphinx *[1977], and* Crystal Gazing *[1982], all with Peter Wollen.) Of paramount importance to the development of a specifically feminist criticism is Mulvey's persuasive demonstration of the inadequacy of criticism that assigns formal or thematic meanings to work that can be described or explained objectively. She argues that scopophilic drives "pursue aims in indifference to perceptual reality creating the imagined, eroticized concept of the world that forms the perception of the subject and makes a mockery of empirical objectivity." Such insight must be the starting-point for any affect-oriented feminist aesthetic.*

I. INTRODUCTION

A. A Political Use of Psychoanalysis

This paper intends to use psychoanalysis to discover where and how the fascination of film is reinforced by pre-existing patterns of fascination already at work within the individual subject and the social formations that have molded him. It takes as starting point the way film reflects, reveals, and even plays on the straight, socially established interpretation of sexual difference which controls images, erotic ways of looking and spectacle. It is helpful to understand what the cinema has been, how its magic has worked in the past, while attempting a theory and a practice which will challenge this cinema of the past. Psychoanalytic theory is thus appropriated here as a political weapon, demonstrating the way the unconscious of patriarchal society has structured film form.

The paradox of phallocentrism in all its manifestations is that it depends on the image of the castrated woman to give order and meaning to its world. An idea of woman stands as lynch pin to the system: it is her lack that produces the phallus as a symbolic presence, it is her desire to make good the lack that the phallus signifies. Recent writing in *Screen* about psychoanalysis and the cinema has not sufficiently brought out the importance of the representation of the female form in a symbolic order in which, in the last resort, it speaks castration and nothing else. To summarize briefly: the function of woman in forming the patriarchal unconscious is two-fold, she first symbolizes the castration threat by her real absence of a penis and, second, thereby raises her child into the symbolic. Once this has been achieved, her meaning in the process is at an end; it does not last into the world of law and language except as a memory, which oscillates between memory of maternal plenitude and memory of lack. Both are posited on nature (or on anatomy, in Freud's famous phrase). Woman's desire is subjected to her image as bearer of the bleeding wound; she can exist only in relation to castration and cannot transcend it. She turns her child into the signifier of her own desire to possess a penis (the condition, she imagines, of entry into the symbolic). Either she must gracefully give way to the word, the Name of the Father and the Law, or else struggle to keep her child down with her in the half-light of the imaginary. Woman then stands in patriarchal culture as signifier for the male other, bound by a symbolic order in which man can live out his fantasies and obsessions through linguistic command by imposing them on the silent image of woman still tied to her place as bearer of meaning, not maker of meaning.

There is an obvious interest in this analysis for feminists, a beauty in its exact rendering of the frustration experienced under the phallocentric order. It gets us nearer to the roots of our oppression, it brings an articulation of the problem closer, it faces us with the ultimate challenge: how to fight the unconscious structured like a language (formed critically at the moment of arrival of language) while still caught within the language of the patriarchy. There is no way in which we can produce an alternative out of the blue, but we can begin to make a break by examining patriarchy with the tools it provides, of which psychoanalysis is not the only but an important one. We are still separated by a great gap from important issues for the female unconscious which are scarcely relevant to phallocentric theory: the sexing of the female infant and her relationship to the symbolic, the sexually mature woman as non-mother, maternity outside the signification of the phallus, the vagina. But, at this point, psychoanalytic theory as it now stands can at least advance our understanding of the status quo, of the patriarchal order in which we are caught.

B. Destruction of Pleasure as a Radical Weapon

As an advanced representation system, the cinema poses questions of the ways the unconscious (formed by the dominant order) structures ways of seeing and pleasure in looking. Cinema has changed over the last few decades. It is no longer the monolithic system based on large capital investment exemplified at its best by Hollywood in the 1930's, 1940's, and 1950's. Technological advances (16mm, etc.) have changed the economic conditions of cinematic production, which can now be artisanal as well as capitalist. Thus it has been possible for an alternative cinema to develop. However self-conscious and ironic Hollywood managed to be, it always restricted itself to a formal mise-en-scène, reflecting the dominant ideological concept of the cinema. The alternative cinema provides a space for a cinema to be born, which is radical in both a political and an aesthetic sense and challenged the basic assumptions of the mainstream film. This is not to reject the latter moralistically, but to highlight the ways in which its formal preoccupations reflect the psychical obsessions of the society which produced it, and further, to stress that alternative cinema must start specifically by reacting against these obsessions and assumptions. A politically and aesthetically avant-garde cinema is now possible, but it can still only exist as counterpoint.

The magic of the Hollywood style at its best (and of all the cinema which fell within its sphere of influence) arose, not exclusively, but in one important aspect, from its skilled and satisfying manipulation of visual pleasure. Unchallenged mainstream film coded the erotic into the language of the dominant patriarchal order. In the highly developed Hollywood cinema, it was only through these codes that the alienated subject, torn in his imaginary memory by a sense of loss, by the terror of potential lack in fantasy, came near to finding a glimpse of satisfaction: through its formal beauty and its play on his own formative obsessions. This article will discuss the interweaving of that erotic pleasure in film, its meaning, and in particular the central place of the image of women. It is said that analyzing pleasure, or beauty, destroys it. That is the intention of this article. The satisfaction and reinforcement of the ego that represent the high point of film history hitherto must be attacked. Not in favors of a reconstructed new pleasure, which cannot exist in the abstract, nor of intellectualized unpleasure, but to make way for a total negation of the ease and plenitude of the narrative fiction film. The alternative is the thrill that comes from leaving the past behind without rejecting it, transcending outworn of oppressive forms, or daring to break with normal pleasurable expectations in order to conceive a new language of desire.

II. PLEASURE IN LOOKING/FASCINATION WITH THE HUMAN FORM

A. The cinema offers a number of possible pleasures. One is scopophilia. There are circumstances in which looking itself is a source of pleasure, just as, in the reverse formation, there is pleasure in being looked at. Originally, in his *Three Essays on Sexuality,* Freud isolated scopophilia as one of the component instincts of sexuality which exist as drives quite independently of the erotogenic zones. At this point, he associated scopophilia with taking other people as objects, subjecting them to a controlling and curious gaze. His particular examples center around the voyeuristic activities of children, their desire to see and make sure of the private and the forbidden (curiosity about other people's genital and bodily functions, about the presence or absence of the penis and, retrospectively, about the primal scene). In this analysis scopophilia is essentially active. (Later, in *Instincts and Their Vicissitudes,* Freud developed his theory of scopophilia further, attaching it initially to pre-genital autoeroticism, after which the pleasure of the look is transferred to others by analogy. There is a close working here of the relationship between the active instinct and its further development in a narcissistic form.) Although the instinct is modified by other factors, in particular the constitution of the ego, it continues to exist as the erotic basis for pleasure in looking at another person as object. At the extreme, it can become fixated into a perversion, producing obsessive voyeurs and Peeping Toms, whose only sexual satisfaction can come from watching, in an active controlling sense, an objectified other.

At first glance, the cinema would seem to be remote from the undercover world of the surreptitious observation of an unknowing and unwilling victim. What is seen on the screen is so manifestly shown. But the mass of mainstream film, and the conventions within which it has consciously evolved, portray a hermetically sealed world which unwinds magically, indifferent to the presence of the audience, producing for them a sense of separation and playing on their voyeuristic fantasy. Moreover, the extreme contrast between the darkness in the auditorium (which also isolates the spectators from one another) and the brilliance of the shifting patterns of light and shade on the screen helps to promote the illusion of voyeuristic separation. Although the film is really being shown, is there to be seen, conditions of screening and narrative conventions give the spectator an illusion of looking in on a private world. Among other things, the position of the spectators in the cinema is blatantly one of repression of their exhibitionism and projection of the repressed desire onto the performer.

B. The cinema satisfies a primordial wish for pleasurable looking, but it also goes further, developing scopophilia in its narcissistic aspect. The conventions of mainstream film focus attention on the human form. Scale, space, stones are all anthropomorphic. Here, curiosity and the wish to look intermingle with a fascination with likeness and recognition: the human face, the human body, the relationship between the human form and its surroundings, the visible presence of the person in the world. Jacques Lacan has described how the moment when a child recognizes its own image in the mirror is crucial for the constitution of the ego. Several aspects of this analysis are relevant here. The mirror phase occurs at a time when the child's physical ambitions outstrip his motor capacity, with the result that his recognition of himself is joyous in that he imagines his mirror image to be more complete, more perfect than he experiences his own body. Recognition is thus overlaid with misrecognition: the image recognized is conceived as the reflected body of the self, but its misrecognition as superior projects this body outside itself as an ideal ego, the alienated subject, which, re-introjected as an ego ideal, gives rise to the future generation of identification with others. This mirror moment predates language for the child. Important for this article is the fact that it is an image that constitutes the matrix of the imaginary, of recognition/misrecognition and identification, and hence of the first articulation of the I, of subjectivity. This is a moment when an older fascination with looking (at the mother's face, for an obvious example) collides with the initial inklings of self-awareness. Hence it is the birth of the long love affair/despair between image and self-image which has found such intense expression in film and such joyous recognition in the cinema audience. Quite apart from the extraneous similarities between screen and mirror (the framing of the human form in its surroundings, for instance), the cinema has structures of fascination are strong enough to allow temporary loss of ego while simultaneously reinforcing the ego. The sense of forgetting the world as the ego has subsequently come to perceive it (I forgot who I am and where I was) is nostalgically reminiscent of that pre-subjective moment of image recognition. At the same time, the cinema has distinguished itself in the production of ego ideals as expressed, in particular in the star system, the stars centering both screen presence and screen story as they act out a complex process of likeness and difference (the glamorous impersonates the ordinary).

C. Sections II, A and B, have set out two contradictory aspects of the pleasurable structures of looking in the conventional cinematic situation. The first, scopophilic, arises from pleasure in using another person as an object of sexual stimulation through sight. The second, developed through narcissism and the constitution of the ego, comes from identification with the image seen. Thus, in film terms, one implies a separation of the erotic identity of the subject from the object on the screen (active scopophilia), the other demands identification of the ego the object on the screen through the spectator's fascination with and recognition of his like. The first is a function of the sexual instincts, the second of ego libido. This dichotomy was crucial for Freud. Although he saw the two as interacting and overlaying each other, the tension between instinctual drives and self-preservation continues to be a dramatic polarization in terms of pleasure. Both are formative structures, mechanisms, not meaning. In themselves, they have no signification, they have to be attached to an idealization. Both pursue aims in indifference to perceptual reality, creating the imagined, eroticized concept of the world that forms the perception of the subject and makes a mockery of empirical objectivity.

During its history, the cinema seems to have evolved a particular illusion of reality in which this contradiction between libido and ego has found a beautifully complementary fantasy world. In reality, the fantasy world of the screen is subject to the law which produces it. Sexual instincts and identification processes have a meaning within the symbolic order which articulates desire. Desire, born with language, allows the possibility of transcending the instinctual and the imaginary, but its point of reference continually returns to the traumatic moment of its birth: the castration complex. Hence the look, pleasurable in form, can be threatening in content, and it is woman as representation/image that crystallizes this paradox.

III. WOMAN AS IMAGE, MAN AS BEARER OF THE LOOK

A. In a world ordered by sexual imbalance, pleasure in looking has been split between active/male and passive/female. The determining male gaze projects its fantasy onto the female figure, which is styled accordingly. In their traditional exhibitionist role, women are simultaneously looked at and displayed, with their appearance coded for strong visual and erotic impact so that they can be said to connote *to-be-looked-at-ness*. Woman displayed as sexual object is the leitmotif of erotic spectacle: from pin-ups to strip-tease, from Ziegfeld to Busby Berkeley, she holds the look, plays to, and signifies male desire. Mainstream film neatly combined spectacle and narrative. (Note, however, how in the musical song-and-dance numbers break the flow of the diegesis.) The presence of woman is an indispensable element of spectacle in normal narrative film, yet her visual presence tends to work against the development of a story line, to freeze the flow of action in moments of erotic contemplation. This alien presence then has to be integrated into cohesion with the narrative.

As Budd Boetticher has put it:

> What counts is what the heroine provokes, or rather what she represents. She is the one, or rather the love or fear she inspires in the hero, or else the concern he feels for her, who makes him act the way he does. In herself, the woman has not the slightest importance.

(A recent tendency in narrative film has been to dispense with this problem altogether; hence the development of what Molly Haskell has called the "buddy movie," in which the active homosexual eroticism of the central male figures can carry the story without distraction.) Traditionally, the woman displayed has functioned on two levels: as erotic object for the characters within the screen story, and as erotic object for the spectator within the auditorium, with a shifting tension between the looks on either side of the screen. For instance, the device of the show-girl allows the two looks to be unified technically without any apparent break in the diegesis. A woman performs within the narrative, the gaze of the spectator and that of the male characters in the film are neatly combined without breaking narrative verisimilitude. For a moment, the sexual impact of the performing woman takes the film into a no-man's-land outside its own time and space. Thus Marilyn Monroe's first appearance in *The River of No Return* and Lauren Bacall's songs in *To Have and Have Not*. Similarly, conventional close-ups of legs (Dietrich, for instance) or a face (Garbo) integrate into the narrative a different mode of eroticism. One part of a fragmented body destroys the Renaissance space, the illusion of depth demanded by the narrative. It gives flatness, the quality of a cut-out or icon rather than verisimilitude to the screen.

B. An active/passive heterosexual division of labor has similarly controlled narrative structure. According to the principles of the ruling ideology and the psychical structures that back it up, the male figure cannot bear the burden of sexual objectification. Man is reluctant to gaze at his exhibitionist like. Hence the split between spectacle and narrative supports the man's role as the active one of forwarding the story, making things happen. The man controls the film fantasy and also emerges as the representative of power in a further sense: as the bearer of the look of the spectator, transferring it behind the screen to neutralize the extra-diegetic tendencies represented by woman as spectacle. This is made possible through the processes set in motion by structuring the film around a main controlling figure with whom the spectator can identify. As the spectator identifies with the main male protagonist, he projects his look onto that of his like, his screen surrogate, so that the power of the male protagonist as he controls events coincides with the active power of the erotic look, both giving a satisfying sense of omnipotence. A male movie star's glamorous characteristics are thus not those of the erotic object of the gaze, but those of the more perfect, more complete, more powerful ideal ego conceived in the original moment of recognition in front of the mirror. The character in the story can make things happen and control events better than the subject/spectator, just as the image in the mirror was more in control of motor coordination. In contrast to woman as icon, the active male figure (the ego ideal of the identification process) demands a three-dimensional space corresponding to that of the mirror recognition, in which the alienated subject internalized his own representation of this imaginary existence. He is a figure in a landscape. Here the function of film is to reproduce as accurately as possible the so-called natural conditions of human perception. Camera technology (as exemplified by deep focus in particular) and camera movements (determined by the action of the protagonist), combined with invisible editing (demanded by realism), all tend to blur the limits of screen space. The male protagonist is free to command the stage: a stage of spatial illusion in which he articulates the look and creates the action.

C.1 Sections III, A and B, have set out a tension between a mode of representation of woman in film and conventions surrounding the diegesis. Each is associated with a look: that of the spectator in direct scopophilic contact with the female form displayed for his enjoyment (connoting male fantasy) and that of the spectator fascinated with the image of his like set in an illusion of natural space and, through him, gaining control and possession of the woman within the diegesis. (This tension and the shift from one pole to the other can structure a single text. Thus both in *Only Angels Have Wings* and in *To Have and Have Not*, the film opens with the woman as object of the combined gaze of spectator and all the male protagonists in the film. She is isolated, glamorous, on display, sexualised. But as the narrative progresses, she falls in love with the main male protagonist and becomes his property, losing her outward glamorous characteristics, her generalized sexuality, her show-girl connotations: her eroticism is subjected to the male star alone. By means of identification with him, through participation in his power, the spectator can indirectly possess her too.)

But in psychoanalytic terms, the female figure poses a deeper problem. She also connotes something that the look continually circles around but disavows: her lack of a penis, implying a threat of castration and hence unpleasure. Ultimately, the meaning of woman is sexual differ-ence, the absence of the penis as visually ascertainable, the material evidence on which is based the castration complex essential for the organization of entrance to the symbolic order and the law of the father. Thus the woman as icon, displayed for the gaze and enjoyment of men, the active controllers of the look, always threatens to evoke the anxiety it originally signified. The male unconscious has two avenues of escape from this castration anxiety: preoccupation with the re-enactment of the original trauma (investigating the woman, demystifying her mystery), counterbalanced by the devaluation, punishment, or saving of the guilty object (an avenue typi-fied by the concerns of the *film noir*); or else complete disavowal of castration by the substitution of a fetish object or turning the represented figure itself into a fetish so that it becomes reas-suring rather than dangerous (hence over-valuation, the cult of the female star). This second avenue, fetishistic scopophilia, builds up the physical beauty of the object, transforming it into something satisfying in itself. The first avenue, voyeurism, on the contrary, has associations with sadism: pleasure lies in ascertaining guilt (immediately associated with castration), assert-ing control, and subjecting the guilty person through punishment or forgiveness. This sadistic side fits in well with narrative. Sadism demands a story, depends on making something happen, forcing a change in another person, a battle of will and strength, victory/defeat, all occurring in a linear time with a beginning and an end. Fetishistic scopophilia, on the other hand, can exist outside linear time as the erotic instinct is focused on the look alone. These contradictions and ambiguities can be illustrated more simply by using works by Hitchcock and Sternberg, both of whom take the look almost as the content or subject matter of many of their films. Hitchcock is the more complex, as he uses both mechanisms. Sternberg's work, on the other hand, provides many pure examples of fetishistic scopophilia.

C.2 It is well known that Sternberg once said he would welcome his films being projected upside down so that story and character involvement would not interfere with the spectator's undiluted appreciation of the screen image. This statement is revealing but ingenuous. Ingenuous in that his films do demand that the figure of the woman (Dietrich, in the cycle of films with her, as the ultimate example) should be identifiable. But revealing in that it emphasizes the fact that for him the pictorial space enclosed by the frame is paramount, rather than narra-tive or identification processes. While Hitchcock goes into the investigative side of voyeurism, Sternberg produces the ultimate fetish, taking it to the point where the powerful look of the male protagonist (characteristic of traditional narrative film) is broken in favor of the image in direct erotic rapport with the spectator. The beauty of the woman as object and the screen space coalesce; she is no longer the bearer of guilt but a perfect product, whose body, stylized and fragmented by close-ups, is the content of the film and the direct recipient of the spectator's look. Sternberg plays down the illusion of screen depth; his screen tends to be one-dimensional, as light and shade, lace, steam, foliage, net, streamers, etc., reduce the visual field. There is little or no mediation of the look through the eyes of the main male protagonist. On the contrary, shadowy presences like La Bessière in *Morocco* act as surrogates for the director, detached as they are from audience identification. Despite Sternberg's insistence that his stories are irrelevant, it is significant that they are concerned with situation, not suspense, and cyclical rather than linear time, while plot complications revolve around misunderstanding rather than conflict. The most important absence is that of the controlling male gaze within the screen scene. The high point of emotional drama in the most typical Dietrich films, her supreme moments of erotic meaning, take place in the absence of the man she loves in the fiction. There are other witnesses, other spectators watching her on the screen, there gaze is one with, not standing in for, that of the audience. At the end of *Morocco*, Tom Brown has already disappeared into the desert when Amy Jolly kicks off her gold sandals and walks after him. At the end of *Dishonored*, Kranau is indifferent to the fate of Magda. In both cases, the erotic impact, sanctified by death, is displayed as a spectacle for the audience. The male hero misunderstands and, above all, does not see.

In Hitchcock, by contrast, the male hero does see precisely what the audience sees. However, in the films I shall discuss here, he takes fascination with an image through scopophilic eroticism as the subject of the film. Moreover, in these cases the hero portrays the contradictions and tensions experienced by the spectator. In *Vertigo*, in particular, but also in *Marnie* and *Rear Window*, the look is central to the plot, oscillating between voyeurism and fetishistic fascination. As a twist, a further manipulation of the normal viewing process, which in some sense reveals it, Hitchcock uses the process of identification normally associated with ideological correctness and the recognition of established morality and shows up its perverted side. Hitchcock has never concealed his interest in voyeurism, cinematic and non-cinematic. His heroes are exemplary of the symbolic order and the law—a policeman (*Vertigo*), a dominant male possessing money and power (*Marnie*)—but their erotic drives lead them into compromised situations. The power to subject another person to the will sadistically or to the gaze voyeuristically is turned onto the woman as the object of both. Power is backed by a certainty of legal right and the established guilt of the woman (evoking castration, psychoanalytically speaking). True perversion is barely concealed under a shallow mask of ideological correctness—the man is on the right side of the law, the woman on the wrong. Hitchcock's skilful use of identification processes and liberal use of subjective camera from the point of view of the male protagonist draw the spectators deeply into his position, making them share his uneasy gaze. The audience is absorbed into a voyeuristic situation within the screen scene and diegesis which parodies his own in the cinema. In his analysis of *Rear Window*, Douchet takes the film as a metaphor for the cinema. Jeffries is the audience, the events in the apartment block opposite correspond to the screen. As he watches, an erotic dimension is added to his look, a central image to the drama. His girlfriend Lisa had been of little sexual interest to him, more or less a drag, so long as she remained on the spectator side. When she crosses the barrier between his room and the block opposite, their relationship is re-born erotically. He does not merely watch her through his lens, as a distant meaningful image, he also sees her as a guilty intruder exposed by a dangerous man threatening her with punishment, and thus finally saves her. Lisa's exhibitionism has already been established by her obsessive interest in dress and style, in being a passive image of visual perfection; Jeffries's voyeurism and activity have also been established through his work as a photo-journalist, a maker of stories and captor of images. However, his enforced inactivity, binding him to his seat as a spectator, puts him squarely in the fantasy position of the cinema audience.

In *Vertigo*, subjective camera predominates. Apart from one flashback from Judy's point of view, the narrative is woven around what Scottie sees or fails to see. The audience follows the growth of his erotic obsession and subsequent despair precisely from his point of view. Scottie's voyeurism is blatant: he falls in love with a woman he follows and spies on without speaking to. Its sadistic side is equally blatant: he has chosen (and freely chosen, for he had been a successful lawyer) to be a policeman, with all the attendant possibilities of pursuit and investigation. As a result, he follows, watches, and falls in love with a perfect image of female beauty and mystery. Once he actually confronts her, his erotic drive is to break her down and force her to tell by persistent cross-questioning. Then, in the second part of the film, he re-enacts his obsessive involvement with the image he loved to watch secretly. He reconstructs Judy as Madeleine, forces her to conform in every detail to the actual physical appearance of his fetish. Her exhibitionism, her masochism, make her an ideal passive counterpart to Scottie's active sadistic voyeurism. She knows her part is to perform, and only by playing it through and then replaying it can she keep Scottie's erotic interest. But in the repetition he does break her down and succeeds in exposing her guilt. His curiosity wins through, and she is punished. In *Vertigo*, erotic involvement with the look is disorientating: the spectator's fascination is turned against him as the narrative carries him through and entwines him with the processes that he is himself exercising. The Hitchcock hero here is firmly placed within the symbolic order, in narrative terms. He has all the attributes of the patriarchal superego. Hence the spectator, lulled into a false sense of security by the apparent legality of his surrogate, sees through his look and finds himself exposed as complicit, caught in the moral ambiguity of looking. Far from being simply an aside on the perversion of the police, *Vertigo* focuses on the implications of the active/looking, passive/looked-at split in terms of sexual difference and the power of the male symbolic encapsulated in the hero. Marnie, too, performs for Mark Rutland's gaze and masquerades as the perfect to-be-looked-at image. He, too, is on the side of the law until, drawn in by obsession with her guilt, her secret, he longs to see her in the act of committing a crime, make her confess and thus save her. So he, too, becomes complicit as he acts out the implications of his power. He controls money and words, he can have his cake and eat it.

IV. SUMMARY

The psychoanalytic background that has been discussed in this article is relevant to the pleasure and unpleasure offered by traditional narrative film. The scopophilic instinct (pleasure in looking at another person as an erotic object), and, in contradistinction, ego libido (forming identification processes) act as formations, mechanisms, which this cinema has played on. The image of woman as (passive) raw material for the (active) gaze of man takes the argument a step further into the structure of representation, adding a further layer demanded by the ideology of the patriarchal order as it is worked out in its favorite cinematic form—illusionistic narrative film. The argument returns again to the psychoanalytic background in that woman as representation signifies castration, inducing voyeuristic or fetishistic mechanisms to circumvent her threat. None of these interacting layers is intrinsic to film, but it is only in the film form that they can reach a perfect and beautiful contradiction, thanks to the possibility in the cinema of shifting the emphasis of the look. It is the place of the look that defines cinema, the possibility of varying it and exposing it, This is what makes cinema quite different in its voyeuristic potential from, say, strip-tease, theatre, shows, etc. Going far beyond highlighting a woman's *to-be-looked-at-ness*, cinema builds the way she is to be looked at into the spectacle itself. Playing on the tension between film as controlling the dimension of time (editing, narrative) and film as controlling the dimension of space (changes in distance, editing), cinematic codes create a gaze, a world, and an object, thereby producing an illusion cut to the measure of desire. It is these cinematic codes and their relationship to formative external structures that must be broken down before mainstream film and the pleasure it provides can be challenged.

To begin with (as an ending), the voyeuristic-scopophilic look that is a crucial part of traditional filmic pleasure can itself be broken down. There are three different looks associated with cinema: that of the camera as it records the pro-filmic event, that of the audience as it watches the final product, and that of the characters at each other within the screen illusion. The conventions of narrative film deny the first two and subordinate them to the third, the conscious aim being always to eliminate intrusive camera presence and prevent a distancing awareness in the audience. Without these two absences (the material existence of the recording process, the critical reading of the spectator), fictional drama cannot achieve reality, obviousness, and truth. Nevertheless, as this article has argued, the structure of looking in narrative fiction film contains a contradiction in its own premises: the female image as a castration threat constantly endangers the unity of the diegesis and bursts through the world of illusion as an intrusive, static, one-dimensional fetish. Thus the two looks materially present in time and space are obsessively subordinated to the neurotic needs of the male ego. The camera becomes the mechanism for producing an illusion of Renaissance space, flowing movements compatible with the human eye, an ideology of representation that revolves around the perception of the subject; the camera's look is disavowed in order to create a convincing world in which the spectator's surrogate can perform with verisimilitude. Simultaneously, the look of the audience is denied an intrinsic force; as soon as fetishistic representation of the female image threatens to break the spell of illusion and the erotic image on the screen appears directly (without mediation) to the spectator, the fact of fetishisation, concealing as it does castration fear, freezes the look, fixates the spectator and prevents him from achieving any distance from the image in front of him.

This complex interaction of looks is specific to film. The first blow against the monolithic accumulation of traditional film conventions (already undertaken by radical film-makers) is to free the look of the camera into its materiality in time and space, and the look of the audience into dialectics, passionate detachment. There is no doubt that this destroys the satisfaction, pleasure, and privilege of the "invisible guest," and highlights how film has depended on voyeuristic active/passive mechanisms. Women, whose image has continually been stolen and used for this end, cannot view the decline of the traditional film form with anything much more than sentimental regret.

NOTE

1. There are films with a woman as main protagonist, of course. To analyze this phenomenon seriously here would take me too far afield. Pam Cook and Claire Johnston's study of *The Revolt of Mamie Stover* in Phil Hardy, ed., *Raoul Walsh,* Edinburgh, 1974, shows in a striking case how the strength of this female protagonist is more apparent than real.

The Oppositional Gaze

Black Female Spectators

By bell hooks

When thinking about black female spectators, I remember being punished as a child for staring, for those hard intense direct looks children would give grown-ups, looks that were seen as confrontational, as gestures of resistance, challenges to authority. The "gaze" has always been political in my life. Imagine the terror felt by the child who has come to understand through repeated punishments that one's gaze can be dangerous. The child who has learned so well to look the other way when necessary. Yet, when punished, the child is told by parents, "Look at me when I talk to you." Only, the child is afraid to look. Afraid to look, but fascinated by the gaze. There is power in looking.

Amazed the first time I read in history classes that white slave owners (men, women, and children) punished enslaved black people for looking, I wondered how this traumatic relationship to the gaze had informed black parenting and black spectatorship. The politics of slavery, of racialized power relations, were such that the slaves were denied their right to gaze. Connecting this strategy of domination to that used by grown folks in southern black rural communities where I grew up, I was pained to think that there was no absolute difference between whites who had oppressed black people and ourselves. Years later, reading Michel Foucault, I thought again about these connections, about the ways power as domination reproduces itself in different locations employing similar apparatuses, strategies, and mechanisms of control. Since I knew as a child that the dominating power adults exercised over me and over my gaze was never so absolute that I did not dare to look, to sneak a peep, to stare dangerously, I knew that the slaves had looked. That all attempts to repress our/black peoples' right to gaze had produced in us an overwhelming longing to look, a rebellious desire, an oppositional gaze. By courageously looking, we defiantly declared: "Not only will I stare. I want my look to change reality." Even in the worse circumstances of domination, the ability to manipulate one's gaze in the face of structures of domination that would contain it, opens up the possibility of agency. In much of his work, Michel Foucault insists on describing domination in terms of "relations of power" as part of an effort to challenge the assumption that "power is a system of domination which controls everything and which leaves no room for freedom." Emphatically stating that in all relations of power "there is necessarily the possibility of resistance," he invites the critical thinker to search those margins, gaps, and locations on and through the body where agency can be found.

Stuart Hall calls for recognition of our agency as black spectators in his essay "Cultural Identity and Cinematic Representation." Speaking against the construction of white representations of blackness as totalizing, Hall says of white presence: "The error is not to conceptualize this 'presence' in terms of power, but to locate that power as wholly external to us—as extrinsic force, whose influence can be thrown off like the serpent sheds its skin. What Franz Fanon reminds us, in *Black Skin, White Masks,* is how power is inside as well as outside:

> … the movements, the attitudes, the glances of the Other fixed me there, in the sense in which a chemical solution is fixed by a dye. I was indignant; I demanded an explanation. Nothing happened. I burst apart. Now the fragments have been put together again by another self. This "look," from—so to speak—the place of the Other, fixes us, not only in its violence, hostility, and aggression, but in the ambivalence of its desire.

Spaces of agency exist for black people, wherein we can both interrogate the gaze of the Other but also look back, and at one another, naming what we see. The "gaze" has been and is a site of resistance for colonized black people globally. Subordinates in relations of power learn experientially that there is a critical gaze, one that "looks" to document, one that is oppositional. In resistance struggle, the power of the dominated to assert agency by claiming and cultivating "awareness" politicizes "looking" relations—one learns to look a certain way in order to resist.

When most black people in the United States first had the opportunity to look at film and television, they did so fully aware that mass media was a system of knowledge and power reproducing and maintaining white supremacy. To stare at the television, or mainstream movies, to engage its images, was to engage its negation of black representation. It was the oppositional black gaze that responded to these looking relations by developing independent black cinema. Black viewers of mainstream cinema and television could chart the progress of political movements for racial equality *via* the construction of images, and did so. Within my family's southern, black, working-class home, located in a racially segregated neighborhood, watching television was one way to develop critical spectatorship. Unless you went to work in the white world, across the tracks, you learned to look at white people by staring at them on the screen. Black looks, as they were constituted in the context of social movements for racial uplift, were interrogating gazes. We laughed at television shows like *Our Gang* and *Amos 'n' Andy,* at these white representations of blackness, but we also looked at them critically. Before racial integration, black viewers of movies and television experienced visual pleasure in a context where looking was also about contestation and confrontation.

Writing about black looking relations in "Black British Cinema: Spectatorship and Identity Formation in Territories," Manthia Diawara identifies the power of the spectator: "Every narration places the spectator in a position of agency; and race, class, and sexual relations influence the way in which this subjecthood is filled by the spectator." Of particular concern for him are moments of "rupture" when the spectator resists "complete identification with the film's discourse." These ruptures define the relation between black spectators and dominant cinema prior to racial integration. Then, one's enjoyment of a film, wherein representations of blackness were stereotypically degrading and dehumanizing, co-existed with a critical practice that restored presence where it was negated. Critical discussion of the film while it was in progress or at its conclusion maintained the distance between spectator and the image. Black films were also subject to critical interrogation. Since they came into being in part as a response to the failure of white-dominated cinema to represent blackness in a manner that did not reinforce white supremacy, they too were critiqued to see if images were seen as complicit with dominant cinematic practices.

Critical, interrogating black looks were mainly concerned with issues of race and racism, the way racial domination of blacks by whites overdetermined representation. They were rarely concerned with gender. As spectators, black men could repudiate the reproduction of racism in cinema and television, the negation of black presence, even as they could feel as though they were rebelling against white supremacy by daring to look, by engaging phallocentric politics of spectatorship. Given the real life public circumstances wherein black men were murdered/lynched for looking at white womanhood, where the black male gaze was always subject to control and/or punishment by the powerful white Other, the private realm of television screens or dark theaters could unleash the repressed gaze. There they could "look" at white womanhood, without a structure of domination overseeing the gaze, interpreting, and punishing. That white supremacist structure that had murdered Emmet Till after interpreting his look as violation, as "rape" of white womanhood, could not control black male responses to screen images. In their role as spectators, black men could enter an imaginative space of phallocentric power that mediated racial negation. This gendered relation to looking made the experience of the black male spectator radically different from that of the black female spectator. Major early black male independent filmmakers represented black women in their films as objects of male gaze. Whether looking through the camera or as spectators watching films, whether mainstream cinema or "race" movies such as those made by Oscar Micheaux, the black male gaze had a different scope from that of the black female.

Black women have written little about black female spectatorship, about our movie-going practices. A growing body of film theory and criticism by black women has only begun to emerge. The prolonged silence of black women as spectators and critics was a response to absence, to cinematic negation. In "The Technology of Gender," Teresa de Lauretis, drawing on the work of Monique Wittig, calls attention to "the power of discourses to 'do violence' to people, a violence which is material and physical, although produced by abstract and scientific discourses as well as the discourses of the mass media." With the possible exception of early race movies, black female spectators have had to develop looking relations within a cinematic context that constructs our presence as absence, that denies the "body" of the black female so as to perpetuate white supremacy and, with it, a phallocentric spectatorship where the woman to be looked at and desired is "white." (Recent movies do not conform to this paradigm but I am turning to the past with the intent to chart the development of black female spectatorship.)

Talking with black women of all ages and classes, in different areas of the United States, about their filmic looking relations, I hear again and again ambivalent responses to cinema. Only a few of the black women I talked with remembered the pleasure of race movies and even those who did felt that pleasure interrupted and usurped by Hollywood. Most of the black women I talked with were adamant that they never went to movies expecting to see compelling representations of black femaleness. They were all acutely aware of cinematic racism—its violent erasure of black womanhood. In Anne Friedberg's essay "A Denial of Difference: Theories of Cinematic Identification," she stresses that "identification can only be made through recognition, and all recognition is itself an implicit confirmation of the ideology of the status quo." Even when representations of black women were present in film, our bodies and being were there to serve—to enhance and maintain white womanhood as object of the phallocentric gaze.

Commenting on Hollywood's characterization of black women in *Girls on Film,* Julie Burchill describes this absent presence:

> Black women have been mothers without children (Mammies—who can ever forget the sickening spectacle of Hattie MacDaniels waiting on the simpering Vivien Leigh hand and foot and enquiring like a ninny, "What's ma lamb gonna wear?") … Lena Horne, the first black performer signed to a long term contract with a major (MGM), looked gutless but was actually quite spirited. She seethed when Tallulah Bankhead complimented her on the paleness of her skin and the non-Negroidness of her features.

When black women actresses like Lena Horne appeared in mainstream cinema, most white viewers were not aware that they were looking at black females unless the film was specifically coded as being about blacks. Burchill is one of the few white women film critics who has dared to examine the intersection of race and gender in relation to the construction of the category "woman" in film as object of the phallocentric gaze. With characteristic wit she asserts: "What does it say about racial purity that the best blondes have all been brunettes (Harlow, Monroe, Bardot)? I think it says that we are not as white as we think." Burchill could easily have said "we are not as white as we want to be," for clearly the obsession to have white women film stars be ultra-white was a cinematic practice that sought to maintain a distance, a separation between that image and the black female Other; it was a way to perpetuate white supremacy. Politics of race and gender were inscribed into mainstream cinematic narrative, from *Birth of a Nation* on. As a seminal work, this film identified what the place and function of white womanhood would be in cinema. There was clearly no place *for black* women.

Remembering my past in relation to screen images of *black* womanhood, I wrote a short essay, "Do you remember Sapphire?" which explored both the negation of black female representation in cinema and television and our rejection of these images. Identifying the character of "Sapphire" from *Amos 'n' Andy* as that screen representation of black femaleness I first saw in childhood, I wrote:

> She was even then backdrop, foil. She was bitch—nag. She was there to soften images of black men, to make them seem vulnerable, easygoing, funny, and unthreatening to a *white* audience. She was there as man in drag, as castrating bitch, as someone to be lied to, someone to be tricked, someone the white and black audience could hate. Scapegoated on all sides. *She was not us.* We laughed with the black men, with the white people. We laughed at this black woman who was not us. And we did not even long to be there on the screen. How could we long to be there when our image, visually constructed, was so ugly. We did not long to be there. We did not long for her. We did not want our construction to be this hated black female

thing—foil, backdrop. Her black female image was not the body of desire. There was nothing to see. She was not us.

Grown black women had a different response to Sapphire; they identified with her frustrations and her woes. They resented the way she was mocked. They resented the way these screen images could assault black womanhood, could name us bitches, nags. And in opposition, they claimed Sapphire as their own, *as* the symbol of that angry part of themselves that white folks and black men could not even begin to understand.

Conventional representations of black women have done violence to the image. Responding to this assault, many black women spectators shut out the image, looked the other way, accorded cinema no importance in their lives. Then there were those spectators whose gaze was that of desire and complicity. Assuming a posture of subordination, they submitted to cinema's capacity to seduce and betray. They were cinematically "gas-lighted." Every black woman I spoke with who was/is an ardent moviegoer, a lover of the Hollywood film, testified that to experience fully the pleasure of that cinema, they had to close down critique, analysis; they had to forget racism. And mostly they did not think about sexism. What was the nature then of this adoring black female gaze—this look that could bring pleasure in the midst of negation? In her first novel, *The Bluest Eye,* Toni Morrison constructs a portrait of the black female spectator; her gaze is the masochistic look of victimization. Describing her looking relations, Miss Pauline Breedlove, a poor working woman, maid in the house of a prosperous white family, asserts:

> The onliest time I be happy seem like was when I was in the picture show. Every time I got, I went, I'd go early, before the show started. They's cut off the lights, and everything be black. Then the screen would light up, and I's move right on in them, picture. White men taking such good care of they women, and they all dressed up in big clean houses with the bath tubs right in the same room with the toilet. Them pictures gave me a lot of pleasure.

To experience pleasure, Miss Pauline sitting in the dark, must imagine herself transformed, turned into the white woman portrayed on the screen. After watching movies, feeling the pleasure, she says, "But it made coming home hard."

We come home to ourselves. Not all black women spectators submitted to that spectacle of regression through identification. Most of the women I talked with felt that they consciously resisted identification with films—that this tension made movie-going less than pleasurable; at times, it caused pain. As one black woman put, "I could always get pleasure from movies as long as I did not look too deep." For black female spectators who have "looked too deep," the encounter with the screen hurt. That some of us chose to stop looking was a gesture of resistance, turning away was one way to protest, to reject negation. My pleasure in the screen ended abruptly when I and my sisters first watched *Imitation of Life*. Writing about this experience in the "Sapphire" piece, I addressed the movie directly, confessing:

> I had until now forgotten you, that screen image seen in adolescence, those images that made me stop looking. It was there in *Imitation of Life,* that comfortable mammy image. There was something familiar about this hard-working, black woman who loved her daughter so much, loved her in a way that hurt. Indeed, as young southern black girls watching this film,

Peola's mother reminded us of the hardworking, churchgoing, Big Mamas we knew and loved. Consequently, it was not this image that captured our gaze; we were fascinated by Peola.

Addressing her, I wrote:

> You were different. There was something scary in this image of young, sexual, sensual black beauty betrayed—that daughter who did not want to be confined by blackness, that "tragic mulatto" who did not want to be negated. "Just let me escape this image forever," she could have said. I will always remember that image. I remembered how we cried for her, for our unrealized desiring selves. She was tragic because there was no place in the cinema for her, no loving pictures. She too was an absent image. It was better, then, that we were absent, for when we were there, it was humiliating, strange, sad. We cried all night for you, for the cinema that had no place for you. And like you, we stopped thinking it would one day be different.

When I returned to films as a young woman, after a long period of silence, I had developed an oppositional gaze. Not only would I not be hurt by the absence of black female presence, or the insertion of violating representation, I interrogated the work, cultivated a way to look past race and gender for aspects of content, form, language. Foreign films and U.S. independent cinema were the primary locations of my filmic looking relations, even though I also watched Hollywood films.

From "jump," black female spectators have gone to films with awareness of the way in which race and racism determined the visual construction of gender. Whether it was *Birth of a Nation* or Shirley Temple shows, we knew that white womanhood was the racialized sexual difference occupying the place of stardom in mainstream narrative film. We assumed white women knew it too. Reading Laura Mulvey's provocative essay, "Visual Pleasure and Narrative Cinema," from a standpoint that acknowledges race, one sees clearly why black women spectators not duped by mainstream cinema would develop an oppositional gaze. Placing ourselves outside that pleasure in looking, Mulvey argues, was determined by a "split between active/male and passive/female." Black female spectators actively chose not to identify with the film's imaginary subject because such identification was disenabling.

Looking at films with an oppositional gaze, black women were able to critically assess the cinema's construction of white womanhood as object of phallocentric gaze and choose not to identify with either the victim or the perpetrator. Black female spectators, who refused to identify with white womanhood, who would not take on the phallocentric gaze of desire and possession, created a critical space where the binary opposition Mulvey posits of "woman as image, man as bearer of the look" was continually deconstructed. As critical spectators, black women looked from a location that disrupted, one akin to that described by Annette Kuhn in *The Power of The Image*:

> … the acts of analysis, of deconstruction, and of reading "against the grain" offer an additional pleasure—the pleasure of resistance, of saying "no": not to "unsophisticated" enjoyment, by ourselves and others, of culturally dominant images, but to the structures of power which ask us to consume them uncritically and in highly circumscribed ways.

Mainstream feminist film criticism in no way acknowledges black female spectatorship. It does not even consider the possibility that women can construct an oppositional gaze via an understanding and awareness of the politics of race and racism. Feminist film theory, rooted in an ahistorical, psychoanalytic framework that privileges sexual difference, actively suppresses recognition of race, reenacting and mirroring the erasure of black womanhood that occurs in films, silencing any discussion of racial difference—of racialized sexual difference. Despite feminist critical interventions aimed at deconstructing the category "woman," which highlight the significance of race, many feminist film critics continue to structure their discourse as though it speaks about "women" when in actuality it speaks only about white women. It seems ironic that the cover of the recent anthology *Feminism and Film Theory* edited by Constance Penley has a graphic that is a reproduction of the photo of white actresses Rosalind Russell and Dorothy Arzner on the 1936 set of the film *Craig's Wife*, yet there is no acknowledgment in any essay in this collection that the woman "subject" under discussion is always white. Even though there are photos of black women from films reproduced in the text, there is no acknowledgment of racial difference.

It would be too simplistic to interpret this failure of insight solely as a gesture of racism. Importantly, it also speaks to the problem of structuring feminist film theory around a totalizing narrative of woman as object whose image functions solely to reaffirm and re-inscribe patriarchy. Mary Ann Doane addresses this issue in the essay "Remembering Women: Psychical and Historical Construction in Film Theory":

> This attachment to the figure of a degeneralizible Woman as the product of the apparatus indicates why, for many, feminist film theory seems to have reached an impasse, a certain blockage in its theorization. In focusing upon the task of delineating in great detail the attributes of woman as effect of the apparatus, feminist film theory participates in the abstraction of women.

The concept "Woman" effaces the difference between women in specific socio-historical contexts, between women defined precisely as historical subjects rather than as a psychic subject (or non-subject). Though Doane does not focus on race, her comments speak directly to the problem of its erasure. For it is only as one imagines "woman" in the abstract, when woman becomes fiction or fantasy, can race not be seen as significant. Are we really to imagine that feminist theorists writing only about images of white women, who subsume this specific historical subject under the totalizing category "woman," do not "see" the whiteness of the image? It may very well be that they engage in a process of denial that eliminates the necessity of revisioning conventional ways of thinking about psychoanalysis as a paradigm of analysis and the need to rethink a body of feminist film theory that is firmly rooted in a denial of the reality that sex/sexuality may not be the primary and/or exclusive signifier of difference. Doane's essay appears in a very recent anthology, *Psychoanalysis and Cinema* edited by E. Ann Kaplan, where, once again, none of the theory presented acknowledges or discusses racial difference, with the exception of one essay, "Not Speaking with Language, Speaking with No Language," which problematizes notions of orientalism in its examination of Leslie Thornton's film *Adynata*. Yet in most of the essays, the theories espoused are rendered problematic if one includes race as a category of analysis.

Constructing feminist film theory along these lines enables the production of a discursive practice that need never theorize any aspect of black female representation or spectatorship. Yet the existence of black women within white supremacist culture problematizes, and makes complex, the overall issue of female identity, representation, and spectatorship. If, as Friedberg suggests, "identification is a process which commands the subject to be displaced by an other; it is a procedure which breeches the separation between self and other and, in this way, replicates the very structure of patriarchy." If identification "demands sameness, necessitates similarity, disallows difference," must we then surmise that many feminist film critics who are "over-identified" with the mainstream cinematic apparatus produce theories that replicate its totalizing agenda? Why is it that feminist film criticism, which has most claimed the terrain of woman's identity, representation, and subjectivity as its field of analysis, remains aggressively silent on the subject of blackness and specifically representations of black womanhood? Just as mainstream cinema has historically forced aware black female spectators not to look, much feminist film criticism disallows the possibility of a theoretical dialogue that might include black women's voices. It is difficult to talk when you feel no one is listening, when you feel as though a special jargon or narrative has been created that only the chosen can understand. No wonder, then, that black women have for the most part confined our critical commentary on film to conversations. And it must be reiterated that this gesture is a strategy that protects us from the violence perpetuated and advocated by discourses of mass media. A new focus on issues of race and representation in the field of film theory could critically intervene on the historical repression reproduced in some arenas of contemporary critical practice, making a discursive space for discussion of black female spectatorship possible.

When I asked a black woman in her twenties, an obsessive moviegoer, why she thought we had not written about black female spectatorship, she commented: "We are afraid to talk about ourselves as spectators because we have been so abused by 'the gaze.'" An aspect of that abuse was the imposition of the assumption that black female looking relations were not important enough to theorize. Film theory as a critical "turf" in the United States has been and continues to be influenced by and reflective of white racial domination. Since feminist film criticism was initially rooted in a women's liberation movement informed by racist practices, it did not open up the discursive terrain and make it more inclusive. Recently, even those white film theorists who include an analysis of race show no interest in black female spectatorship. In her introduction to the collection of essays *Visual and Other Pleasures,* Laura Mulvey describes her initial romantic absorption in Hollywood cinema, stating:

> Although this great, previously unquestioned and unanalyzed love was put in crisis by the impact of feminism on my thought in the early 1970s, it also had an enormous influence on the development of my critical work and ideas and the debate within film culture with which I became preoccupied over the next fifteen years or so. Watched through eyes that were affected by the changing climate of consciousness, the movies lost their magic.

Watching movies from a feminist perspective, Mulvey arrived at that location of disaffection that is the starting point for many black women approaching cinema within the lived harsh reality of racism. Yet her account of being a part of a film culture whose roots rest on a founding relationship of adoration and love indicates how difficult it would have been to enter that world from "jump" as a critical spectator whose gaze had been formed in opposition.

Given the context of class exploitation, and racist and sexist domination, it has only been through resistance, struggle, reading, and looking "against the grain," that black women have been able to value our process of looking enough to publicly name it. Centrally, those black female spectators who attest to the oppositionality of their gaze deconstruct theories of female spectatorship that have relied heavily on the assumption that, as Doane suggests in her essay "Woman's Stake: Filming the Female Body," "woman can only mimic man's relation to language, that is, assume a position defined by the penis-phallus as the supreme arbiter of lack." Identifying with neither the phallocentric gaze nor the construction of white womanhood as lack, critical black female spectators construct a theory of looking relations where cinematic visual delight is the pleasure of interrogation. Every black woman spectator I talked to, with rare exception, spoke of being "on guard" at the movies. Talking about the way being a critical spectator of Hollywood films influenced her, black woman filmmaker Julie Dash exclaims, "I make films because I was such a spectator!" Looking at Hollywood cinema from a distance, from that critical politicized standpoint that did not want to be seduced by narratives reproducing her negation, Dash watched mainstream movies over and over again for the pleasure of deconstructing them. And of course there is that added delight if one happens, in the process of interrogation, to come across a narrative that invites the black female spectator to engage the text with no threat of violation.

Significantly, I began to write film criticism in response to the first Spike Lee movie, *She's Gotta Have It*, contesting Lee's replication of mainstream, patriarchal cinematic practices that explicitly represents woman (in this instance, black woman) as the object of a phallocentric gaze. Lee's investment in patriarchal filmic practices that mirror dominant patterns makes him the perfect black candidate for entrance to the Hollywood canon. His work mimics the cinematic construction of white womanhood as object, replacing her body as text on which to write male desire with the black female body. It is transference without transformation. Entering the discourse of film criticism from the politicized location of resistance, of not wanting, as a working-class black woman I interviewed stated, "to see black women in the position white women have occupied in film forever," I began to think critically about black female spectatorship.

For years, I went to independent and/or foreign films where I was the only black female present in the theater. I often imagined that in every theater in the United States there was another black woman watching the same film wondering why she was the only visible black female spectator. I remember trying to share with one of my five sisters the cinema I liked so much. She was "enraged" that I brought her to a theater where she would have to read subtitles. To her it was a violation of Hollywood notions of spectatorship, of coming to the movies to be entertained. When I interviewed her to ask what had changed her mind over the years, led her to embrace this cinema, she connected it to coming to critical consciousness, saying, "I learned that there was more to looking than I had been exposed to in ordinary (Hollywood) movies." I shared that though most of the films I loved were all white, I could engage them because they did not have, in their deep structure, a subtext reproducing the narrative of white supremacy. Her response was to say that these films demystified "whiteness," since the lives they depicted seemed less rooted in fantasies of escape. They were, she suggested, more like "what we knew life to be, the deeper side of life as well." Always more seduced and enchanted with Hollywood cinema than me, she stressed that unaware black female spectators must "break out," no longer be imprisoned by images that enact a drama of our negation. Though she still sees Hollywood films, because "they are a major influence in the culture," she no longer feels duped or victimized.

Talking with black female spectators, looking at written discussions either in fiction or academic essays about black women, I noted the connection made between the realm of representation in mass media and the capacity of black women to construct ourselves as subjects in daily life. The extent to which black women feel devalued, objectified, dehumanized in this society determines the scope and texture of their looking relations. Those black women whose identities were constructed in resistance, by practices that oppose the dominant order, were most inclined to develop an oppositional gaze. Now that there is a growing interest in films produced by black women and those films have become more accessible to viewers, it is possible to talk about black female spectatorship in relation to that work. So far, most discussions of black spectatorship that I have come across focus on men. In "Black Spectatorship: Problems of Identification and Resistance," Manthia Diawara suggests that "the components of difference" among elements of sex, gender, and sexuality give rise to different readings of the same material, adding that these conditions produce a "resisting" spectator. He focuses his critical discussion on black masculinity.

The recent publication of the anthology *The Female Gaze: Women as Viewers of Popular Culture* excited me, especially as it included an essay, "Black Looks," by Jacqui Roach and Petal Felix that attempts to address black female spectatorship. The essay posed provocative questions that were not answered: Is there a black female gaze? How do black women relate to the gender politics of representation? Concluding, the authors assert that black females have "our own reality, our own history, our own gaze—one which sees the world rather differently from 'anyone else.'" Yet, they do not name/describe this experience of seeing "rather differently." The absence of definition and explanation suggests they are assuming an essentialist stance wherein it is presumed that black women, as victims of race and gender oppression, have an inherently different field of vision. Many black women do not "see differently" precisely because their perceptions of reality are so profoundly colonized, shaped by dominant ways of knowing. As Trinh T. Minh-ha points out in "Outside In, Inside Out": "Subjectivity does not merely consist of talking about oneself … be this talking indulgent or critical."

Critical black female spectatorship emerges as a site of resistance only when individual black women actively resist the imposition of dominant ways of knowing and looking. While every black woman I talked to was aware of racism, that awareness did not automatically correspond with politicization, the development of an oppositional gaze. When it did, individual black women consciously named the process. Manthia Diawara's "resisting spectatorship" is a term that does not adequately describe the terrain of black female spectatorship. We do more than resist. We create alternative texts that are not solely reactions. As critical spectators, black women participate in a broad range of looking relations, contest, resist, revision, interrogate, and invent on multiple levels. Certainly when I watch the work of black women filmmakers Camille Billops, Kathleen Collins, Julie Dash, Ayoka Chenzira, Zeinabu Davis, I do not need to "resist" the images even as I still choose to watch their work with a critical eye.

Black female critical thinkers concerned with creating space for the construction of radical black female subjectivity, and the way cultural production informs this possibility, fully acknowledge the importance of mass media, film in particular, as a powerful site for critical intervention. Certainly Julie Dash's film *Illusions* identifies the terrain of Hollywood cinema as a space of knowledge production that has enormous power. Yet, she also creates a filmic narrative wherein the black female protagonist subversively claims that space. Inverting the "real-life" power structure, she offers the black female spectator representations that challenge stereotypical notions that place us outside the realm of filmic discursive practices. Within the film she uses the strategy of Hollywood suspense films to undermine those cinematic practices that deny black women a place in this structure. Problematizing the question of "racial" identity by depicting passing, suddenly it is the white male's capacity to gaze, define, and know that is called into question.

When Mary Ann Doane describes in "Woman's Stake: Filming the Female Body," the way in which feminist filmmaking practice can elaborate "a special syntax for a different articulation of the female body," she names a critical process that "undoes the structure of the classical narrative through an insistence upon its repressions." An eloquent description, this precisely names Dash's strategy in *Illusions,* even though the film is not unproblematic and works within certain conventions that are not successfully challenged. For example, the film does not indicate whether the character Mignon will make Hollywood films that subvert and transform the genre or whether she will simply assimilate and perpetuate the norm. Still, subversively, *Illusions* problematizes the issue of race and spectatorship. White people in the film are unable to "see" that race informs their looking relations. Though she is passing to gain access to the machinery of cultural production represented by film, Mignon continually asserts her ties to black community. The bond between her and the young black woman singer Esther Jeeter is affirmed by caring gestures of affirmation, often expressed by eye-to-eye contact, the direct unmediated gaze of recognition. Ironically, it is the desiring, objectifying, sexualized white male gaze that threatens to penetrate her "secrets" and disrupt her process. Metaphorically, Dash suggests the power of black women to make films will be threatened and undermined by that white male gaze that seeks to re-inscribe the black female body in a narrative of voyeuristic pleasure where the only relevant opposition is male/female and the only location for the female is as a victim. These tensions are not resolved by the narrative. It is not at all evident that Mignon will triumph over the white supremacist capitalist imperialist dominating "gaze."

Throughout *Illusions,* Mignon's power is affirmed by her contact with the younger black woman whom she nurtures and protects. It is this process of mirrored recognition that enables both black women to define their reality, apart from the reality imposed upon them by structures of domination. The shared gaze of the two women reinforces their solidarity. As the younger subject, Esther represents a potential audience for films that Mignon might produce, films wherein black females will be the narrative focus. Julie Dash's recent feature-length film *Daughters of the Dust* dares to place black females at the center of its narrative. This focus caused critics (especially white males) to critique the film negatively or to express many reservations. Clearly, the impact of racism and sexism so overdetermine spectatorship—not only what we look at but who we identify with—that viewers who are not black females find it hard to empathize with the central characters in the movie. They are adrift without a white presence in the film.

Another representation of black females nurturing one another *via* recognition of their common struggle for subjectivity is depicted in Sankofa's collective work *Passion of Remembrance.* In the film, two black women friends, Louise and Maggie, are, from the onset of the narrative, struggling with the issue of subjectivity, of their place in progressive black liberation movements that have been sexist. They challenge old norms and want to replace them with new understandings of the complexity of black identity, and the need for liberation struggles that address that complexity. Dressing to go to a party, Louise and Maggie claim the "gaze." Looking at one another, staring in mirrors; they appear completely focused on their encounter with black femaleness. How they see themselves is most important, not how they will be stared at by others. Dancing to the tune "Let's get Loose," they display their bodies not for a voyeuristic colonizing gaze but for that look of recognition that affirms their subjectivity—that constitutes them as spectators. Mutually empowered, they eagerly leave the privatized domain to confront the public. Disrupting conventional racist and sexist stereotypical representations of black female bodies, these scenes invite the audience to look differently. They act to critically intervene and transform conventional filmic practices, changing notions of spectatorship. *Illusions, Daughters of the Dust,* and *A Passion of Remembrance* employ a deconstructive filmic practice to undermine existing grand cinematic narratives even as they re-theorize subjectivity in the realm of the visual. Without providing "realistic" positive representations that emerge only as a response to the totalizing nature of existing narratives, they offer points of radical departure. Opening up a space for the assertion of a critical black female spectatorship, they do not simply offer diverse representations, they imagine new transgressive possibilities for the formulation of identity.

In this sense, they make explicit a critical practice that provides us with different ways to think about black female subjectivity and black female spectatorship. Cinematically, they provide new points of recognition, embodying Stuart Hall's vision of a critical practice that acknowledges that identity is constituted "not outside but within representation" and invites us to see film "not as a second-order mirror held up to reflect what already exists, but as that form of representation which is able to constitute us as new kinds of subjects, and thereby enable us to discover who we are." It is this critical practice that enables production of feminist film theory that theorizes black female spectatorship. Looking and looking back, black women involve ourselves in a process whereby we see our history as counter-memory, using it as a way to know the present and invent the future.

The West and the Rest: Discourse and Power

By Stuart Hall

WHERE AND WHAT IS "THE WEST"?

This question puzzled Christopher Columbus and remains puzzling today. Nowadays, many societies aspire to become "Western"—at least in terms of achieving Western standards of living. But in Columbus's day (the end of the fifteenth century) going West was important mainly because it was believed to be the quickest route to the fabulous wealth of the East. Indeed, even though it should have become clear to Columbus that the New World he had found was *not* the East, he never ceased to believe that it was, and even spiced his reports with outlandish claims: on his fourth voyage, he still insisted that he was close to Quinsay (the Chinese city now called Hangchow), where the Great Khan lived, and probably approaching the source of the Four Rivers of Paradise! Our ideas of "East" and "West" have never been free of myth and fantasy, and even to this day they are not primarily ideas about place and geography.

We have to use short-hand generalizations, like "West" and "Western" but we need to re-member that they represent very complex ideas and have no simple or single meaning. At first sight, these words may seem to be about matters of geography and location. But even this, on inspection, is not straightforward since we also use the same words to refer to a type of society, a level of development, and so on. It's true that what we call "the West," in this second sense, *did* first emerge in Western Europe. But "the West" is no longer only in Europe, and not all of Europe is in "the West." The historian John Roberts has remarked that, "Europeans have long been unsure about where Europe 'ends' in the east. In the west and to the south, the sea provides a splendid marker ... but to the east the plains roll on and on and the horizon is awfully remote"

Excerpted from Stuart Hall, "The West and the Rest: Discourse and Power," in S. Hall and B. Gieben (eds.), *Formations of Modernity* (Cambridge: Polity Press, 1992), pp. 275–331.

(Roberts 1985: 149). Eastern Europe doesn't (doesn't yet? never did?) belong properly to "the West"; whereas the United States, which is not in Europe, definitely does. These days, technologically speaking, Japan, is "Western" though on our mental map it is about as far "East" as you can get. By comparison, much of Latin America, which is in the Western hemisphere, belongs economically to the Third World, which is struggling—not very successfully—to catch up with "the West." What are these different societies "east" and "west" of, exactly? Clearly, "the West" is as much an idea as a fact of geography.

The underlying premise of this chapter is that "the West" is a *historical,* not a geographical, construct. By "Western" we mean […] a society that is developed, industrialized, urbanized, capitalist, secular, and modern. Such societies arose at a particular historical period—roughly, during the sixteenth century, after the Middle Ages and the break-up of feudalism. They were the result of a specific set of historical processes—economic, political, social, and cultural. Nowadays, any society, wherever it exists on a geographical map, which shares these characteristics, can be said to belong to "the West." The meaning of this term is therefore virtually identical to that of the word "modern." […]

"The West" is therefore also an idea, a concept […] How did the idea, the language, of "the West" arise, and what have been its effects? What do we mean by calling it a *concept?*

The concept or idea of "the West" can be seen to function in the following ways:

First, it allows us to characterize and classify societies into different categories—i.e., "Western" "non-Western." It is a tool to think with. It sets a certain structure of thought and knowledge in motion.

Secondly, it is an image, or set of images. It condenses a number of different characteristics into one picture. It calls up in our mind's eye—it *represents* in verbal and visual language—a composite picture of what different societies, cultures, peoples, and places are like. It functions as part of a language, a "system of representation." (I say "system" because it doesn't stand on its own, but works in conjunction with other images and ideas with which it forms a set: for example, "Western" = urban = developed: or "non-Western" = non-industrial = rural = agricultural = underdeveloped.)

Thirdly, it provides a standard or model of comparison. It allows us to compare to what extent different societies resemble, or differ from, one another. Non-Western societies can accordingly be said to be "close to" or "far away from" or "catching up with" the West. It helps to explain *difference.*

Fourthly, it provides criteria of evaluation against which other societies are ranked and around which powerful positive and negative feelings cluster. (For example, "the West" = developed = *good* = desirable: or the "non-West" = underdeveloped = *bad* = undesirable.) It produces a certain kind of *knowledge* about a subject and certain attitudes towards it. In short, it functions as an *ideology.* […]

We know that the West itself was produced by certain historical processes operating in a particular place in unique (and perhaps unrepeatable) historical circumstances. Clearly, we must also think of the *idea* of "the West" as having been produced in a similar way. These two aspects are in fact deeply connected, though exactly how is one of the big puzzles in sociology. We cannot attempt to resolve here the age-old sociological debate as to which came first: the idea of "the West," or Western societies. What we can say is that, as these societies emerged, so a concept and language of "the West" crystallized. And yet, we can be certain that the idea of "the West" did not simply reflect an already established Western society: rather, it was essential to the very formation of that society.

What is more, the idea of "the West," once produced, became productive in its turn. It had real effects: it enabled people to know or speak of certain things in certain ways. It produced knowledge. It became *both* the organizing factor in a system of global power relations *and* the organizing concept or term in a whole way of thinking and speaking.

The central concern […] is to analyze the formation of a particular pattern of thought and language, a "system of representation" which has the concepts of "the West" and "the Rest" at its center.

The emergence of an idea of "the West" was central to the Enlightenment […] The Enlightenment was a very European affair. European society, it assumed, was the most advanced type of society on earth, European man *(sic)* the pinnacle of human achievement. It treated the West as the result of forces largely *internal* to Europe's history and formation.

However, […] we argue that the rise of the West is also a *global* story. As Roberts observes, "'Modern' history can be defined as the approach march to the age dominated by the West" (Roberts 1985: 41). The West and the Rest became two sides of a single coin. What each now is, and what the terms we use to describe them mean, depend on the relations which were established between them long ago. The so-called uniqueness of the West was, in part, produced by Europe's contact and self-comparison with other, non-Western, societies (the Rest), very different in their histories, ecologies, patterns of development, and cultures from the European model. The difference of these other societies and cultures from the West was the standard against which the West's achievement was measured. It is within the context of these relationships that the idea of "the West" took on shape and meaning.

The importance of such perceived difference needs itself to be understood. Some modern theorists of language have argued that *meaning* always depends on the relations that exist between the different terms or words within a meaning system[…] Accordingly, we know what "night" means because it is different from—in fact, opposite to—"day." The French linguist who most influenced this approach to meaning, Ferdinand de Saussure (1857–1912), argued that the words "night" and "day" on their own can't mean anything; it is the *difference* between "night" and "day" which enables these words to carry meaning (to signify).

Likewise, many psychologists and psychoanalysts argue that an infant first learns to think of itself as a separate and unique "self" by recognizing its separation—its difference—from others (principally, of course, its mother). By analogy, national cultures acquire their strong sense of identity by contrasting themselves with other cultures. Thus, we argue, the West's sense of itself—its identity—was formed, not only by the internal processes that gradually molded Western European countries into a distinct type of society, but also through Europe's sense of difference from other worlds—how it came to represent itself in relation to these "others." In reality, differences often shade imperceptibly into each other. (When exactly does "night" become "day"? Where exactly does "being English" end and "being Scottish" begin?) But, in order to function at all, we seem to need distinct, positive concepts many of which are sharply polarized towards each other [… S]uch "binary oppositions" seem to be fundamental to all linguistic and symbolic systems and to the production of meaning itself.

This […] is about the role which "the Rest" played in the formation of the idea of "the West" and a "Western" sense of identity. At a certain moment, the fates of what had been, for many centuries, separate and distinct worlds became—some would say, fatally—harnessed together in the same historical time-frame. They became related elements in the same *discourse,* or way of speaking. They became different parts of one global social, economic, and cultural system, one interdependent world, one language.

A word of warning must be entered here. In order to bring out the distinctiveness of this "West and the Rest" discourse, I have been obliged to be selective and to simplify my representation of the West, and you should bear this in mind as you read. Terms like "the West" and "the Rest" are historical and linguistic constructs whose meanings change over time. More importantly, there are many different discourses, or ways in which the West came to speak of and represent other cultures. Some, like "the West and the Rest," were very Western-centered, or Eurocentric. Others, however, which I do not have space to discuss here, were much more culturally relativistic. I have elected to focus on what I call the discourse of "the West and the Rest" because it became a very common and influential discourse, helping to shape public perceptions and attitudes down to the present.

Another qualification concerns the very term "the West," which makes the West appear unified and homogeneous—essentially one place, with one view about other cultures and one way of speaking about them. Of course, this is not the case. The West has always contained many internal differences—between different nations, between Eastern and Western Europe, between the Germanic Northern and the Latin Southern cultures, between the Nordic, Iberian, and Mediterranean peoples, and so on. Attitudes towards other cultures within the West varied widely, as they still do between, for example, the British, the Spanish, the French, and the German.

It is also important to remember that, as well as treating non-European cultures as different and inferior, the West had its own *internal* "others." Jews, in particular, though close to Western religious traditions, were frequently excluded and ostracized. West Europeans often regarded Eastern Europeans as "barbaric," and, throughout the West, Western women were represented as inferior to Western men.

The same necessary simplification is true of my references to "the Rest." This term also covers enormous historical, cultural, and economic distinctions—for example, between the Middle East, the Far East, Africa, Latin America, indigenous North America and Australasia. It can equally encompass the simple societies of some North American Indians and the developed civilizations of China, Egypt, or Islam.

These extensive differences must be borne in mind as you study the analysis of the discourse of "the West and the Rest" in this chapter. However, we can actually use this simplification to make a point about discourse. For simplification is precisely what this discourse itself *does*. It represents what are in fact very differentiated (the different European cultures) as homogeneous (the West). And it asserts that these different cultures are united by one thing: the fact that *they are all different from the Rest*. Similarly, the Rest, though different among themselves, are represented as the same in the sense that *they are all different from the West*. In short, the discourse, as a "system of representation," *represents* the world as divided according to a simple dichotomy—the West/the Rest. That is what makes the discourse of "the West and the Rest" so destructive—it draws crude and simplistic distinctions and constructs an oversimplified conception of "difference." [...]

WHAT IS A DISCOURSE?

In common-sense language, a discourse is simply "a coherent or rational body of speech or writing; a speech, or a sermon." But here the term is being used in a more specialized way

[…] By "discourse," we mean a particular way of *representing* "the West," "the Rest," and the relations between them. A discourse is a group of statements which provide a language for talking about—i.e., a way of representing—a particular kind of knowledge about a topic. When statements about a topic are made within a particular discourse, the discourse makes it possible to construct the topic in a certain way. It also limits the other ways in which the topic can be constructed.

A discourse does not consist of one statement, but of several statements working together to form what the French social theorist, Michel Foucault (1926–84), calls a "discursive formation." […] The statements fit together because any one statement implies a relation to all the others: "They refer to the same object, share the same style and support 'a strategy … a common institutional … or political drift or pattern'" (Cousins and Hussain 1984: 84–5).

One important point about this notion of discourse is that it is not based on the conventional distinction between thought and action, language and practice. Discourse is about the production of knowledge through language. But it is itself produced by a practice: "discursive practice"—the practice of producing meaning. Since all social practices entail *meaning*, all practices have a discursive aspect. So discourse enters into and influences all social practices. Foucault would argue that the discourse of the West about the Rest was deeply implicated in practice i.e., in how the West behaved towards the Rest.

To get a fuller sense of Foucault's theory of discourse, we must bear the following points in mind.

1. A discourse can be produced by many individuals in different institutional settings (like families, prisons, hospitals, and asylums). Its integrity or "coherence" does not depend on whether or not it issues from one place or from a single speaker or "subject." Nevertheless, every discourse constructs positions from which alone it makes sense. Anyone deploying a discourse must position themselves as *if they* were the subject of the discourse. For example, we may not ourselves believe in the natural superiority of the West. But if we use the discourse of "the West and the Rest" we will necessarily find ourselves speaking from a position that holds that the West is a superior civilization. As Foucault puts it, "To describe a … statement does not consist in analysing the relations between the author and what he *[sic]* says … ; but in determining what position can and must be occupied by any individual if he is to be the subject of it [the statement]" (Foucault 1972: 95–6).
2. Discourses are not closed systems. A discourse draws on elements in other discourses, binding them into its own network of meanings. Thus […] the discourse of "Europe" drew on the earlier discourse of "Christendom," altering or translating its meaning. Traces of past discourses remain embedded in more recent discourses of "the West."
3. The statements within a discursive formation need not all be the same. But the relationships and differences between them must be regular and systematic, not random. Foucault calls this a "system of dispersion": "Whenever one can describe, between a number of statements, such a system of dispersion, whenever … one can define a regularity … [then] we will say … that we are dealing with a *discursive formation*" (Foucault 1972: 38). […]

DISCOURSE AND IDEOLOGY

A discourse is similar to what sociologists call an "ideology": a set of statements or beliefs which produce knowledge that serves the interests of a particular group or class. Why, then, use "discourse" rather than "ideology"?

One reason which Foucault gives is that ideology is based on a distinction between *true* statements about the world (science) and *false* statements (ideology), and the belief that the facts about the world help us to decide between true and false statements. But Foucault argues that statements about the social, political, or moral world are rarely ever simply true or false; and "the facts" do not enable us to decide definitively about their truth or falsehood, partly because "facts" can be construed in different ways. The very language we use to describe the so-called facts interferes in this process of finally deciding what is true, and what false.

For example, Palestinians fighting to regain land on the West Bank from Israel may be described either as "freedom fighters" or as "terrorists." It is a fact that they are fighting; but what does the fighting *mean?* The facts alone cannot decide. And the very language we use— "freedom fighters/terrorists"—is part of the difficulty. Moreover, certain descriptions, even if they appear false to us, can be *made* "true" because people act on them believing that they are true, and so their actions have real consequences. Whether the Palestinians are terrorists or not, if we think they are, and act on that "knowledge," they in effect become terrorists because we treat them as such. The language (discourse) has real effects in practice: the description becomes "true." Foucault's use of "discourse," then, is an attempt to side-step what seems an unresolvable dilemma—deciding which social discourses are true or scientific, and which false or ideological. Most social scientists now accept that our values enter into all our descriptions of the social world, and therefore most of our statements, however factual, have an ideological dimension. What Foucault would say is that knowledge of the Palestinian problem is produced by competing discourses—those of "freedom fighter" and "terrorist"—and that each is linked to a contestation over power. It is the outcome of *this* struggle which will decide the "truth" of the situation.

You can see, then, that although the concept of "discourse" side-steps the problem of truth/ falsehood in ideology, it does *not* evade the issue of power. Indeed, it gives considerable weight to questions of power since it is power, rather than the facts about reality, which make things "true": "We should admit that power produces knowledge. ... That power and knowledge directly imply one another; that there is no power relation without the correlative constitution of a field of knowledge, nor any knowledge that does not presuppose and constitute ... power relations" (Foucault 1980: 27).

CAN A DISCOURSE BE "INNOCENT"?

Could the discourse which developed in the West for talking about the Rest operate outside power? Could it be, in that sense, purely scientific—i.e., ideologically innocent? Or was it influenced by particular class interests?

Foucault is very reluctant to *reduce* discourse to statements that simply mirror the interests of a particular class. The same discourse can be used by groups with different, even contradictory, class interests. But this does *not* mean that discourse is ideologically neutral or "innocent." Take, for example, the encounter between the West and the New World. There are several reasons why this encounter could not be innocent, and therefore why the discourse which emerged in the Old World about the Rest could not be innocent either.

First, Europe brought its own cultural categories, languages, images, and ideas to the New World in order to describe and represent it. It tried to fit the New World into existing conceptual frameworks, classifying it according to its own norms, and absorbing it into Western traditions of representation. This is hardly surprising: we often draw on what we already know about the world in order to explain and describe something novel. It was never a simple matter of the West just looking, seeing, and describing the New World/the Rest without preconceptions.

Secondly, Europe had certain definite purposes, aims, objectives, motives, interests, and strategies in setting out to discover what lay across the "Green Sea of Darkness." These motives and interests were mixed. The Spanish, for example, wanted to:

a. get their hands on gold and silver,
b. claim the land for Their Catholic Majesties, and
c. convert the heathen to Christianity.

These interests often contradicted one another. But we must not suppose that what Europeans said about the New World was simply a cynical mask for their own self-interest. When King Manuel of Portugal wrote to Ferdinand and Isabella of Spain that "the principal motive of this enterprise [da Gama's voyage to India] has been … the service of God our Lord, and our own advantage" (quoted in Hale 1966: 38)—thereby neatly and conveniently bringing God and Mammon together into the same sentence—he probably saw no obvious contradiction between them. These fervently religious Catholic rulers fully believed what they were saying. To them, serving God and pursuing "our advantage" were not necessarily at odds. They lived and fully believed their own ideology.

So, while it would be wrong to attempt to reduce their statements to naked self-interest, it is clear that their discourse was molded and influenced by the play of motives and interests across their language. Of course, motives and interests are almost never wholly conscious or rational. The desires which drove the Europeans were powerful; but their power was not always subject to rational calculation. Marco Polo's "treasures of the East" were tangible enough. But the seductive power which they exerted over generations of Europeans transformed them more and more into a myth. Similarly, the gold that Columbus kept asking the natives for very soon acquired a mystical, quasi-religious significance.

Finally, the discourse of "the West and the Rest" could not be innocent because it did not represent an encounter between equals. The Europeans had outsailed, outshot, and outwitted peoples who had no wish to be "explored," no need to be "discovered," and no desire to be "exploited." The Europeans stood *vis-à-vis* the Others in positions of dominant power. This influenced what they saw and how they saw it, as well as what they did not see.

Foucault sums up these arguments as follows. Not only is discourse always implicated in *power,* discourse is one of the "systems" through which power circulates. The knowledge which a discourse produces constitutes a kind of power, exercised over those who are "known." When that knowledge is exercised in practice, those who are "known" in a particular way will be subject (i.e., subjected) to it. This is always a power-relation. (See Foucault 1980: 201.) Those who produce the discourse also have the power to *make it true*—i.e., to enforce its validity, its scientific status.

This leaves Foucault in a highly relativistic position with respect to questions of truth because his notion of discourse undermines the distinction between true and false statements—between science and ideology—to which many sociologists have subscribed. These epistemological issues (about the status of knowledge, truth, and relativism) are too complex to take further here [...] However, the important idea to grasp now is the deep and intimate relationship which Foucault establishes between discourse, knowledge, and power. According to Foucault, when power operates so as to enforce the "truth" of any set of statements, then such a discursive formation produces a "regime of truth":

> Truth isn't outside power ... Truth is a thing of this world; it is produced only *by* virtue of multiple forms of constraint ... And it induces regular effects of power. Each society has its regime of truth, its "general polities" of truth; that is, the types of discourse which it accepts and makes function as true; the mechanisms and instances which enable one to distinguish "true" and "false" statements; the means by which each is sanctioned; and the techniques and procedures accorded value in the acquisition of truth; the status of those who are charged with saying what counts as true. (Foucault 1980:131)

REFERENCES

Cousins, M. and Hussain, A. 1984: *Michel Foucault*. London: Macmillan.

Foucault, M. 1972: *The Archaeology of Knowledge*. London: Tavistock.

Foucault, M. 1980: *Power/Knowledge*. Brighton: Harvester.

Hale, J. R. et al. 1966: *Age of Exploration*. The Netherlands: Time-Life International.

Roberts, J. M. 1985: *The Triumph of the West*. London: British Broadcasting Corporation.

Disjuncture and Difference in the Global Cultural Economy

By Arjun Appadurai

The central problem of today's global interactions is the tension between cultural homogenization and cultural heterogenization. A vast array of empirical facts could be brought to bear on the side of the 'homogenization' argument, and much of it has come from the left end of the spectrum of media studies (Hamelink, 1983; Mattelart, 1983; Schiller, 1976), and some from other, less appealing, perspectives (Gans, 1985; Iyer, 1988). Most often, the homogenization argument subspeciates into either an argument about Americanization, or an argument about 'commoditization', and very often the two arguments are closely linked. What these arguments fail to consider is that at least as rapidly as forces from various metropolises are brought into new societies they tend to become indigenized in one or other way: this is true of music and housing styles as much as it is true of science and terrorism, spectacles and constitutions. The dynamics of such indigenization have just begun to be explored in a sophisticated manner (Barber, 1987; Feld, 1988; Hannerz, 1987, 1989; Ivy, 1988; Nicoll, 1989; Yoshimoto, 1989), and much more needs to be done. But it is worth noticing that for the people of Irian Jaya, Indonesianization may be more worrisome than Americanization, as Japanization may be for Koreans, Indianization for Sri Lankans, Vietnamization for the Cambodians, Russianization for the people of Soviet Armenia and the Baltic Republics. Such a list of alternative fears to Americanization could be greatly expanded, but it is not a shapeless inventory: for polities of smaller scale, there is always a fear of cultural absorption by polities of larger scale, especially those that are near by. One man's imagined community (Anderson, 1983) is another man's political prison.

This scalar dynamic, which has widespread global manifestations, is also tied to the relationship between nations and states, to which I shall return later in this essay. For the moment let us note that the simplification of these many forces (and fears) of homogenization can also be exploited by nation-states in relation to their own minorities, by posing global commoditization (or capitalism, or some other such external enemy) as more 'real' than the threat of its own hegemonic strategies.

The new global cultural economy has to be understood as a complex, overlapping, disjunctive order, which cannot any longer be understood in terms of existing center-periphery models (even those that might account for multiple centers and peripheries). Nor is it susceptible to simple models of push and pull (in terms of migration theory) or of surpluses and deficits (as in traditional models of balance of trade), or of consumers and producers (as in most neo-Marxist theories of development). Even the most complex and flexible theories of global development which have come out of the Marxist tradition (Amin, 1980; Mandel, 1978; Wallerstein, 1974; Wolf, 1982) are inadequately quirky, and they have not come to terms with what Lash and Urry (1987) have recently called 'disorganized capitalism'. The complexity of the current global economy has to do with certain fundamental disjunctures between economy, culture and politics which we have barely begun to theorize.[1]

I propose that an elementary framework for exploring such disjunctures is to look at the relationship between five dimensions of global cultural flow which can be termed: (a) ethnoscapes; (b) mediascapes; (c) technoscapes; (d) finanscapes; and (e) ideoscapes.[2] I use terms with the common suffix scape to indicate first of all that these are not objectively given relations which look the same from every angle of vision, but rather that they are deeply perspectival constructs, inflected very much by the historical, linguistic and political situatedness of different sorts of actors: nation-states, multinationals, diasporic communities, as well as sub-national groupings and movements (whether religious, political or economic), and even intimate face-to-face groups, such as villages, neighborhoods and families. Indeed, the individual actor is the last locus of this perspectival set of landscapes, for these landscapes are eventually navigated by agents who both experience and constitute larger formations, in part by their own sense of what these landscapes offer. These landscapes thus, are the building blocks of what, extending Benedict Anderson, I would like to call 'imagined worlds', that is, the multiple worlds which are constituted by the historically situated imaginations of persons and groups spread around the globe (Appadurai, 1989). An important fact of the world we live in today is that many persons on the globe live in such imagined 'worlds' and not just in imagined communities, and thus are able to contest and sometimes even subvert the 'imagined worlds' of the official mind and of the entrepreneurial mentality that surround them. The suffix scape also allows us to point to the fluid, irregular shapes of these landscapes, shapes which characterize international capital as deeply as they do international clothing styles.

By 'ethnoscape', I mean the landscape of persons who constitute the shifting world in which we live: tourists, immigrants, refugees, exiles, guest workers and other moving groups and persons constitute an essential feature of the world, and appear to affect the politics of and between nations to a hitherto unprecedented degree. This is not to say that there are not anywhere relatively stable communities and networks, of kinship, of friendship, of work and of leisure, as well as of birth, residence and other filiative forms. But it is to say that the warp of these stabilities is everywhere shot through with the woof of human motion, as more persons and groups deal with the realities of having to move, or the fantasies of wanting to move. What is more, both these realities as well as these fantasies now function on larger scales, as men and women from villages in India think not just of moving to Poona or Madras, but of moving to Dubai and Houston, and refugees from Sri Lanka find themselves in South India as well as in Canada, just as the Hmong are driven to London as well as to Philadelphia. And as international capital shifts its needs, as production and technology generate different needs, as nation-states shift their policies on refugee populations, these moving groups can never afford to let their imaginations rest too long, even if they wished to.

By 'technoscape', I mean the global configuration, also ever fluid, of technology, and of the fact that technology, both high and low, both mechanical and informational, now moves at high speeds across various kinds of previously impervious boundaries. Many countries now are the roots of multinational enterprise: a huge steel complex in Libya may involve interests from India, China, Russia and Japan, providing different components of new technological configurations. The odd distribution of technologies, and thus the peculiarities of these technoscapes, are increasingly driven not by any obvious economies of scale, of political control, or of market rationality, but of increasingly complex relationships between money flows, political possibilities and the availability of both low and highly-skilled labor. So, while India exports waiters and chauffeurs to Dubai and Sharjah, it also exports software engineers to the United States (indentured briefly to Tata-Burroughs or the World Bank), then laundered through the State Department to become wealthy 'resident aliens', who are in turn objects of seductive messages to invest their money and know-how in federal and state projects in India. The global economy can still be described in terms of traditional 'indicators' (as the World Bank continues to do) and studied in terms of traditional comparisions (as in Project Link at the University of Pennsylvania), but the complicated technoscapes (and the shifting ethnoscapes), which underlie these 'indicators' and 'comparisions' are further out of the reach of the 'queen of the social sciences' than ever before. How is one to make a meaningful comparision of wages in Japan and the United States, or of real estate costs in New York and Tokyo, without taking sophisticated account of the very complex fiscal and investment flows that link the two economies through a global grid of currency speculation and capital transfer?

Thus it is useful to speak as well of 'finanscapes', since the disposition of global capital is now a more mysterious, rapid and difficult landscape to follow than ever before, as currency markets, national stock exchanges, and commodity speculations move mega-monies through national turnstiles at blinding speed, with vast absolute implications for small differences in percentage points and time units. But the critical point is that the global relationship between ethnoscapes, technoscapes and finanscapes is deeply disjunctive and profoundly unpredictable, since each of these landscapes is subject to its own constraints and incentives (some political, some informational and some techno-environmental), at the same time as each acts as a constraint and a parameter for movements in the other. Thus, even an elementary model of global political economy must take into account the shifting relationship between perspectives on human movement, technological flow, and financial transfers, which can accommodate their deeply disjunctive relationships with one another.

Built upon these disjunctures (which hardly form a simple, mechanical global 'infrastructure' in any case) are what I have called 'mediascapes' and 'ideoscapes', though the latter two are closely related landscapes of images. 'Mediascapes' refer both to the distribution of the electronic capabilities to produce and disseminate information (newspapers, magazines, television stations, film production studios, etc.), which are now available to a growing number of private and public interests throughout the world; and to the images of the world created by these media. These images of the world involve many complicated inflections, depending on their mode (documentary or entertainment), their hardware (electronic or pre-electronic), their audiences (local, national or transnational) and the interests of those who own and control them. What is most important about these mediascapes is that they provide (especially in their television, film and cassette forms) large and complex repertoires of images, narratives and 'ethnoscapes' to viewers throughout the world, in which the world of commodities and the world of 'news' and politics are profoundly mixed. What this means is that many audiences throughout the world experience the media themselves as a complicated and interconnected repertoire of print, celluloid, electronic screens and billboards. The lines between the 'realistic' and the fictional landscapes they see are blurred, so that the further away these audiences are from the direct experiences of metropolitan life, the more likely they are to construct 'imagined worlds' which are chimerical, aesthetic, even fantastic objects, particularly if assessed by the criteria of some other perspective, some other 'imagined world'.

'Mediascapes', whether produced by private or state interests, tend to be image-centered, narrative-based accounts of strips of reality, and what they offer to those who experience and transform them is a series of elements (such as characters, plots and textual forms) out of which scripts can be formed of imagined lives, their own as well as those of others living in other places. These scripts can and do get disaggregated into complex sets of metaphors by which people live (Lakoff and Johnson, 1980) as they help to constitute narratives of the 'other' and proto-narratives of possible lives, fantasies which could become prologemena to the desire for acquisition and movement.

'Ideoscsapes' are also concatenations of images, but they are often directly political and frequently have to do with the ideologies of states and the counter-ideologies of movements explicitly oriented to capturing state power or a piece of it. These ideoscapes are composed of elements of the Enlightenment world-view, which consists of a concatenation of ideas, terms and images, including 'freedom', 'welfare', 'rights', 'sovereignty', 'representation' and the master-term 'democracy'. The master-narrative of the Enlightenment (and its many variants in England, France and the United States) was constructed with a certain internal logic and presupposed a certain relationship between reading, representation and the public sphere (for the dynamics of this process in the early history of the United States, see Warner, 1990). But their diaspora across the world, especially since the nineteenth century, has loosened the internal coherence which held these terms and images together in a Euro-American master-narrative, and provided in-stead a loosely structured synopticon of politics, in which different nation-states, as part of their evolution, have organized their political cultures around different 'keywords' (Williams, 1976).

As a result of the differential diaspora of these keywords, the political narratives that govern communication between elites and followings in different parts of the world involve problems of both a semantic and a pragmatic nature: semantic to the extent that words (and their lexical equivalents) require careful translation from context to context in their global movements; and pragmatic to the extent that the use of these words by political actors and their audiences may be subject to very different sets of contextual conventions that mediate their translation into public politics. Such conventions are not only matters of the nature of political rhetoric (viz. what does the aging Chinese leadership mean when it refers to the dangers of hooliganism? What does the South Korean leadership mean when it speaks of 'discipline' as the key to democratic industrial growth?).

These conventions also involve the far more subtle question of what sets of communica-tive genres are valued in what way (newspapers versus cinema for example) and what sorts of pragmatic genre conventions govern the collective 'readings' of different kinds of text. So, while an Indian audience may be attentive to the resonances of a political speech in terms of some key words and phrases reminiscent of Hindi cinema, a Korean audience may respond to the subtle codings of Buddhist or neo-Confucian rhetorical strategy encoded in a political document. The very relationship of reading to hearing and seeing may vary in important ways that determine the morphology of these different 'ideoscapes' as they shape themselves in different national and transnational contexts. This globally variable synaesthesia has hardly even been noted, but it demands urgent analysis. Thus 'democracy' has clearly become a master-term, with powerful echoes from Haiti and Poland to the Soviet Union and China, but it sits at the center of a variety of ideoscapes (composed of distinctive pragmatic configurations of rough 'translations' of other central terms from the vocabulary of the Enlightenment). This creates ever new terminological kaleidoscopes, as states (and the groups that seek to capture them) seek to pacify populations whose own ethnoscapes are in motion, and whose mediascapes may create severe problems for the ideoscapes with which they are presented. The fluidity of ideoscapes is complicated in particular by the growing diasporas (both voluntary and involuntary) of intellectuals who continuously inject new meaning-streams into the discourse of democracy in different parts of the world.

This extended terminological discussion of the five terms I have coined sets the basis for a tentative formulation about the conditions under which current global flows occur: *they occur in and through the growing disjunctures between ethnoscapes, technoscapes, finanscapes, mediascapes and ideoscapes*. This formulation, the core of my model of global cultural flow, needs some explanation. First, people, machinery, money, images, and ideas now follow increasingly non-isomorphic paths: of course, at all periods in human history, there have been some disjunctures between the flows of these things, but the sheer speed, scale and volume of each of these flows is now so great that the disjunctures have become central to the politics of global culture. The Japanese are notoriously hospitable to ideas and are stereotyped as inclined to export (all) and import (some) goods, but they are also notoriously closed to immigration, like the Swiss, the Swedes and the Saudis. Yet the Swiss and Saudis accept populations of guestworkers, thus creating labor diasporas of Turks, Italians and other circum-mediterranean groups. Some such guestworker groups maintain continuous contact with their home-nations, like the Turks, but others, like high-level South Asian migrants tend to desire lives in their new homes, raising anew the problem of reproduction in a deterritorialized context.

Deterritorialization, in general, is one of the central forces of the modern world, since it brings laboring populations into the lower class sectors and spaces of relatively wealthy societies, while sometimes creating exaggerated and intensified senses of criticism or attachment to politics in the home-state. Deterritorialization, whether of Hindus, Sikhs, Palestinians or Ukranians, is now at the core of a variety of global fundamentalisms, including Islamic and Hindu fundamentalism. In the Hindu case for example (Appadurai and Breckenridge, forthcoming) it is clear that the overseas movement of Indians has been exploited by a variety of interests both within and outside India to create a complicated network of finances and religious identifications, in which the problems of cultural reproduction for Hindus abroad has become tied to the politics of Hindu fundamentalism at home.

At the same time, deterritorialization creates new markets for film companies, art impressarios and travel agencies, who thrive on the need of the deterritorialized population for contact with its homeland. Naturally, these invented homelands, which constitute the mediascapes of deterritorialized groups, can often become sufficiently fantastic and one-sided that they provide the material for new ideoscapes in which ethnic conflicts can begin to erupt. The creation of

'Khalistan', an invented homeland of the deterritorialized Sikh population of England, Canada and the United States, is one example of the bloody potential in such mediascapes, as they interact with the 'internal colonialisms' (Hechter, 1974) of the nation-state. The West Bank, Namibia and Eritrea are other theaters for the enactment of the bloody negotiation between existing nation-states and various deterritorialized groupings.

The idea of deterritorialization may also be applied to money and finance, as money managers seek the best markets for their investments, independent of national boundaries. In turn, these movements of monies are the basis of new kinds of conflict, as Los Angelenos worry about the Japanese buying up their city, and people in Bombay worry about the rich Arabs from the Gulf States who have not only transformed the prices of mangoes in Bombay, but have also substantially altered the profile of hotels, restaurants and other services in the eyes of the local population, just as they continue to do in London. Yet, most residents of Bombay are ambivalent about the Arab presence there, for the flip side of their presence is the absence of friends and kinsmen earning big money in the Middle East and bringing back both money and luxury commodities to Bombay and other cities in India. Such commodities transform consumer taste in these cities, and also often end up smuggled through air and sea ports and peddled in the gray markets of Bombay's streets. In these gray markets, some members of Bombay's middle-classes and of its lumpenproletariat can buy some of these goods, ranging from cartons of Marlboro cigarettes, to Old Spice shaving cream and tapes of Madonna. Similarly gray routes, often subsidized by the moonlighting activities of sailors, diplomats, and airline stewardesses who get to move in and out of the country regularly, keep the gray markets of Bombay, Madras and Calcutta filled with goods not only from the West, but also from the Middle East, Hong Kong and Singapore.

It is this fertile ground of deterritorialization, in which money, commodities and persons are involved in ceaselessly chasing each other around the world, that the mediascapes and ideoscapes of the modern world find their fractured and fragmented counterpart. For the ideas and images produced by mass media often are only partial guides to the goods and experiences that deterritorialized populations transfer to one another. In Mira Nair's brilliant film, *India Cabaret*, we see the multiple loops of this fractured deterritorialization as young women, barely competent in Bombay's metropolitan glitz, come to seek their fortunes as cabaret dancers and prostitutes in Bombay, entertaining men in clubs with dance formats derived wholly from the prurient dance sequences of Hindi films. These scenes cater in turn to ideas about Western and foreign women and their 'looseness', while they provide tawdry career alibis for these women. Some of these women come from Kerala, where cabaret clubs and the pornograpic film industry have blossomed, partly in response to the purses and tastes of Keralites returned from the Middle East, where their diasporic lives away from women distort their very sense of what the relations between men and women might be. These tragedies of displacement could certainly be replayed in a more detailed analysis of the relations between the Japanese and German sex tours to Thailand and the tragedies of the sex trade in Bangkok, and in other similar loops which tie together fantasies about the other, the conveniences and seductions of travel, the economics of global trade and the brutal mobility fantasies that dominate gender politics in many parts of Asia and the world at large.

While far more could be said about the cultural politics of deterritorialization and the larger sociology of displacement that it expresses, it is appropriate at this juncture to bring in the role of the nation-state in the disjunctive global economy of culture today. The relationship between states and nations is everywhere an embattled one. It is possible to say that in many societies, the nation and the state have become one another's projects. That is, while nations (or more properly groups with ideas about nationhood) seek to capture or co-opt states and state power, states simultaneously seek to capture and monopolize ideas about nationhood (Baruah, 1986; Chatterjee, 1986; Nandy, 1989). In general, separatist, transnational movements, including those which have included terror in their methods, exemplify nations in search of states: Sikhs, Tamil Sri Lankans, Basques, Moros, Quebecois, each of these represent imagined communities which seek to create states of their own or carve pieces out of existing states. States, on the other hand, are everywhere seeking to monopolize the moral resources of community, either by flatly claiming perfect coevality between nation and state, or by systematically museumizing and representing all the groups within them in a variety of heritage politics that seems remarkably uniform throughout the world (Handler, 1988; Herzfeld, 1982; McQueen, 1988). Here, national and international mediascapes are exploited by nation-states to pacify separatists or even the potential fissiparousness of all ideas of difference. Typically, contemporary nation-states do this by exercising taxonomical control over difference; by creating various kinds of international spectacle to domesticate difference; and by seducing small groups with the fantasy of self-display on some sort of global or cosmopolitan stage. One important new feature of global cultural politics, tied to the disjunctive relationships between the various landscapes discussed earlier, is that state and nation are at each's throats, and the hyphen that links them is now less an icon of conjuncture than an index of disjuncture. This disjunctive relationship between nation and state has two levels: at the level of any given nation-state, it means that there is a battle of the imagination, with state and nation seeking to cannibalize one another. Here is the seedbed of brutal separatisms, majoritarianisms that seem to have appeared from nowhere, and micro-identities that have become political projects within the nation-state. At another level, this disjunctive relationship is deeply entangled with the global disjunctures discussed throughout this essay: ideas of nationhood appear to be steadily increasing in scale and regularly crossing existing state boundaries: sometimes, as with the Kurds, because previous identities stretched across vast national spaces, or, as with the Tamils in Sri Lanka, the dormant threads of a transnational diaspora have been activated to ignite the micro-politics of a nation-state.

In discussing the cultural politics that have subverted the hyphen that links the nation to the state, it is especially important not to forget its mooring in the irregularities that now characterize 'disorganized capital' (Lash and Urry, 1987; Kothari, 1989). It is because labor, finance and technology are now so widely separated that the volatilities that underlie movements for nationhood (as large as transnational Islam on the one hand, or as small as the movement of the Gurkhas for a separate state in the North-East of India) grind against the vulnerabilities which characterize the relationships between states. States find themselves pressed to stay 'open' by the forces of media, technology, and travel which had fueled consumerism throughout the world and have increased the craving, even in the non-Western world, for new commodities and spectacles. On the other hand, these very cravings can become caught up in new ethnoscapes, mediascapes, and eventually, ideoscapes, such as 'democracy' in China, that the state cannot tolerate as threats to its own control over ideas of nationhood and 'peoplehood'. States throughout the world are under siege, especially where contests over the ideoscapes of democracy are fierce and fundamental, and where there are radical disjunctures between ideoscapes and technoscapes (as in the case of very small countries that lack contemporary technologies of production and information); or between ideoscapes and financscapes (as in countries, such as

Mexico or Brazil where international lending influences national politics to a very large degree); or between ideoscapes and ethnoscapes (as in Beirut, where diasporic, local and translocal filiations are suicidally at battle); or between ideoscapes and mediascapes (as in many countries in the Middle East and Asia) where the lifestyles represented on both national and international TV and cinema completely overwhelm and undermine the rhetoric of national politics: in the Indian case, the myth of the law-breaking hero has emerged to mediate this naked struggle between the pieties and the realities of Indian politics, which has grown increasingly brutalized and corrupt (Vachani, 1989).

The transnational movement of the martial-arts, particularly through Asia, as mediated by the Hollywood and Hongkong film industries (Zarilli, forthcoming) is a rich illustration of the ways in which long-standing martial arts traditions, reformulated to meet the fantasies of contemporary (sometimes lumpen) youth populations, create new cultures of masculinity and violence, which are in turn the fuel for increased violence in national and international politics. Such violence is in turn the spur to an increasingly rapid and amoral arms trade which penetrates the entire world. The worldwide spread of the AK-47 and the Uzi, in films, in corporate and state security, in terror, and in police and military activity, is a reminder that apparently simple technical uniformities often conceal an increasingly complex set of loops, linking images of violence to aspirations for community in some 'imagined world'.

Returning then to the 'ethnoscapes' with which I began, the central paradox of ethnic politics in today's world is that primordia, (whether of language or skin color or neighborhood or of kinship) have become globalized. That is, sentiments whose greatest force is in their ability to ignite intimacy into a political sentiment and turn locality into a staging ground for identity, have become spread over vast and irregular spaces, as groups move, yet stay linked to one another through sophisticated media capabilities. This is not to deny that such primordia are often the product of invented traditions (Hobsbawm and Ranger, 1983) or retrospective affiliations, but to emphasize that because of the disjunctive and unstable interplay of commerce, media, national policies and consumer fantasies, ethnicity, once a genie contained in the bottle of some sort of locality (however large) has now become a global force, forever slipping in and through the cracks between states and borders.

But the relationship between the cultural and economic levels of this new set of global disjunctures is not a simple one-way street in which the terms of global cultural politics are set wholly by, or confined wholly within, the vicissitudes of international flows of technology, labor and finance, demanding only a modest modification of existing neo-Marxist models of uneven development and state-formation. There is a deeper change, itself driven by the disjunctures between all the landscapes I have discussed, and constituted by their continuously fluid and uncertain interplay, which concerns the relationship between production and consumption in today's global economy. Here I begin with Marx's famous (and often mined) view of the fetishism of the commodity, and suggest that this fetishism has been replaced in the world at large (now seeing the world as one, large, interactive system, composed of many complex subsystems) by two mutually supportive descendants, the first of which I call production fetishism, and the second of which I call the fetishism of the consumer.

By production fetishism I mean an illusion created by contemporary transnational production loci, which masks translocal capital, transnational earning-flows, global management and often faraway workers (engaged in various kinds of high-tech putting out operations) in the idiom and spectacle of local (sometimes even worker) control, national productivity and territorial sovereignty. To the extent that various kinds of Free Trade Zone have become the models for production at large, especially of high-tech commodities, production has itself become a fetish, masking not social relations as such, but the relations of production, which are increasingly transnational. The locality (both in the sense of the local factory or site of production and in the extended sense of the nation-state) becomes a fetish which disguises the globally dispersed forces that actually drive the production process. This generates alienation (in Marx's sense) twice intensified, for its social sense is now compounded by a complicated spatial dynamic which is increasingly global.

As for the fetishism of the consumer, I mean to indicate here that the consumer has been transformed, through commodity flows (and the mediascapes, especially of advertising, that accompany them) into a sign, both in Baudrillard's sense of a simulacrum which only asymptotically approaches the form of a real social agent; and in the sense of a mask for the real seat of agency, which is not the consumer but the producer and the many forces that constitute production. Global advertising is the key technology for the worldwide dissemination of a plethora of creative, and culturally well-chosen, ideas of consumer agency. These images of agency are increasingly distortions of a world of merchandising so subtle that the consumer is consistently helped to believe that he or she is an actor, where in fact he or she is at best a chooser.

The globalization of culture is not the same as its homogenization, but globalization involves the use of a variety of instruments of homogenization (armaments, advertising techniques, language hegemonies, clothing styles and the like), which are absorbed into local political and cultural economies, only to be repatriated as heterogeneous dialogues of national sovereignty, free enterprise, fundamentalism, etc. in which the state plays an increasingly delicate role: too much openness to global flows and the nation-state is threatened by revolt—the China syndrome; too little, and the state exits the international stage, as Burma, Albania and North Korea, in various ways have done. In general, the state has become the arbiter of this *repatriation of difference* (in the form of goods, signs, slogans, styles, etc.). But this repatriation or export of the designs and commodities of difference continuously exacerbates the 'internal' politics of majoritarianism and homogenization, which is most frequently played out in debates over heritage.

Thus the central feature of global culture today is the politics of the mutual effort of sameness and difference to cannibalize one another and thus to proclaim their successful hijacking of the twin Enlightenment ideas of the triumphantly universal and the resiliently particular. This mutual cannibalization shows its ugly face in riots, in refugee-flows, in state-sponsored torture and in ethnocide (with or without state support). Its brighter side is in the expansion of many individual horizons of hope and fantasy, in the global spread of oral rehydration therapy and other low-tech instruments of well-being, in the susceptibility even of South Africa to the force of global opinion, in the inability of the Polish state to repress its own working-classes, and in the growth of a wide range of progressive, transnational alliances. Examples of both sorts could be multiplied. The critical point is that both sides of the coin of global cultural process today are products of the infinitely varied mutual contest of sameness and difference on a stage characterized by radical disjunctures between different sorts of global flows and the uncertain landscapes created in and through these disjunctures.

NOTES

A longer version of this essay appears in *Public Culture 2* (2), Spring 1990. This longer version sets the present formulation in the context of global cultural traffic in earlier historical periods, and draws out some of its implications for the study of cultural forms more generally.

1. One major exception is Fredric Jameson, whose (1984) essay on the relationship between postmodernism and late capitalism has in many ways, inspired this essay. However, the debate between Jameson (1986) and Ahmad (1987) in *Social Text* shows that the creation of a globalizing Marxist narrative, in cultural matters, is difficult territory indeed. My own effort, in this context, is to begin a restructuring of the Marxist narrative (by stressing lags and disjunctures) that many Marxists might find abhorrent. Such a restructuring has to avoid the dangers of obliterating difference within the 'third world', of eliding the social referent (as some French postmodernists seem inclined to do) and of retaining the narrative authority of the Marxist tradition, in favor of greater attention to global fragmentation, uncertainty and difference.

2. These ideas are argued more fully in a book I am currently working on, tentatively entitled *Imploding Worlds: Imagination and Disjuncture in the Global Cultural Economy*.

REFERENCES

Ahmad, A. (1987) 'Jameson's Rhetoric of Otherness and the "National Allegory"', *Social Text* 17: 3–25.

Amin, S. (1980) *Class and Nation: Historically and in the Current Crisis*. New York and London: Monthly Review.

Anderson, B. (1983) *Imagined Communities: Reflections on the Origin and Spread of Nationalism*. London: Verso.

Appadurai, A. (1989) 'Global Ethnoscapes: Notes and Queries for a Transnational Anthropology', in R. G. Fox (ed.), *Interventions: Anthropology of the Present*.

Appadurai, A. and Breckenridge, C.A. (forthcoming) *A Transnational Culture in the Making: The Asian Indian Diaspora in the United States*. London: Berg.

Barber, K. (1987) 'Popular Arts in Africa', *African Studies Review* 30(3).

Baruah, S. (1986) 'Immigration, Ethnic Conflict and Political Turmoil, Assam 1979–1985', *Asian Survey* 26 (11).

Chatterjee, P. (1986) *Nationalist Thought and the Colonial World: A Derivative Discourse*. London: Zed Books.

Feld, S. (1988) 'Notes on World Beat', *Public Culture* 1(1): 31–7.

Gans, Eric (1985) *The End of Culture: Toward a Generative Anthropology*. Berkeley: University of California.

Hamelink, C. (1983) *Cultural Autonomy in Global Communications*. New York: Longman.

Handler, R. (1988) *Nationalism and the Politics of Culture in Quebec*. Madison: University of Wisconsin.

Hannerz, U. (1987) 'The World in Creolization', *Africa* 57(4): 546–59.

Hannerz, U. (1989) 'Notes on the Global Ecumene', *Public Culture* 1(2): 66–75.

Hechter, M. (1974) *Internal Colonialism: The Celtic Fringe in British National Development, 1536–1966*. Berkeley and Los Angeles: University of California.

Herzfeld, M. (1982) *Ours Once More: Folklore, Ideology and the Making of Modern Greece*. Austin: University of Texas.

Hobsbawm, E. and Ranger, T. (eds) (1983) *The Invention of Tradition*. New York: Columbia University Press.

Ivy, M. (1988) 'Tradition and Difference in the Japanese Mass Media', *Public Culture* 1(1): 21–9.

Iyer, P. (1988) *Video Night in Kathmandu*. New York: Knopf.

Jameson, F. (1984) 'Postmodernism, or the Cultural Logic of Late Capitalism', *New Left Review* 146 (July–August): 53–92.

Jameson, F. (1986) 'Third World Literature in the Era of Multi-National Capitalism', *Social Text* 15 (Fall): 65–88.

Kothari, R. (1989) *State Against Democracy: In Search of Humane Governance*. New York: New Horizons.

Lakoff, G. and Johnson, M. (1980) *Metaphors We Live By*. Chicago and London: University of Chicago.

Lash, S. and Urry, J. (1987) *The End of Organized Capitalism*. Madison: University of Wisconsin.

McQueen, H. (1988) 'The Australian Stamp: Image, Design and Ideology', *Arena* 84 Spring: 78–96.

Mandel, E. (1978) *Late Capitalism*. London: Verso.

Mattelart, A. (1983) *Transnational and Third World: The Struggle for Culture*. South Hadley, MA: Bergin and Garvey.

Nandy, A. (1989) 'The Political Culture of the Indian State', *Daedalus* 118(4): 1–26.

Nicoll, F. (1989) 'My Trip to Alice', *Criticism, Heresy and Interpretation (CHAI)*, 3: 21–32.

Schiller, H. (1976) *Communication and Cultural Domination*. White Plains, NY: International Arts and Sciences.

Vachani, L. (1989) 'Narrative, Pleasure and Ideology in the Hindi Film: An Analysis of the Outsider Formula', MA thesis, The Annenberg School of Communication, The University of Pennsylvania.

Wallerstein, I. (1974) *The Modern World-System* (2 volumes). New York and London: Academic Press.

Warner, M. (1990) *The Letters of the Republic: Publication and the Public Sphere*. Cambridge, MA: Harvard.

Williams, R. (1976) *Keywords*. New York: Oxford.

Wolf, E. (1982) *Europe and the People Without History*. Berkeley: University of California.

Yoshimoto, M. (1989) 'The Postmodern and Mass Images in Japan', *Public Culture* 1(2): 8–25.

Zarilli, P. (Forthcoming) 'Repositioning the Body: An Indian Martial Art and its Pan-Asian Publics' in C.A. Breckenridge, (ed.), *Producing the Postcolonial: Trajectories to Public Culture in India*.

The New International Information Order

By Sean MacBride and Colleen Roach

Resolutions, meetings, and manifestos calling for a "new order" in international information structures and policies became a feature of the world scene in the early 1970s and often generated intense dispute. The original impulse came from the nonaligned nations, many of which had gained independence in the postwar years. To many the euphoria of independence was turning to a sense of disillusionment. In spite of international assistance programs, the economic situation in many developing countries had not improved, and in some it had actually deteriorated. For certain countries foreign trade earnings could not cover interest due on foreign loans. These same years witnessed the rapid development of new communications media, and the era was constantly characterized as the Information Age—one in which information would be a key to power and affluence. To the developing countries it was increasingly clear that the "flow of information" (a term that seemed to subsume ideas and attitudes and followed a one-way direction from rich to poor countries) was dominated by multinational entities based in the most powerful nations. The resulting disparities tended to set the framework for discussion even within developing countries. Clearly political independence was not matched by independence in the economic and sociocultural spheres. A number of nonaligned countries saw themselves as victims of "cultural colonialism." The imbalances it involved, and what might be done about them, became the focus of debate for the nonaligned countries.

EVOLUTION OF THE DEBATE

The nonaligned nations movement took form in 1955 at a meeting in Bandung, Indonesia, that brought together world leaders from Asia and Africa. Subsequent meetings—in some cases, summit meetings of nonaligned leaders—were held in Bangkok, Algiers, Tunis, Havana, and elsewhere. During the 1970s the membership grew to more than 90 countries plus several regional groups and represented a majority in various United Nations bodies, with strong influence over their agendas. These UN agencies embraced a "development ideology," meaning that high priority would be given to the development needs of the Third World.

A nonaligned summit held in Algiers in 1973 adopted a resolution calling for a "new international economic order," which was endorsed the following year by the UN General Assembly. This served as precedent and model for a similar resolution focusing on information, which was articulated as a 1976 nonaligned news symposium in Tunis. A leading figure at this meeting was Mustapha Masmoudi, Tunisian secretary of state for information, who demanded a reorganization of existing communication channels that are a legacy of the colonial past. This "decolonization" of information, he said, must lead to a "new order in information matters." In subsequent meetings this phrase evolved into *a new international information order* and, at a later stage, into *a new world information and communication order*.

That same year UNESCO's General Conference in Nairobi also discussed information issues, in a context that produced sharp confrontation between the interests of developed and developing countries. The focus was on free-flow-of-information doctrine. UNESCO's mandate in the area of communications is explicit in its constitution, adopted in 1946, which enjoined the agency to "collaborate in the work of advancing the mutual knowledge and understanding of peoples, through all means of mass communication and to that end recommend the free flow of Ideas by word and image." The free-flow doctrine was, developed by the United States and other Western nations after World War II. As viewed, by supporters, the unhampered flow of information would be a means of promoting, peace and understanding and spreading technical advances. The doctrine had ties with other Western libertarian principles such as freedom of the press. However, critics of the doctrine came to view it as part of a global strategy for domination of communication markets and for ideological control by the industrialized nations. They saw it as serving the interests of the most powerful countries and transnational corporations and helping them secure economic and cultural domination of less powerful, nations. A rewording of the doctrine was urged by nonaligned spokespersons calling for a free *and balanced* flow of information. The suggestion stirred deep suspicion in developed countries. If it meant that Third World nations would ordain a proper balance and control or limit the flow, this would be—according to Western spokespersons—the very antithesis of a free flow. "Free and balanced flow" and "free flow" seemed at this meeting to be irreconcilable concepts.

An important outcome of this 1976 UNESCO meeting was the appointment by Amadou-Mahtar M'Bow, Director-General of UNESCO, of a 16-person commission—broadly representative of the world's economic and geographic spectrum and headed by Sean MacBride of Ireland—to study "the totality of communication problems in modern societies." Its members held different opinions about what sort of new order was needed but all were in agreement that the existing information order was far from satisfactory. They began their work late in 1977 and, after two years of fact-gathering committee hearings, and debate, submitted their final report—known as the MacBride Report—to the 1980 UNESCO General Conference in Belgrade. Published in English as *Many Voices, One World*, It has been translated yo many languages. Along with a resolution adopted at the same conference confirming UNESCO's support for a *new information and communication order* (see table 40.1), the report became the focus of debate during the following years—a rallying point as well as a target for attack.

Table 40.1 Resolution 4/19 adopted by the Twenty-first Session of the UNESCO General Conference, Belgrade, 1980

The General Conference considers that

(a) this new world information and communication order could be based among other considerations, on:

(i) elimination of the imbalances and inequalities which characterize the present situation;

(ii) elimination of the negative effects of certain monopolies, public or private, and excessive concentrations;

(iii) removal of the internal and external obstacles to a free flow and wider and better balanced dissemination of information and ideas;

(iv) plurality of sources and channels of information;

(v) freedom of the press and of information;

(vi) the freedom of journalists and all professionals in the communication media, a freedom inseparable from responsibility;

(vii) the capacity of developing countries to achieve improvement of their own situations, notably by providing their own equipment, by training their personnel, by improving their infrastructures and making their information and communication media suitable to their needs and aspirations;

(viii) the sincere will of developed countries to help them attain these objectives;

(ix) respect for each people's cultural identity and for the right of each nation to inform the world about its interests, its aspirations and its social and cultural values;

(x) respect for the right of all peoples to participate in international exchanges of information on the basis of equality, justice and mutual benefit;

(xi) respect for the right of the public, of ethnic and social groups and of individuals to have access to information sources and to participate actively in the communication process;

(b) this new world information and communication order should be based on the fundamental principles of international law, as laid down in the Charter of the United Nations;

(c) diverse solutions to information and communication problems are required because social, political, cultural and economic problems differ from one country to another and, within a given country, from one group to another.

THEMES

The debate had at first centered on the news-flow question. The major Western international news services—AP and UPI of the United States, the French Agence France Presse, and Reuters of the United Kingdom—were consistently described as having *monopoly* control over the flow of news to and from developing countries, and exercising it from a limited perspective reflecting the economic and cultural interests of the industrialized nations. Expressions such as "coups and earthquakes" were frequently used to describe reporting of Third World events. In 1976 Indira Gandhi the prime minister of India, expressed the prevailing view: "We want to hear Africans on events in Africa. You should similarly be able to get an Indian explanation of events in India. It is astonishing that we know so little about leading poets, novelists, historians, and editors of various Asian, African, and Latin American countries while we are familiar with minor authors and columnists of Europe and America." The need for policies and structures to develop communications between developing nations (sometimes referred to as "South-South dialogue") was constantly stressed.

The flow of television programming, including *entertainment* programming, was soon incorporated into the debate, in large measure owing to a study conducted by two Finnish researchers, Kaarle Nordenstreng and Tapia Varis, and published by UNESCO in 1974. The study demonstrated that a few Western nations controlled the international flow of television programs, with the United States, the United Kingdom, France, and the Federal Republic of Germany accounting for the largest shares. The implications of this domination, in both financial and ideological terms, received increasing attention.

The integration of television with new technologies such as the communications *satellite*—including direct broadcast satellites—and telecommunications networks that were channels for an increasing volume of transborder data flow difficult or impossible to control, extended the range of topics covered in the debate. Here the questions also included imbalances in the assignment of spectrum frequencies and of orbital slots for future satellites.

The international flow of *advertising*, under similar multinational controls, was another issue that entered the debate, It was described by many as furthering not only products and services but also a way of life, generally centered on the acquisition of consumer goods. Some saw this as diverting attention from necessities to luxuries, and others saw it as a serious threat to indigenous culture.

In 1978 a new element was added to the debates with the passage of a UNESCO Declaration on the Mass Media. It was the result of six years of negotiation to achieve a consensus text, which finally carried the title *The Declaration of Fundamental Principles concerning the Contribution of the Mass Media to Strengthening Peace and International Understanding, to the Promotion of Human Rights and to Countering Racialism, Apartheid and Incitement to War*. Regarded by the nonaligned nations as furthering the new order movement, it was the first international instrument referring directly to moral, social, and professional responsibilities of mass media in the context of "the universally recognized principles of freedom of expression information and opinion." Hovering over the debate once again was the issue of the role of government. The final version of the resolution did not include because of Western demands—proposals to make national governments responsible for the actions of communications companies working within their jurisdictions.

COLLISION COURSE

In the early 1980s the nature of the debate underwent decisive changes. Nonaligned nations were no longer as unified as they had been; amid a widespread economic recession some leaned toward a more militant, others toward a more conciliatory, stance. Differences in political systems came more sharply into, focus. In the developed nations a trend toward *deregulation* of information media and attention of public-sector enterprises was gaining momentum. The industrialized nations were increasingly attentive to information markets, including those in the Third World. Because the continued growth of the private sector seemed vital to this strategy, "government-controlled media" were viewed as particularly ominous.

The importance of this issue was evident at a 1981 UNESCO-sponsored meeting on the protection of journalists. For two decades attempts had been made by international organizations of journalists and publishers—such as the International Federation of Journalists, the International Federation of Newspaper Editors, and the International Press Institute—to draft and have adopted an international convention for the protection of journalists. At the UNESCO meeting the concerns of the journalists' organizations were quickly obscured by the recurring issue of the role of governments, this time revolving around licensing. Most governments were prepared to recognize the importance of safeguarding journalists, even though few seemed to cherish the activities of "investigative reporters." The status of journalists and the special protections proposed for them would presumably be based on professional credentials—but issued by whom? In raising this issue, Third World leaders were accused of wishing to license journalists, an idea that was anathema to Western nations.

Nonetheless, attempts were made during the early 1980s to steer the *new order* debates away from such divisive issues. This was especially evident in the creation of a new organization based on an earlier initiative of the United States: the International Program for the Development of Communication (IPDC). The IPDC was designed to be a key instrument for organizing international technical cooperation, helping in the creation and implementation of operational projects, and mobilizing the resources needed for those purposes. Although officially launched in 1980, its first meeting was not held until June 1981. It soon became apparent, however, that contributions from donor countries were much more limited than had been expected. The IPDC was faced with the same dilemma confronting a number of international development agencies: a necessary curtailment of expectations and plans.

The 1982 and 1983 UNESCO General Conferences, held in Paris, did not witness the heated polemics of similar meetings held in 1978 and 1980. At the 1983 conference the call for a new information and communication order was formally designated as "an evolving and continuous process"—a concession to Western interests intent on ensuring that the new order should not be viewed as requiring a sudden and radical transformation of existing communication structures.

A 1983 United Nations-UNESCO Round Table on a New World Information and Communication Order held in Igls, Austria, was another promising sign of dialogue. At the first official United Nations-UNESCO meeting on the issue, the Austrian round table was noteworthy for the absence of political rhetoric and the determination of participants to establish specific mechanisms for assisting the developing countries. Communications technology, rather than news flow alone, was now the primary concern of developing countries.

The year 1983 was to end with two paradoxical but not unrelated events. In early December the nonaligned nations movement held in New Delhi its first Media Conference. It opened with a call to intensify efforts to promote the proposed new order. Weeks later, as December came to a close, Secretary of State George P. Schultz of the United States sent a letter to the director-general of UNESCO informing him that, after the required one-year notification period, in December 1984 the United States would withdraw from UNESCO. An indirect reference to the *new order* campaign was evident in a passage referring to the necessity of maintaining "such goals as individual human rights and the free flow of information." The US decision to withdraw from UNESCO surprised observers who had taken note of the apparent absence of conflict in 1982 and 1983. However, it was clear that throughout the early 1980s there was significant bipartisan congressional opposition to UNESCO, not only because of its efforts to promote a new information order but also because of disputes relating to Israel, UNESCO's examination of the issues of peace and disarmament, and a new generation of "people's rights," as well as various financial and organizational reasons. This opposition was widely backed by the US press and other groups.

CHALLENGES

Two decades of debates and resolutions had done little to solve underlying problems of the international flow of information, although they had made the world community more aware of the issues involved. Those issues would be a continuing presence, posing a diversity of challenges, many of which had been spelled out in the MacBride Commission's report. A notable aspect of the report was that it went beyond immediate needs and brought to the fore the overall significance of communications in modern society and the implications of media policies for the world's future.

Meanings of Technology

The commission noted that technological needs had been a central concern at many meetings but urged that they not be allowed to overshadow the social, political, and economic implications. The importance of the new communications technologies was seen to lie to a large extent in the fundamental transformations they impose on society. Governments and private companies alike have long been inclined to think of technology as a means available to serve their particular needs without consideration of the impact on humanity at large. Use of technical developments cannot and should not be slowed, in the view of the commission, but their implications should be constantly assessed. Technology "is seldom neutral—its use is even less so"—for use is influenced by political, financial, and other considerations. Therefore, decisions about communications policies and priorities should not be made solely by technocrats but should involve wide public participation and discussion. "We must beware of the temptation to regard technology as an all-purpose tool capable of superseding social action." The commission noticed a widespread feeling that "technological progress is running ahead of man's capacity to interpret its implications and direct it into the most desirable channels," and cited the fear expressed by Albert Schweitzer that humankind has "lost the capacity to foresee and forestall the consequences" of its actions.

Ways of Freedom

The commission noted the perilous status of freedom of expression around the world. The fact "that there is said to be freedom of expression in a country does not guarantee its existence in practice." The commission further noted that "even where freedom is not openly attacked by authority, it may be limited by self-censorship on the part of communicators themselves. Journalists may fail to publish facts which have come into their possession for several reasons: sheer timidity, an excessive respect for the power structure or in some instances lest they give offence to officialdom and thus risk losing access to their sources of information." Self-censorship, like censorship itself, was seen by the commission as a constantly distorting factor in the flow of communication.

The commission emphasized its view that the exercise of freedom in the communications field involves responsibilities. "We need to ask, moreover, on what grounds a claim for freedom is being made. The freedom of a citizen or social group to have access to communication, both as recipients and contributors, cannot be compared to the freedom of an investor to derive profits from the media. One protects a fundamental human right, the other permits the commercialization of a social need."

The report observed that because of the overwhelming importance of communication today, the state imposes some degree of regulation in virtually all societies. It can intervene in many diverse ways—through the allocation of broadcast licenses and newsprint and through visa policies, import restriction, and many other procedures. "Some governments find it natural to assume total control over the content of information, justifying themselves by the ideology in which they believe. Even on purely pragmatic standards, it is doubtful if this system can be called realistic."

Democratization of Communication

Surveying the "spectrum of communication in modern society," the commission found that it almost defies description because of its immense variety. Barriers could readily be seen: monopolistic controls, technical disparities, restrictive media practices, exclusion of disadvantaged groups, blacklist, censorship. Nevertheless, a tendency toward democratization seemed to be taking place—for example, in the growing role of public opinion. Governments throughout the world were becoming increasingly aware that they must take into account not only national opinion but "world public opinion," because today's media are capable of diffusing "information on international questions to every part of the world." Occasionally opinion crystallizes on some issue with enough force to compel action. This happened, as the commission saw it, on the issues of colonialism, apartheid, and nuclear proliferation. But a meaningful process of opinion formation will in the long run require richer media fare, development of widespread "critical awareness," assertion of the "right to reply," the establishment of "alternative channels of communication," and public participation in decision making on media policies. The goal, the commission felt, should be that everyone would be both "producer and consumer of communication." [...]

Peripheral Vision

By John Sinclair, Elizabeth Jacka, and Stuart Cunningham

Instead of the image of "the West" at the centre dominating the peripheral "Third World" with an outward flow of cultural products, we see the world as divided into a number of regions which each have their own internal dynamics as well as their global ties. Although primarily based on geographic realities, these regions are also defined by common cultural, linguistic, and historical connections which transcend physical space. Such a dynamic, regionalist view of the world helps us to analyse in a more nuanced way the intricate and multi-directional flows of television across the globe.

NEW PATTERNS OF TELEVISION FLOW

Public discourse about television and the media-studies literature are both replete with anxiety about the supposed cultural effects of the global spread of programmes like *Dallas* or, more recently, *Beverly Hills 90210*. The unquestioned basis for this anxiety is expressed in the orthodox critical paradigm for analysing the connection between international power relations and the media, the thesis of "cultural imperialism", or more particularly, "media imperialism". According to this view, world patterns of communication flow, both in density and in direction, mirror the system of domination in the economic and political order. Thus, world centres like New York, Los Angeles, London, and Tokyo are major nodes for international telecommunications traffic, as well as for other kinds of flows, such as television programmes. The media imperialism perspective more particularly sees that the major world sources for programme exports are located in the USA and secondarily in Europe, mainly the UK, and that these centres act as nodes through which all flows of cultural products must pass, including those from one peripheral part of the world to another.

The *locus classicus* of the cultural imperialism thesis is found in the work of Herbert Schiller. As recently as 1991, in an article tellingly entitled "Not Yet the Post-Imperialist Era", he has restated his position in the following way: "The role of television in the global arena of cultural domination has not diminished in the 1990s. Reinforced by new delivery systems—communication satellites and cable networks—the image flow is heavier than ever. Its source of origin also has not changed that much in the last quarter of the century". The classic study for UNESCO by Nordenstreng and Varis in 1974 documented the dominance of the USA in world television programme exports at that time. Television programme flows became an integral issue for the New World Information Order movement and its debate within UNESCO. As this continued into the 1980s the cultural imperialism view of international domination stood challenged only by those who were seen as apologists for the USA and its demand for a "free flow" international regime for trade in cultural products. Neither critics nor apologists questioned the oft-quoted factoid that entertainment is second only to aerospace as an export industry for the USA.

Indeed, as long as the flows of television programme exports seemed to continue along the "one-way street" from the West (and the USA in particular) to the rest of the world, the critical discourse of cultural imperialism was a plausible theoretical response, at least in its more subtle variations, notably that of "cultural dependence, and media Imperialism." In an essential respect, the cultural imperialism perspective was the then-current neo-Marxist analysis of capitalist culture projected on to an international scale: the "dominant ideology" thesis writ large. As such, it had the all-embracing appeal of a comprehensive theory, and also provided the high moral ground from which the international activities of USA networks and the ideological content of their television programmes could be analysed, and then denounced.

However, by the mid-1980s, it became evident that the cultural imperialism discourse had serious inadequacies, both as theory and in terms of the reality which the theory purported to explain. Actual transformation of the world television system made it less and less sustainable on the empirical level, and shifting theoretical paradigms, including postmodernism, postcolonialism, and theories of the, active audience, made its conceptual foundations less secure. To take the empirical aspect first, Jeremy Tunstall had long since pointed out that the "television imperialism thesis," of such writers as Schiller and Wells was based on the quite correct, assumption that the high levels of USA programme imports into Latin America in the 1960s were a permanent condition rather than a transitional stage in the development of television in these regions. The other empirical development which ought to have given pause to theorists of cultural imperialism was the research reported by Varis as an update of the, original "one-way street" project, in which he noted a trend toward greater regional exchanges", in spite of continued USA and European dominance in television programme flows. This finding was reinforce by other studies around the same time which, although absurdly exaggerated in their estimation on how far the flows had formed new patterns, were able nevertheless to document just how one such regional market was taking shape in the case of Latin America.

Thus, even in Latin America, virtually the cradle of the theorization of cultural imperialism, USA Imports were prominent only in the early stages. As the industry matured in Latin America, and as it developed "critical mass", USA imports were to some extent replaced by local products, a pattern that can be found repeated many times over around the world, and which is currently shaping Europe's new privately owned services. Of course, not all countries in Latin America have the capacity, to develop sizeable indigenous television production industries. Rather, the matter in Latin America, as in Asia and the Middle East, is that each "geolinguistic region, as we shall call them, is itself dominated by one or two centres of audio-visual production—Mexico and Brazil for Latin America, Hong Kong and Taiwan for the Chinese-speaking populations of Asia, Egypt for the Arab world, and India for the Indian population of Africa and Asia. The Western optic through which the cultural imperialism thesis was developed literally did not see these non-Western systems of regional exchange, nor understand what they represented. Yet by the late 1980s, Tracey could observe that the "very general picture of TV flows … is not a one-way street; rather there are a number of main thoroughfares, with a series of not unimportant smaller roads".

We have noted how, as theory, the cultural imperialism critique tended to identify the USA as the single centre of a process of media centric capitalist cultural influence which emanated out to the rest of the world in the form of television programmes. It also assumed that these programmes had an inevitable and self sufficient ideological effect upon their helpless audiences in the periphery. Although this rationale established a theoretical connection between US television programmes and "consumerism", it did not address the question of just how such a mechanism of effect might work, nor how it could be observed in action upon actual audiences. In the discourse of cultural imperialism, the mystique of television entertainment's multivalent appeal for its audiences, and how specific audiences responded to it, were never on the agenda.

Other shortcomings arose from the theory's emphasis on external forces from the USA, and the corresponding disregard for the internal sociological factors within the countries seen to be subject to them. In its eagerness to hold US companies, and behind them, the US government, responsible for regressive sociocultural changes in the "Third World", the cultural imperialism critique neglected the internal historical and social dynamics within the countries susceptible to their influence. This left out of consideration the strategic social structural position of the individuals and interest groups who benefited from facilitating US market entry or even from taking their own initiatives. Some of these have subsequently built up their own international media empires, such as Mexico and Brazil. Other players have more recently joined the game, such as some Saudi investors, while investment in the new channels in India by expatriates shows that media entrepreneurism also can be widespread on a small scale. The cultural imperialism theory failed to see that, more fundamental than its supposed ideological influence, the legacy of the USA in world television development was in the implantation of its systemic model for television as a medium—the exploitation of entertainment content so as to attract audiences which could then be sold to advertisers. American content may have primed this process, but as the experience of many parts of the peripheral world shows, it is not required to sustain it.

We should also note that with its dichotomized view of "the West" versus the "Third World", the cultural imperialism theory was unable to give an adequate account of semi-peripheral settler societies such as Australia and Canada, where the experience of colonialism, and postcolonialism, has been quite distinct from that of nations in other former colonized zones, a distinctiveness manifest in the television systems which they developed.

The basic assumption of Western domination via television is worth further comment. Paradoxically, even though the cultural imperialism thesis has been articulated in the name of defending the "Third World" against domination by audiovisual products from the USA, it is more inclined to reinforce Western cultural influence by taking it as given, when it should be challenging it, A more postcolonial perspective in theory has forced us to realize that USA domination always was limited, either by cultural or political "screens", or both. A related weakness or "blind spot" of the cultural imperialism thesis has been its over-emphasis on the significance of imported *vis-à-vis* local television. Television has always been more of a local than a global medium, and remains so, although the increasingly multichannel and globalized nature of the industry may alter the balance at the margin in the longer term. According to figures from 1989, the volume of purely domestic material in national markets is twenty-nine times higher than that which is traded. Television is still a gloriously hybrid medium, with a plethora of programming of an inescapably and essentially local, untranslatable nature.

Although US programmes might lead the world in their transportability across cultural boundaries, and even manage to dominate schedules on some channels in particular countries, they are rarely the most popular programmes where viewers have a reasonable menu of locally produced material to choose from. And even where there is imported content, it is no longer acceptable to read off from that fact alone any presumed effects of a cultural or political kind. Hamid Naficy captures this vividly in his brilliant study of television amongst Iranian exiles in Los Angeles. Describing how his exclusively English-speaking Iranian daughter, Shayda, and his exclusively German-speaking Iranian niece, Setarah, communicated through the Disney film *The Little Mermaid*, he goes on to comment:

> The globalization of American pop culture does not automatically translate into globalization of American control. This globalized culture provides a shared discursive space where transnationals such as Setarah and Shayda can localize it, make their own uses of it, domesticate and indigenize it. They may think with American cultural products but they do not think American. [...]

"GATEKEEPERS" AND CULTURAL INDUSTRY FACTORS IN TELEVISION FLOWS

Many cross-cultural studies emphasize the diverse, localized character of international audience responses, and are imbued with a sense of the viability and integrity of the cultures of peripheral or "small" nations. So it is somewhat ironic, because of the dominance of American programmes at highly visible though only provisionally premium places in schedules, that such studies should focus on US programmes almost exclusively. As Ellen Seiter argues strongly with regard to the theoretical field from which this position draws, "in our concern for audiences' pleasures ... we run the risk of continually validating Hollywood's domination of the worldwide television market".

Far more than for the USA, the success or otherwise of peripheral nations' exports is contingent on factors other than those captured by established modes of audience study. This explains why so little audience reception research has been able to be conducted on their products in international markets, and why we need instead middle-range analysis to do so. In the middle range between political economy approaches and reception analysis, a number of factors are mediating. How are programmes acquired overseas? Who engages in their appraisal and acquisition and what perceptions have they formed of peripheral programming? This "primary audience" is the major source of informed "gatekeeping" which regulates (in the widest sense) the flow of peripheral programming in international markets. And what are the characteristics of the major territories which influence the success or failure of such programmes internationally? All these mediating factors embody legitimate, indeed central, aspects of cultural exchange, as virtually all the significant research on non-dominant nations' television production and reception indicates.

The actual structure of major international television trade markets is central to middle-range analysis. There is an ever-wider variety of modes of contracting for international programme production and exchange: offshore, co-production, official co-production, co-venture (including presales), and straight purchase of territorial rights for completed programmes in the major trade markets such as MIP-TV and MIPCOM. These run on annual cycles suited to the programming and scheduling patterns of the major northern hemisphere territories, but a notable shift in the patterns of global television traffic was indicated in 1994 when the first MIP-Asia was held, a trade market specifically for the Asian region. At such events, programming is often bought (or not bought) on the basis of company reputation or distributor clout, in job lots and sight-unseen. Very broad, rough-and-ready genre expectations are in play; judgements may seem highly "subjective" and arbitrary.

Universalist explanations may prove useful in accounting for the international successes of historically universal forms like US series drama, but there is solid evidence that cultural specificities, along with other middle-range industrial factors, are unavoidable and, at times, enabling factors for international success in peripheral countries' export activity. Studies which compare viewers' engagement with US as against other sources of television programming confirm that there tends to be a more distanced realm of "pure entertainment" within which US programmes are processed—as markers of modish modernity, as a "spectacular" world—compared to more culturally specific responses made to domestic and other sources.

The capacity for peripheral countries to export their programmes across diverse markets is to some extent based on their substitutability or non-substitutability for US material, although this also depends in part on the type of channel they are purchased for. Australian productions have provided useful models from which the protocols of commercial popularity may be learnt in rapidly commercializing European broadcasting environments, but the fact that Australian programmes are perceived as imitations of US formats constitutes a problem for both commentators and regulators in Europe.

To be sure, the structure of content and the form of internationally popular serial drama in particular are widely shared and may even be "borrowed" from US practice, as the *telenovela* was decades ago. But the "surface" differences, nevertheless, almost always are consequential, and contribute to the acceptance or rejection of non-US material, depending on whether the "primary audience" of gatekeepers and the viewing audience respond positively or negatively to those differences. As Anne Cooper-Chen has shown, even that most transparently internationalized of television formats, the game show, contains significant differences in the widely variant cultures in which it is popular. After looking at popular game shows in fifty countries, she regards them as having at least three structural variants—the East Asian, Western, and Latin models—and innumerable surface particularities. Hamid Mowlana and Mehdi Rad show that the Japanese programme *Oshin* found acceptance in Iran because its values of perseverance and long suffering were compatible with cultural codes prevalent in what might appear a distinctly different society. The evidence for the popularity of *Neighbours* in Britain demonstrates that, while Australian soaps arguably were brought into the market as substitutes for US material, their popularity built around textual factors based on projections and introjections of Australian "life-style". Australia has served in many ways as a kind of "other" to Britain—the younger, more upstart and hedonistic vision of how the British might like to see themselves.

The "export of meaning" is not just a matter of viewer reception. Many nations, both core and peripheral, place special importance on the international profile they can establish with their audiovisual exports. These are fostered both as a form of cultural diplomacy, and for intrinsic economic reasons, although national cultural objectives and audiovisual industry development are not always compatible, as Australia and Canada have long been aware, and some Asian countries are now learning. In the case of the Middle East, one commentator has observed that the popularity of Egyptian television exports in the Arab states has a number of cultural and even political "multiplier effects". This popularity was preceded by the success of Egyptian films, and carries with it a potential acceptance and recognition of Egyptian accents and performers that can operate as "a soft-sell commercial for Egyptian values" which then carries over into indirect political leverage. While it might be difficult to isolate and measure them, it is not unreasonable to infer cultural, trade, and political multiplier effects from what can be seen of peripheral nations' products on the world's television screens. [...]

Even amongst the globalization theorists, it is becoming a commonplace to observe that the globalizing forces towards "homogenization", such as satellite television, exist in tension with contradictory tendencies towards "heterogenization", conceived pessimistically as fragmentation, or with postmodernist optimism, as pluralism. Thus, "identity and cultural affiliation are no longer matters open to the neat simplifications of traditional nationalism. They are matters of ambiguity and complexity, of overlapping loyalties and symbols with multiple meanings". To the extent that we can assume that television is in fact a source of identity, and that audiences for the same programme derive similar identities from it, it becomes possible to think of identities which are multiple, although also often contradictory, corresponding to the different levels from which the televisual environment is composed in a given market. An Egyptian immigrant in Britain, for example, might think of herself as a Glaswegian when she watches her local Scottish channel, a British resident when she switches over to the BBC, an Islamic Arab expatriate in Europe when she tunes in to the satellite service from the Middle East, and a world citizen when she channel surfs on to CNN. [...]

The Production of Mobilities at Schiphol Airport, Amsterdam

By Tim Cresswell

> Description is more valuable than metaphor.
> —Text on Jenny Holzer installation at Schiphol Airport, Amsterdam

I t has been a central aim of this book to connect discussions of mobility from the blood cells coursing around the body to the movement of people across international boundaries. We have encountered a number of thinkers who have tried to enact just such an overarching story of mobility—from Etienne-Jules Marey in his Paris laboratory, to Thomas Hobbes pondering the definition of liberty, to spatial scientists equating the flow of rain into gutters with commuters entering a highway. These thinkers, in one way or another, have produced bodies of knowledge that have looked for similarities between moving things—to extract, if you like, an essence of mobility.

In this book I have had a slightly different aim. While I insist connections need to be made among mobilities at different scales, a central plank of my argument is that difference is an important but paradoxical theme connecting mobilities. A fully social notion of mobility, I have argued, is one that acknowledges the production of mobilities as an activity that occurs in a context of social and cultural difference within a systematically asymmetrical field of power. Mobility as a social and cultural resource gets distributed unevenly and in interconnected ways. One theme that connects mobilities, in other words, is not essential similarity, but the role mobility plays in the differentiation of society.

In this chapter, I make these connections-through-difference more concrete by exploring the way they are played out in the space par-excellence of postmodern, post-national flow—the international airport. In the airport, I argue, we can see a place where the micro-management of human bodies extolled by Taylor and the Gilbreths meets the control and ordering of traffic from cars to planes—where the passenger standing in a line, moving slowly if at all, becomes the enactment of a discourse on mobility rights constructed at the transnational level. Mobilities from the body to the globe pulse and circulate through and around the airport. But before considering the production of corporeal mobilities in and around Schiphol Airport in Amsterdam, consider the role the airport-as-metaphor has performed in the emergent nomadic metaphysics of the late twentieth and early twenty-first centuries.

THE AIRPORT AS METAPHOR

The airport has become something of an iconic space for discussions of modernity and postmodernity, and its central role in literature on mobility makes it an ideal place to consider the ways in which geographies of human mobility have developed.[1] As Mike Crang has recently suggested, in order to understand a globalized world of transitory experience, we need to understand the points and nodes at which mobilities are produced: "Of all the spaces of a globalised world," he writes, "airports may be the most emblematic."[2]

What, exactly, airports are emblematic of is a matter for debate. In one reading they are seen as the opposite of authentic, rooted, bounded place—as placeless places or non-places. Take Marc Augés discussion *of non-place* for instance.

> The multiplication of what we may call empirical non-places is characteristic of the contemporary world. Spaces of circulation (freeways, airways), consumption (department stores, supermarkets), and communication (telephones, faxes, television, cable networks) are taking up more room all over the earth today. They are spaces where people coexist or cohabit without living together.[3]

Augé's discussion of the "anthropology of super-modernity" starts from the perspective of an air traveler and flits in and out of airports throughout. It asks anthropologists to come to terms with the reality of a mobile world. Other writers are even more enamored with the airport world. Consider the enthusiasm of the architect Hans Iberlings:

> Airports are to the 1990s what museums were to the postmodern 1980s: the arena where numerous contemporary themes converge and all kinds of interesting developments take place. … Mobility, accessibility and infrastructure are seen as fundamental themes of the age, unlimited access to the world as the ideal of the moment.[4]

Iberlings describes the airport as "an attractive model for the kind of existence that is nowadays associated with globalization, a world where 'jet lag' is built into everybody's biological clock and time and place have become utterly relative."[5] This enthusiasm is shared by cultural theorists, such as Iain Chambers, who sees a place such as the airport lounge as a contemporary symbol of flow, dynamism, and mobility. Chambers delights in a postmodern world that finds its ultimate expression in the international airport. "With its shopping malls, restaurants, banks, post-offices, phones, bars, video games, television chairs and security guards," he writes, "it is a miniaturised city. As a simulated metropolis it is inhabited by a community of modern nomads: a collective metaphor of cosmopolitan existence where the pleasure of travel is not only to arrive, but also not to be in any particular place."[6] This vision of the airport is shared by the feminist theorist Rosi Braidotti who writes:

> But I do have special affection for the places of transit that go with travelling: stations and airport lounges, trams, shuttle buses, and check-in areas. In between zones where all ties are suspended and time stretched to a sort of continuous present. Oases of non-belonging, spaces of detachment. No-(wo)man's land.[7]

Much of the fetishization of speed and mobility comes from male commentators, and has more than a touch of "boys and their toys" about it. In this respect, Braidotti's "special affection" is unusual. But clearly the airport has become the site par excellence of musing about the world of flow.

Typical of the contemporary gloss on the significance of airports is the claim made by architectural critic Deyan Sudjic that airports are the contemporary substitute for the public square—a place where strangers come together and cross paths. Architectural consultant M. Gordon Brown clearly believes this. "Travel is no longer the special and liberating activity it once was," he writes, "it is becoming normalized as a part of everyday urban life for many people. Airports have developed into self-contained cities that boast more activity and a greater diversity of people than most American downtowns."[8]

Travel writer Pico Iyer seems to agree with this diagnosis. Los Angeles International Airport (affectionately known as LAX by the people who pass through) is, he argues, a self-sufficient community complete with chapel, gym, and museum. Airports to him are "the new epicenters and paradigms of our dawning post-national age … bus terminals in the global village … prototype, in some sense, for our polyglot, multicoloured, user-friendly future."[9] Mobility, of course, plays a key role in the construction of these new public spaces, where they are "merely stages on some great global Circle Line, shuttling variations on a common global theme. Mass travel has made L.A. contiguous to Seoul and adjacent to Sao Paulo, and has made all of them now feel a little like bedroom communities for Tokyo."[10] Typical of the assumptions made by Western writers and academics jetting around the world, Iyer notes that: "We eat and sleep and shower in airports, we pray and weep and kiss there." Who *we* consists of is left to the reader's imagination.

Perhaps we can see the airport terminal as a specific kind of site from which global mobility is theorized. Kevin Hetherington has suggested that the airport may be the (post)modern equivalent of the coffee house of the eighteenth century or the street of the nineteenth century.

> Perhaps now we see a shift of site of intellectual endeavour to the kinds of non-places that Augé has associated with our future sense of solitary existence (we all know that intellectual writing is largely a solitary exercise): the airport lounge, Bonaventure hotels, conference centres, motorways and of course the aircraft itself.[11]

These are the spaces from which people write the postmodern global experience. Clearly, business people and intellectuals spend a lot of time in airport terminals between meetings and conferences. They are avatars of what Pico Iyer has called the "Global Soul."[12] Perhaps these members of the kinetic elite are mistaking their experience—their particular geographical trajectories—for a general global condition.

If the new airport boosterism is to be believed, a space such as Heathrow, Schiphol, Changhi, or LAX is a kind of transnational Utopian space of flows where nationality has been abolished and class erased—where people are generally contented. While it is possible to see how these conclusions might have been arrived at, they are also somewhat surprising. They are surprising because they erase other features of the airport experience highlighted by an approach that takes the politics of mobility seriously. Clearly, not all passengers in terminals are mobile in quite the same way. As Mike Crang has argued, the image of the airport as global, transnational space "may speak to a globe-trotting semiotician, but says little to the family with overtired children delayed by lack of connecting buses in Majorca."[13] Indeed, as Jenny Holzer's art installation at Schiphol Airport suggests, perhaps description is sometimes better than metaphor.

Consider, for instance, the various mobilities that produce and are produced by the airport spaces around the world. First, consider the passengers waiting to board their planes. The airport lounge is indeed the space of the privileged business traveler, in addition to those who have recently purchased discount tickets on the Internet for an EasyJet flight. There is no system on Earth that quite so explicitly makes the existence of a kinetic hierarchy so clear. On Virgin Atlantic, those who travel in the most luxury are traveling "upper class." On other airlines, such travelers are classified as "connoisseur" or "elite." If you travel "upper class," a limousine can pick you up at home. Your mobility will be seamless. On arrival at Heathrow the Virgin upper-class traveler can take the fast lane through immigration. In the airport there are lounges for this kinetic elite. Many of the people traveling through airports are familiar with them. Others have never flown before and still find the very idea of flying miraculous. So the airport is the space of the global kinetic elite as well as occasional flyers, budget airline flyers, and charter flight package tourists, such as the family en route to Majorca, that Crang reminds us of. Also making their way through the airport are immigrants, refugees, and asylum seekers. People who have been forced to smuggle drugs with condoms full of cocaine filling their stomachs. Then there is the workforce of pilots, flight attendants, mechanics, check-in workers, janitors. Major airports support a huge workforce whose members commute in daily patterns to and from the airport and its suburbs. The already differentiated traveler, the immigrant workers, and the airport workers are all mobile. Their mobilities are all enabled by the construction of the airport as a node in a network, but their mobilities are brimming over with different forms of significance. The general observation that the world is a more mobile place does not do justice to this richness. The suggestion that airports erase class and nationality seem, frankly, bizarre in an instrumental space where you are literally divided into classes and so frequently asked to show your passports as evidence of where you come from and where you are allowed to go. In the airport the corporeality of mobility—the way the body feels—intersects with categorizations of types—citizen, alien, tourist, business traveler, commuter.

Now think of the division of spaces in an airport—spaces that are themselves increasingly the product of assumptions about mobility built into modeling software.[14] Think of the lines at check-in—the long line of economy check-in and the non-line at upper-class check-in. Then there are the departure lounges and shops catering to different travelers. Arrival halls (in Europe) are divided into European and non-European immigration lines traveling at different speeds. Not long ago I arrived in Bologna and was rushed through immigration without so much as a glance at my passport. A plane from Albania had arrived at the same time and the line of people at immigration was more or less stationary. My traveling companions were American citizens and therefore had to stand in line with the Albanians until a policeman noticed their passports and moved them through the "European" line. Here was the politics of mobility and immobility—the geopolitics of mobility at a microscale. Once immigration has been negotiated, there is customs. Who gets stopped and why? What kinds of immobility are imposed on those subjected to body cavity searches? Many people every year are sent on the next plane home.

In short, very few places are more finely differentiated according to a kinetic hierarchy than an international airport. The airport also illustrates how the politics of mobility draws our attention to interrelating scales of mobility. While airports are most often mobilized as symbols of globalization and transnational identity, they also illustrate the politics of mobility at the scale of the body. Airports and air travel in general are replete with stories of comfort and illness, pampering and torture—bodies stopped and examined interminably. Some glide through the fast lane and have complimentary massages in the business lounge. Some bodies are found frozen in undercarriage wells. Once on the plane, upper-class passengers get more oxygen and more toilets. Economy-class passengers are left with a full bladder and a headache.

Clearly then, the airport as a symbol of global, postmodern nomadism needs to be unpacked. Seeing it as a space where motion, meaning, and power come together enacts such an unpacking. A politics of mobility directs our attention to the relations among different experiences of mobility and the relations between mobility and obduracy. It recognizes the importance of mobility in the modern world, but does not mistake it for a techno-utopian general condition. It insists on the importance of particular contexts for the production and consumption of mobility.

IT ALL COMES TOGETHER IN SCHIPHOL—FROM ROOTS TO ROUTES

Writing about the airport runs the risk of generalizing the airport experience in a way I would not want to repeat. Clearly, the experience of Singapore's Changhi or London's Heathrow is vastly different from that of Salisbury, Maryland, or Liverpool's John Lennon. The kind of airport that seems to frequent the writings of contemporary theorists is clearly an international hub. A place the world passes through. The following, then, is an account of one particular airport, Schiphol Airport in Amsterdam. In 2004 it was Europe's fourth busiest airport, and one of the world's two or three most popular if web polls are accurate.

Networks, nodes, and mobilities are often presented to us in abstract form as spatialities outside of history. It is as if they have suddenly appeared out of thin air. This ahistorical approach is partly behind the assumption made by theorists of the present that the world is more homogeneous than it once was. These networks, it is argued, make place and time less and less important. Manuel Castells, for instance, writes that for the global elite "there is the construction of a (relatively) secluded space across the world along the connecting lines of the space of flows: international hotels whose decoration, from the design of the room to the color of the towels, is similar all over the world to create a sense of familiarity with the inner world, while inducing abstraction from the surrounding world; airports' VIP lounges, designed to maintain the distance *vis-à-vis* society in the highways of the space of flows."[15] This space of flows is contrasted with traditional notions of place replete with a sense of history and bounded-ness within which the majority of people are said to live. On the one hand there is a largely ahistorical and non-placebound space of flows, and on the other there is the rooted and historical space of place. But, as we shall see, the space of flows that is Schiphol has a very clear history—a history that permeates the networks that pass through it.

Schiphol's origins lie in its use as a military airport during World War I. It was built in an area known as Haarlemmermeer, an arable area (polder) situated near Amsterdam, Rotterdam, the Hague, and Harlaam. The site had to be reclaimed from a 30,000 acre lake and is 13 feet below sea level. To the northeast was a funnel-shaped section of coastline that became very dangerous when gales blew in from the southwest. This was called Schipshol, or the ship's hole, in reference to the number of ships that sunk there. The lake was drained and dykes were built around it in the years leading up to 1848, the year the work was completed. The first structure there was a military garrison. Growers of root vegetables taking advantage of the fertile soil soon farmed it.

The first commercial flight was on May 17, 1920, and the first scheduled service was between London and Amsterdam on July 5, 1920. This was quickly followed by scheduled service between Amsterdam and Hamburg and Copenhagen (September 1920), Amsterdam and Paris (May 1921), and Amsterdam and Berlin (April 1923). Not surprisingly, given the origins of the area, the airport was frequently a quagmire and passengers were carried from plane to terminal. Occasionally local farmers, whose land was being progressively eaten up by the airport complex, would throw various root crop products at the passengers as they were transported. On October 1, 1924 crowds gathered to watch the first occasional flight from Schiphol to the Dutch East Indies.[16] By 1929 four airlines flew out of Schiphol.

In 1920, 400 passengers passed through Schiphol. By World War II, when Schiphol was destroyed, the figure was close to 100,000. In 1938 Schiphol became the national airport of the Netherlands; Douglas DC-3s and DC-2s used the airport. They had a range of 1,000 kilometers and regularly took passengers to North Africa, and twice a week to the Batavia (Djakarta) in the Dutch East Indies. The trip took five and one-half days, but was no longer an occasion for large crowds to gather.[17] Up until World War II the Amsterdam-Batavia route was the longest timetabled commercial air voyage available in the world, and for a long time it was the only route from Schiphol to anywhere outside of Europe. The first Batavia flight left Schiphol on October 1, 1924; it was a Fokker F.VII. The flight was scheduled to take twenty-two days, but due to a crash landing and mechanical problems did not arrive in Batavia until November 25. Nevertheless the successful delivery of Dutch mail to the far reaches of empire was a cause for considerable celebration in the Netherlands. On May 23, 1935 the first Douglas DC-2 flight to Batavia left Schiphol and landed on May 31, reducing the flight time to a mere eight days. A few weeks later, KLM started flying to Batavia twice a week, and within a year the flight time had decreased still further to five and one-half days, stopping overnight at Athens, Baghdad, Jodhpur, Rangoon, and Singapore. A ticket included all hotels and travel insurance as well as meals. The logistical challenge for KLM was extraordinary. They had to provide spare parts at all twenty-two airfields used by the aircraft, as well as deal with visas and overflight permission in eighteen countries. There were no international agreements on airspace or sophisticated air traffic control staff to help them out. The mere existence of this mammoth flight, however, encouraged the development of directional radio transmissions, night lighting at airfields, and speedy refueling drills. It was these developments, as much as innovations in aircraft manufacture, that led to the effective annihilation of distance.

The success of the Schiphol-Batavia route was celebrated iconographically in an array of publicity material for Schiphol Airport, for KLM and for a number of other companies attached to the endeavor, such as Shell—who provided the fuel at all the refueling stations along the way. The ever expanding network of routes that centered on Schiphol was also represented in Schiphol publicity material. After World War II there was again debate over where the national airport would be sited due to the bombing of Schiphol, but it rose from the ashes and in 1945 was referred to as the World Airport of the Netherlands. A series of runways at tangents to one another were built there. In 1958 it became a public limited company with 76 percent of the shares owned by the government. It was not until 1979 that the government completely gave up on building a national airport elsewhere.

In the 1960s the airport continued to grow, and by 1964 had two runways and a standard terminal. In addition to the passengers, 1.5 million sightseers visited the airport to watch the planes—the Boeing 707s and Douglas DC-8s equipped with sophisticated instrument landing systems, which could fly from New York or Chicago. For the first time Schiphol was being referred to in its own promotional literature as an "Aviation City" complete with banks, rental car facilities, showers, and duty-free shopping. It was just fifteen minutes from Amsterdam and employed 15,000 people. Schiphol was beginning to advertise itself as a gateway to Europe. Most passengers do not begin or end a journey in Amsterdam. It is much more likely to serve as a hub or connection point between flights. Indeed, the local population on its own could never sustain a large airport. Realizing this, Schiphol pioneered a simplified system for transit passengers that eliminated passport checks and encouraged shopping at the proliferating duty-free outlets.

It was also in the 1960s that the new airport terminal was constructed. The major impetus for this was the invention of the Boeing 747 Jumbo Jet, which carried over 400 passengers and needed new terminal docking points to accommodate its massive bulk. The new terminal (1967) had twenty-five gates on three piers. In addition to the new terminal, four new runways were built swallowing up more and more of the polder, where the farmers continued to farm root vegetables. It was only recently, as David Pascoe points out, that "the justification for the polder's existence—farming as a stabilizing force on the landscape—has, to some extent, faded, thus providing new opportunities to reclaim the ground for transport."[18]

By the early 1970s the arrival of jumbo jets led to a further extension of the arrivals hall and the extension of the piers that were used to provide births for the new leviathan. In 1971 the handling capacity of the airport was 8 million passengers a year. The new D pier was constructed specially for the new wider body jets. By 1974 the capacity had risen to 18 million passengers with 42 docking positions for aircraft, and a railway connection to the airport was developed for the first time. Over 350 businesses were located in and around the airport, and 24,000 people were employed there. By 1977, 9,114,974 passengers used Schiphol from all corners of the globe (See Table 24-1 and Table 24-2).

Table 24-1. *Schiphol Airport Statistics*

	Passengers	Airlines	Connected Cities
1929	14,000	4	18
1936	58,000	9	—
1964	2,141,000	26	115
1977	9,114,000	50	140
2003	40,000,000	102	—

Table 24-2. *Schiphol Airport Passenger Figures (1977)*

Origination Point	Number of Passengers
Europe	6,823,459
London	1,023,570
North America	1,068,291
Far East	391,582
Middle East	333,673
Africa	264,716
Mid and South America	233,253

Schiphol had successfully made itself into a gateway to Europe—it had shifted from an airport to a *mainport*. By the 1990s it was Europe's fourth busiest airport servicing 18 million passengers on 350,000 flights; 508 companies were based at the airport employing 36,000 people.[19] It competes successfully with London, Frankfurt, and Paris for passenger traffic on the basis of transfer traffic (people who do not leave the airport as they change planes). It has been able to market itself as a hub because it only has one terminal building and the passengers only need 50 minutes between planes. Take away the transfer traffic and Schiphol would only rank tenth among Europe's airports. It has excellent transport connections to the rail network, which now has a station under the terminal. It is well known for its retail outlets and duty-free shopping. As air traffic continues to grow, the terminal building evolves, growing new fingers to accommodate more planes. As the terminal expands its reach, so the air-traffic-control towers become higher and higher. Road networks and rail development occur to handle the traffic at Schiphol, and a kerosene pipeline from Rotterdam provides fuel for the planes.

Today's Schiphol is a truly remarkable kind of place. As well as being a very successful and extremely busy airport, it is also a retail space, place of entertainment, and office park. The Burger King at Schiphol is the world's busiest fast food outlet. Retail space in the airport can expect a turnover of ten times that of the most successful equivalent in downtown Amsterdam. The offices in the attached World

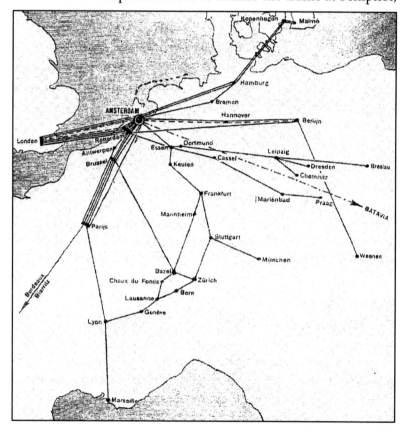

Figure 24-1. *Map of the airline route network centered on Schiphol from 1929.*

Figure 24-2. *Map of the airline route network centered on Schiphol from 1936.*

Trade Centre can demand considerably higher rents than their downtown competitors. In addition to shops, restaurants, and offices, you can find a museum, a casino, hotels, a massage parlor, a conference center, and a place for children to play. There are areas where you can check out the Internet from your own laptop due to the provision of wireless Internet services (provided by the appropriately named Nomadix company). Below the airport is a rail station that can take you to Amsterdam in ten minutes or further afield.

Schiphol's place in the world can be read as a simple tale of expansion. It has certainly become one of the world's busiest and most successful airports. It is extremely popular with passengers and is often voted the world's best airport. One scale of mobility impacted (produced) by Schiphol then, is the global scale. It has been a place from which the process of time-space compression has been produced, just as time-space compression was producing this place. As early as 1936 the airport brochures were advertising this fact in very graphic form as they sought to advertise the possibility of travel to the Dutch East Indies in only five and one-half days. This is the most obvious narrative of mobility at Schiphol Airport, but there are other scales at which this place is implicated in the production of mobilities.

SCHENGEN SPACE(S)

It is tempting to think of buildings in general, and airports in particular, as accomplishments—finished spaces that have been built with a particular purpose and a particular aesthetics in mind. But buildings are constantly used. People move through them in new and sometimes unpredictable ways. The space of Schiphol is thus very much in process. Schiphol's current architect, Jan Benthem, described his vision of Schiphol as a place that is never finished but always *becoming*. "What makes an airport different is that it is not a finished building. It's always being built. It's never finished or it's always finished. It's always as it is. You are always building.

It is never a case of 'you're not ready yet.'"[20] It is difficult for an architect like Benthem to plan the construction of the airport over the medium and long term, as "you will never know what it is going to be because it will always be something different." Benthem's experience of working with and on Schiphol underlines his conviction that airports are never finished. He started, twenty years previously, by designing a bicycle shed for one of the outbuildings; this was soon followed by a temporary bus station that was never used. By the time it was finished time had moved on.

> We started with small buildings and then got some bigger jobs. Our first involvement with the main terminal was building a temporary bus station. … The big architect was too involved with the extension of the airport and they needed a bus station in five months time! It had to be there because of a certain growth in air traffic. We did that within cost and within time. … they never used it … they changed their minds so—they don't like to put people on buses they like to put people on planes and if things go well you don't need it. And in 1988 there was a large leap forward because, well, there was a sudden growth in air traffic and there was the problem of European unity they had to solve in the medium and long time. In 1988 there was the decision that in 1993 there would be one control system and they had to change this airport—because basically it was an international airport—into an airport that has both [international and domestic] … and that was a very difficult situation and there was no scheme for the future and there was a need to build up the airport in four or five years. They wanted someone with a new vision for the airport as well.

Here the production of mobilities at Schiphol clashed; first, through the production of a never-to-be-used bus terminal, and second, through the rearrangement of space to make room for a new arrangement of mobilities at the continental scale.

Consider the scale of European mobility. Since its inception, the European Union (EU, formally the European Economic Community) has placed the right to mobility at the heart of its constitution. The development of the EU can be seen as the gradual reduction in barriers to the movement of people, goods, information, and capital.[21] Border controls were gradually abolished and replaced by more limited passport and document checks. This process was solidified in the Schengen Agreement, which was signed in 1985 and implemented in most states a decade later.[22] The purpose of the agreement was to stimulate free-market forces by reducing the time and effort needed to move. In this way, it was believed, Europe could compete with the United States and Japan. The Schengen Agreement was also underlined by an ideological commitment to a sense of European "community" that would transcend national allegiances and reduce the chance of conflict between member states.

But alongside this commitment to freedom of movement in "Schengen space," came an equal commitment of fortifying Europe's external borders against illegal immigrants, terrorists, and drug traffic. As Ginette Verstraete puts it, "new frontiers had to be implemented to be able to distinguish between Europeans and non-Europeans, and between (authorized) travel and (unauthorized) migration. The freedom of mobility for some (citizens, tourists, business people) could only be made possible through the organized exclusion of others forced to move around as illegal 'aliens', migrants, or refugees."[23] This differentiation of mobilities at a continental scale could only be operationalized through a multitude of local spatial reorganizations and practices of surveillance. The "external borders" of Schengen space in the age of hypermobility were not simply the land borders of the Schengen states but, clearly, the airports and seaports. Airports in particular are a strange kind of border marking a crossing point in vertical rather than horizontal space. Few would think of the borders of Europe as being in Manchester, Amsterdam, or Bologna, but there they are—a multitude of dispersed nodal borders. It is in these transport nodes that Schengen space was enacted and, indeed, materially produced.

The Schengen accords were represented as the abolition of borders, but they can also be seen as the multiplication of borders and the production of new kinds of borders. Just as the borders were being created, so were the mobilities. While it became easier for the Italian business-woman to enter Germany or the Belgian tourist to backpack to Greece, it became significantly more difficult to enter from the outside.

The Schengen Agreement, an agreement about mobility and its control at the scale of Europe, produced Schengen space—the space of the states in Europe through which it was now possible to travel "freely." It also raised a series of issues that had to be dealt with at Schiphol Airport, as in other airports throughout Europe. Other kinds of Schengen space were produced at the local and micro scales. The agreement was made to allow freedom of movement between the Schengen states. For Schiphol this meant that there were now two distinct categories of flights and passengers—Schengen passengers and non-Schengen passengers. In the local context of Amsterdam's airport, this was a particularly significant moment in the production of mobilities. Pre-Schengen Schiphol was more or less an international airport with international passengers in transit. Unlike London's Heathrow or Paris's Charles de Gaulle, for instance, Schiphol never catered to a large number of domestic passengers—there are very few flights that operate within the Netherlands and Amsterdam is a relatively small source of outbound passengers. Schiphol had built its success on the basis of being a mainport or hub—an extremely successful node in a global network. Suddenly a large number of passengers effectively became "domestic" passengers, who would not have to pass through passport control on arrival. This was the problem that faced Jan Benthem as he became the lead architect at Schiphol:

> Well you have to change your structure because on the air side of your original airport you have the international and the European passengers mixed in one level … departure and arrivals mixed on one level … everybody is mixed there … and if you have to take one category of Schengen people out then you have to make divisions somewhere or you have to make a second level and make every gate have the possibility of a switch and it was very difficult to solve the problem and of course it was very difficult if you don't know what your future is and you have to double the airport physically in five years time.

Part of the problem Benthem faced was due to the fact that Schiphol is different from other large airports in that it is based on the concept of a single terminal building. In practice this had given it the advantage of making the location of aircraft, in relation to the flows of passengers and baggage, relatively immaterial. It also had the advantage of being popular with passengers who could make quick connections between planes. The effect of the Schengen Agreement on the architectural space of Schiphol was to demand the separation of passenger streams for the first time. There was considerable debate about how to accomplish this. Although Schiphol has only one terminal building, it is split into three connected sections referred to as Terminals 1 to 3. The first plan was to designate Terminal 2 as a Schengen traffic space. This was resisted by the airport's home airline, KLM, which did not want its operations divided between terminals at great expense. In 1992 the airport directorate decided to divide space based on airlines rather than origins and destinations of passengers. Terminal 3 was allocated to airlines with few or no European routes, Terminal 2 to KLM, and all other airlines (operating in both Schengen space and non-Schengen space) to Terminal 1. Just as the terminal was divided in this way, so the piers became Schengen or non-Schengen; B and C piers became Schengen piers and E, F, and G piers were designated non-Schengen traffic spaces. The most difficult space was D pier, which marked the boundary between Schengen space and non-Schengen space. It also acts as a switch space between the two global spaces. Thus an aircraft arriving from the United States and flying on to Frankfurt would not have to switch piers between legs of the flight.

In order to accommodate both kinds of traffic, pier D had to be split both horizontally and vertically. Originally the pier corridor was divided horizontally by a vertical glass wall. In 1996 a second level was added to the pier thus dividing the space vertically.

Finally the process of customs and immigration had to be divided in new ways. Where once there was simply a universal passport check procedure, there now had to be one set of lines for non-Schengen passengers and another set of lines for Schengen passengers, who would not have to have their passports checked. The production of space within the airport thus ensured the entanglement of bodies moving in lines with the structure of material space and European Union ideologies of free movement. In this way, the production of Schiphol Airport helped to ensure a space of flows for emerging European citizens.

These citizens, through the reiterative practice of mobility in airport space, were performing European identity. This has been made quite explicit in European Union documentation. The recent European Convention documents, for instance, confirmed the long-established idea that the right to mobility is perhaps the most significant fundamental right in Europe. European Commission documentation is quite clear about the significance of this right to mobility.

> The freedom to travel or to go about one's business throughout Europe as in one's own country is for the citizen the most potent symbol of the existence of the European Union.[24]

> Barriers to the free movement of people within the European Union have tumbled over the past 25 years. Queues of vehicles at borders between EU countries are a thing of the past. Citizens of the Union can now travel or go about their business throughout Europe almost as if it were one country.[25]

The promotion of mobility as a way of being a free European citizen extends well beyond formal rights. A pamphlet on European citizenship produced by the European Commission makes this clear:

> Everyone nowadays recognizes the sky-blue banner with 12 gold stars symbolizing European unification, which we see more and more often flying alongside national flags in front of public buildings. … What Community national does not enjoy following the "European Community" sign in airport arrival halls, and passing through simply by showing the uniform passport adopted in 1985?[26]

The pamphlet goes on to list the different technologies and practices of mobility that will ensure a feeling of European identity through constant reiterative use. These include common driving licenses, agreements for provision of health care, a frontier free mobile phone transmission zone, a lack of customs checks, the EU channel at airports and border crossings without passports. There is a clear sense here that it is the practice of mobility that will produce a feeling of freedom, citizenship, and European identity—that citizenship will be produced through the practice of freedom of/as mobility. Representations and ideologies of mobility pervade many aspects of European iconography. The Euro, for instance, features images of bridges and gateways—but not real bridges and gateways for fear of appearing to favor one country over others. Rather, they are made to represent a generic Europeanness.[27]

So as the creation of a space of mobility at a European level (and at an airport and pier level) was enacted, the final point of impact was the human body, which either had to wait in line or pass smoothly through. Suddenly a large number of passengers became "domestic" and could pass relatively smoothly through a non-passport check line while others had to wait in lines that moved slowly, if at all. The comfortable mobility of some, European, citizens is dependent on the establishment of new boundaries and frontiers between different kinds of space and different kinds of mobility.

MANAGING MOBILE BODIES

Clearly Schiphol, as a node in a network, is both produced by and productive of both global and continental forms of mobility. Indeed, they are the "customised spaces *par excellence* for organising and housing global flows."[28] But as anyone who has waited in line at immigration knows, it is at the scale of the body that the production of mobilities is brought home. In addition to being sites that enable global travel, airports are places where the motion of human bodies is finely managed. They are machines for mobility. There are few sites on earth where the individual motions of human bodies are so consistently monitored and micromanaged. Just as the ideology of mobility as a right of citizenship is reproduced in airport space, so the models of motion developed by Taylor, the Gilbreths, and others find their logical end-point in the management of mobile bodies in the airport. Consider the interconnected roles of information technology, signs, and architecture, and their impact on the body.

Information Technology

Elaborate software programs are used to both design the architecture of airports and predict and manage the movement of passengers once they are built. Surveillance, simulation, and security are mingled into a hybrid space of code, people, and physical structures.[29] As Martin Dodge and Rob Kitchin put it, "Progress from buying a ticket, to moving through an airport, to travel on a plane is mediated through code/space—space produced through code."[30] In the airport, the construction of material space and the programming of software have become inseparable. The architecture itself is produced using software models: flows in and out of the airport space are modeled, and surveillance systems monitor the use of space in great detail. In addition, passports have become computer readable and tickets are more often than not e-tickets, for the most part unintelligible to the average passenger. As you move through the airport you are processed—you move through real space and code space simultaneously.[31] The use of modeling and surveillance is combined to both model future movement through the airport and monitor existing mobility. Trustworthy mobilities need to be differentiated from untrustworthy ones. Passenger profiling, for instance, uses complicated and increasingly biometric indicators to choose who should be searched when boarding the aircraft. Airport authorities, in the wake of 9/11, are increasingly looking for travelers who should be prevented from traveling. The new American system called CAPPS II (Computer Assisted Passenger Prescreening System) performs exactly this function. A system such as this "relies on stories about activities that are proper and ones that are improper, about activities that belong in particular places and activities that do not. Each in the end relies on a simple and unstable story, of the treacherous—or trusted—traveller."[32]

Modeling mobility has been central to the planning and engineering of airport environments. This has grown ever more sophisticated as computing power has increased. Peter Adey has shown how the use of modeling systems in airport environments has developed from simple generalized models of flow to complicated three-dimensional envisionings of passenger mobility. In the process, specific human bodies have been made to disappear and reappear at will.[33] To most people in airport management, passengers become mere PAX. PAX are passengers—generic passengers with no identifying marks. Once you have invented PAX, you can then produce models of PAX movements in airport space. PAX are a symptom of a synoptic perspective on space that enacts a transformation of mobile bodies into a legible record that can be analyzed by the panoptic gaze of the architect, planner, and engineer. The ways in which mobile bodies are made to disappear bring to mind the work of Muybridge, Marey, Taylor, and the Gilbreths. Indeed, there is a clear logic that links early efforts to make mobility legible with the models used by airport planners today. Again, movement is abstracted and standardized through the removal of the clumsy fleshiness of real bodies. Bodies are thus transformed "into a phantom in order to establish a space of reason."[34] The meaningful mobility of people is abstracted into the movement of PAX.

Airport managers used a model known as Critical Path Analysis (CPA) to model the movements of PAX in airport space. Passengers were given cards that could be punched at various points in the airport in order to log the time taken to travel between points. These times would then be used to record the longest time in which a sequence of events would occur. The term *critical path* referred to the longest path in a particular network—the longest time it took for particular events to occur. Architects and planners could then reengineer the space to shorten the critical path—to make things happen *faster* and more efficiently.[35] Contemporary airport modeling programs construct sophisticated 3-dimensional animated images of PAX wandering around beautiful and functional terminals as well as moving smoothly between exits, entrances, and check-in. Meanwhile the airplanes land and take off like clockwork in order to transport the animated PAX to their final destination.

While PAX enact abstract, disembodied movement within flow models, other forms of hardware and software rely on the very specificity of particular kinds of bodies in order to police mobility at various points within the airport. The airport enacts a series of thresholds for mobility allowing some (most) people to move on while effectively immobilizing others. Passports have to be shown and identities revealed. Codes have to match identities. Suspicious movements are watched and monitored. During a tour of Schiphol given to me by its chief architect, Jan Bentham, we were stopped on emerging from the baggage handling area. We both had passes (Bentham had arranged one for me), but were nevertheless recognized as unauthorized mobile bodies among the machines and luggage. Jan explained our interview and identified himself as the architect. We were allowed to proceed, but only after being told that even the building's architect did not have permission to take visitors into the baggage handling underworld. So much for architects as gods. There is nowhere in Schiphol where mobilities are not being monitored.

Schiphol is more advanced than most airports in that it has introduced a biometric monitoring scheme for frequent passengers willing to submit to it and pay an appropriate fee (about $100).[36] Starting in 2001 the scheme, called Privium, allows approved travelers to move at speed through immigration by simply submitting to an iris scan. Members not only travel through the airport more quickly, they are also allotted guaranteed parking at the closest car park and are provided with dedicated check-in services at certain airline check-in desks. The technique of iris scanning is explained on the Privium website:

> The technology used in the iris scan is based on the recognition of specific characteristics of the iris. The iris scan is more reliable and faster than other forms of biometric identification, such as fingerprint or hand palm recognition. This is because the iris never changes and irises are rarely damaged or injured. Just a tiny injury to the finger or to the palm of the hand can hamper biometric recognition.[37]

There are limits to membership in the scheme. You have to be a member of the European Economic Area (EU plus Iceland, Switzerland, and Norway) and over 1.5 meters tall. Images of people using the scheme on the web and in pamphlets available at the airport are all of smartly dressed white people—mostly men. Signing up for this form of voluntary surveillance is seen as a privilege that allows highly mobile (the literature states it is useful for people who enter Schiphol over eight times a year) business travelers to effectively bypass immigration. These members of the kinetic elite are granted what amounts to a fast lane from home to meeting and back again. The absence of people in the Privium line is very noticeable as you stand in line at passport control.

Biometric schemes for monitoring identities as they pass through mobility thresholds work on the basis of linking a particular unique body (more precisely—a metonymic part of it, such as the iris or a fingerprint) to an identity. So while closed circuit television monitors mobility everywhere through the logic of the gaze, biometrics works to track movement by logging identities at particular points or thresholds. What is at stake, at these thresholds, is the ability of particular bodies to move in speed and comfort. As one observer has put it, "[b]iometrics is concerned with keeping people in or out: of buildings; of websites; of countries. It is a method of controlling the chaos of movement, of protecting capital from contagion—the harmful touch of an unauthorized ingress—and streamlining the flow for those with the right password."[38] As acceptable passengers are allowed to enact their mobility unmolested, so human security officials are freed up to monitor life in the slow lane of non-Privium members. The speed of some is logically related to the slowness of others.

Biometric schemes like Privium are implicated in the construction of various forms of citizenship as particular types of passengers are separated from others. As the scheme's members are more than likely to be European business travelers, they fall neatly into established notions of what constitutes a citizen in Europe—bodies that are easily understood within liberal framings of mobility in a free-trade zone. The excluded are those who, to a greater or lesser degree, do not match such a framing—"[t]he improved mobility of these Privium cardholders is therefore paired with the promise that illegal aliens and potential terrorist threats will be deterred."[39] As Martha Rosler has argued, "information manipulation—which includes the construction and dissemination of social narratives as well as covert surveillance and other forms of data gathering and management—has come into focus as the most visible and consistent form of social control. This impulse to control is part and parcel of the air transport system."[40] Representation, ideology, and practice cohere around a scheme such as Privium and the mobilities it manages. As Rosler suggests, behind the seemingly neutral technology lie social narratives—ideologies—of mobility. These ideologies course through the mundane practices of passenger mobilities as they are practiced on a day-to-day basis in Schiphol. They connect the patterns of the Iris to notions of transnational citizenship.

Signs

The sophisticated computational world of code space is not the only "code" in the airport. There is also the more familiar code of conventional directional signage. While these signs, which Schiphol is justly famous for, work because they are visible, their mundane obviousness makes them paradoxically just as invisible as the computational code space. Simple directional markers are rarely the subject of admiration. Most of us do not even notice them. When you arrive at Schiphol you enter a world full of signs letting you know how to get where you want to go. Similarly, once you are past the security check and have entered the departure lounge, you are surrounded by signs informing you of how to get to your gate and what you might want to buy along the way.

The vast majority of the signs you see in Schiphol were designed by Paul Mijksenaar. In 1963 Mijksenaar was an art student at the Gerrit Rietveld Academy in Amsterdam when he noticed the newly standardized British road signs designed by Jock Kinnear. He was impressed by their simplicity and their beauty. Previously he had thought of signs as the products of government officials rather than designers. Now, Mijksenaar is something of a global transport sign design guru. He has designed the signs for both Schiphol and the new Amsterdam Metro System. The success of the Schiphol sign system has led to him being commissioned to produce a standardized system for all of New York's airports. Heathrow has also copied Mijksenaar's system.

The spatial location of signs is calculated in relation to the patterns of flow in the airport. As the architect, Jan Benthem, told me: "[a] simple rule is that when you have commercial signs you put them parallel to the flows. And if you have a sign for directions you put it at right angle to the flows. … We try to put commercial messages on a lower level … when it is getting busier, commercial messages blend in with people and with all the excitement. The higher line is for the real signing messages."

The signs are colorful. The original interior designer employed at Schiphol was Kho Liang Ie, who believed that the interior spaces of airports should be largely neutral. In a busy and anxiety-provoking place, there would be more than enough color and excitement without adding to it. It is against this neutral backdrop that the colorful signs stand out. As Mijksenarr suggested to me. "Airport is a kaleidoscopic space already, so the architecture should be neutral and the signs should stand out from the architecture."[41]

All the signs are back-lit and carefully color coded. The most prominent are the yellow signs with black writing and symbols that Mijksenaar refers to as "primary process" signs. These are the signs that tell you where to go—they are signs for flow. Then there are the black signs with yellow writing that Mijksenaar refers to as the "secondary process" or "waiting/staying" signs. These mark the locations of things such as the museum, toilets, and chapel. Green signs refer to emergency exits and other important emergency functions. Finally, there are completely different blue signs that point to commercial enterprises. These are made to look like city street signs with many signs on a single pole. These remind passengers of the well-known tourist signs that tell you how many miles it is to Chicago or Tokyo. To Mijksenaar, the yellow signs are the most important and therefore the most prominent. "[I]n the yellow sign the yellow background in itself is the main thing—it gives the signal "I'm a sign." These signs unconsciously direct the traveler and process him or her through the airport. The contrast of yellow and black has the highest measurable contrast (86 percent) against black and white, which is the next best (82 percent). Benthem told me that passengers are not supposed to notice this coding. It is supposed to work at an unconscious level—to become embodied. This confirms a point made by Gillian Fuller. "These signs don't merely represent the airport," she writes, "they create it. In other words, the textualised cartographies and myriad jurisdictions of the airport are to be obeyed, not believed."[42]

Signs are a central part of what the anthropologist Marc Augé calls non-place.[43] Non-places, often spaces of transit, refer to other places without taking you there. Schiphol Airport, read through its signs, is consumed by the need to keep moving. The combinations of letters, arrows, and (helpfully) times are part of the code that produces a space of incredibly intricate flows. They are built into the architecture of mobility. The sheer number of signs reaffirms the idea that the airport is a processing machine for mobile bodies. Ideally, Mijksenaar told me, there would be a one-to-one relationship between a sign and a location or thing it referred to. In the world of the airport, however, this is not possible.

> The ideal situation will be that you choose your destination and the signs will direct you to your destination—it's one to one. But of course that never happens. There are thousands of users and there are thousands of destinations—so it is impossible—so how can you approach this? It is a stop by stop—first you have to go there and then you have to … it is like a menu of information.

The signs at Schiphol are located at crucial decision points. You do not enter the front of the airport and see a sign directing you to your gate. You are given a choice between departure and arrivals. Then you are directed to your check-in desk, then to security, and so on. They form a set of nested categories at crucial decision points within the building. The passenger simply has to give in to the process and act accordingly. It is for this reason that there are few large maps on Schiphol signs—they tend to be hidden away or featured on handy little pocket pamphlets that are available widely in the airport. To Mijksenaar, maps are not useful technologies for way-finding in airports.

Cresswell: You don't like maps do you?

Mijksenaar: Maps are only for getting an idea of your topographical environment or how big it is … you shouldn't use it as a way-finding instrument. It's more of an opening—a window.

Cresswell: So in the kind of places we are talking about like airports and hospitals—places where I never know where I am—

Mijksenaar: It is hard to make any sense of where you are—the place where you are is a non-place—you are somewhere in the lounge—what does it say? You only want to know where you are in the process. Am I before or after immigration? Is baggage claim after or before? What is between me and the gates?

Cresswell: Don't you think that sometimes people in an airport might like to feel a sense of security about—more like a normal place? In a sense Schiphol is like a public square. And so it's more like a city space than most airports.

Mijksenaar: In a city it is more stretched, there are more squares and there are neighborhoods. That's a difference. The difference is they call an airport city an airport city—that is how it is marketed—its more that it has one of everything—a square, a main street, a hospital—a real city has neighborhoods with different squares, different streets … Then it is important what this neighborhood is like compared to the other neighborhood … airports are more about process.

In Schiphol they hold meetings and use the hotel. They are not interested in where the hotel is—they want to know the direction and how far it is.

Developing signs that do the work they are supposed to in an international airport involves producing a universal language in a polyglot world. As it is impossible to write out directions in every language on earth, the signs have to work across differences. Like computer software, they have to become universal and ubiquitous. In addition to linguistic differences, there are all the other differences in modes of mobility that must be accounted for. Blind people, slow people, anxious people, and mobility-impaired people all have to find their way. The signs have to speak to all of them. Despite the ingenuity of the pictograms on Schiphol's signs, they remain firmly European in their origins, "restaurant pictograms display plates, knives and forks (not bowls and chopsticks, or hands), our universal female generally wears an a-line knee-length skirt (who herself is a sign for a toilet), and arrival and departure signs are designed to follow the vectoral logic of left to right literacy systems, such as English."[44]

Mijksenaar's Schiphol signs are all in English and are often combined with innovative pictograms depicting the function referred to by the sign—aircraft leaving and arriving, baggage, and so forth. The decision was made in 2001 that it was only necessary to use one language, as having Dutch on the signs simply made them more confusing. This says something about the expected PAX. As Mijksennar puts it, "the lingua franca of the international traveller is not Esperanto, but English—the language used at airports and railway stations worldwide."[45] All the signs were changed to English only.

There is no doubt that the sign system used at Schiphol is extremely efficient. In addition to directing PAX smoothly through the system, it produces a modernist uniform aesthetic against the neutral backdrop of the interior design. In addition, Mijksenaar's scheme has received the attention of numerous designers and been exported abroad. Heathrow was one of the first airports to import the color coding system, and Mijksenaar is now in the process of developing a similar standardized system for all the airports in New York. When he first examined the signage in and around JFK airport, Mijksenaar was perplexed by the idiosyncrasy of what he found. There were no signs to Manhattan—only to the Van Wyck Expressway—a meaningless piece of information for anyone who was not local. Even more confusing was the sign that read "W/B BQE Closed," which apparently meant that the Westbound Brooklyn Expressway was closed. Inside the seventeen terminals of New York's airports there are hundreds of directional signs, each with different styles. Individual airlines have frequently dominated the appearance of signs in the terminals they are associated with. The signs are often made up of white letters on dark backgrounds. Soon they will all look something like Schiphol. "Level A" will become "Ground Floor" and "Courtesy Vans" will become "Hotel Shuttles."[46] JFK is beginning to look a lot more like Schiphol. Thus an international aesthetic of air mobility is radiating out from Amsterdam.

Architecture

In Schiphol Plaza, mobility is subtly coded into the fabric of the architecture. As you enter the public square that forms the front entrance to the airport, there are surprisingly few obvious signs directing you one way or another. This was a deliberate decision by the architects. As Jan Bentham put it: "[i]n this area we tried to use all kinds of models for flow and we experimented with all kinds of signage and in the end we removed all signing from this area as we had to get used to the idea that this is a square and on a square you don't need signage—you need signage on street or on roads but on a square it is impossible to sign—it's much better to give names to the buildings around the square and to the different elements and find your own way because the traffic here has all kinds of directions." So while it is possible to see the entrances to different parts of the terminal (the buildings around the square) and the entrances descending into the rail station below, there are not arrows sending you one way or another. The space appears devoid of directional markings. Rather than signs, the architects built visual clues into the very structure of the plaza.

The floor of the plaza is made of a neutral colored grid that immediately indicates two directions for movement at ninety degrees to each other. One of these directions leads from the entrances and exits into the airport, and the other leads the passengers past the entrances to the rail terminal.

The columns supporting the roof also form passages and the roofing material is made of a striated material that runs diagonal to the flooring. Between them they indicate the "three main directions in the building in the construction because this is parallel with one terminal—this is parallel with the other terminal, and this is on a right angle with the railway track." To Bentham, the plaza is completely different from the terminal itself. While the terminal is marked by an overabundance of signs, the plaza is a space with flows coded directly into it. "An airport is an interior—it may be a building, but the passengers don't experience it as a building—they experience it as one large interior and that is a different problem because you have to find some kind of order in the interior to make it readable properly, and that is one of the reasons why we changed the atmosphere in this part of the building [the plaza]—almost completely opposite to the terminals upstairs. The common airline building—especially the departure check-in area—this is not so much the airport—the building of the airlines."

It has repeatedly been pointed out that airports are machines for mobility—spaces of process and becoming rather than location and identity. At Schiphol it is quite clearly the case that architecture, information technology, and signs form a seamless machine with each operating in coordination with the other.

INHABITING SPACE OTHERWISE

"Space is the ongoing possibility of a different inhabitation."   —Elizabeth Grosz[47]

So Schiphol is both a node in the production of global mobilities and a place that frames and orders new hierarchies of mobility through the internal organization of its spaces of flow. It is designed to enable and constrain particular kinds of mobile practice by particular kinds of people. But there are other kinds of mobility we need to consider to properly describe Schiphol. Here I turn to the homeless and the taxi drivers.

Homeless People

In his essay on Martha Rosler's images of airports, Anthony Vidler notes how airports are places where "all travellers are for a moment subject to the powerlessness of the unemployed, and a once excited thrill of spatial exploration has been regularized into a controlled mechanism of calculated flows and uneasy, unwanted delays."[48] The space of the airport, he argues, is an abstract, regulated space in which mobilities are closely and carefully channeled. In this sense the airport, with its security apparatus, "ensures that the airport, like the shopping mall, the theme park, and the new gambling palaces of multimedia combines, will remain free of the disturbing presence of the truly homeless, leaving them open to the vicarious and temporary homelessness of the privileged nomadism."[49] One of the most surprising things about Schiphol, therefore, is the number of homeless people that inhabit it. Within minutes of sitting down in the terminal, I was approached by a homeless man carrying a huge bag overflowing with bits and pieces. He asked me for a cigarette. "There's nowhere to buy cigarettes around here," he gestured, ignoring the many places that do, in fact, sell cigarettes. I did not have any to give. I could not recall seeing a homeless person in an airport before and his presence surprised me. Over the next few days I became accustomed to seeing some familiar faces. A black man with a green towel wrapped around his head rummaging through the bins. Four people sitting near one of the entrances. Several people talking to themselves and moving strangely—out of sync with the general sense of ordered movement that surrounded me. On the face of it, the airport was not designed for these people. I raised this with the architect, Jan Benthem. Benthem, it turns out, is quite proud of what he sees as the "public space" ambience of Schiphol Plaza. "We very much tried to give it the atmosphere of a public area," he insisted, "and this is how the front entrance to an airport should be—the public square of this city." When I mentioned the homeless people to him he smiled, adding, "yes, this is the city—it is a public square. The nice thing is that the airport authorities—they have already changed their business statement. Their business statement is not managing an airport—it is creating airport cities. They have changed not only an airport to an airport city, but they changed their own profession also from only managing an airport to creating this kind of urban quality and opportunities around the airport." Part of this urban quality, for Benthem, is the toleration of homelessness.

Nevertheless, the homeless experience of Schiphol as a place would be entirely different from the members of the kinetic elite the airport was designed to serve. So what do homeless people make of the airport?

As I sat in the Burger King seating area watching and writing, I began to see homeless people everywhere. One black, balding man sat in a public seating area marked "no smoking" and proceeded to light up nonchalantly. No one paid any attention. He seemed to be watching people as closely as I was. Occasionally he would stroll up and down and, at opportune moments, lift the top off the cylindrical bins and rummage through their contents. Once he found a magazine and sat reading it for over an hour as the world passed him by. A large white man with grey hair, dressed in an enormous bright orange coat, was sitting near me drinking cola and smoking cigarettes. He occasionally gestured to people and laughed loudly. He took a television remote control out of his green plastic bag and acted as though he was changing channels. Passengers waiting for planes looked past and through him. I offered him another drink and a burger and he talked to me as best he could in English. He said he frequently came to the airport as it was warm and easy to get to. He liked to watch the planes from the viewing platform. He gave me the name Nick. He looked about fifty years old. He had no socks and occasionally made sudden gestures with his head or hands that made little sense. At one point he suddenly started running his finger along the table as though drawing a map for me. The Burger King seating area was, it turns out, one of the favorite places for homeless people in the airport. People in a hurry leave drinks, fries, and burgers that can be picked up by a watchful homeless person before the Burger King employee who is paid to clean the tables and, presumably, police the activities of the homeless. Nick saw people leave at the other side of the seating area and ran over to rummage through the wrappers. He found a burger and more Pepsi and wolfed it down between sudden articulations in Dutch to no one in particular. Perhaps the caffeine was influencing him unduly, but his motions and speech were becoming more and more dramatic. The Burger King employee, a very young black man, approached him gingerly and began to clear up the litter around him quite deliberately. He went away and came back to sweep around Nick's feet. Nick was the only person who got this treatment—he occasionally waved his arms at the employee. His head movements became more and more dramatic, and he certainly seemed to be speaking to someone who no one else could see. Eventually a more senior employee arrived and told him to leave. It strikes me that the airport has a fairly relaxed attitude to the obviously homeless people who inhabit it, but Nick's bodily movements exceeded some sort of pact between the authorities and the homeless allowing them to stay. It was Nick's sudden head movements and waving arms that crossed the line and brought the sanction of the Burger Kind hierarchy. These movements caused unease and anxiety.

Over another burger I spoke to James, a talkative and eloquent homeless black man who spoke excellent English. He had moved to Amsterdam from the former Dutch colony of Curaçao ten years earlier to live with some family members and attempt a new life. That was the first time he had seen Schiphol. Now James spends almost every day of the year in the airport. He had been separated from his wife and (grown-up) children and become homeless. He gets sleep during the day in an area of Terminal 2 near the viewing panorama platform. Between midnight and 4:00 a.m., when the building is closed to all those without tickets, he gets the train into Amsterdam and hangs out in the Red Light District "watching people having fun." It is easy to catch the train because no one ever checks tickets in the short time between the airport and the city. He told me the airport is a good place for him. Security guards don't bother him. He has friends to keep him company. There is plenty of food, warmth, shelter, and reading material left by people in a hurry. He said he felt free with no one telling him what to do or playing loud music. But, he admitted, his dreams are like those of anyone, a nice house and car and lots of money. He dreams of returning to Curaçao but dislikes hot weather. He asked me questions, too. He enquired about my children and asked what life in Britain is like.

He was curious about why I should be so interested in airports and homeless people. It is obvious why the homeless like airports, he told me. They are warm, dry, and interesting. They are easy to sleep in. He came across as a man of the world.

The homeless feature in Michael Serres' haunting book *Angels*.

> Airports are built on the outskirts of cities, in the suburbs, what we call the *banlieue:* a place of banishment. Excluded and pushed out to the margins, the down and outs end up here. It's almost a law of nature. When they arrive, they're amazed to discover they can actually sleep here, in the dry, on benches, like ordinary travelers … their movement is like the movement of passengers arriving and departing—it never ceases. They stay for a while and then they move on, like everyone else.[50]

There are other reasons why a homeless person may be relatively comfortable in an airport terminal, other than the obvious benefits of shelter and warmth. No one looks twice at people carrying lots of bags around in airports, and it is not unusual to see people sleeping. It is possible to see airport space as a kind of liminal space where unusual activities (at least ones that do not threaten security) are allowed to occur—even expected. As Kim Hopper, an astute writer on homelessness, has observed, "airports occupy a singular place in the American night: Nowhere else may one observe, as accepted practice, ordinary citizens—some in quite casual attire, many with bags, and most looking a little worse for the wear—bedding down for the night in full public view. A reasonably clean and decently dressed homeless person has no trouble fitting in with the impromptu sleepers scattered about."[51] In addition, as Hopper notes, "legitimate" travelers, like the homeless, frequently need to go through their bags to reorganize their possessions, momentarily making their private belongings a public spectacle.

Accounts of the presence of homeless people at Schiphol are sketchy. Leon Deben has been researching homelessness in Amsterdam for many years. Every two years since 1995 he has conducted censuses of the homeless. There have, he notes, been stories circulating about a large number of homeless people sleeping in Schiphol Airport. In 1999, Schiphol was included in the census despite the fact that it lies outside the city. They counted fifteen to twenty homeless people—a number that led them to believe that homelessness was "not that bad" at the airport.[52] By 2001, however, a homeless man was able to point out forty or so homeless people who regularly slept in the terminal to Deben and his colleagues. News stories indicated numbers of between one and two hundred. Deben concurs with Hopper that airports are a logical place for homeless people to seek shelter and food. Even after 2001, when a homeless man was blamed for a small fire in one of the toilets in the arrival hall and the toilets were subsequently closed after midnight to anyone without a ticket, numbers of homeless people in the airport continued to rise. "Schiphol is an attractive place to stay for some of them," Deben writes, "as it is not only warm and dry; there are also lots of things to find there. Many travellers throw away their telephone cards, train tickets or even their weed … thus providing smart homeless people with something on the side. With a train ticket they can, for instance, legally make a round trip to Utrecht, Rotterdam, and the Hague (with coffee breaks) after midnight then resume their sleep, returning to Schiphol around 4 A.M."[53] A student of Deben's, Frank Groot, spent months undertaking participant observation at Schiphol. He made contact with twenty-eight homeless people who used the airport regularly. About half of these were there almost permanently. Twenty-three were male and five female.[54] He noted the use of innovative strategies to make do in the airport. One person would go to sleep with a large label attached to him reading "Please wake me up at 10:00 P.M.—I have a plane to catch."

Taxi Drivers

Homeless people are not the only unorthodox users of Schiphol Airport. As I sat in the terminal, I became aware of a repeated announcement made every fifteen minutes. "Disregard taxis offering unofficial services—use the official taxi rank," the recorded voice said. Intrigued by the possibility of unofficial taxi drivers, I decided to take some rides and ask the drivers about this. It did not take long to discover more.

My first ride was with a white, fifty-something driver who was more than happy to explain the situation to me. He explained to me that his taxi is a special "Schiphol Taxi," which means that his company pays about €400 a month for a licence that allows them to pick up people at Schiphol. I suggest that he probably doesn't have to wait long to pick up travelers at the airport:

Driver 1: Sometimes you have to wait too long.

Cresswell: Yes?

Driver 1: Because there are too many taxis.

Cresswell: Oh, right.

Driver 1: We are an official Schiphol taxi but our government would like to see more competition in the trade.

Cresswell: Right. So are there unofficial taxis?

Driver 1: Uh yes—they call them "cockroach."

Cresswell: Cockroach?

Driver 1: Cockroach—they are not 100 percent qualified like Schiphol taxis.

Cresswell: But are they legal?

Driver 1: They are legal—yes, in a way you know.

Cresswell: Right.

Driver 1: But we are paying an awful lot of contribution for the airport … and those people who are called the cockroach—they are paying just by passenger—and it is all organized by a transponder in the car.

Driver 1: Another problem that is very common is that we do have—we call them snorders.

Cresswell: Snorders?

Driver 1: And they are completely illegal—because they are going at the arrivals and trying to take some passengers in their cab or in their private cars I should say. You must have an expression in English for these kind of people. And they are completely illegal.

Cresswell: Pirates, maybe? That's interesting—at the airport there is an announcement that tells you to disregard people asking you for taxi rides.

Driver 1: And they are mainly from foreign nationalities—nationality of abroad—like Moroccans.

On another occasion—again with a white male taxi driver (I never met a female driver) I mentioned that I noticed an article in a local paper about a taxi war and asked him what that meant.

Driver 2: There is a taxi war coming up, yes.

Cresswell: What does that mean?

Driver 2: This is about—Snorders—too many taxis at Schiphol—more or less legal, illegal—so there must be a quality certificate—because it is very dishonest—we have to pay so much contribution to the airport we should be protected.

Cresswell: So how much do you pay Schiphol then?

Driver 2: I think it is about €400 a month.

Cresswell: Wow—that is a lot.

Driver 2: To get license at Schiphol—and you have to have not less than Mercedes 200E.

Cresswell: Yes, and that's the other thing that is amazing—the cars are so good—you don't get this in London.

Driver 2: You cannot drive along in a fifteen-year-old Toyota or whatsoever—it is crazy.

Cresswell: No.

Driver 2: Even when he has arrived and gets his certificate from the government, you cannot do it—it is as simple as that—not very honest against the customer at all because the car is not clean and 100 percent safe car.

Cresswell: Yes—that's true.

An Introduction to Communication

Driver 2: But if you are taking a taxi in Amsterdam—8 of 10 times you will find there is people from abroad driving the taxi. And Amsterdam used to have 2,500 taxis driving around now there are 4,000—so you can imagine that.

Clearly there is a great deal of tension between these official Mercedes-driving, white, Schiphol taxi drivers and the incomers in their old Toyotas. The word *snorder* does not translate into English, but is a slang term used only among taxi drivers to refer to illegal (mostly migrant) drivers who have operated without a license. Eventually I managed to locate some immigrant taxi drivers who may or may not have been the so-called cockroaches or snorders. While not driving Mercedes cars, these drivers nevertheless offered a perfectly good service in reasonably clean and new cars. One such driver came to Amsterdam from Turkey eleven years earlier. He had driven taxis in Istanbul and moved to Amsterdam in order to marry his girlfriend—also a Turkish immigrant. He had help from within the Turkish community to find his job and set him up with a taxi. He could tell me about members of his family in the United Kingdom, the United States, and Spain who also drive taxis. Another Turkish driver I spoke to spoke Dutch, English, Turkish, and a little French. He had been in Amsterdam five years and planned to move to London in order to work in his uncle's restaurant. Clearly these drivers were part of fairly elaborate and extensive transnational family networks of taxi drivers and others. There also appeared to be a significant degree of mobility around this network as people moved from job to job and place to place.

So what do these accounts of homeless people and taxi drivers tell us about airports? The most important thing I think they point to is the way different networks and experiences of mobility intersect in this particular place. The metaphorical construction of airports as placeless places or non-places constitutes them as spaces of pure motion—uninhabited and inauthentic. Similarly, the celebration of airports as avatars of a brave new classless and postnational world feature a largely uncritical celebration of global nomadism, as if everyone were moving in more or less the same ways. Even when a difference is noted between those who move and those who do not move, it appears to miss the sheer variability of mobility experiences. Manuel Castells, in *The Network Society,* makes the following observation.

> In short elites are cosmopolitan, people are local. The space of power and wealth is projected throughout the world while people's life and experience is rooted in places, in their culture, in their history. Thus, the more a social organization is based upon ahistorical flows, superseding the logic of any specific place, the more the logic of global power escapes the socio-political control of historically specific local/national societies.[55]

This observation clearly indicates the link between the mobility of some and immobility of others. Its suggestion that only the elite are cosmopolitan, however, hides the considerable cosmopolitanism of the kinetic underclass. Everywhere that the kinetic elite travel, they are serviced by a mobile workforce who do not share in the luxury of the business travelers Castells writes of. They drive their taxis, clean their rooms, and look after their children. They, too, are mobile. They, too, are cosmopolitan. The general celebration of the nomadic in contemporary theory too often levels out agency so that these differences in the experience of mobility disappear. Not only are there snorders at the airport, driving Toyotas rather than Mercedes, there are also the truly homeless moving side by side with the kinetic elite. Zygmunt Bauman has metaphorically described the mobilities of globalization through the two mobile figures who mark the end points of a scale of mobilities—the vagabond and the tourist. He argues that the globalized society we inhabit is just as stratified as any other. The dimension along which we are plotted is our "degree of mobility."[56] It is not just the degree of mobility, however, it is the nature of the experience of mobility. Often those "high up" in a kinetic hierarchy "travel through life by their heart's desire and pick and choose their destinations according to the joys they offer. Those "low down" happen time and again to be thrown out from the site they would rather stay in."[57] So while both the metaphorical vagrant and the metaphorical tourist are mobile, they are in different experiential worlds. The globally mobile kinetic elite inhabit a world in which space is less and less of a constraint, while the kinetic underclass are often thrown into a mobile world they did not choose or are tied to spaces which, In Bauman's terms, "close in on them." Space for them is not disappearing but has to be transcended painfully.

> For the inhabitants of the first world—the increasingly cosmopolitan, extraterritorial world of global businessmen, global culture managers or global academics, state borders are levelled down, as they are dismantled for the world's commodities, capital and finances. For the inhabitant of the second world, the walls built of immigration controls, of residence laws and of "clean streets" and "zero tolerance" policies, grow taller; the moats separating them from the sites of their desire and of dreamed of redemption grow deeper. … The first travel at will, get much fun from their travel … are cajoled or bribed to travel and welcomed with smiles and open arms when they do. The second travel surreptitiously, often illegally, sometimes paying more for the crowded steerage of a stinking unseaworthy boat than others pay for business-class gilded luxuries—and are frowned upon, and, if unlucky, arrested and promptly deported, when they arrive.[58]

The kinetic elite are voluntarily mobile. They take pleasure in their mobility and experience mobility as freedom, while the kinetic underclass—the vagabonds—are confined or forced to move out of necessity and experience mobility as survival. Bauman's point, however, is not just that these experiences of global mobility are different, but that they are tied up in the same logic. Globalization, he argues, is tied to the dreams and desires of the kinetic elite who inhabit the luxurious space of flows, and who need the kinetic underclass to service it. There are no *tourists* without *vagabonds*.

CONCLUSIONS

In conclusion, there are five points to make about Schiphol. First, like Heathrow or Paris it is clearly an important node in a global network of air travel that has connected first world places to distant ex-colonies and effectively made them closer. Second, it is a local place that enacts the continental construction of a space of free mobility in most of Europe, while keeping a close eye on those who come from outside. Just as ancient Chinese cities were designed as scale models of the wider cosmos, so Schiphol has been designed as a map of continental and European distinctions between acceptable and unacceptable mobilities. Third, Schiphol has ghosts in its mobility machine. The homeless man from the Dutch Antilles once arrived in Schiphol on a flight and now lives there. The Turkish taxi driver also arrived at Schiphol in order to marry his sweetheart and become a taxi driver shuttling the kinetic elite to and from the airport.

Fourth, these nested mobilities take place in Schiphol. Schiphol is clearly a place of movement, but it is not a place that easily becomes a metaphor. It does not do justice to the many-layered complexity of the place to call it a non-place or a new transnational Utopia. Paying attention to the politics of mobility begins to undo the equation that links a generalized celebration of mobility to sites such as the airport. Schiphol is a complicated kind of space on which an intricate "place-ballet" of multiple movements takes place on a daily basis. It is not simply a part of the life-world of the kinetic elite, but a place of shelter and livelihood. The people who service the kinetic elite are every bit as cosmopolitan as the jet-lagged business-class passengers who need their rooms tidied, their taxis driven, and their food cooked.

Finally, the fact that this is Schiphol and not Paris, London, or Chicago matters. Airports as metaphors appear as spaces of equivalence—places that could be anywhere—non-places. But clearly, Schiphol, like any other kind of place, is situated and has its own history and own sets of connections. Its geographical location makes a difference to the experience of the mobilities that are produced there. This can be seen in the connections between Schiphol and Batavia, in the mapping of Schengen space onto the airport, and in the fact that a homeless man from Curaçao inhabits it on a daily basis. Schiphol may be a node in a global space of flows, but it is still uniquely Schiphol—still a place.

All of these point to the incredibly complicated nature of mobility in the modern West. At various points in this book we have considered moving bodies, social narratives about mobility, arguments about meaning, domination, resistance, conformity, and transgression. All of these are jumbled up in a place like Schiphol where the movement of bodies is tied to notion of rights to mobility, social narratives of the acceptable and unacceptable, and increasingly sophisticated technologies of mobility.

In addition to all this, the experience of Schiphol makes it quite clear that people continue to be remarkably creative in mobile ways. The homeless people and semi-legal taxi drivers of Schiphol reveal the complex ways in which people can exercise power against the grain of the acceptable and expected. Workers, no doubt, continued to work in ways that deviated from the expectations of those studying their time and motion. Dancers continued to dance wildly in London despite the best efforts of Victor Silvester and others. Bus riders in Los Angeles continue to ask awkward questions about ideologies of mobility (public and otherwise) in urban America. Suffragists took to the road in automobiles, whether or not male observers were shocked by their actions. The story of mobility in modernity is one in which creativity continues to play an important role. Virtual, ideal, mobilities are still being produced and real, fleshy people continue to refuse to comply.

NOTES

1. For recent discussions of airports, see Mark Gottdiener, *Life in the Air: Surviving the New Culture of Air Travel* (Lanham, MD: Rowman & Littlefield, 2000); David Pascoe, *Airspaces* (London: Reaktion, 2001).
2. Mike Crang, "Between Places: Producing Hubs, Flows, and Networks," *Environment and Planning a* 34 (2002): 569–74, 571.

3. Marc Augé, *Non-Places: Introduction to an Anthropology of Supermodernity* (London; New York: Verso, 1995), 110. This idea of airports as a kind of non- place is now commonplace. The artist Robert Smithson referred to the air port as a "non-site" in "Towards the Development of an Air Terminal Site," in Robert Smithson and Nancy Holt, *The Writings of Robert Smithson: Essays with Illustrations* (New York: New York University Press, 1979).

4. Hans Ibelings, *Supermodernism: Architecture in the Age of Globalization* (Rotterdam: NAi, 1998), 78–79.

5. Ibid., 80.

6. Iain Chambers, *Border Dialogues: Journeys in Postmodernity* (London; New York: Routledge, 1990), 57–58.

7. Rosi Braidotti, *Nomadic Subjects: Embodiment and Sexual Difference in Contemporary Feminist Theory* (New York: Columbia University Press, 1994), 18.

8. M. Brown, "A Flying Leap into the Future," *Metropolis,* July/August (1995): 50–79, 79.

9. Pico Iyer, "Where Worlds Collide," *Harper's Magazine,* August 1995, 51.

10. Ibid.

11. Kevin Hetherington, "Whither the World?—Presence, Absence and the Globe," in *Mobilizing Place, Placing Mobility: The Politics of Representation in a Globalized World,* ed. Tim Cresswell and Ginette Verstraete (Amsterdam: Rodopi, 2002), 173–88, 179.

12. Pico Iyer, *The Global Soul: Jet Lag, Shopping Malls, and the Search for Home* (New York: Knopf, 2000).

13. Crang, "Between Places: Producing Hubs, Flows, and Networks," 573.

14. See Peter Adey, "Secured and Sorted Mobilities: Examples from the Airport," *Surveillance and Society* 1, no. 4 (2004): 500–19.

15. Manuel Castells, *The Rise of the Network Society* (Oxford: Blackwell Publishers, 1996), 417.

16. This information is given in: Municipal Airport of Amsterdam, *Schiphol: Gemeente Luchthaven Amsterdam (Illustrated Guide of Municipal Airport of Amsterdam)* (1929). This and other guides to the airport are available in the Municipal Archives of Amsterdam.

17. This information is from: Municipal Airport of Amsterdam, *Gemeente Luchthaven Amsterdam (Illustrated Guide to Municipal Airport of Amsterdam)* (1936). Municipal Archives of Amsterdam.

18. Pascoe, *Airspaces,* 75.

19. This recent information is from Reinier Gerritsen and Luuk Kramer, *Schiphol Airport* (Rotterdam: NAi Publishers, 1999).

20. This and the following quotations are taken from an interview with Jan Benthem, November 18, 2003 at Schiphol Airport.

21. For a perceptive account of this, on which I draw here, see Ginette Verstraete, "Technological Frontiers and the Politics of Mobility in the European Union," *New Formations* 43 (spring 2001): 26–43.

22. The original signatories of the Schengen Agreement were Belgium, France, Germany, Luxemburg, and the Netherlands. These countries have been joined by Austria, Denmark, Finland, Greece, Iceland, Italy, Portugal, Nor way, Spain, and Sweden.

23. Verstraete, "Technological Frontiers and the Politics of Mobility in the European Union," 29.

24. European Commission, *Freedom of Movement, Europe* (Brussels: Office for Official Publications of the European Communities, 1994), 3.

25. Ibid., 1.

26. Pascal Fontaine, *A Citizen's Europe* (Luxembourg: 1993), 7–8.

27. For insightful commentary on the role of mobility in European identity construction, see Ginette Verstraete, "Heading for Europe: Tourism and the Global Itinerary of an Idea," in *Mobilizing Place, Placing Mobility: The Politics of Representation in a Globalized World,* ed. Tim Cresswell and Ginette Verstraete (Amsterdam: Rodopi, 2002), 33–52; Verstraete, "Technological Frontiers and the Politics of Mobility in the European Union."

28. Stephen Graham and Simon Marvin, *Splintering Urbanism Networked Infrastructures, Technological Mobilities and the Urban Condition* (London: Routledge, 2001), 364.

29. See Adey, "Secured and Sorted Mobilities: Examples from the Airport"; Peter Adey, "Surveillance at the Airport: Surveilling Mobility/Mobilising Surveillance," *Environment and Planning A* (2004); Michael Curry, "The Profiler's Question and the Treacherous Traveler: Narratives of Belonging in Commercial Aviation," *Surveillance and Society* 1, no. 4 (2004): 475–99; Martin Dodge and Rob Kitchin, "Flying through Code/Space: The Real Virtuality of Air Travel," *Environment and Planning A* 36 (2004): 195–211.

30. Dodge and Kitchin, "Flying through Code/Space: The Real Virtuality of Air Travel," 198.

31. For a wider interpretation of this phenomenon, see N. J. Thrift and S. French, "The Automatic Production of Space," *Transactions of the Institute of British Geographers* 27 (2002): 309–35.

32. Curry, "The Profiler's Question and the Treacherous Traveler: Narratives of Belonging in Commercial Aviation," 488.

33. Adey, "Surveillance at the Airport: Surveilling Mobility/Mobilising Surveillance."

34. Jonathan Crary, *Techniques of the Observer: On Vision and Modernity in the Nineteenth Century* (Cambridge, MA: MIT Press, 1990), 41.

35. Adey, "Surveillance at the Airport: Surveilling Mobility/Mobilising Surveillance"; Albert Battersby, *Network Analysis for Planning and Scheduling* (New York: Wiley, 1970).

36. A similar program (INSPASS) based on a scan of the hand is in operation in the United States with over 50,000 participants.

37. Privium website, http://www.schiphol.nl/schiphol/privium/privium_home.jsp (accessed June 14, 2004).

38. Gillian Fuller, "Perfect Match: Biometrics and Body Patterning in a Networked World," *Fibreculture Journal* 1 (2004). http://journal.fibreculture. org/issue1/issue1_fuller.html.

39. Adey, "Surveillance at the Airport: Surveilling Mobility/Mobilising Surveillance."

40. Martha Rosier, *Martha Rosier: In the Place of the Public: Observations of a Frequent Flyer* (New York: Cantz, 1998), 32.

41. This and all other quotations from Mijksenaar are taken from an interview conducted on November 20, 2003.

42. Gillian Fuller, "The Arrow-Directional Semiotics; Wayfinding in Transit," *Social Semiotics* 12, no. 3 (2002): 131–44, 131.

43. Augé, *Non-Places: Introduction to an Anthropology of Supermodernity.*

44. Fuller, "The Arrow—Directional Semiotics; Wayfinding in Transit," 135.

45. P. Mijksenaar, "Signs of the Times," *Airport World* 8, no. 4 (August–September 2003) http://www. mijksenaar.com/pauls_corner/index.html (accessed June 21, 2004).

CPSIA information can be obtained at www.ICGtesting.com
Printed in the USA
BVOW050339210912

301025BV00001B/2/P